Addressing Cyber Instability

Addressing Cyber Instability

Cyber Conflict Studies Association

*Edited by Dr. James C. Mulvenon and
Dr. Gregory J. Rattray*

*Authors: Matt Devost, Maeve Dion, Jason Healey,
Bob Gourley, Samuel Liles, James C. Mulvenon,
Hannah Pitts, Gregory J. Rattray*

*Contributors: Julia Dizhevskaya, Karl Grindal,
Gregory Russo, Eneken Tikk*

ISBN 978-1-300-30741-9

Contents

Capstone: Deepening the Foundations of the Cyber Conflict Field of Study

Introduction

The emergence of cyberspace is the tectonic event of the 21st century. It has fundamentally altered politics, economics, social interaction, and national security, providing dramatic new opportunities, capabilities, vulnerabilities, and threats. With each passing day, cyberspace becomes an indispensible, even irreplaceable, part of the daily lives of individuals, companies, and entire nations. Yet this rapidly growing dependence on the "network" is bedeviled by two core problems, one technical and the other policy-related:

- *The core technical problem at the heart of cyberspace is that the underlying architecture was never designed with security in mind; indeed, the original designers never imagined that the network would be used for malicious purposes.* The priorities were and generally remain openness, ease of interconnection and facilitating technical innovation. Meanwhile, the threat environment has quickly metastasized from relatively harmless webpage defacements in the mid-1990s to state-level network exploit activities, such as the Silicon Valley hacks in late 2009 and early 2010, that challenge the very heart of the American innovation economy. The vulnerabilities that make cyber space an insecure environment and have allowed the emergence of significant malicious activity and conflict that stem ultimately from a lack of priority on security in the fundamental building blocks of cyberspace. In response to these threats, we have done the best we can with an imperfect architecture, gluing security onto the network and attempting to mitigate the damage.

- *The core policy problem in cyberspace is that the evolution of the technological architecture has vastly outpaced the corresponding set of conceptual, doctrinal, organizational and legal structures, resulting in a reactive and atavistic policy dynamic where today's ideas and organizations are often chasing yesterday's problems with no flexibility to deal with the future problems created by the introduction of as-yet uninvented technologies.* For national security strategists, it therefore feels like many other periods where new weapons (nuclear, chemical, biological) or modes of delivery (airplanes, ballistic missiles) were developed, and the capability was far ahead of conceptual thinking about their use and implications.

Definitions and Scope

Before delving deeper, it is first necessary to define key terms. Indeed, one of the fundamental problems over the past decades has been deciding what to include in the definition of "cyberspace." In the 1990s, the term was used to categorize something seen as separate and different from the physical world.[1] Over time, this point of view has evolved into viewing cyberspace as a domain, similar to land, sea, air, and space, which has in turn led to a debate about whether cyberspace can be considered a "global commons."[2]

Other definitions are much less abstract, emphasizing the physical environment of cyberspace defined by its architectures and components.[3] The US Department of Defense definition of

---

[1] Gregory J. Rattray, "An Environmental Approach to Understanding Cyberpower," in *Cyberpower and National Security*, ed. Franklin D. Kramer, Stuart H. Starr, Larry K. Wentz, (Dulles, VA: NDU Press, 2009), 254.

[2] Gregory J. Rattray, Chris Evans, Jason Healey, "American Security in the Cyber Commons," in *Contested Commons: The Future of American Power in a Multipolar World*, ed. Abraham M. Denmark and Dr. James Mulvenon, (Center for a New American Security: Jan. 2010), 137-176.

[3] Rattray, "An Environmental Approach to Understanding Cyberpower."

cyberspace, for example, emphasizes the technical infrastructure: "A global domain within the information environment consisting of the interdependent network of information technology infrastructures, including the Internet, telecommunications networks, computer systems, and embedded processors and controllers."[4] An alternative, simpler definition is that cyberspace is all interconnected information technologies.[5] The 2003 National Strategy to Secure Cyberspace calls cyberspace "the nervous system of [US] critical infrastructures—the control system of our country. Cyberspace comprises hundreds of thousands of interconnected computers, servers, routers, switches, and fiber optics cables...."[6]

Whether viewed as a physical or virtual domain, it is important to note that the US and other countries see cyberspace as a critical operating environment filled with complex contradictions. On the one hand, cyberspace offers dramatically exciting opportunities to unite and bind individuals and entire societies, yet on the other hand it simultaneously presents new grave challenges to individual and collective security. As articulated by the recent US International Strategy for Cyberspace: "The reach of networked technology is pervasive and global. For all nations, the underlying digital infrastructure is or will soon become a national asset."[7] As a result, it is also important to understand the dynamics and consequences of conflict within that cyberspace.

What is Cyber Conflict?

As defined in the initial CCSA research agenda in 2005, cyber conflict *"is the conduct of large scale, politically motivated conflict based on the use of offensive and defensive capabilities to disrupt*

---

4   Deputy Secretary of Defense Memorandum, Subject: *The Definition of Cyberspace*, May 12, 2008.

5   This definition is often used by Bob Gourley, one of the authors of the current volume.

6   U.S. Executive Office of the President, *The National Strategy to Secure Cyberspace* (February 2003), 1.

7   U.S. Executive Office of the President, *International Strategy of Cyberspace: Prosperity, Security, and Openness in a Networked World* (May 2011), http://www.whitehouse.gov/sites/default/files/rss_viewer/international_strategy _for_cyberspace.pdf (accessed 25 May 2011).

digital systems, networks, and infrastructures, including the use of cyber-based weapons or tools by non-state/transnational actors in conjunction with other forces for political ends."[8] Cyber conflict includes activities conducted by both state and non-state actors against a variety of targets. In this sense, "cyber conflict" is a useful term as it encompasses a number of activities that pose threats to individuals, organizations, and nation states as well as consideration with traditional military and intelligence operations. An alternative definition notes that cyber conflict is "broader than cyber warfare, including all conflicts and coercion between nations and groups for strategic purposes utilizing cyber space where software, computers, and networks are both the means and the targets."[9] At its most basic level, cyber conflict encompasses activities conducted by many kinds of actors in order to achieve a strategic gain.

The first task of a cyber conflict studies research agenda is to refine the definition of cyber conflict itself, in particular the difficult task of categorizing formal cyber-based activity between countries (that is, cyber warfare) vice intelligence collection, covert action, crime, terrorism, and conventional war. An important, but no less difficult, categorization problem involves distinguishing between largely technology-focused research and efforts focused at the level of strategic studies. The current literature is largely divided into two different camps, with one sub-canon focused on technical issues with little concern for strategic issues and vice versa. This effort is unashamedly focused on strategic issues.

One useful distinction is to differentiate between cyber conflict and cyber crime. In a military and intelligence context, cyber conflict can largely be subsumed under a finite set of categories agreed upon most actors, though sometimes with different names. In the US Department of Defense, Computer Network Operations (CNO) includes three primary elements: Computer Network Defense (CND), Computer Network Exploitation (CNE), and Computer Network Attack (CNA). According to the revised Joint Publication 3.13 *Information Operations*:

---

[8]   Mulvenon, "Towards a Cyberconflict Studies Research Agenda," 52-55.

[9]   Jason Healey, "Advanced Intelligence Support to Cyber Conflict," Delta Risk Fundamentals for Cyber Warfare (Course Presentation, Needham, MA, 28-30 September 2010).

CNA consists of actions taken through the use of computer networks to disrupt, deny, degrade, or destroy information resident in computers and computer networks, or the computers and networks themselves. CND involves actions taken through the use of computer networks to protect, monitor, analyze, detect, and respond to unauthorized activity within DOD information systems and computer networks. CND actions not only protect DOD systems from an external adversary but also from exploitation from within, and are now a necessary function in all military operations. CNE is enabling operations and intelligence collection capabilities conducted through the use of computer networks to gather data from target or adversary automated information systems or networks.[10]

Even though we are using the definitions of the world's most powerful military, all of these CNO activities can be conducted by state actors, non-state actors or even proxies conducting such activities on behalf of the first two. For our purposes, cyber crime does not fall within cyber conflict when the goal is commercial or direct monetary gain. For example, high-end cyber crime, including stealing vast quantities of credit card information, are not included within our definition, but cyber conflict does include "economic warfare" like embargoes, economic sabotage, or espionage to favor national defense industries.

We do not directly address issues related to the "soft" side of information-gathering operations, such as perception management (actions to convey or deny selected information, and indicators to influence emotions, motives, and objective reasoning), deception (measures designed to mislead the enemy by manipulation, distortion, or falsification of evidence to induce a reaction), and other psychological operations (activities to convey selected information and indicators to foreign audiences to influence their emotions, motives, objective reasoning, and ultimately the behavior of foreign governments, organizations, groups, and

---

[10] U.S. Joint Staff, *Information Operations*, Joint Publication 3.13 (13 February 2006).

individuals). These are generally considered "information operations (IO)" or "military information support operations" (MISO), in United States military parlance. The broader IO construct does include CNO and cyberspace will be an essential medium for the conduct of the other aspects of IO.

The strategic implications of cyber conflict also reach far beyond the military, intelligence and economic sectors – extending into realm of diplomacy and statecraft. As states increasingly recognize the utility of cyberspace as a tool of national security, it is necessary to examine the implications of cyber conflict for bilateral and multilateral relations, civil society, and international legal regimes. Allegations of cross-border hacking, whether the cyber operation is classified as an attack or as espionage, have a profound effect on both official and unofficial channels of diplomacy. Additional diplomatic ramifications of cyber conflict include the recent increased attention to the problems of Internet freedom,[11] soft power,[12] the role of cyberspace in uprisings around the world, and the release of classified data on a major scale.[13] All of these phenomena complicate the roles and responsibility for the world's leaders. As summarized by Nye, "States will remain the dominant actor on the world stage, but they will find the stage far more crowded and difficult to control."[14] As such, the entry costs

---

[11] See Executive Office of the President, *International Strategy of Cyberspace*, *supra* note 7. Evgeny Morozov, *The Net Delusion: The Dark Side of Internet Freedom*, New York: PublicAffairs, 2011. Hillary Clinton, "Remarks on Internet Freedom," Remarks at the Newseum, 21 January, 2010. Available at: http://www.state.gov/secretary/rm/2010/01/135519.htm. Hillary Clinton, "Internet Rights and Wrongs: Choices and Challenges in a Networked World," Remarks at George Washington University, 15 February 2011. Available at: http://www.state.gov/secretary/rm/2011/02/156619.htm.

[12] See, for example, Joseph S. Nye, *The Future of Power*, (New York: PublicAffairs, 2011); Ed. Leigh Armistead, *Information Operations: Warfare and the Hard Reality of Soft Power*, (Dulles, VA: Brassey's, 2004); Joseph S. Nye, Jr., "The Information Revolution and American Soft Power," *Asia-Pacific Review*, vol. 1, no. 1, (2002); Shanthi Kalathil, "China's Soft Power in the Information Age: Think Again," ISD Working Papers, (New Diplomacy, May 2011).

[13] John Markoff, "The Asymmetrical Online War," Bits Blog, *New York Times*, 3 April 2011, http://bits.blogs.nytimes.com/2011/04/03/the-asymmetrical-online-war.

[14] Nye, *The Future of Power*, 116.

decline and "world politics will not be the sole province of governments."[15]

Beyond the strategic implications of cyberspace, its profound impact on societal developments is apparent. The Internet and cyberspace decentralizes communication and information, increasing capacity, speed, and directness.[16] Social media and other communications media, including Facebook, Twitter, blogs, and messaging, are reshaping how individuals relate to information and each other. Chatting online with a friend in Tokyo is just as easy if she were sitting a few city blocks away. While not all developments in cyberspace are positive, it has already expanded the global commons and increased our ability to communicate more easily and more quickly. We can see the effects of this social interaction in the uprisings of the so-called "Arab Spring" across North Africa and the Middle East, but these same examples also demonstrate the continued roles of states to use information technology against its citizens and disrupt social development.[17] While these issues are not a major focus of this monograph, they are increasingly the fundamental concerns of leaders around the globe that will impact the relative openness of cyberspace as well as other features that will shape the cyber conflict environment.

The Threat Environment

Even as the world becomes more dependent on cyberspace in every facet of life, the threat environment has become more dire, driven by both fundamental flaws in the underlying architecture and the desire to prioritize connectivity over security. The spectrum of cyber threats ranges widely from lower level threats like defacements to intermediate threats like botnets and malware, to a new threshold of cyber attacks established by the Stuxnet

---

[15] Ibid.

[16] Ibid.

[17] See, for example, James Cowie, "Egypt Leaves the Internet," *Renesys* (blog), 27 January 2011, http://www.renesys.com/blog/2011/01/egypt-leaves-the-internet.shtml.

worm.[18] Not only is the spectrum of threats wide in breadth, but the potential actors and adversaries are proliferating at the speed of the network. States and non-state actors, including state-sponsored organizations or proxies, have varying levels of capability and intent, but still comprise a significant level of threat in cyberspace. Increasing dependence on cyberspace across all dimensions of national power (political, economic, military, diplomatic, social) only increases our vulnerability and the potential negative consequences of not adequately understanding the threats.

While Stuxnet is considered the new pinnacle of cyber threats, cyber espionage, not cyber attack, or "cyber war," is currently the most pressing risk for the United States in cyberspace. Strategic espionage against political, military and intelligence targets can change the outcome of interstate conflicts and even alter the balance of power, while economic espionage can result in substantial economic losses and can endanger future competitive advantage.[19] Within the espionage realm, Advanced Persistent Threat poses the most significant, sustained challenge to actors in cyberspace. Advanced Persistent Threat, or APT, consists of highly sophisticated intrusion activities, best documented in efforts targeted at the US Government or companies in the Defense Industrial Base (DIB) but expanding to include companies at the core of the innovation economy such as Google.[20] Threats against

---

[18] William J. Broad and David E. Danger, "Worm Was Perfect for Sabotaging Centrifuges," *New York Times*, 18 November 2010, http://www.nytimes.com/2010/11/19/world/middleeast/19stuxnet.html. For more information on Stuxnet, see Ralph Langner, "Cracking Stuxnet, a 21st-century cyber weapon," *TED*, March 2011, http://www.ted.com/talks/ralph_langner_cracking_stuxnet_a_21st_century_cyberweapon.html?awesm=on.ted.com_Langner&utm_content=awesm-publisher&utm_medium=on.ted.com-static&utm_source=langner.com.

[19] Nye, *The Future of Power*, 145. For a specific example of cyber espionage, see Brian Grow and Mark Hosenball, "Special Report: In cyberspy vs. cyberspy, China has the edge," *Reuters*, 14 April 2011. Available at: http://www.reuters.com/article/2011/04/14/us-china-usa-cyberespionage-idUSTRE73D24220110414.

[20] "Under Cyberthreat: Defense Contractors," *Businessweek*, 6 July 2009, http://www.businessweek.com/technology/content/jul2009/tc2009076_873512.htm. See also, Brian Grow, Keith Epstein and Chi-Chu Tschang, "The New E-spionage Threat," *Businessweek*, 10 April 2008, http://www.businessweek.com/magazine/content/08_16/b4080032218430.htm.

the DIB and the government are only compounded by serious and known vulnerabilities in critical infrastructure, which are often privately held but are crucial for government services.

Another important class of threats against states include activities designed to deny access to cyber resources, such as the Distributed Denial of Service attacks (DDoS) against Estonia in 2007, which took down the websites of many Estonian organizations, including the parliament, banks, and media following increased tensions with Russia. The Estonian disruption also included defacements and other lower level methods, although the DDoS attacks caused the most significant, sustained damage. While some Russian hackers have taken responsibility for the attacks, no official connection with the Russian government has been uncovered. The Estonian experience was repeated during the 2008 cyber disruptions before and during the brief war between Georgia and Russia, including defacement and DDoS attacks against Georgian government and media websites, again presumably by Russian-backed actors.

Taken together, these various classes of cyber threats present a significant threat to the viability of cyberspace as a useable domain by states, groups or individuals, necessitating a systematic examination of the dynamics of cyber conflict.

The Evolution of Cyber Thinking

Cyber conflict studies, though embryonic, represent an attempt to comprehensively identify and analyze the origins, modes and possible consequences of conflict in cyberspace, fusing together a wide range of interdisciplinary approaches. Though the field of cyber conflict studies has clearly matured over time, it has not kept pace with the rapid technological developments that have accelerated the evolution of this type of conflict. This section provides an overview of the state of the field before the establishment of the CCSA and how it has evolved through the years. It is not intended to be a literature review of cyber conflict studies, as more detailed overviews of existing scholarship are included in the relevant chapters.

Since the creation of the foundational technologies themselves, decades of books, monographs, think-tank studies, presidential commissions, and industry reports have contributed to the body of cyber conflict knowledge. Many of these writings have not stood the test of time, overcome by events or rendered obsolete by the advance of technology. In general, they all share a deep concern about the vulnerabilities of the network, and, to a lesser extent, have offered possible solutions. As global dependencies on the network proliferate, writings have increasingly warned of the potential for strategic cyber attacks, including the potential of a catastrophic cyber attack against the United States. Others have warned about the theft of money and intellectual property through cyber attack. Yet very little of this literature could be considered a contribution to a field, since the articles rarely referenced each other and therefore were not building systematized knowledge. With so many issues to explore and policies to establish or optimize, cyber conflict research needs to a more cumulative approach and the following survey is meant to capture this foundation of cyber conflict research to date.

Although the network was born in the 1960s with the work of Paul Baran and the initial ARPANET projects, cyber conflict did not become an issue of concern until the late 1980s, when two significant events raised concerns about the security and reliability of the Internet.[21] In 1987 researcher Cliff Stoll uncovered a hacker using the Lawrence Berkeley National Laboratory Network to hack into other networks, including military bases and defense contractors.[22] One year later Robert Morris, Cornell University graduate student and the son of an NSA scientist, unleashed the first worm onto the Internet. He was convicted under the 1986 Computer Fraud and Abuse Act, although Morris stated that he wrote the worm to measure the size of the Internet and his stated intent was not malicious.[23] As a result of the Morris Worm, the CERT/CC was established, beginning the evolution of offense-defense interactions that continues to this day.[24]

[21] Katie Hafner, *Where Wizards Stay Up Late: The Origins of the Internet*, (New York: Simon & Schuster, 1998).
[22] Cliff Stoll, *The Cuckoo's Egg*, (New York: Gallery Books, 2005).
[23] Ted Eisenberg et al., "The Cornell Commission: On Morris and the Worm," *Communications of the ACM*, vol. 32, no. 6 (June 1989).
[24] Hilarie Orman, "The Morris Worm: A Fifteen-Year Perspective," *IEEE Security & Privacy,* vol. 1, no. 5, (September/October 2003): 35-43.

The early literature was also marked by a series of prescient theorizing that in retrospect had a clear view of the coming cyber conflict environment. In their series of books including *Future Shock* (1970), *The Third Wave* (1984), and *War and Anti-War* (1993), futurists Alvin and Heidi Toffler unveiled a vision for an Information Age built on information and communication technologies that would overturn the status quo of nation-state power and precipitate "the deepest social upheaval and creative restructuring of all times."[25] The Tofflers also understood these new technologies would empower non-state groups in more violent ways as well: "The Second Wave [Industrial Age] idea that national governments are the only ones that can wield military force is now obsolete."[26] In their view, small groups in the future would be able to militarily challenge states and societies with the nuclear material and knowledge streaming out of the then-destitute former Soviet Union, with portable biological labs, and, yes, with cyber attacks. Other early important theoretical contributions were offered by John Arquilla and David Ronfeldt, whose *Networks and Netwars* (2001), *In Athena's Camp* (1997), and *Cyberwar is Coming!* (1993) offer some of the most innovative and cross-disciplinary analyses of the subject to date, especially through their application of network theory to cyber conflict.[27][28][29] Arquilla and Ronfeldt added early clarification to what was meant by "cyber war," which they defined as "conducting, and preparing to conduct, military operations according to information-related principles."[30] Finally, cyber gadflies like Winn Schwartau in his 1994 book *Information Warfare* offered the first examination of the construct of information warfare.[31]

---

25   Alvin and Heidi Toffler, *The Third Wave*, (New York, NY: Bantam, 1984), 10.

26   Toffler, *War and Anti-War* (New York, NY: Grand Central Publishing, 1993), 270.

27   John Arquilla and David Ronfeldt, *Networks and Netwars: The Future of Terror, Crime, and Militancy* (Santa Monica, CA: RAND, 2001).

28   John Arquilla and David Ronfeldt, *In Athena's camp: Preparing for Conflict in the Information Age,* (Santa Monica, CA: RAND, 1997).

29   Arquilla and Ronfeldt, "Cyberwar is coming!" *Comparative Strategy,* vol. 12, no. 2, (1993): 141-165.

30   Ibid., 144.

31   Winn Schwartau, *Information Warfare*, (New York, NY: Thunder's Mouth Press, 1994).

In the early 1990s, the policy community began to systematically explore the early symptoms of cyber conflict. In 1991, the National Research Council produced "Computers at Risk," a still relevant articulation of the importance of security in the face of advanced threats.[32] "Computers at Risk" also addressed the importance of non-state actors in information security, describing the "high-grade threat" in perhaps the first unclassified description of what is today called the Advanced Persistent Threat. Significant policy contributions in the 1990s were also made by Roger Molander and Peter Wilson, whose monograph *Strategic Information Warfare Rising* attempted to formulate a common Department of Defense strategy and policy framework for addressing the challenge of strategic information warfare.[33]

Researchers of this period also articulated clear, compelling rational for enhancing our ability to defend systems. In 1995 Bruce Berkowitz wrote that cyber attacks could degrade both civilian and military networks, emphasizing the importance of mounting an information warfare 'civil defense': "Civilian information systems are prime candidates for attack...Just as cities are targeted in strategic bombing, in future wars we can expect civilian information systems to be hacked, tapped, penetrated, bugged, and infected with computer viruses."[34] In 1996 a RAND team that included Roger Molander clearly laid out the vulnerabilities and stakes involved: "Civilian data encryption and system protection are rudimentary. Talented computer hackers in distant countries may be able to gain access to large portions of the information infrastructure underlying both US economic well being and defense logistics and communications."[35] At a more general level, Dorothy Denning's *Information Warfare and Security* provides a comprehensive and detailed look at three categories of information warfare:

---

[32] National Research Council, *Computers at Risk: Safe Computing in the Information Age* (Washington, DC: National Academies Press, 1991).

[33] Roger C. Molander, *Strategic Information Warfare Rising* (Santa Monica, CA: RAND, 1998).

[34] Bruce Berkowitz, "Warfare in the Information Age," *Issues in Science and Technology*, (University of Texas at Dallas, 1995), 59-66.

[35] Gregory J. Rattray, *Strategic Warfare in Cyberspace* Cambridge, MA: The MIT Press, 2001).

computer crime, cybercrime, and information terrorism.[36] It discusses government use of information warfare for law enforcement investigations and for military and intelligence operations, conflicts arising in the areas of free speech and encryption, offensive information warfare, deceptive exploitation of information, denial of access to information, and defensive information warfare, especially information security principles and practices.

By the mid 1990s, the US government had recognized the growing problem of cyber conflict and its various departments began to tackle key aspects of the issue. The Defense Science Board (DSB) issued two important reports on cyber conflict, particularly their 1996 report "Information Warfare – Defense" and their 2000 report "Defensive Information Operations," placing an important official DoD stamp on what was still an insurgent doctrinal movement. Other parts of the government, especially the White House staff under the leadership of CCSA initiator Richard Clarke, recognized that the nation had become increasingly reliant on civilian infrastructures, not just for the Internet and communications, but also on the electrical and financial industries. These themes of threat, vulnerability, dependence and cooperation were first introduced in the President's Commission on Critical Infrastructure Protection (PCCIP) (1997). The PCCIP report, a product of a 15-month effort, focused on requirements for ensuring the security, continuity, and availability of critical infrastructures.[37] The commission was widely credited for highlighting the fact that all infrastructures share a collective dependence on information and communication capabilities, calling for enhanced means to protect the nation from cyber threats. Many of the structures for information sharing and analysis in place today were established based on this report's recommendations and it remains a key reference for cyber studies.

At the same time that the government was paying greater attention to cyber conflict issues, the academic literature on the topic matured significantly, bringing methodological rigor and

---

[36] Dorothy Denning, *Information Warfare and Security*, (New York: Addison-Wesley Professional, 1998).

[37] *Critical Foundations: Protecting America's Infrastructures,* The Report of the President's Commission on Critical Infrastructure Protection (October 1997).

interdisciplinary breadth. Gregory Rattray's 2001 *Strategic Warfare in Cyberspace* was the first comprehensive treatment of cyber conflict that placed the phenomena within the terminological and theoretical constructs of the strategic literature, establishing a framework for examining the dynamics of warfare in the emerging cyberspace environment.[38] The book examines the nature of the cyberspace environment, the potential for disruptive action in cyberspace and the dynamics of cyber conflict. The work compares cyber with other forms of strategic warfare such as nuclear, strategic air strikes and naval blockades, and then applies the frameworks for successful conduct of strategic offense and defense to the realm of cyber conflict. The growing maturity of the cyber conflict field was also marked by the arrival of articulate skeptics of prevailing assumptions and shibboleths. Martin Libicki's 1997 monograph, *Defending Cyberspace and Other Metaphors* [39] incisively questions many of the core assumptions of the cyber warfare literature. His 2007 work, *Conquest in Cyberspace: National Security and Information Warfare* argues that the possibilities of hostile attacks are less threatening than mainstream analysts assert, and his 2009 book *Cyberdeterrence and Cyberwar* raises serious questions about the applicability of strategic theory to cyber conflict.[40]

After 9/11, the world naturally focused on counter-terrorism but the rapidly evolving and growing threats in cyberspace did not give policymakers the luxury of only focusing on kinetic terrorism. Then-Director of National Intelligence Mike McConnell's stark warning to President George W. Bush that a cyber attack against Wall Street could produce more economic damage than 9/11 led the Administration to promulgate the National Strategy to Secure Cyberspace (2003), Homeland Security Presidential Directive 7 (2003), and the Comprehensive National Cybersecurity Initiative at the end of the Administration.

---

[38] Rattray, *Strategic Warfare in Cyberspace.*

[39] Martin C. Libicki, *Defending Cyberspace and Other Metaphors,* (Washington, DC: U.S. G.P.O., 1997).

[40] Martin Libicki, *Conquest in Cyberspace: National Security and Information Warfare,* (New York, NY: Cambridge University Press, 2007); Martin Libicki, *Cyberdeterrence and Cyberwar,* (Santa Monica, CA: RAND Corporation, 2009).

Since the end of the Bush Administration, largely as a function of the growing realization of the scale of APT and its potential damage to US national power, the policy community has arguably seized upon cyber conflict as one of the top national security threats. In the run-up to the 2008 presidential election, the CSIS Commission on Cybersecurity for the 44th Presidency published "Securing Cyberspace for the 44th Presidency."[41] This report focused on issues beyond the scope of cyber conflict, but emphasized the importance of cyber security for US domestic and international policy. Following a 60-Day Cyber Review in 2009, President Obama encapsulated many of these lessons in a major speech on cyber policy, which eventually resulted in the creation of the White House "cyber czar" position.

After the issuance of the White House strategy, national institutions published three significant cyber publications. In 2009, the National Research Council published *Technology, Policy, Law, and Ethics Regarding US Acquisition and Use of Cyberattack Capabilities*, edited by William Owens, Kenneth Dam and Herbert Lin.[42] This first major review of how the US acquires and might use cyber attack capabilities provides an excellent overall description of the cyber environment and how it enables asymmetric attacks, but is limited in its treatment of non-state actors. The National Defense University's 2009 edited volume *Cyberpower and National Security* provided a significant baselining of current military-associated academic thought regarding cyber conflict.[43] Chapters covered a wide range of topics, including technology issues, military operations, crime, Internet governance, law, and critical infrastructure protection. In his policy recommendations, Franklin Kramer, continues a plea echoed for the last two decades: "Since cyber conflict and cyber power is a fundamental fact of global life, the United States must create an effective national and international strategic framework for

---

41   Center for Strategic and International Studies, *Securing Cyberspace for the 44th President: A Report on Cybersecurity for the 44th President,* (Washington DC: 8 December 2008).

42   William A. Owens, Kenneth W. Dam, and Herbert S. Lin, eds., *Technology, Policy, Law, and Ethics Regarding U.S. Acquisition and Use of Cyberattack Capabilities,* (Washington, DC: National Academies Press, 2009).

43   Franklin D. Kramer, Stuart H. Starr, and Larry Wentz, *Cyberpower and National Security,* (Washington, DC: Potomac Books, Inc., 2009).

the development and use of cyber conflict as part of an overall national security strategy." In their 2010 study *Proceedings of a Workshop on Deterring Cyberattacks: Informing Strategies and Developing Options*, the National Research Council emphasized the problem of offense, examining how, for example, attribution might be improved to better deter non-state actors. Looking at challenges of attribution, strategy policy and doctrine, deterrence concepts, and law and regulation broadly, this workshop and the associated volume of research put forward a very cohesive body of research into the social and political aspects of cyber conflict from a nation-state perspective.

Perhaps the best evidence of the emerging centrality of cyber issues in the national security policy debate is the fact that the subject has been integrated into the writings of senior national security strategists. Richard Clarke and Robert Knake's *Cyber War* traces earlier examples of cyber conflict and proposes domestic and international solutions for improving global cyber security.[44] The book also criticizes current US policy and argues that even though the US pioneered the Internet and cyberspace, it is being left behind by new developments and imperiled by new threats. Similarly, Joseph Nye discusses cyberspace and international security dynamics in his new magnum opus, *The Future of Power*.[45] The primary contribution of Nye's book is that it takes cyber conflict out of its usual self-referential mode and places it within the larger context of national security concerns for the United States and the international system.

The latest exciting, emerging theme in the cyber conflict literature highlights the reassertion of governments in cyberspace. In the early days of the Internet, self-described prophets like John Perry Barlow told governments that cyberspace was "naturally independent of the tyrannies you seek to impose on us." While it remains generally true that "governance in cyberspace resembles the American Wild West ... with limited governmental authority and engagement,"[46] governments have increasingly been able to reassert

---

[44] Richard A. Clarke and Robert Knake, *Cyber War*, (New York: Ecco, 2010).
[45] Nye, *Future of Power*.
[46] Ed. Abe Denmark and James Mulvenon, *Contested Commons: The Future of American Power in a Multipolar World*, (Center for a New American Security: Jan. 2010).

their dominance in the cyber domain, just as they do in the air, sea, space and maritime domains. Re-assertion of government sovereignty in cyberspace, while driven by every nation's increasing dependence on the network for prosperity and security, also derives from the realization that every switch, every router, every node in the network lies within the boundaries of a sovereign nation-state or travels over cable or satellite owned by a company governed by the laws of a sovereign nation-state. Authoritarian regimes, such as China, Saudi Arabia, or Iran, have been quicker to operationalize this revelation for the benefit of the state. Jack Goldsmith and Tim Wu wrote convincingly in *Who Controls the Internet* that nations were imposing borders into cyberspace to control content, whether it was China blocking content that criticized the regime or France blocking the sale of Nazi memorabilia in online auctions.[47] More recently, Evgeny Morozov argued in *The Net Delusion* that the "idea that the Internet favors the oppressed rather than the oppressor is marred by ... a naïve belief in the emancipatory nature of online communication."[48] The recent, near total shutdown of the Egyptian Internet will surely generate more significant research both into the government control of the Internet– as well as whether such control will be effective.[49]

Chapter Summaries

Given the review of our understanding of cyber conflict and its dynamics is growing but at a nascent stage, we now turn to a summary of the chapters of our monograph, which aims to synthesize previous insights and create systematic knowledge about cyber conflict.

---

[47] Jack Goldsmith and Tim Wu, *Who Controls the Internet? Illusions of a Borderless World* (New York: Oxford University Press, 2006).

[48] Evgeny Morozov, *The Net Delusion: The Dark Side of Internet Freedom* (New York: PublicAffairs, 2011), xiii.

[49] See the excellent blogs from Renesys which tracked these developments as they happened: James Cowie, "Egypt Leaves the Internet," 27 January 2011 http://www.renesys.com/blog/2011/01/egypt-leaves-the-internet.shtml and "Egypt Returns to the Internet," (accessed 22 September 2011); James Cowie, "Egypt Returns to the Internet," 2 February 2011, http http://www.renesys.com/blog/2011/02/egypt-returns-to-the-internet.shtml.

Chapter One: Strategic-Level Issues

The emergence of cyber conflict is the strategic challenge of the 21st century, adding to the ongoing dilemmas posed by nuclear warfare and terrorism. When examining the core strategic issues posed by cyber conflict, one must first begin with definitional problems and progressing through the core elements of the historical canon, exploring the cyber dimensions of concepts such as deterrence, compellence, escalation control, command and control, and war termination. While inspired by the works of Kahn, Wohlstetter, Schelling, Ellsberg, et al, one must also explicitly delineate the fundamental similarities and differences with the nuclear analogy, building a conceptual structure that does not simply attempt to pound a square cyber peg into a round nuclear hole. This chapter begins first by placing cyber conflict within the current strategic environment, highlighting two core problems, one technical and the other policy-related. The second section directly confronts the strengths and weaknesses of the nuclear analogy for cyber, adopting useful concepts and translating them to a very different technological phenomenon. The third and central section applies the "big concepts" (deterrence, compellence, etc.) to cyber, and analyzes the dynamics across a range of actors, including nation-states, non-state actors and hybrids.

The chapter concludes by asserting that the cyberspace domain is inherently unstable, and teases out the strategic implications of that finding. The current strategic cyber environment is marked by an inability to establish credible deterrence and effectively prevent the emergence of adversaries and conflicts in cyberspace detrimental to US interests. The sources of this instability are manifold. First, the technical architecture undergirding cyberspace is highly permissive of cyber intrusions and attacks, resulting in a system that is extremely hard to defend and confers dominance to the offense. The defender can mitigate the asymmetry by reducing the degree of interconnectivity, or even disconnecting networks, but this move is very costly given the growing reliance of the United States and advanced nations on these networks for a wide range of economic activity and military operations. Second, the design of the architecture often provides the attacker with anonymity and plausible deniability, exacerbated by the lack of effective governance of the network focused on mitigating malicious activity. Third, the relatively low cost of technology and operations significantly lowers the barriers to entry for the attacker, enabling a wide range of actors to acquire capabilities. Fourth, cyber operations running at the rapid "speed of the network" deny defenders and the political leadership sufficient time for assessment and decision-making. Automation may mitigate this problem, but the risks are both high and unknown. Fifth, the pace of technological change and the breadth of network connectivity are outpacing both defensive approaches at the enterprise or engineering level as well as the policy and legal constructs promulgated to guide their operations.

Moreover, these conditions are only getting worse with the proliferation of social media, mobile communications, and the migration to cloud computing. The Internet underground capable of exploiting these trends is alive and well, with pirates and mercenaries thriving in a swampy ecosystem that makes hiding and attacking too easy. And lastly, while the issues are acknowledged, little progress is being made in terms of improving security and resilience as a key aspect of Internet governance. The implications of this conclusion are explored in the final section of this monograph.

What are the implications of this cyber instability? First, it undermines deterrence, especially against non-state actors, who have the significant strategic advantage of being able to limit options for cyber retaliation and may seek to foster an unstable cyber conflict environment. Second, it leads to the temptation to consider preventive war or preemptive war options that would remove the enemy's capacity for effective cyber operations before it can raise its defenses and perhaps even degrade conventional military operations assuming the adequate intelligence exists to enable effective preemption. Third, it provides strong incentives for escalation to the use of other military capabilities once conflict has begun, primarily to prevent these options from being paralyzed by use of cyber attack. Thus, it is clear that this instability is highly dangerous, especially for status quo cyber actors like the United States who have so much to lose. Indeed, the United States desperately seeks cyber stability for a range of reasons, including continuing economic prosperity, wielding global soft power, and avoiding asymmetric security vulnerabilities with state and non-state adversaries.

Yet despite the hopes and focus of most current approaches to managing cyber security, we cannot expect to achieve cyber stability alone. The US Government has limited influence on the fundamental causes of cyber instability, which also look as if they will only worsen for an extended period. We cannot construct a safe haven nor does a cyber high ground exist to seize and hold. Worse, there are difficult tradeoffs in achieving our objectives. Core principles of Internet freedom, tech innovation, and openness/connectivity conflict with the security imperative, and our open political system demands that the former be accorded at least equal status with the latter. In response, we must therefore implement a national or even global strategy in cyberspace to create stability through resilience and efforts to clean up the ecosystem. The recent White House strategy is a positive if belated move in this direction, but we must acknowledge limits to current approaches and boldly move to claim strategic advantage.

The implications of cyber instability, the current state of United States and global efforts to address this concern, and examination of alternative approaches constitute major themes addressed throughout the remainder of the work.

Chapter Two: Military and Operational

Chapter Two explores cyber conflict at the operational level, focusing particularly on how military and intelligence strategy, doctrine, and organizations have evolved in the United States, culminating in the formation of a Cyber Command (CYBERCOM). While CYBERCOM has provided a coherent construct for the organization of US military cyber operations it has also resulted in the perception that the US seeks to militarize and dominate cyber space. The chapter also highlights the continuing strains between the cyber-related activities and roles of the military on the one hand and the intelligence community on the other, which is complicated by the increasing use of cyber capabilities to further intelligence collection and constraints posed by current domestic legal frameworks to effectively integrate such operations.

Given the nature of the cyber environment, what sort of military and intelligence organizations or capabilities are needed? As a first principle, bureaucracies and people in this environment must develop new capabilities to adapt to new threats in a fast and agile way. Second, military cyber defense must be increasingly collaborative with other actors, including non-governmental organizations, researchers, corporations, and other groups outside traditional national security communities. This collaboration must be focused on developing resilience in the face of a continuously evolving threat that has demonstrated that it *will* penetrate defenses. Third, those combating cyber threats must ensure that they maintain sufficient knowledge capture to build upon existing experience and lessons. The chapter concludes with the assessment that current US military and intelligence approaches must demonstrate significant continued evolution in light of the challenges posed by strategic instability, with a focus on removing policy and operational barriers to defensive collaboration and avoiding generating perceptions of the US as a source of threats and instability in cyberspace.

Chapter Three: Non-State Actors in Cyberspace

Current CCSA research on the "new security agenda" sector focuses on the role of non-state actors in cyber conflict and the challenges of managing conflicts that will necessarily involve much greater roles for non-state actors. By highlighting the common misperception regarding the dominance of state actors in the dynamics of conflict in cyberspace, this chapter focuses instead on developing new thinking about cyber conflict management and mitigation, emphasizing the current and potential role of non-states. CCSA research covers substantial ground in considering the new roles for non-state actors and their implications on traditional and new security considerations.

The potential emergence of significant cyber threats based on non-state actors conducting guerilla campaigns against economic and social centers of gravity is discussed along with the limitations of traditional national security and law enforcement approaches in addressing such threats. The research concludes with the need to develop mechanisms to foster defensive collaboration as a means to more effectively address concerns of cyber instability that involves a wide range of non-state actors – network operators, vendors, security researchers, CERTs, and other operational responders. Such collaboration will prove an essential aspect of both national security-focused strategies as well as help improve global capacity to reduce the number and mitigate the consequences of cyber conflict. The policy and operational consequences of such a multi-stakeholder collaborative defense will require more in-depth research and thought.

Chapter Four: Domestic and International Law

This chapter explores the domestic and international legal framework for cyber operations. While taking a positivist approach to US and international law, the main legal findings frame growing consensus on a number of legal issues. First, the relatively immaturity of applying international and domestic legal constructs to malicious activity in cyberspace has also resulted in a hesitancy of both governmental and private sector actors to take steps to reduce malicious activity that is contributing to the instability of the cyber environment. Additionally, norms and customs related to behavior in cyberspace and obligations for managing cyber conflict must be developed over time. While the process of norm maturation will be potentially difficult and contentious, it is important to begin that dialogue now with both states and non-state actors. Like-minded states must also begin acting on agreed-upon foundations, but the basis for agreement requires broader, more comprehensive thinking about the causes and dynamics of cyber conflict, which can then translate into more-focused regime building efforts and policies. Remaining research issues for in the legal and ethical field include exploring the effects of legal norms for cyberspace upon traditional political, social, and economic frameworks. Even more broadly, this chapter begins to assess the potential contributions of international, regional, and bilateral treaties in governing conflict in cyberspace, especially the interplay between international legal norms and the current attempts to develop policy norms to govern cyber security. Future CCSA research may focus on the maturation of international cyber norms through the implementation of legal regimes and varying models, as norms may play a fundamental role in terms of governance of both state and non-state actors in seeking cyber stability.

Chapter Five: Approaches for Mitigating Cyber Conflict

The monograph's final chapter proposes three approaches for more effective management of cyber conflict challenges. These approaches are not mutually exclusive and may have complementary features regarding their use by the United States and others seeking cyber security. As core assumptions, the models incorporate earlier analysis about cyber instability and the importance of non-state actors, both in their development and their subsequent policy recommendations.

Firstly, the public health model considers how useful norms for states and non-state actors, like hygiene, can limit the spread of disease. Furthermore, the mandatory reporting of infectious diseases can provide a model for early warning, prevention, and intervention in cyberspace. The second proposed "environmental model" also focuses on cyber clean-up. It suggests the application of a legal regime to deal with problems such as pollution and provides for a meaningful role for non-state actors, while touching upon similarities with the global development agenda. Finally, the irregular warfare approach illustrates how an existing military mindset may be leveraged to provide new insight onto cyber conflict management and mitigation. This approach demonstrates the parallels between the asymmetric and indirect means and tactics employed by irregular warfare and cyber conflict actors. This not to say, however, that our adversaries are engaging in an irregular war in cyberspace – though some may have indeed adopted this as a primary goal/strategy – merely that examining the tactics and strategies of irregular operations on the ground can provide useful insight into conflicts in cyberspace. We believe that the ability to adapt current approaches and think more in terms of management of conflict, as well as developing approaches that prioritize addressing a wide range of actors and the role of collaboration will be essential in informing US policy and meeting the challenges of cyber instability.

The Future of the Cyber Conflict Research Agenda

Each chapter of this book asks new questions or highlights challenges that require more analysis, demonstrating the continued need for innovative, multidisciplinary coordination and research on cyber conflict.

Regarding strategic-level issues from Chapter One, the posited concept of inherent cyber instability has broad, far-reaching implications for academics, policymakers, and strategists. If decision makers accept that cyberspace is inherently unstable from a strategic conflict management perspective and abandon attempting to create a stable cyber environment, this may naturally result in an increased emphasis on resilience, risk management and mitigation, and the potential creation of risk reduction centers.

The analysis in Chapter Two raised many important questions about the future of military and intelligence cyber operations, such as: How can the balance of intelligence gain and intelligence loss in cyberspace be better optimized? What research can be conducted into the supply chain dimensions of cyber conflict? How can cyber warfare capabilities be best integrated with other military forces? How can the nation enhance the relationships between and among Department of Defense, Department of Homeland Security, and other key cyber players? How can we find ways to convert research from academia into actionable recommendations for implementation by government?

Chapter Three highlighted the critical importance of non-state actors, leading to new questions about their role in cyber conflict: How can we better incorporate the offensive and defensive intent and capability of non-state actors in cyber conflict research? Because the majority of cyberspace is primarily owned, operated, and populated by private actors, what role will they play in cyber conflict? How will the role of the state change vis-à-vis the variety of actors in the cyber ecosystem? What role will non-state actors play in cyber risk reduction?

Chapters Four and Five emphasize the importance of norm development and the ground rules for global collaboration. Future research should explore the boundaries between domestic and international strategy, as well as the different categories for norm development, including the relevant legal, policy, technical, and economic concerns.

While these recommendations may seem daunting when combined together, the CCSA cyber conflict research agenda and its further development provides discipline in answering new questions as well as those that have not yet been addressed. One of the key challenges of this field is its interdisciplinary nature, which is reflected in the large number of questions that still remain open for dialogue and discussion. We hope the monograph you are about to read both stimulates thought and helps make a cumulative addition to the body of knowledge in this field.

Closing Call to Action

The Cyber Conflict Studies Association's two-year study has lead to the sobering conclusion that the current strategic cyber environment is fundamentally unstable. What are the implications of this cyber instability? First, it undermines deterrence, especially against non-state actors, who have the significant strategic advantage of being able to limit options for cyber retaliation and may seek to foster an unstable cyber conflict environment. Second, it leads to the temptation to consider preventive war or preemptive war options that would remove the enemy's capacity for effective cyber operations before it can raise its defenses and perhaps even degrade conventional military operations, assuming the adequate intelligence exists to enable effective preemption. Third, it provides strong incentives for escalation to the use of other military capabilities once conflict has begun, primarily to prevent these options from being paralyzed by use of cyber attack. Thus, it is clear that this instability is highly dangerous, especially for status quo cyber actors like the United States who have so much to lose. Indeed, the United States desperately seeks cyber stability for a range of reasons, including continuing economic prosperity, wielding global soft power, and avoiding asymmetric security vulnerabilities with state and non-state adversaries.

Yet despite the hopes and focus of most current approaches to managing cyber security, we cannot expect to achieve cyber stability alone. The US Government has limited influence on the fundamental causes of cyber instability and they look to get worse for extended period. We cannot construct a safe haven nor does a cyber high ground exist to seize and hold. Worse, there are difficult tradeoffs in achieving our objectives. Core principles of Internet freedom, tech innovation, and openness/connectivity conflict with the security imperative, and our open political system demands that the former be accorded at least equal status with the latter. In response, we must therefore implement a national or even global strategy in cyberspace to create stability through resilience and efforts to clean up the ecosystem. The White House strategy is a positive if belated move in this direction, but we must acknowledge limits to current approaches and boldly move to claim strategic advantage.

Chapter One

Strategy and Cyber Conflict

Introduction

The emergence of cyber conflict is one of the strategic challenges of the 21st century, adding to the ongoing dilemmas posed by nuclear warfare and terrorism. This chapter addresses the core strategic issues posed by cyber conflict, beginning with definitional problems and progressing through the core elements of the historical canon, exploring the cyber dimensions of concepts such as deterrence, compellence, escalation control, command and control, and war termination. While inspired by the works of Kahn, Wohlstetter, Schelling, Ellsberg, et al, this study also seeks to explicitly delineate the fundamental similarities and differences with the nuclear analogy, building a conceptual structure that does not simply attempt to pound a rough-fitting cyber peg into a nuclear hole. This chapter begins first by placing cyber conflict within the current strategic environment, highlighting two core problems, one technical and the other policy-related. The second section directly confronts the strengths and weaknesses of the nuclear analogy for cyber, adopting useful concepts and translating them to a very different technological phenomenon. The third and central section applies the big concepts (i.e. deterrence and compellence) to cyber, and analyzes the dynamics across a range of actors, including nation-states, non-state actors and hybrids. The final section lays out a roadmap for building credible deterrence, assessing the limits of the possible in the short- and long-term given the inherently unstable cyber environment.

The Emergence of Cyber in the New Strategic Environment

The emergence of cyberspace is a tectonic event of the 21st century. It has fundamentally altered politics, economics, social interaction, and national security, providing dramatic new opportunities, capabilities, vulnerabilities, and threats. With each passing day, cyberspace becomes an indispensible, even irreplaceable, part of the daily lives of individuals, companies and entire nations. Yet this rapidly growing dependence on the "network" is bedeviled by two core problems, one technical and the other policy-related:

The core technical problem at the heart of cyberspace is that the underlying architecture was never designed with security in mind; indeed, the original designers never imagined that the network would be used for malicious purposes. Meanwhile, the threat environment has quickly metastasized from relatively harmless webpages defacements in the mid-1990s to state-level network exploit activities, such as the Silicon Valley hacks in late 2009 and early 2010, representing a serious and potentially growing challenge to the success of the American innovation economy. The vulnerabilities that facilitate these and other cyber attacks stem mostly from the original design of the network. In response to these threats, we have done the best we can with an imperfect architecture, gluing security onto the network and attempting to mitigate the damage.

The core policy problem in cyberspace is that the evolution of the technological architecture has vastly outpaced the corresponding set of conceptual, doctrinal, bureaucratic and legal structures, resulting in a reactive and atavistic policy dynamic where today's ideas and organizations are addressing yesterday's problems (i.e., privacy, intellectual property, cyberwar) with no flexibility to deal with the future problems created by the introduction of as-yet uninvented technologies and applications. For national security strategists, it therefore feels like 1946 in cyber, where atomic weapons have been invented and we have only begun to think conceptually about their use and implications.[1] While the cupboard is not entirely bare (books like

---

[1]   For a discussion of lessons and parallels to nuclear strategy see Joseph S. Nye, Jr., "Nuclear Lessons for Cyber Security?" *Strategic Studies Quarterly* (Forthcoming 2012).

Gregory Rattray's *Strategic Warfare in Cyberspace* and Martin Libicki's *Cyberdeterrence* are two early examples that could reasonably be described as our generation's equivalent of Bernard Brodie's 1946 classic *The Absolute Weapon*), the cyber conflict literature is certainly not as well-developed, nuanced and mature as the nuclear warfare canon of Kahn, Wohlstetter, Schelling and Ellsberg. We lack consensus on even basic terminology, and suffer from a dearth of meaningful case studies other than the proto-conflicts in Estonia in 2007 and Georgia in 2008. Indeed, we find ourselves in the same embryonic state with respect to organizational development. The recent standup of US Cyber Command (CYBERCOM), for example, parallels the establishment of Strategic Air Command in 1946 at the dawn of the nuclear age, but it was not until Secretary of Defense Robert McNamara conducted a top-down review in the early 1960s that nuclear warfare strategy began to move beyond its relatively primitive "strike first with everything" posture.

Ill-Fitting Clothes: Historical Analogies for Cyber Conflict

When examining any new form of conflict or warfare, it is understandable to look for historical analogies or pre-existing frameworks, if only to find some useful insights or a path to the creation of wisdom and knowledge.[2] For cyber, given its potential global and potentially existential impact, many strategists have naturally turned to the Cold War and the thousands of pages in the nuclear canon. An extensive review of this literature reveals many, many important insights that can be applied to cyber conflict, and also many ideas that cannot be easily expropriated, though primarily because of technological incompatibilities.

Before embarking on a comprehensive exercise in comparisons and contrasts, however, it is important to define terms and boundaries. For our purposes, we focus on "cyber conflict," defined as "the conduct of large- scale, politically motivated conflict based on the use

---

[2]   For the sake of completeness, it is important to note that some analysts (perhaps theocrats would be a better term) of cyber conflict continue to believe that cyber conflict is distinctly unique phenomenon, with no historical antecedents.

of offensive and defensive capabilities to disrupt digital systems, networks, and infrastructures, including the use of cyber-based weapons or tools by non- state/transnational actors in conjunction with other forces for political ends." We use the phrase "cyber conflict" advisedly, following a long series of debates about the utility of popular phrases like "cyber war." We judge the latter to have two main flaws: (1) it is too limiting in scope, excluding important cyber-based conflicts that fall short of a "war" threshold, such as hacktivism and cyberterrorism; and (2) it is premature, in the sense that the vast majority of malicious behavior we see on the network is cyber-espionage, not destabilizing militarized conflict between nation-states or between nation-states and non-state actors.[3]

What, then, are the key similarities and differences between cyber conflict and nuclear warfare?

Table 1.1: Key Similarities Between Cyber and Nuclear Conflict

1.   Both operate at all three levels of military operations: strategic,[4] operational and tactical, with the potential to have effects ranging from small- to population-scale.

2.   While nuclear weapons have unique kinetic capabilities, both cyber and nuclear conflicts have the capacity to create large-scale, even existentially, disruptive effects.

3.   Both can be conducted between nation-states, between a nation-state and non-state-actors, or between hybrids involving nation-states and non-state-actor proxies.

4.   Both nuclear and cyber conflict "could present the adversary with decisive defeat, negating the need to fight conventional wars."[5]

---

[3]   For a solid definition of cyber attack, see the definition in William A. Owens, Kenneth W. Dam, and Herbert S. Lin, eds., *Technology, Policy, Law, and Ethics Regarding US Acquisition and Use of Cyberattack Capabilities* (Washington, DC: National Academies Press, 2009), 1: "Cyberattack refers to deliberate actions to alter, disrupt, deceive, degrade, or destroy computer systems or networks or the information and/or programs resident in or transiting these systems or networks."

[4]   The term "strategic" is defined here to mean warfare designed to "defeat opponents through attacks on centers of gravity without fighting fielded forces." See Gregory Rattray, *Strategic Warfare in Cyberspace* (Cambridge, MA: MIT Press, 2001), 20.

5. Both can intentionally or unintentionally cause "cascade effects" beyond the scope of the original attack target.

Table 1.2: Key Differences Between Cyber and Nuclear Conflict

1. Attribution of the attacker was never a problem in the mature phases of nuclear conflict, thanks to technologies like the DEW line and the DSP constellation, but it is one of the central problems in cyber conflict.

2. The medium for cyber conflict is man-made, largely in private sector hands, and would likely traverse infrastructure of non-combatants, while the medium for nuclear conflict includes only sovereign domains (nation's airspace, land, coastal waters) and the global commons (airspace, sea, and space).

3. Low cost and ease of availability means that millions of people around the world have potential access to potent cyber attack tools, whereas access to operational nuclear weapons was historically limited to a small number of nation-states with sufficient resources to build them.

4. Whereas nuclear warfare can only be conducted in a violent way, cyber conflict can be conducted in "either a physically violent or nonviolent way," creating both physical destruction (e.g., "blanking the screen of air traffic controllers so that airliners crash") as well as virtual destruction (e.g., deleting data).[6]

5. Computer network attack can be conducted covertly, whereas the dramatic, overt effects of nuclear attack make covertness impossible.

6. Use of nuclear weapons is unambiguously viewed as an act of aggression justifying retaliation, whereas significant ambiguities continue to bedevil attempts to define clear legal and ethical boundaries in cyber conflict.

7. Offensive and defensive weapons are generally easier to distinguish in nuclear combat, while knowledge of "the tools

---

[5]   Ibid.

[6]   Ibid., 19.

and techniques used to conduct digital warfare are often useful to both attackers and defenders."[7]

8. Cyber attack and defense tools have significant dual-use applications (i.e. military and civilian), whereas there are no appreciable dual-use applications for nuclear weapons.

9. Whereas the effects of nuclear weapons can be scientifically delineated from the laws of physics (see *Effects of Nuclear Weapons*), cyber attacks are much more uncertain because of the potential of cascading effects.

10. Since US government and military networks are scanned and pinged every second, *thresholds* is a much more difficult problem for retaliation and escalation to cyber attack than the "acknowledged threshold" of nuclear attack.[8]

11. In nuclear war, "the 1000th bomb could be as powerful as the first," whereas in cyber the second attack could be thwarted by the results of the first.[9]

12. In nuclear conflict, counterforce was possible, but there are real questions as to whether you can really attack a nation's offensive cyber capabilities.[10]

13. In nuclear war, one has a clear understanding about the intervention of third parties but a large and ever shifting range of third parties are intrinsically involved in cyber conflict whether the primary participants want them to be or not.[11]

14. Private firms were not expected to defend themselves in nuclear war, whereas they are responsible for their own defense in cyber conflict.[12]

15. Finally, no higher level of war existed in nuclear conflict, whereas cyber can always escalate to nuclear war.[13]

---

[7]   Ibid., 135.
[8]   Martin Libicki, *Cyberdeterrence and Cyberwar* (Santa Monica, CA: RAND, 2009), xvi.
[9]   Ibid.
[10] Ibid.
[11] Ibid.
[12] Ibid.
[13] Ibid.

The differences listed in Table 1.2 cannot be dismissed as minor, since some strike at the very heart of core dynamics of nuclear conflict. *But the terminology and conceptual vocabulary of the strategic conflict canon remains a critical resource for understanding cyber conflict once it is modified to accommodate cyber's different technological characteristics and modalities.*

Cyber and the Big Concepts: Deterrence and the Dynamics of Deterrence Failure

In order to test the applicability of the core concepts of the strategic canon to cyber conflict, it is necessary to systematically define terms and then adapt them to the new dynamics in cyberspace, much as earlier generations applied the lessons of the two world wars and centuries of military history to the emerging nuclear age. Given the asymmetric vulnerability of the United States to cyber exploitation and attack, we must give top priority to the very difficult challenges of cyber deterrence. Our early experience with cyber conflict, however, tells us that cyber deterrence will be difficult if not impossible to implement in the near-term, so we must also discuss key post-deterrence concepts that traverse the entire spectrum of conflict, including signaling, thresholds, escalation, and even the dynamics of war termination.

Deterrence

While the United States wisely retains the intention and capability to initiate cyber conflict at a time and place of its own choosing, it naturally seeks to deter other adversaries from the same goal, particularly given the asymmetric dependence of the United States on cyberspace for economic, political, and technological power. While it is well-known that US government, military, and corporate networks have been the target of sustained computer network exploit activities over the last ten years, it must be noted that the country has not yet been the target of the type of large-scale computer network attack envisioned by Richard Clarke and others in their writings. How can we explain this apparent gap? Why have adversaries not taken advantage of clear vulnerabilities to launch cyber attacks against the United States? Have they not developed sufficient capabilities to do so? Hard to believe given the sophistication of the intrusion sets. Has there not yet been the right combination of strategic circumstance and perceived payoff, such as the China-Taiwan contingency involving US military intervention discussed later in the chapter, to justify using known capabilities? Or, despite its strategic confusion, does the United States currently enjoy a form of tacit cyber deterrence from computer network attack, and if so, what is the basis for this tacit deterrence?

Before proceeding further, rigor demands that we define what we mean by cyber deterrence. Fortunately, we do not need to till new ground, as recent work by Libicki and Kugler and others have provided a sufficient definitional foundation for further work. The most useful general definition of deterrence is offered by William Kaufmann:

> Deterrence consists of essentially two basic components: first, the expressed intention to defend a certain interest; secondly, the demonstrated capability actually to achieve the defense of the interest in question, or to inflict such a cost on the attacker that, even if he should be able to gain his end, it would not seem the effort to him.[14]

More simply, "deterrence is simply the persuasion of one's opponent that the costs and/or risks of a given course of action he might take outweigh its benefits."[15] For militaries, organizations dedicated to use the force to defense national interests, deterrence ironically aims to avoid the use of force:

> Deterrence is concerned with the exploitation of potential force. It is concerned with persuading a potential enemy that he should in his own interests avoid certain courses of activity...A theory of deterrence would be, in effect, a

---

[14]   William Kaufmann, "The Evolution of Deterrence, 1945-1958," unpublished RAND research (1958), cited in Libicki, *Cyberdeterrence and Cyberwar*, 7.

[15]   Alexander George and Richard Smoke, *Deterrence in American Foreign Policy: Theory and Practice*, (New York: Columbia University Press, 1974), 11.

theory of the skillful non-use of military forces, and for this purpose deterrence requires something broader than military skills.[16]

Translating these conceptual ideas into language resonant with US interests, DoD defines it thus:

Deterrence [seeks to] convince adversaries not to take actions that threaten US vital interests by means of decisive influence over their decision-making. Decisive influence is achieved by credibly threatening to deny benefits and/or impose costs, while encouraging restraint by convincing the actor that restraint will result in an acceptable outcome.[17]

The strategic canon points out that deterrence comes in at least two distinct forms, deterrence by punishment and deterrence by denial:

Deterrence by punishment threatens to inflict unacceptable costs on an adversary that takes aggressive actions. If he knows he will suffer such costs should he take such actions, he will refrain from taking them. Deterrence by denial seeks to deny the adversary success from his aggressive actions. If he knows his aggressive actions will not result in success, he will refrain from taking them.[18]

Yet deterrence is also not a single move in a game. As Schelling argues in *The Strategy of Conflict*, "each party must be confident that the other will not jeopardize future opportunities by destroying trust at the outset. This confidence does not always exist; and one of the purposes of piecemeal bargains is to cultivate

---

[16]   Thomas Schelling, *The Strategy of Conflict* (Cambridge, MA: Harvard University Press, 1981), 7.

[17]   United States Department of Defense, *Deterrence Operations: Joint Operating Concept*, Version 2.0, December 2006, www.dtic.mil/futurejointwarfare/concepts/do_joc_v20.doc.

[18]   Owens, Dam, and Lin, eds., *Cyberattack Capabilities,* 40.

the necessary mutual expectations."[19] Indeed Schelling asserts that deterrence "requires that there be both conflict and common interest between the parties involved,"[20] and concerns itself with "influencing the choices that another party will make, and doing it by influencing his expectations of how we will behave."[21] As a result, deterrence can be single or iterated; involving adversary dynamics that are either asymmetric or symmetric, and past actions (or lack of actions) can deeply influence adversary calculations of risk and gain.[22]

When applied to our subject, however, nuclear deterrence, even conventional deterrence, looks in retrospect much easier to achieve than cyber deterrence. Following the framework above, the remainder of this section will explore cyber deterrence through denial and then punishment, followed by an examination of the temporal dynamics of sustaining either over time.

Cyber Deterrence Through Denial?

Deterrence through denial is primarily a defensive game. During the Cold War, efforts to achieve deterrence through denial focused on basing and deployment modes, civil defense, and the triad, with the goal of denying the adversary the ability to launch a decapitating first strike. Ironically, deterrence through denial was one of the primary impetuses for the development of the packet-switched network itself, growing out of a concern about the vulnerability of nuclear command and control.[23] Cyber deterrence through denial is also primarily based on computer network defense. One piece of good news is that the "attribution problem," which occupies center stage in the discussion of the dilemmas posed by cyber deterrence by punishment, is not as significant an issue in cyber deterrence by denial, because it is not critical to know who might attack, only whether you are vulnerable to attack. Also, two primary methods for

---

[19]   Schelling, *The Strategy of Conflict*, 45.

[20]   Ibid., 11.

[21]   Ibid., 13.

[22]   Martin Libicki, *Cyberdeterrence and Cyberwar* (Santa Monica, CA: RAND Corporation, 2009).

[23]   See Paul Baran's 11-volume "On Distributed Communications" series (1964), http://www.rand.org/about/history/baran-list.html (accessed September 23, 2011).

protecting retaliatory forces are mobility and concealment.[24] Cyber forces, by virtue of their form factor, (i.e., a laptop is easier to conceal than a ballistic missile submarine) are already more mobile and more concealed than nuclear forces ever were. Finally, the inability to disarm an adversary's cyber attack capability has three benefits: (1) reduced incentives for preemption; (2) retaliation can be more focused and proportional; and (3) reduced demand for immediate retaliation ("use it or lose it").[25]

But the cyber offense-defense balance *is* a huge problem for cyber deterrence by denial. As discussed earlier, fundamental security was not built into the architecture design of cyberspace, and we have been gluing security onto the side of the network ever since. Without fundamental re-architecting of the network, which is unlikely in the short-term, is deterrence by denial even possible? In the short-term, Rattray argues that these defensive dilemmas put a greater onus on risk management than impenetrable protection:

> Diffuse vulnerabilities and limited resources also require defensive efforts predicated on managing the risks of attacks rather than establishing comprehensive defenses capable of assured protection.[26]

In fact, Owens, et al, writes in the NRC study that "the gap between the attacker's capability to attack many vulnerable targets and the defender's inability to defend all of them is growing rather than diminishing."[27] Additionally, cyber offensive capabilities are dramatically cheaper than effective cyber defensive capabilities. As is often pointed out, the cyber warrior, armed perhaps with a minimal kit (computer, Internet connection, and publicly available tools) only needs to find one way in, but the cyber defender, protecting perhaps a huge network of thousands of heterogeneous nodes with dozens of access points, needs to stop every possible

---

[24] Schelling, *The Strategy of Conflict*, 243.

[25] Libicki, *Cyberdeterrence and Cyberwar*, 61-62. At the same time, there may be pressure for prompt retaliation in some circumstances, i.e. using intelligence before the information goes stale by virtue of configuration changes in the attacker's systems.

[26] Rattray, *Strategic Warfare in Cyberspace*, 474.

[27] Owens, Dam, and Lin, eds., *Cyberattack Capabilities,* 44.

avenue of approach. Thus, deterrence by denial in cyber is also cost-prohibitive. For both of these reasons, it appears that cyber deterrence by denial may be less credible than deterrence by punishment, which likely has a much higher chance of success.

Cyber Deterrence Through Punishment

Deterrence through punishment is primarily an offensive game, based on the threat of credible and painful retaliation for attacks. In the nuclear era, this was a numbers game, calculated through drawdown curves and force exchange models for land-, sea-, and air-based weapons. Strategic "stability" was achieved when both sides had the ability to inflict significant second-strike punishment on the other, creating "absolute certainty in the opponent's mind that nuclear attack would draw severe reprisal."[28] In the early nuclear period, officials argued that deterrence could be achieved through the threat of "massive retaliation,"[29] such that any attack would result in "mutually assured destruction" (MAD).[30] By the 1960s, however, this was rejected as an unrealistic concept with no limited war thresholds and was replaced by a doctrine of Flexible Response, championed by Secretary of Defense Robert McNamara.[31] Flexible response encompassed using the full range of military response to respond to aggression, without necessarily escalating to the nuclear

---

[28]   Bruce Blair, *Strategic Command and Control: Redefining the Nuclear Threat* (Washington, DC: Brookings Institution Press, 1985), 19.

[29]   In 1954, John Foster Dulles argued that the US intended in the future to deter aggression by depending "primarily upon a great capacity to retaliate, instantly, by means and at places of our own choosing." See John Foster Dulles, "The Evolution of Foreign Policy," Department of State Bulletin, Vol. 30, (January 1954), 25.

[30]   MAD is defined as "the ability to deter a deliberate nuclear attack upon the United States or its allies by maintaining at all time a clear and unmistakable ability to inflict an unacceptable degree of damage upon any aggressor, or combination of aggressors, even after absorbing a first strike." See Alain Enthoven and K. Wayne Smith, *How Much is Enough? Shaping the Defense Program, 1961-1969*, (Santa Monica, CA: RAND, 1971), 174.

[31]   For a discussion of the theory behind flexible response and its implementation, see Chapter Eight, "Kennedy, Johnson, and Flexible Response," and Chapter Nine, "Implementing the Flexible Response: Vietnam as a Test Case" in John Lewis Gaddis, *Strategies of Containment* (New York: Oxford University Press, 1982).

option. As Bruce Blair asserts, "because it is assumed that neither side can disarm the opponent, choosing to attack risks nuclear annihilation; attack would thus be irrational and both sides are deterred,"[32] since "the expected costs of a first strike will always outweigh the benefits."[33] As a result, "the study of nuclear strategy is...the study of the non-use of these weapons."[34]

On the other hard, instability arises and "mutual deterrence dissolves when one or both sides can remove the opponent's ability to inflict severe damage in retaliation."[35] This leads to the temptation to strike preemptively, which is the "worst of all hypothetical worlds."[36] Yet MAD prevailed and perversely succeeded in preventing nuclear war during the Cold War, and as a consequence, "...meaningful military victory in the modern nuclear era came to be regarded as unrealizable."[37] As a result, strategic forces were used as "instruments of threat, coercion, and intimidation rather than of military victory."[38]

In the cyber realm, deterrence by punishment theoretically offers better chances of success, especially against adversaries that have well-developed cyber infrastructure. As Owens, et al, argue:

> Deterrence by punishment is more likely to be an effective strategy against nations that are highly dependent on information technology, because such nations have a much larger number of potential targets that can be attacked. Nevertheless, even nations with a less technologically sophisticated national infrastructure are probably vulnerable to cyberattack in selected niches.[39]

Moreover, the will to retaliate is arguably less of a factor in cyber attack than nukes, given its plausible deniability, potentially covert nature, and less physically destructive effects.[40]

---

[32]   Blair, *Strategic Command and Control,* 16.
[33]   Ibid.
[34]   Lawrence Freedman, "The First Two Generations of Nuclear Strategists," *Makers of Modern Strategy: From Machiavelli to the Nuclear Age,* ed. Peter Paret (Princeton: Princeton University Press, 1986), 735.
[35]   Blair, *Strategic Command and Control,* 17.
[36]   Ibid.
[37]   Ibid., 18.
[38]   Ibid., 17.
[39]   Owens, Dam, and Lin, eds., *Cyberattack Capabilities,* 41.
[40]   Libicki, *Cyberdeterrence and Cyberwar,* 69-71.

Yet cyber deterrence through punishment is also highly problematic. The main challenges for cyber deterrence through punishment are: (1) the so-called "attribution problem," which makes it difficult to identify the attacker in the first place; and (2) a series of credibility problems, including automaticity of response, unavailability of retaliatory targets, demonstration of effect, uncertainty of cyber effects, repeatability of effect, survivability of retaliatory capability, thresholds, signaling, command and control, and extended deterrence. None of these challenges can be solved alone through policy measures like stated declaratory policies. *All of these challenges lead to a fundamental strategic instability in cyber conflict, and undermine the utility of deterrence through punishment.*

Issue #1: The Cyber Attribution Problem

The single greatest challenge to effective cyber deterrence through punishment is the difficulty of exactly attributing the origin and perpetrator of the attack. For most of the Cold War, attribution was not a key concern in the nuclear balance, as billions of dollars were expended deploying sensors like the Defense Support Program (DSP) satellite constellation[41] and the DEW line[42] that provided highly accurate attribution of the source and trajectory of incoming nuclear weapons. Instead, nuclear strategists concentrated their attention on the difficult problems posed by offense-defense racing, throw-weight, basing modes, among other issues.

In cyber conflict, by contrast, the very nature of the medium or battlefield, the network itself, offers an attacker multiple layers of anonymity and obfuscation. He can attack from addresses within his own country that are not officially assigned to the government or military, and then claim that the attack was carried out by a third party transiting his network. Or he can route attacks through third countries himself, constraining US response options or even worse, bringing down retaliation on an innocent party. While some technical specialists argue that the attribution problem is getting better with the

---

[41]   *Defense Support Program*, Federation of American Scientists, 14 February 2000, http://www.fas.org/spp/military/program/warning/dsp.htm.

[42]   F. Robert Naka and William W. Ward, "Distant Early Warning Line Radars" The Quest for Automatic Signal Detection", *Lincoln Laboratory Journal*, vol. 12, no. 2 (2000): 181-204.

deployment of IPv6 and its corresponding improvements in securing DNS and BGP, others argue that the attribution problem is keeping pace with technological change or actually getting worse. Even if stronger authentication is employed, "there is always the risk that an authenticated computer could be improperly compromised to conduct aggressive action."[43] Regardless of the trend line, an inability to attribute the attack systematically undermines almost all of the key pillars of strategic stability, because the victim does not know who to punish and therefore does not have any way to signal intent, choose retaliatory targets, establish appropriate thresholds, calculate (dis)proportionality of response, manage escalation, or even negotiate war termination. Thus, cyber conflict blurs a key question asked by Schelling: "what communication is required in a deterrence situation, and what means of authenticating the evidence communicated?[44]

Some authors have pushed pack on this depressing view, making four counterarguments. Kugler rightly points out that attackers may forgo anonymity if the purpose is overt coercion, and therefore having credible deterrence through punishment posture is necessary.[45]

A second counter-argument addresses the atmospherics surrounding a cyber attack, insisting that national decision makers in some cases will be able to attribute an attack given the nature of the crisis and the expected beneficiary of the attack. As one senior military official told me years ago: "If China is rattling sabers around Taiwan, using bellicose language and exercising missiles, and then I see a determined but unattributable attack against PACOM's computer networks, I will put two and two together and then 'katy bar the door'!"

Thirdly, Lin argues that while theoretical attackers may be perfectly untraceable, in practice attribution remains possible. He writes:

> It is commonly said that attribution of hostile cyber operations is impossible. The statement does have an

---

[43]   Owens, Dam, and Lin, eds., *Cyberattack Capabilities*, 41.

[44]   Thomas Schelling, *The Strategy of Conflict*, 13.

[45]   Richard Kugler, "Deterrence of Cyber Attacks," in *Cyberpower and National Security*, eds. Franklin D. Kramer, Stuart H. Starr, and Larry K. Wentz (Dulles, VA: Potomac Books, 2009).

essential kernel of truth: if the perpetrator makes no mistakes, uses techniques that have never been seen before, leaves behind no clues that point to himself, does not discuss the operation in any public or monitored forum, and does not conduct his actions during a period in which his incentives to conduct such operations are known publicly, then identification of the perpetrator may well be impossible.

Indeed, sometimes all of these conditions are met, and policy makers rightly despair of their ability to act appropriately under such circumstances. But in other cases, the problem of attribution is not so dire, because one or more of these conditions are not met, and it may be possible to make some useful (if incomplete) judgments about attribution.[46]

This leaves open the possibility for analysts and investigators to uncover or piece together enough information to functionally attribute malicious activity, providing policy makers with enough information to guide response.[47]

A fourth counter is that surrendering to attribution problem is simply not feasible, given the requirements of national defense, and calls for the redoubling of technical and policy efforts to improve enumeration of attacks or at least mitigate the problem. How could that be achieved? Most proposed solutions seek to get closer to the point of origin of the attack, leveraging greater use of offensive cyber capabilities for forward-leaning collection and I&W. Of course, such aggressive computer network exploit activities run the risk of provoking the very attacks they are designed to prevent. Overall, therefore, attribution remains the principal obstacle to credible cyber deterrence through punishment. Owens, et al, probably said it best "it is too strong a statement to say that plausible attribution of an adversary's cyberattack is impossible, but it is also too strong to say that definitive and certain attribution of an adversary's cyberattack will always be possible."[48]

---

[46]   Herbert Lin, "Thoughts on Threat Assessment in Cyberspace," *I/S: A Journal of Law and Policy for the Information Society*, Vol. 8, Issue 2 (2012).

[47]   Ibid.

[48]   Owens, Dam, and Lin, eds., *Cyberattack Capabilities,* 41.

Issue #2: Credibility of Cyber Deterrence Through Punishment

Cyber deterrence through punishment confronts nine primary credibility questions, addressed in turn below:

1. Will retaliatory cyber capability survive the first strike?

This question was a primary focus of the nuclear era. In one of this canonical works on the subject, Sir Lawrence Freedman writes that first strike "refers not simply to the first shots...but to an attack directed against the enemy's means of retaliation."[49] By contrast, "a second-strike capability represented the ability to absorb a first strike and still inflict a devastating retaliation on the enemy."[50] As a result, he argued that "the key requirement for a second-strike force was that it should be survivable." [51] Survivability of cyber retaliation capability must be examined at two levels: the capability itself and the means of delivering the retaliation. The survivability problem related to the means of delivering the retaliation derives from the nature of cyberspace as a medium or battlefield. In nuclear conflict, retaliation did not require sharing the same pathways as the adversary's first strike. The air, water and space dimensions would remain relatively open after the initial attack.[52]

In cyber conflict, by contrast, retaliation would likely take place over the same network infrastructure as the original destructive attacks, so it is not guaranteed that these pathways will be able in the retaliatory phase. Similarly, the adversary may make his own networks unreachable after the attack, eliminating viable cyber targets. For example, China's networks are reachable only through three state-controlled gateways, located in Beijing, Shanghai, and Guangzhou. While suboptimal, China could close those gateways or filter them in such a way as to reduce US cyber retaliatory options. This would not eliminate all retaliation options, for example, the threat of a cyber attack launched from a US operative inside of China, but would constrain the available

---

[49] Freedman, "The First Two Generations of Nuclear Strategists," 753.
[50] Ibid.
[51] Ibid.
[52] Debris from ground-bursted weapons could fratricide incoming warheads, as could scintillating detonations in the atmosphere or space.

retaliation strategies. At the same time, the upstream DNS for China's backbone network largely resides at the US end of Pacific submarine cable infrastructure. The implications of these problems create a perverse incentive to fire first, since it is the only way to guarantee the full range of offensive options. In other words, cyber conflict, like nuclear conflict in its early years, appears to still be vulnerable to a disarming first strike, and therefore strategic logic would drive an observer to seek to neutralize the enemy's cyber capabilities rather than conceive of a posture of deterrence. This is but one element of the current cyber "instability."

2. What is the threshold for cyber retaliation?

Paraphrasing Freedman, thresholds are defined as "the point at which restraints on...employment are abandoned."[53] In cyber conflict, this means the point at which the national command authority authorizes the use of computer network attack, or even a kinetic attack, in retaliation for adversary attacks. But the nature of the cyber security environment creates a huge problem for this strategic response dynamic. US government and military networks are scanned and pinged every second, millions of times a day, by IP addresses all over the world. The "noise" level in cyber indications and warning is therefore much higher than in the nuclear era, where the world existed in a Manichean environment where one was either in a nuclear war or not. Yet most of these probes are related to computer network exploit rather than preparations for attack, and espionage is not an accepted casus belli. For example, the alleged Chinese intrusion set does not reach the threshold of retaliation through computer network attack. Additional problems for cyber thresholds are primarily legal in origin, reducing the question to one of effects rather than modalities:

> the essential framework for the legal analysis of cyberattack is based on the principle that notions related to "use of force" and "armed attack" (terms of special relevance to the Charter of the United Nations) should be judged primarily by the effects of an action rather than its modality. That is, the fact that an attack is carried out through the use of cyberweapons rather than kinetic

---

[53]   Freedman, "The First Two Generations of Nuclear Strategists," 762.

weapons is far less significant than the effects that result from such use, where "effects" are understood to include both direct and indirect effects.[54]

STRATCOM/CYBERCOM use a similar effects-based standard, judging that "an incoming cyberattack must have a material impact on the DOD's ability to perform a mission or to carry out an operation, and that cyberattacks that merely cause inconvenience or that are directed only at intelligence gathering do not rise to the threshold of warranting such a response."[55]

Two immediate problems with an effects-based I&W system are perceptual and procedural. As Jervis taught us in the nuclear era, strategic stability demands that we first understand whether our adversaries view the situation in the same way.[56] Therefore, we must anticipate their answers to a range of parallel questions:

1. What activities constitute a cyberattack?
2. How might damage or harm from a cyberattack be assessed?
3. What activities might constitute evidence of hostile intent?
4. How should cyberexploitation and intelligence gathering be differentiated from cyberattacks?
5. How, if at all, should exploitations for economic purposes be differentiated from exploitations for national security purposes?"

If we are confident that we know the answers to these questions, which is highly doubtful, then it is imperative to make sure that both sides recognize the location and consequences of the cyber tripwire. As Schelling argues, "A threat has to be credible to be efficacious, and that its credibility may depend on the costs and risks associated with fulfillment for the party making the threat. We have develop the idea of making a threat credible by getting ourselves committed to its

---

[54] Owens, Dam, and Lin, eds., *Cyberattack Capabilities,* 21.
[55] Ibid., 52.
[56] For the classic work on the subject, see Robert Jervis, *Perception and Misperception in International Politics* (Princeton, NJ: Princeton University Press, 1976).

fulfillment, through the stretching of a "trip wire" across the enemy's path of advance, or by making fulfillment a matter of national honor and prestige...[57] What kinds of Berlin-like trip wires could we build in cyber conflict? For instance, is it possible to distinguish military from civilian networks and therefore create a threshold to distinguish armed conflict from other forms of cyber conflict? Perhaps even more vexing is the boiling frog problem. What if the adversary slowly increases the tempo of his computer network exploit activities, lulling us into a false sense of security and making it more difficult to discern the fulcrum point where exploit becomes attack? Much as we would prefer strategic ambiguity to retain operational options, the potential for escalation problems in the strategic cyber environment suggests that clarity, even declared thresholds, may be more in US interest.

3. Declaratory Policies: Should Cyber Retaliation Be "Automatic"?

Beyond declared thresholds, should the United States have a declaratory policy on cyber conflict overall? The DOD Information Operations Roadmap of 2003 recommended that the US government should have a declaratory policy on the use of cyberspace for offensive cyber operations. In 2008 SECDEF Gates concurred in a speech, asserting that "[f]uture administrations will have to consider new declaratory policies about what level of cyberattack might be considered an act of war and what type of military response is appropriate." [58] On one level, a cyber declaratory policy could be simple, direct, and retain strategic flexibility, asserting "The United States reserves at a time and manner of its own choosing to respond to a strategic-level cyber attack with the full measure of US national power." This type of declaration need not define "strategic-level," leaving it to the National Command Authority to determine, depending on the circumstance. Moreover, the emphasis on the "full measure of US national power" offers the flexibility to respond to the attack not

---

[57]   Schelling, *The Strategy of Conflict*, 6.

[58]   Robert Gates, "Nuclear Weapons and Deterrence in the 21st Century," address to the Carnegie Endowment for International Peace, 28 October 2008.

with cyber, where the US arguably does not enjoy escalation dominance, to a domain where it does enjoy escalation dominance, whether conventional or nuclear.

The policy process behind this declaration needs to go deeper, of course, and some policymakers might even desire to promulgate a more detailed policy paper at its conclusion. Owens, et al, identify eight excellent questions that such a policy review should answer: "[f]or what purposes does the United States maintain a capability for cyberattack? Do cyberattack capabilities exist to fight wars and to engage in covert intelligence or military activity if necessary or do they exist primarily to deter others (nation-states, terrorist groups) from launching cyberattacks on the United States? If they exist to fight wars, are they to be used in a limited fashion? Under what circumstances would what kinds of cyberattack be launched? What legal regimes are relevant to different levels of cyber conflict? How and when is cyber conflict to be stopped? To the extent that cyberattack is part of the US deterrent posture, how can its use be established as a credible threat? What, if any, role do cyberattack capabilities have in law enforcement efforts directed against transnational criminal groups?[59] Most of these questions are embedded in the structure of this paper, but the embryonic nature of cyber conflict and the rapidly changing technological base suggests a more general declaratory policy not tied to a particular technology or vector of attack would have greater strategic longevity and power.

4. Is Signaling Possible During Cyber Conflict?

Signaling, whether prior to the initiation of conflict or during its various escalatory and de-escalatory phases, is critical to understanding the dynamics of strategic conflict. In the nuclear era, Schelling argued:

> ...violence is most successful when held in reserve and made contingent upon the adversary's behavior. Nuclear diplomacy is the manipulation of latent violence – violence that can be withheld or inflicted in the future. It is also understood, however, that the power to hurt and

---

[59]   Owens, Dam, and Lin, eds., *Cyberattack Capabilities,* 57.

the credibility of threats to do so may be communicated by some actual violence.[60]

Most nuclear strategists concentrated their attention on signaling of intent below the nuclear threshold, primarily through words or conventional forces. Here again Jervis' work on perception and misperception as well as Mearsheimer's work on conventional deterrence are dispositive.[61] Edgier strategists, such as Herman Kahn, believed that intra-nuclear war was not only possible but desirable, and laid out highly detailed escalation control theories based on the ability to communicate to the adversary with both words and weapons at every stage of nuclear conflict.

While signaling in nuclear conflict was hardly easy, cyber conflict contains additional complexities. On the level of deterrence signaling, Libicki identifies "three sources of confusion": (1) attribution; (2) BDA [battle damage assessment], and (3) third-party interference.[62] The first and last of these have been touched on earlier in this chapter, and BDA is discussed below in the sections on "uncertainty" and "repeatability" of cyber-based effects. For his part, Libicki recommends full disclosure of cyber attack, at least to bolster the credibility of retaliation. For once, Schelling supports Libicki when the former argues:

> In the case of a planned, deliberate, surprise attack, the aggressor has every reason to disguise the truth. But in the case of 'inadvertent war,' both sides have a strong interest in conveying the truth if the truth can in fact be conveyed in a believable way in time to prevent the other side's mistaken decision.[63]

Yet this view is strongly contested by those unwilling to sacrifice sources and methods for a single iterative move in a longer game.[64]

---

[60]   Blair, *Strategic Command and Control,* 18.
[61]   Ibid.
[62]   Libicki, *Cyberdeterrence and Cyberwar*, 62.
[63]   Schelling, *The Strategy of Conflict*, 247.
[64]   Libicki, *Cyberdeterrence and Cyberwar*, 92.

Perhaps the more interesting signaling issue is cyber's possible use as sub-nuclear signaling. Cyber, for example, could be used as a vector to establish the credibility of future violence. However, the plausible deniability of cyber attacks cuts both ways in this situation. On the positive side a cyber signal could communicate the credible threat of escalatory violence, but the deniability could give the adversary necessary relief from an automatic or mechanistic escalatory response. On the negative side, a deniable cyber signal could simply complicate the signaling by introducing more ambiguity about the attacker's identity, intentions, and thresholds. Indeed, it is difficult to distinguish between cyber attacks meant to influence decisions and cyber attacks geared to limit the victims' options for retaliation. Worse yet, a cyber signaling attack could unintentionally damage communications infrastructure and therefore undermine its very utility as a means to signal. Finally, cyber signaling runs into major problems with respect to adversaries with underdeveloped cyber capabilities or those who use cyber proxies, since the target of the signal may be too unintelligent to comprehend it or too weak to enforce his will on those he represents.[65] Perversely, the important role of these wild-card proxies, such as those pro-Russian hackers who were allegedly involved in the 2007 Estonia attacks and the 2008 Georgia attacks, may in fact lend more credence to Schelling's notion of the "threat that leaves something to chance," which requires participants to credibly communicate threats in which "the final decision is not altogether under the control of the entity making the threat."[66]

5. Will Cyber Retaliatory Targets Be Available?

In state-to-state nuclear conflict, targeting problems were often a poverty of riches. While early nuclear analysis worried about whether the bomber would always get through, the development of the missile legs of the triad fundamentally changed the equation. If one's strategy called for counterforce targeting, then the dilemmas revolved around which military forces to strike and in what order. For countervalue targeting, one had to decide between cities,

---

[65]   Schelling, *The Strategy of Conflict*, 22-23.
[66]   Ibid., 188.

industrial centers, or key infrastructure like bridges. In either case, there were always far more targets than available weapons. Only in the realm of nuclear terrorism did things get complicated, as one could suffer a nuclear attack and have no meaningful adversary targets to hit in retaliation.

In cyber conflict, by contrast, targeting is complicated against both state and non-state actors. Let's look at the best-case scenario. Even if state-based cyber attacks originate in an adversary's networks, and we have exquisite attribution that the attacks were carried out deliberately by the government, the adversary could block all retaliatory cyber strikes by filtering packets from the target country, or shutting down its network gateways entirely. However, it is unlikely that the location of the adversary's offensive capabilities would be known, preventing retaliation. Further, if the paths to targets are left open, it is highly unlikely that one could keep the adversary's computer network attack capabilities at risk, since they could be as simple as a laptop and an Internet connection, not fixed positions like silos or submarines. It is therefore tempting to conclude that cyber attack targets can only be countervalue, not counterforce.[67] This circumstance severely limits a retaliator's strategic options, and again creates perverse incentives for preemptive first strikes.

Owens, et al, lay out a strong corresponding case for the different set of difficulties related to targeting non-state hackers:

> Against non-state hackers, deterrence by punishment may be particularly ineffective...First, a non-state group may be particularly difficult to identify. Second, it is likely to have few if any information technology assets that can be targeted. Third, some groups (such as organized hacker groups) regard counterattacks as a challenge to be welcomed rather than something to be feared. Fourth, a non-state group such as a terrorist or insurgent group might seek to provoke cyber-retaliation in order to galvanize public support for it or to antagonize the public against the United States.[68]

---

[67]   Libicki, *Cyberdeterrence and Cyberwar*, 120.

[68]   Owens, Dam, and Lin, eds., *Cyberattack Capabilities,* 42.

As a result of these problems, it is difficult to implement "tailored deterrence" for non-state actors, because

> that concept is premised on an understanding and a knowledge of specific adversaries. Indeed, it presumes that such knowledge is available in advance as the basis for tailoring a deterrence strategy against that particular adversary. But by definition, deterrence cannot be tailored to an adversary about whom nothing is known.[69]

Bottom line: those seeking credible cyber deterrence by punishment must deal with the fact that there may few if any comparable targets for retaliation.

6. Is Command and Control of Cyber Conflict Possible?

In nuclear warfare, command and control was critical for maintaining the credibility to use weapons. Bruce Blair and others argued convincingly that nuclear C4I was potentially a weak link in our nuclear deterrent, declaring, "command performance is quite possibly not just an important factor but the key determinant of real strategic capability."[70] Deterrence theory argues that adversaries will not attack C3I systems in order to maintain channels for diplomacy, negotiation and coercion, but "command vulnerabilities could encourage deliberate, direct attack intended to achieve purely military rather than politico-diplomatic objectives."[71] Deficiencies in C2 create "strong incentives on both sides to launch a first strike [...], which undermines crisis stability."[72] If damage limitation is the objective of an adversary's attack, Blair and others asserted that the adversary might be better served by attacking US C3I systems instead of weapons.[73]

In cyber conflict, command and control is also critical for credibility. Like nuclear weapons, an adversary's preemptive

---

[69]   Ibid.
[70]   Blair, *Strategic Command and Control,* 3.
[71]   Ibid., 7.
[72]   Ibid., 3.
[73]   Ibid.

cyber attack could potentially cut off cyber retaliation forces from the national command authority, raising traditional deterrence and warfighting questions about contingency operations and delegation of authority in crisis. But there are also some key structural command and control differences between cyber and nuclear conflict. Nuclear weapons do not travel to their targets along the same pathways as their command and control networks, but, in cyber conflict, the C4I infrastructure broadly speaking is not only the command and control network for the cyber attack but also the main pathway for the attack itself. As a result, the degradation of C4I networks in conflict could directly degrade retaliatory cyber weapons capability and employment. Another key difference relates to the deterrence requirement for launch on warning/launch under attack, which was a critical command and control challenge for nuclear combat but seems impossible in cyber conflict, since an attack payload could arrive in milliseconds rather than 20 minutes over the Pole. This poses serious challenges about the level of command authorization for various degrees of response to attack and to what extent this process will, or should, be automated.

7. Does Credible Cyber Deterrence Require Demonstration Effects?

The detonations of the atomic bombs over Nagasaki and Hiroshima in 1945 served as horrifying proof of the United States' nuclear weapons capabilities. Subsequent nuclear tests during the Cold War by the major nuclear powers offered further demonstration effects to potential adversaries. Recent underground tests by India, Pakistan, and North Korea were designed principally as deterrent signals of capability. While some insist cyberwar could also have similarly catastrophic effects upon modern, information-driven societies, the lack of demonstrated large-scale cyber effects complicates effective cyber deterrence. In the absence of detailed information about actual US capabilities, the good news is that potential adversaries will likely overestimate and exaggerate US capabilities, providing a form of deterrence. The bad news is that those demonstrations, if forced to occur, could potentially undermine deterrence, though it could be argued that the recent Stuxnet episode only serves to bolster the credibility of US capabilities.[74] Still Owens, et al, correctly argue:

> the fragility of cyberweapons...provide disincentives for the United States to provide such demonstrations. These disincentives may raise the thresholds at which the United States is willing to use those particular weapons.[75]

At the same time, a perceived ability to carry out effective preemptive attacks does not mean that the United States is capable of carrying out effective cyber retaliation, given the known deficiencies of the architecture.

8. Can Cyber Deterrence Be Credible if Effects Are Uncertain and Unrepeatable?

A deeper credibility problem with cyber deterrence through punishment is the overall uncertainty of cyber effects. Whereas the effects of nuclear weapons can be scientifically delineated from the laws of physics (see *Effects of Nuclear Weapons*[76]), cyber attacks are much more uncertain and unpredictable, as described at length in Chapter 3 of Libicki's *Cyberdeterrence*.[77] If you cannot calculate the "expected costs" of a cyber first strike, direct damage as well as lost productivity, capability, confidence, and other factors, then it would be difficult to determine if the costs of a first strike outweigh the benefits. Moreover, cyber has a repeatability problem.

Even if you could calculate the effect of a first strike, the subsequent remediation of network vulnerabilities significantly reduces the possibility of achieving the same effect with a later attack against a now-alerted adversary. As Libicki pithily puts it, "deterrence can be fragile if hitting back today prevents hitting back tomorrow

---

[74] For an example of a scenario in which the US was "forced" to demonstrate capability, see the US-193 BURNT FROST shootdown of a defunct and potentially dangerous US reconnaissance satellite, which had the desultory benefit of demonstrating to Beijing that they were not the only country in possession of anti-satellite weapons.

[75] Owens, Dam, and Lin, eds., *Cyberattack Capabilities,* 42.

[76] Samuel Glasstone and Philip J. Dolan, *The Effects of Nuclear Weapons* (Washington, DC: US Government Printing Office, 1983).

[77] Libicki, *Cyberdeterrence and Cyberwar,* 53

and thereafter."[78] If neither the value of neutralizing the threat nor the likely collateral damage of the counterattack can be calculated, or even reliably estimated, with mathematical precision, then neither side of a potential cyber conflict achieve strategic stability of any sort, much less mutually assured destruction.

9. Can Cyber Deterrence Be Extended to Third Parties?

During the Cold War, a crucial point of contention in NATO and other alliances was the credibility of US promises of extended nuclear deterrence. Despite public declarations, exercises, and posture changes, doubt persisted that Washington would trade New York for Paris, particularly given if the conflict started in the conventional realm. Given the problems outlined above for a credible US cyber deterrent, extended cyber deterrence really seems like "a bridge too far," especially given the even greater challenge of attributing and enumerating a cyber attack conducted against a third-party.

10. Can Cyber Deterrence Through Punishment Be Controlled or Stopped?

The relationship between cyber deterrence through punishment and escalation control is complex, and ultimately unsatisfying. On the one hand, credibility is perversely bolstered when the adversary fears that retaliation will be total and relentlessly destructive. On the other hand, the adversary needs to believe that, should she seek to sue for peace, the retaliator has the ability to de-escalate its attacks and even terminate them, especially if the initial attack was an accidental launch, the unauthorized actions of an individual on either, or, most important in cyber, the spoofed intervention of an unrelated third party. Otherwise, the strategic balance changes from the potential stability of credible and secure retaliatory forces to the Doomsday Machine of Dr. Strangelove fame, condemning the world to darkness.

Thus, we must ask ourselves: are modern cyber theorists Kahnians (i.e., they think that cyber war can be conducted in a controlled, discriminating manner) or are they Schellingians (i.e.

---

[78]   Ibid., 56.

they think that the uncertainties inherent in the escalation process will produce deterrence by warning the other side that things could get out of control)? Kahn's complex theories on escalation do not seem to fit cyber well: how do you know which rung you are on? Which rung your opponent is on? How can you estimate the scale of the attack when you are blinded by the attack? How do you know whether your opponent is actually escalating or whether a third party is spoofing escalation? How can you make distinctions between strikes against military targets and strikes against non-military targets, given dual-use cyber infrastructure and the possible intended cascade effects on infrastructure? Schelling appears more appropriate for cyber, given his emphasis that "violence, especially in war, is a confused and uncertain activity, highly unpredictable depending on decisions taken by fallible human beings organized into imperfect governments depending on fallible communications and warning systems and on the untested performance of people and equipment. It is furthermore a hot-headed activity, in which commitments and reputations can develop a momentum of their own."[79] For example, escalation control and intrawar deterrence rely on accurate battle damage assessment, which is highly challenging in cyber conflict due to the nature of the systems involved:

> The smallest change in the configuration and interconnections of an IT system can result in completely different system behavior, and the direct effects of a cyberattack on a given system may be driven by the behavior and actions of the human system operator and the specific nature of that system as well as the intrinsic characteristics of the cyberweapon involved. Furthermore, these relatively small and/or obscure and/or hidden characteristics are often important in cyber targeting, and information about these things are difficult to obtain through remote intelligence collection methods such as photo reconnaissance, which means that substantial amounts of

---

[79]   Thomas Schelling, *Arms and Influence* (New Haven, CT: Greenwood Press Reprint, 1966), 93.

relevant information may not be available to the attacker...
An additional complication to the prediction problem is the
possibility of cascading effects that go further than expected.
For example, in analyzing the possible effects of a
cyberattack, there may be no good analog to the notion of a
lethal radius within which any target will be destroyed.[80]

Next, given the unpredictable nature of cyber weapons, it is
not clear that cyber conflict can be easily stopped:

[S]ome tools such as corrupted software products or viruses
might prove difficult, if not impossible, to stop. Also, if
insiders or surrogate organizations were involved, adequate
means to communicate with, and control, such entities to stop
their activities would be necessary….Attacks on information
infrastructures   that   degraded   communications   with
subordinate forces might also impede cessation of a conflict.[81]

Also, the unintended cascade effects from attacks might make
it more difficult for the adversary to assess their own untenable
position, tell their own forces to stand down, or even communicate
their willingness to concede.

Finally, even if the primary actors want to stop, intervening
third parties could so muddy the waters with spoofing attacks
and chaos that the conflict continues against everyone's wishes.
Further, third-party intervention increases the difficulty of
verifying that the adversary has ended its attacks, pressuring the
conflict to continue despite the intentions of the primary
actors.[82]

---

[80]   Owens, Dam, and Lin, eds., *Cyberattack Capabilities,* 122. By contrast,
"munitions effects in the kinetic world can often be calculated on the basis
of computational models that are based on physics-based algorithms. That
is, the fundamental physics of explosives technology and of most targets is
well known, and so kinetic effects on a given target can be calculated with
acceptable confidence. Thus, many of the uncertainties in kinetic targeting
can be theoretically calculated and empirically validated (e.g., at weapons
effects test ranges), and the remaining uncertainties relate to matters such as
target selection and collocation of other entities with the intended target."

[81]   Rattray, *Strategic Warfare in Cyberspace,* 145-146.

[82]   Owens, Dam, and Lin, eds., *Cyberattack Capabilities,* 311.

Addressing Strategic Instability in Cyberspace

The current strategic cyber environment is structurally unstable, marked by an inability to establish credible deterrence and strong incentives to strike preemptively. The sources of this instability are many-fold.

1. The technical architecture undergirding cyberspace is fundamentally flawed, resulting in a system that is extremely hard to defend and confers dominance to the offense. The defender can mitigate the asymmetry by shutting down (i.e., disconnecting the network), but this move is very costly given the likely reliance of the defender on the network for operations and does not address certain hardware vulnerabilities, which present another set of security issues and vulnerabilities.

2. The design of the architecture often provides the attacker with anonymity and plausible deniability, exacerbated by the lack of central governance of the network and the nascent state of international law and norms regarding attribution and responsibility.

3. The relatively low cost of technology and operations significantly lowers the barriers to entry for the attacker, enabling a wide range of actors to acquire capabilities.

4. Operations running at the rapid "speed of the network" deny defenders sufficient time for assessment and decision-making. Automation may mitigate this problem but the risks are both high and unknown.

5. The pace of technological change and the breadth of network connectivity are outpacing both defensive approaches at the enterprise or engineering level as well as the policy and legal constructs promulgated to guide their operations. Moreover, these conditions are only getting worse with the proliferation of social media, mobile communications, and the migration to cloud computing. The Internet underground capable of

exploiting these trends is also alive and well, with pirates and mercenaries thriving in a swampy ecosystem that makes hiding and attacking too easy.

6.   There is a vacuum in Internet governance, with no one seemingly in change of security.

Yet it is important to note that the strategic instability of the current cyber environment is not unprecedented. While it can be contrasted with the "stability" of the late Cold War, it does resemble the early nuclear era and its omnipresent "window of vulnerability."[83] As Sir Lawrence argues,

> By the end of the 1950s, the dominant theme was the risk of sliding into an inadvertent war through military logic, a la August 1914.[84]

Thomas Schelling called this mindset the "reciprocal fear of surprise attack," whereby "a modest temptation on each side to sneak in a first blow" would become "compounded through a process of interacting expectations," leading to successive cycles of "he thinks we think he thinks we think...he thinks we think he'll attack; so he thinks we shall; so he will; so we must."[85] As a result, the late 1960s saw a determined quest for deterrence stability; "wherein neither side felt compelled to take the initiative in a crisis or exploit its own first-strike capability, and the answer was invulnerable retaliatory forces."[86] According to Schelling:

> There is a difference between a balance of terror in which either side can obliterate the other and one in which *both* sides can do it no matter who strikes first. It is not the "balance" – the sheer equality or symmetry in the situation – that constitutes mutual deterrence; it is the stability of the balance. The balance is stable only when neither, in striking first, can destroy the other's ability to strike back.[87]

---

[83]   Blair, *Strategic Command and Control,* 3.
[84]   Freedman, "The First Two Generations of Nuclear Strategists," 754.
[85]   Schelling, *The Strategy of Conflict,* 207.
[86]   Freedman, "The First Two Generations of Nuclear Strategists," 754.
[87]   Schelling, *The Strategy of Conflict,* 232.

Eventually nuclear weapons reached a stability plateau where populations could not be protected against an attack, but weapons could. Schelling again:

> The special significance of surprise attack thus lies in the possible vulnerability of retaliatory forces. If these forces were themselves invulnerable – if each side were confident that its own forces could survive an attack, but also that it could not destroy the other's power to strike back – there would be no powerful temptation to strike first. And there would be less need to react quickly to what might prove to be a false alarm. Thus schemes to avert surprise attack have as their most immediate objective the safety of the weapons rather than the safety of people.[88]

In the current cyber era, by contrast, the "window of vulnerability" is still wide open, presenting pressures and incentives for launching a cyber attack first.

What are the implications of this cyber instability? First, it undermines deterrence, especially against non-state actors, who gain significant strategic advantages in an unstable environment. Second, it leads to temptation to consider preventive war or preemptive war options that would remove the enemy's capacity for effective cyber retaliation before it can raise its defenses, and perhaps even degrade conventional military operations. Third, it provides strong incentives for escalation once conflict has begun. Thus, it is clear that this instability is highly dangerous, especially for status quo cyber actors like the United States who have so much to lose. Indeed, the United States desperately needs cyber stability for a range of reasons, including continued economic prosperity, to wield global soft power, and to avoid asymmetric security vulnerabilities with state and non-state adversaries.

Yet despite hopes and focus of most current approaches, we cannot expect to achieve cyber stability alone. The US Government has limited influence on the fundamental causes of cyber instability and they look to get worse for extended period.

---

[88]   Ibid., 233.

We cannot construct a safe haven nor does a cyber high ground exist to seize and hold. Worse, there are difficult tradeoffs in achieving our objectives. Core principles of Internet freedom, tech innovation, and openness/connectivity conflict with the security imperative, and our open political system demands that the former be accorded equal status with the latter. A strategy of total control and safety would be unreasonably costly and would likely prove to be ineffective. Instead, we must implement a national/global strategy in cyberspace to create stability through resilience, collaboration, risk mitigation, and efforts to clean up the cyber ecosystem. The recent White House strategy is a positive, if belated, move in this direction, but we must acknowledge limits to current approaches and boldly move to claim strategic advantage.

Chapter Two

US Operational Military Aspects of Cyber Conflict

Introduction

This chapter explores the operational aspects of cyber conflict in the United States military, and to a lesser extent, the intelligence community. The United States military, recognizing both the challenges and opportunities in cyberspace, has long cast about for the right balance and solutions. Though it has not been fully recognized, the troubles finding the best strategies and operational policies reflect the underlying instability of cyber conflict.

In the 2005 National Military Strategy for Cyberspace Operations, then-Secretary of Defense Donald Rumsfeld looked for solutions against "adversaries a ready avenue of approach to exploit cyberspace to gain strategic, operational, and tactical advantages over the United States."[1]

More recently, DoD has centralized cyber operations under United States Cyber Command and is working to "normalize" cyber operations, as expressed in the latest policy the *Department of Defense Strategy for Operating in Cyberspace* (or DSOC). As this chapter will describe, this strategy has five key components:

---

[1]   Peter Pace, "The National Military Strategy for Cyberspace Operations," *Berlin Information Center for Transatlantic Security*, DoD, 12 2006, http://www.bits.de/NRANEU/others/strategy/07-F-2105doc1.pdf (accessed September 24, 2011).

- Cyber must be recognized as a warfare domain equal to land, sea, and air, requiring its own organization, equipment, and training;

- Defensive postures must employ new operating concepts like active defense and advanced sensors, which go beyond "good hygiene" to include sophisticated and accurate operations that allow, as former Deputy Secretary of Defense William Lynn described, rapid response in "milliseconds";

- Cyber defenses must reach beyond .mil, partnering with other government agencies and private industry, including Homeland Security and the commercial defense industry, to enable a whole-of-government approach;

- Cyber defenses must be pursued with international allies to strengthen collective cyber security, which Lynn emphasizes must include effective "shared warning" of threats; and

- DoD must help leverage the cyber workforce and rapid innovation to maintain US technological superiority.[2]

To contextualize the current state of US cyber operations, this chapter briefly surveys how the military got to where it is today: from signals intelligence and electronic warfare, through information warfare and operations, to the centralization of cyber operations under a Joint Task Force organization. This discussion then focuses on eventual creation of Cyber Command and the current state of cyber operations, including the five strategic components in the latest DoD strategy. The chapter concludes with other important issues, such as rules of engagement, and a final summary of military cyber operations.

Underlying Drivers of Military Doctrine, Policy, and Operations in Cyber Conflict

During the two-decades-long struggle of the US military to grapple with conflict in cyberspace, a number of doctrinal, policy and

---

2   William Lynn, "Defending a New Domain," *Foreign Affairs* (September/October 2010): 97-108.

operational issues have been continually visited and revisited. There are a several underlying drivers of change that have fed this dynamic and seem to be central for understanding military policies and organizations for cyber conflict.

As this chapter will explore, the organizational response within the DoD has changed over time to each of these, either implicitly or explicitly, and there is little reason to assume that the current response –- the DSOC – will be the final and best response. Future cyber conflicts and new technologies may easily force different responses. These drivers of change include the following:

1. **Centralization or decentralization** of cyber forces, operations, and capabilities. For example, should cyber forces be centrally commanded (like modern air forces) or should individual commanders have organic capability (such as the early Army Air Corps, chopped to different division commanders)?

2. **Normalization or differentiation** of cyber forces, operations, and capabilities. For example, should cyber be treated as a special capability similar to Special Forces or integrated into traditional military operations? Should it they be conducted in stand-alone operations or integrated with other kinds of kinetic or information operations?

3. **Limited or expansive military goal**. Should the military seek military superiority in cyberspace or some lesser goal, such as freedom of action or local superiority?

4. **Operational coordination** of offense, defense, and intelligence. Given the global range, accelerated pace of cyber operations, and overlapping organizational responsibilities, how should different forces remain coordinated?

5. **Legal Authorities** How do domestic laws cover US cyber operations (e.g. can intelligence organizations perform warlike cyber operations?) and when must cyber operations comply with the laws of armed conflict?

6.   **Coordination with Private Sector** The great majority of networks are owned and operated by the private sectors, as are many other legitimate critical infrastructure targets in cyberspace. How should the military work accordingly?

These issues are analyzed throughout the chapter.

Operational US Military History of Cyber Conflict

A Beginning: Electronic Warfare

The US military has long engaged in practices similar to what is now called cyber conflict. Militaries have used different means of information storage and transmission and "battles" between intelligence services are nothing new, the American Civil War in the 1860s unveiled a new chapter. Indeed, the first use of a military electronic "attack" probably occurred then, when telegraphs were used to pass commands and information about enemy and friendly forces.[3] Both sides quickly recognized the importance of long-range electronic communications and both sought to disrupt the other's use of the telegraph,[4] as well as penetrate opposing telegraph lines to pass false messages.[5]

Both sides in the Russo–Japanese War of 1904-1905 used telegraph and radio extensively including the first use of at-sea vessels conducting wireless relay and intelligence collection.[6] This war was also a proving ground for technologies that would be later used in World War I, continuing the fundamental

---

[3]   Tom Wheeler, *Mr. Lincoln's T-Mails* (New York, NY: HarperCollins Publishers, 2006).

[4]   Tom Standage, *The Victorian Internet* (New York, NY: Walker and Company, 1998).

[5]   A.W. Greely, *The Military Telegraph Service*. Retrieved 9 15, 2011, from Signal Corp Association 1860-1865:
http://www.civilwarsignals.org/pages/tele/telegreely/telegreely.html

[6]   Bob Gourley, "The Laurels of Victory: Information Warfare in the Russo-Japanese War (1904-1905)," (April 1997). Available at:
http://papers.ssrn.com/sol3/papers.cfm?abstract_id=1726342.

changing the nature of command and control which enabled leadership over larger and more geographically dispersed military forces.

The use of information technology in the military and its exploitation by intelligence professionals grew especially rapidly after that. World War II saw multiple benefits of focused cyber attack and cyber defense that contributed to battlefield victory, with one of the most instructive cases being from the use of encryption, decryption, and signal intelligence. German cryptographers created the Enigma cipher, to secure messages between German High Command, U-boats, commanders, and other forces. In response, the Allies developed their own electromechanical devices to attack the German Enigma cipher, such as was the British Bombe, developed by Alan Turing.[7] Allied cryptanalysis of the German encryption Enigma led to direct successes in combat, including a dramatic turnaround in the initially disastrous Battle of the Atlantic.[8] The penetration and misdirection efforts involving telegraphs and radio described above were a clear precursor to some forms of modern cyber attack with the aims of direct manipulation of adversary networks and data.

Over the next several decades, particularly with the invention of integrated circuitry in the late 1950s and early 1960s, the use and the dependency on computers increased exponentially. Decades of research focused on increasing functionality and survivability led to continuing enhancements of information technology, including communication protocols like TCP/IP. These most famous and now most ubiquitous protocols, developed by the military, enabled the broad interconnections of the Internet.

These operational and technological changes led to important conceptual and policy developments. Perhaps one of the earliest known in-depth studies of such issues was the 1970 Ware Report,

---

[7] Michael Smith, *Station X: Decoding Nazi Secrets* (TV Books, 2001). The original bomb had been developed by Polish cryptographers who passed their secrets to the British.

[8] Kenneth Wynn, *U-Boat Operations of the Second World War* (Annapolis, MD: Naval Institute Press, 1998).

released by the United States' Defense Science Board.[9] A product
of a Task Force set up in 1967 by the Advanced Research Projects
Agency (now the Defense Advanced Research Projects Agency),
the report summarized key findings and recommendations with
regards to computer security safeguards that would protect
classified information in multi-access, resource-sharing computer
systems. This policy research preceded the widespread commercial
adoption of the Internet in the early 1990s and addressed the
inherently challenging task of keeping secure a network designed
for sharing. This is one of the core contradictions that makes
cyberspace instable.

The Rise of Information Warfare

Following lessons from the first Gulf War (which showed the
combat power that resulted from information dominance), military
services began pushing new doctrines and organizations to attempt
to grapple with information warfare. Literature, previously focused
on operational security or computer security, shifted with
increasing emphasis put on state use of information capabilities as
a tool of power projection. Important documents include Joint
Publications 3-13 (1998) and 6.0 (1995), CJCSI 6510.01 (1993),[10]
and DoD Directives 5200 (1997) and S-3600.1 (1996) as well as
the Air Force Cornerstones of Information Warfare (1995), and Air
Force Doctrine Document 2-5 (1998). The Defense Science Board
Report also released influential reports in 1996 on "Information
Warfare – Defense" and on "Defensive Information Operations"
highlighting the themes of DoD's heavy reliance on information
systems to carry out operations.

These service and joint documents were written separately
and updated quickly, which created a wealth of ideas and
doctrines, many of which were not well coordinated or did not

---

[9]   Willis H. Ware, *Security Controls for Computer Systems: Report of Defense
Science Board Task Force on Computer Security* (Santa Monica, CA:
RAND, 1979).

[10]   As an example of how quickly policies were updated during this time, the
original CJSCI 6510.01 was issued in 1993 and by 1997 had already been
superseded twice. One version, 6510.01B lasted little more than a year, being
issued in May 1996 and was made obsolete by 6510.01C by August 1997.

stand the test of time. Even though "information warfare" and "information operations" were the most central concepts of this time, both of these have been eclipsed more recently by "cyber." This differentiation of cyber forces and information warfare has been a critical trend in cyber history. Whereas cyber offense and defense capabilities had been earlier part of each Service's "information" forces, this now is increasingly less the case. [11] Additionally, most of these documents set a goal of military "superiority" or "dominance" of the information realm.

In the early 1990s, the various US services each independently decided to centralize information (and by extension, cyber) forces in the US. Within the United States, the Navy merged fleet deception and electronic warfare capabilities in 1992, laying the foundation for what would later become the Fleet Information Warfare Command. The Navy also added additional capabilities to its cyber force and integrated offensive capabilities under the Navy Information Warfare Activity (NIWA).[12] The Air Force organized cyber units into the Air Force Information Warfare Center in 1993 and created the first Air Force operational cyber warfighting unit, combining defensive and offensive capabilities with the 609th Information Warfare Squadron in 1995.[13] The Army established a focused effort on information warfare in 1995 by creating the Land Information Warfare Activity (LIWA).[14] By the late 1990s, the National Security Agency created the Information Operations Technology Center to help bring together the capabilities being separately developed in each of the services.[15]

During this time, there had been significant doctrinal distinctions between the military services which were cleared up with the issuance of the common joint terms of CNA, CND, CNE

---

[11]   With the Navy's "Information Dominance Corps" a notable exception.

[12]   National Defense University, *Information Operations Timeline*, http://www.jfsc.ndu.edu/schools_programs/jc2ios/io/io_timeline.asp (accessed August 29, 2011).

[13]   609th Information Warfare Squadron, "609 IWS: A Brief History, October 1995-August 1997" (September 1997).

[14]   *United States Army Intelligence and Security Command*, August 29, 2011, http://www.inscom.army.mil/Default.aspx?text=off&size=12pt (accessed August 29, 2011).

[15]   William Arkin, "The Cyber Bomb in Yugoslavia," *Washington Post*, October 25, 1999.

and CNO that are still in place. Understanding these terms is critical to understanding US military cyber operations:

- Computer Network Attack or CNA: "Actions taken through the use of computer networks to disrupt, deny, degrade, or destroy information resident in computers and computer networks, or the computers and networks themselves."

- Computer Network Defense or CND: Actions taken to protect, monitor, analyze, detect, and respond to unauthorized activity within the Department of Defense information systems and computer networks.

- Computer Network Exploitation or CNE: Enabling operations and intelligence collection capabilities conducted through the use of computer networks to gather data from target or adversary automated information systems or networks.

- Computer Network Operations or CNO: Comprised of computer network attack, computer network defense, and related computer network exploitation enabling operations.[16]

These definitions would be used immediately in the next generation of military operational organizations.

The Creation of a Cyber Joint Task Force

The Joint Task Force for Computer Network Defense (JTF-CND) was established on December 30, 1998 by the DoD as a joint warfighting unit to enhance the military's ability to defend against strategic computer network attacks, as well as coordinate and direct responses to other CND missions.[17] JTF-CND quickly developed being rebranded first as JTF-CNO then JTF-GNO (to be defined later) eventually becoming the core of today's Cyber Command. The JTF Concept of Operations emphasized the unit was to mount defenses

---

[16]   Definitions of CNA, CND, CNE and CNO from Joint Publication 1-02, Department of Defense Dictionary of Military and Associated Terms, p65-66.

[17]   Ellen Nakashima, "Warriors in the battle for cyberspace," *Washington Post*, September 24, 2010.

against computer networks that might attack using combatant command lines of operation or across Service or agency lines.[18] According to the Concept of Operations for the unit,

> The Joint Task Force-Computer Network Defense (JTF-CND) is responsible for the defense of DOD computer networks from strategic Computer Network Attack (CNA) and other Secretary of Defense (SECDEF) Computer Network Defense (CND) missions. A strategic CNA is an attack that crosses Command-in-Chiefs (CINCs), Services, and Agencies (C/S/A) borders or have widespread or critical effects on the Defense Information Infrastructure (DII).

> The JTF-CND will coordinate and direct DOD wide CND operations. The JTF-CND is responsible for collecting data on CNAs against critical DOD computer networks, formulating courses of action (COA) to thwart CNAs, coordinating and directing DOD actions for defense, and prioritizing recovery actions and mission critical "work arounds" for the DII.[19]

As such, the JTF-CND started to address critical questions about what military doctrine, policy, and operations should look like in cyber conflict – all of which can be seen in more robust form in today's Cyber Command. With Major General John Campbell as its commander, JTF-CND centralized forces and authority by having a two-star general in charge that reported directly to the Deputy Secretary of Defense. The unit also started to assert operational control and coordination between defensive (but not offensive or intelligence) missions. JTF-CND also addressed legal limitations, establishing a Judge Advocate General to help address policy issues.[20] It also quickly established strong ties with the National Infrastructure Protection Center at the Federal Bureau of Investigation to coordinate with other agencies and, to a much lesser degree, the

---

[18]   U.S. Strategic Command, *JTF-CND Concept of Operations* (1998).
[19]   U.S. Strategic Command, *JTF-CND Concept of Operations* (1998).
[20]   Ensuring the JTF-CND had a JAG was a critical concern for the Air Force when standing up the unit.

private sector. The organizational diagram below shows these relationships.

Figure 2.1: Organizational Chart for Joint Task Force – Computer Network Defense[21]

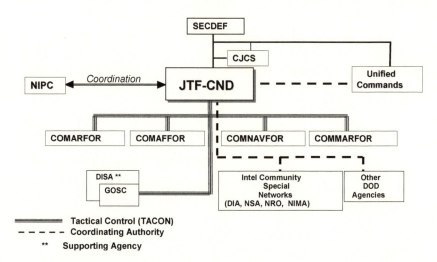

While the changes helped to centralize cyber operations, within two years the Joint Task Force's role had changed. First, the reporting chain shifted to report to Space Command (later Strategic Command) rather than directly to the Office of the Secretary of Defense, based on Space Command's experience with a global, digital-centric mission.[22] This helped to normalize cyber operations, as JTFs don't generally report to the Pentagon but to other military commanders, and continued centralization and operational coordination with other military forces.

At the same time, the unit's mission expanded. The defensive role stayed the same, but after 2000 the JTF would also coordinate offensive cyber operations and accordingly had its name changed to Joint Task Force Computer Network Operations (JTF-CNO).

---

21   "Fact File: Joint Task Force - Computer Network Operations," *The Information Warfare Site*, February 2003, http://www.iwar.org.uk/iwar/resources/jtf-cno/factsheet.htm.

22   Richard B. Myers and Malcolm McConnell, *Eyes on the Horizon: Serving on the Front Lines of National Security,* (New York: Threshold Editions, 2010.

According to a fact sheet from Strategic Command, the offensive mission was as follows:

> CNA mission: coordinate, support and conduct, at the direction of the president, CNA operations in support of US objectives. For this mission, JTF-CNO is responsible for ensuring that CNA capabilities can be efficiently employed in support of US National Security objectives. Along with the USSTRATCOM staff, services, other combatant commanders, and defense agencies, is working to develop and implement comprehensive policies, structures, roles and missions for computer network operations. The initial US Strategic Command concept of operations calls for the supported commander, assisted by the JTF-CNO, to integrate service-provided forces into military plans and operations. USSTRATCOM will coordinate the use of all DOD CNA assets for the supported commander.[23]

To address these additional responsibilities, the JTF-CNO expanded to 122 authorized positions from the original 20 authorized for JTF-CND in 1998.[24] By adding an offensive mission to JTF-CNO, the agency was given permission, if not significant opportunity, to utilize the instability of cyberspace to the military's advantage.

In 2003, the JTF-CND lost this offensive mission to the Joint Functional Component Command – Network Warfare of Strategic Command (JFCC-NW), but added significant roles for network operations and defense. With new responsibilities, the JTF-CND was renamed the Joint Task Force for Global Network Operations (JTF-GNO) in 2004. It eventually grew to nearly 400 authorized personnel. This arrangement kept centralized control (under Strategic Command) over both offensive and defensive operations but gave more responsibility to both sides.

---

[23]   "Fact File: Joint Task Force - Computer Network Operations," *The Information Warfare Site*, February 2003, http://www.iwar.org.uk/iwar/resources/jtf-cno/factsheet.htm.

[24]   "Fact File: Joint Task Force - Computer Network Operations," *The Information Warfare Site*, February 2003, http://www.iwar.org.uk/iwar/resources/jtf-cno/factsheet.htm.

The Director of the National Security Agency (NSA), then Lt General Michael Hayden, commanded the new JFCC-NW. The NSA's extended capabilities allowed JFCC-NW more operational coordination between offense and signals intelligence. The Director of the Defense Information Systems Agency (DISA) also served as the commander of the JTF-GNO allowing similar integration for network defense and operations.

In addition to these organizational changes, equally important developments during the 2000s included the normalization of cyber as an issue, its differentiation from "information operations," and its increasingly centralized authority in ever-higher ranking generals. For the next several years, however, the most important operational military developments related to policy and strategy. While the details remain largely classified, in 2004 the National Security Council at the White House issued a National Security Presidential Directive, NSPD-38, which outlined means for operational coordination of offensive cyber operations. [25] Moreover, the 2005 National Military Strategy for Cyber Operations (NMS-CO) was intended to provide a comprehensive framework for the conduct of cyber operations, focused on ensuring superiority in cyberspace, for the Department of Defense. The strategy presented the official, government perception of the cyber domain, the threat environment, strategic considerations for operating in the domain, and laid out a military strategic framework that sought to ensure future US military strategic superiority in cyberspace. [26] Network Operations, Information Operations, Kinetic Operations, Law Enforcement and Counterintelligence and Themes and Messages were deemed crucial to cyber operations and to the achievement of US superiority in the domain.

The decade-old theme of achieving superiority in cyberspace continued as the NMS-CO sought to ensure the DoD would "have cyberspace superiority to ensure our freedom of action and deny the same to our adversaries through integration of network defense,

---

[25]   William J. Lynn, "Speech on Cyber Security at the Center for Strategic and International Studies," US *Department of Defense*, June 15, 2009, http://www.defense.gov/speeches/speech.aspx?speechid=1365.

[26]   Peter Pace, "The National Military Strategy for Cyberspace Operations," *Berlin Information Center for Transatlantic Security*, DoD, 12 2006, http://www.bits.de/NRANEU/others/strategy/07-F-2105doc1.pdf (accessed 9 24, 2011).

exploitation, and attack.[27] This was only the latest in a series of doctrinal back-and-forth variations on the proper goal of military action in cyberspace. Sometimes, this was superiority (implying merely a 51% advantage) to dominance or supremacy (implying a complete "overmatch") of the adversary, as the United States showed in the 1991 Gulf War.[28]

While the early years of this debate centered on "information" superiority or dominance, at least since the 2005 National Military Strategy for Cyberspace Operations, "cyber" was the centerpiece and other kinds of information operations were increasingly ignored. According to NMS-CO, strategic superiority in cyberspace was a major goal for the military.[29]

However, Cyber Command has backed away from "dominance" or "superiority" to put emphasis on "freedom of action" in cyberspace.[30] Freedom of action implies the ability to exert localized or temporary control to achieve objectives; not superiority but perhaps sufficiency. Though little has been written on this very realistic change in emphasis, assumedly the scale of the domain makes it costly and unnecessary to maintain constant strategic superiority over the Internet as a whole. Though Cyber Command has the mission of "freedom of action" in cyberspace, the Navy still believes in information dominance, having created a new corps to better organize and train the more than 44,000 people the Navy has with "extensive skills in information-intensive fields".[31]

---

[27] Pace, "The National Military Strategy for Cyberspace Operations," *Berlin Information Center for Transatlantic Security*, DoD, 12 2006, http://www.bits.de/NRANEU/others/strategy/07-F-2105doc1.pdf (accessed 9 24, 2011).

[28] For example, see the Army TRADOC Issue Paper, "Information Dominance vs. Information Superiority," 1997, available at http://www.iwar.org.uk/iwar/resources/info-dominance/issue-paper.htm.

[29] Chairman of the Joint Chiefs of Staff, "The National Military Strategy for Cyberspace Operations," 2005
Michael W. Wynne, "Senior Leader Perspectives," *Air & Space Power Journal,* Spring 2007, http://www.airpower.au.af.mil/airchronicles/apj/apj07/spr07/wynnespr07.html#wynne (accessed December 16, 2011).

[30] Briefing, "US Cyber Command: Integrating Cyber Operations," undated command brief available at http://www.afcea.org/smallbusiness/files/CommitteeMeetings/PODCAST_Cyber_Command_Brief_February_2011/USCC%20Brief_unclass_AFCEA.pdf.

[31] Chief of Naval Personnel Public Affairs, "Information Dominance Corps Warfare Insignia Approved", 22 February 2010, available at http://www.navy.mil/search/display.asp?story_id=51448

To codify the larger national security policies for cyber, in January 2008, the Bush Administration issued the Comprehensive National Cybersecurity Initiative, also known as CNCI and NSPD-54/HSPD-23.[32] Originally this initiative was classified, but the Obama Administration has since declassified the twelve key tenets, some of which dealt with operational military issues:

1. Manage the Federal Enterprise Network as a single network enterprise with Trusted Internet Connections.

2. Deploy an intrusion detection system of sensors across the Federal enterprise.

3. Pursue deployment of intrusion prevention systems across the Federal enterprise.

4. Coordinate and redirect research and development (R&D) efforts.

5. Connect current cyber operations centers to enhance situational awareness.

6. Develop and implement a government-wide cyber counterintelligence (CI) plan.

7. Increase the security of our classified networks.

8. Expand cyber education.

9. Define and develop enduring "leap-ahead" technology, strategies, and programs aiming far beyond traditional R&D.

10. Define and develop enduring deterrence strategies and programs.

11. Develop a multi-pronged approach for global supply chain risk management.

12. Define the Federal role for extending cybersecurity into critical infrastructure domains.

Past US strategies tried to simultaneously solve cyber security problems in both the public and private sectors. With CNCI, the government decided to focus their efforts on the solutions that

---

[32]   U.S. White House, "The Comprehensive National Cybersecurity Initative," *Whitehouse.gov*, March 2, 2010, http://www.whitehouse.gov/cybersecurity/ comprehensive-national-cybersecurity-initiative (accessed 9 23, 2011).

were most under their own control, fixing the Federal government, and money flooded into these 12 areas. Within the military context, these principles drove a consolidation of authority in a single unified command with relevant authorities and capabilities.

The Formation of Cyber Command

The creation of Cyber Command occurred on June 23, 2010 when Secretary of Defense Robert Gates directed Strategic Command to form a sub-unified command that would focus on cyberspace.[33] Gates' order declared that the director of the NSA would serve as commander. The agency received initial operating capability on May 21, 2010, and achieved full operating capability less than half a year later in November.[34] Gates' memo also charged the Under Secretary of Defense for Policy to review cyber policy and strategy to come to up with a "comprehensive approach to cyber operations." The resulting *Department of Defense Strategy for Operating in Cyberspace* was only completed in July 2011.[35]

The Current State of US Cyber Operations

With the fulfillment of Gates' initial memo, it seems appropriate to reflect on the Department of Defense's new operational structure. Cyber Command doesn't operate in a vacuum; its creation has provided some clarity on important issues in the field of cyber conflict research. It has been a definitive answer to the issues of centralization vs. decentralization, offense vs. defense, established military goals, detailed the operational coordination and chain of command, resolved some legal questions, and articulated the

---

[33]   U.S. Cyber Command Fact Sheet, October 2010,
       http://www.stratcom.mil/factsheets/Cyber_Command/.
[34]   U.S. Department of Defense, "Cyber Command Achieves Full Operational
       Capability," News Release, 3 November 2010,
       http://www.defense.gov/releases/release.aspx?releaseid=14030.
[35]   U.S. Department of Defense, *Strategy for Operating in Cyberspace*, June
       2011 http://www.defense.gov/home/features/2011/0411_cyberstrategy/docs/
       DoD_Strategy_for_Operating_in_Cyberspace_July_2011.pdf.

relationship between military cyber efforts and the private sector. While answering some questions and moving the policy discussion forward, it has also invited a whole new set of questions around action in cyberspace.

Military Cyber Operations

Little has been officially published that gives much insight into the military cyber operations of the United States. Perhaps the most instructive is a draft doctrine publication of the Air Force, AFDD 2-11 of 2008, a document that was never published. AFDD 3-11, Cyberspace Operations, revealed details of how the Air Force viewed offensive and defensive operations:

> Execution in cyberspace comprises two types of thought: offensive and defensive. For example, we engage in offensive operations to attack a vulnerability gained through access. We engage in defensive actions to close a vulnerability resulting from an adversary's access. Therefore, access is the "on ramp" for both sides' offensive actions. We protect access through a variety of means, such as password protection, firewalls, closed networks, or certificates—all of these predicated on the vigilance of individual network users.[36]

The document went on to describe how the Air Force saw that in cyberspace, activities fell into "a minimum of ten broad categories." This view of activities mapped against offensive and defensive thinking are illustrated in AFDD 3-11, as shown in Figure 2.2.

---

[36]   United States Air Force, AF Doctrine Document 3-11, Cyberspace Operations, Draft, 2008, 35.

Figure 2.2: Anatomy of a Cyberspace Operation[37]

Anatomy of a Cyberspace Operation

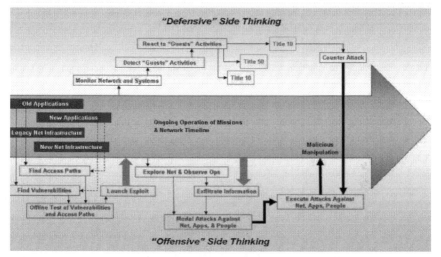

This figure shows the key activities in defensive operations, monitoring, detecting and reacting to an adversary, deciding to respond either through law enforcement (Title 18), intelligence or counterintelligence (Title 50) or ultimately through military action (Title 10) – as described in the legal section of this chapter.

On the offensive side, the key activities in AFDD 3-11 start with finding access paths and vulnerabilities. Only after the military conducts offline tests of these vulnerabilities and access paths does it launch the appropriate exploit which will hopefully give control of the adversary computers. After the successful exploitation, the operation turns to listening and learning by exploring within the adversary's networks and observing the information therein to learn about their operations. The information is then "exfiltrated" or taken from the adversaries network and brought back to friendly networks.

Before taking any destructive actions within the adversary's network – moving from taking information to deleting it or breaking systems – the military models the effects

---

[37]   Ibid.

of the attack to determine if their payloads will have the desired effect and only the desired effect. Modeling should reveal if the attack is likely to be successful and if so, for how long. However the modeling should also hopefully reveal other information. If the attack is likely to cascade or otherwise cause disproportionate harm to civilians or break the laws of armed conflict (see the legal section of this chapter), the offensive team will have to find another, less disruptive, means of attack.

Up to this point, all of these activities fall into the military definition of CNE, or intelligence activities, as the military has not disrupted or otherwise "attacked" in the military sense. The military will continue to collect information until a commander gives the order to take the next step and only then will the military operators execute the attack.

Current US Structures for DoD and Intelligence in Cyber Conflict

Testimony to Congress and speeches by senior DoD leaders provides insight into how they and the Intelligence Community are organizing for cyber conflict. Other open reporting, including academic and journalistic articles have helped flesh out current leadership's intent. DoD directives also provide important context relevant to understanding issues in this area.

Within the Department of Defense, the following are the key organizations involved in cyber conflict:

- Office of the Secretary of Defense,
- Joint Staff,
- Strategic Command (which oversees cyber issues as part of its overall role for global strike missions, such as by intercontinental missiles and bombers),
- Cyber Command (a sub-command of Strategic Command),
- Defense Information Systems Agency (responsible for the DoD's IT systems),
- National Security Agency (responsible for information assurance and cyber-based signals intelligence collection,

providing deep support for the co-located Cyber Command),

- Military Services (Army, Navy, Air Force, and Marines),
- Geographic combatant commands (GCCs, such as European Command or Pacific Command responsible for warfighting in a particular part of the world) and
- Functional component commands (FCCs, like Transportation Command, overseeing a critical DoD function).

In addition to these military organizations, the US government has other civilian groups, including the Office of the Director of National Intelligence, Federal Bureau of Investigations, and with the biggest role of all, the Department of Homeland Security.

Each of these organizations, whether military or civilian, can be binned into at least one of the following six categories:

1. Policy Organizations: Led by senior government officials with clear mandate to coordinate and approve policy.

2. Command Organizations: Military and intelligence commands with authority to execute operations under the US Constitution and Law either (Title 10 Title 18 Title 50 Title 22).

3. Internal CND: Organizations tasked to defend their own internal information systems and networks

4. CNA Capability Provider: Entities capable of conducting attack operations, including those that provide forces to others for execution.

5. Investigation/Forensics Provider: Closely related to internal defense organizations, but with deep expertise in computer forensics and cyber crime investigation.

6. Adversary threat prediction/intelligence: Collectors and analyzers of adversary information.

These types of functions are performed at multiple levels in the community. An overview, simplified to make the distinctions clearer, is provided in the table below:

Table 2.1: Cyber Organizations and their Focus

Organization	Policy	Command	CND	CNA	Forensics	Intel
MILITARY AGENCIES						
OSD	X				X	
Joint Staff	X					
USSTRATCOM	X	X	X			
Cyber Command	X	X	X	X	X	X
DIA			X	X		X
DISA			X			
Services			X	X	X	
NSA			X			X
Geographic Commands		X	X			
Functional Commands			X			
CIVILIAN AGENCIES						
ODNI	X					
CIA		X	X	X		X
DHS	X		X		X	
FBI		X	X	X		

Structurally, the most important new construct in military and intelligence dimensions is the creation of US Cyber Command. Based on the chart above, it becomes instantly apparent how Cyber Command has centralized a variety of functions, which should create a larger pool of resources, improve cooperation and coordination, and provide an expanded range of capabilities.

US Cyber Command: Integrating Offense, Defense and Exploitation

The creation of US Cyber Command, a sub-unified command under US Strategic Command, is meant to bring more centralization and normalization to cyber operations. Cyber Command's missions include:

- "Planning, coordinating, integrating, synchronizing, and directing activities to operate and defend the Department of Defense information networks."[38] This includes the Global Information Grid (GIG). [39]

- "[Conducting] full-spectrum military cyberspace operations (in accordance with all applicable laws and regulations) in order to ensure US and allied freedom of action in cyberspace, while denying the same to our adversaries."[40]

While the creation of Cyber Command clearly emphasizes the importance the Department of Defense places on cyber operations, it is not necessarily a signal that the United States will be more aggressive in cyberspace. Though some voices, such as retired general James Cartwright, former vice chairman of the Joint Chiefs of Staff, emphasize the offensive mission and deterrence[41] as table 2.3 would suggest, Cyber Command has a broad focus with significant defensive missions. General Keith Alexander, the first commander of CYBERCOM, has made clear that while the defensive missions need to be conducted day and night, every day with "80 to 90% of their effort." The offensive mission, he noted, "is very seldom used, is very specific."[42] This seems fitting as the US military's "heavy joint reliance on advanced communications systems," means that cyber attacks "will be a central element of any enemy antiaccess/area-denial strategy, requiring a higher degree of protection for friendly command and control systems," according to a 2012 DoD document.

---

[38] US Strategic Command, "US Cyber Command Fact Sheet."

[39] US Department of Defense, Office of the Assistant Secretary of Defense, "Deputy Assistant Secretary of Defense for Cyber, Identity, and Information Assurance Strategy," August 2009, http://iase.disa.mil/policy-guidance/dasd_ciia__strategy_aug2009.pdf.

[40] US Strategic Command, "US Cyber Command Fact Sheet."

[41] Tony Capaccio and David Lerman, "New Cyber Strategy Defends, Not Deters, Cartwright Says," *Bloomberg*, July 14, 2011, http://www.bloomberg.com/news/2011-07-14/new-cyber-strategy-is-defense-not-deterrence-cartwright-says.html (accessed December 16, 2011).

[42] Keith Alexander, "Advance Questions for Lieutenant General Keith Alexander," US *Senate*, April 15, 2010, http://armed-services.senate.gov/statemnt/2010/04%20April/Alexander%2004-15-10.pdf.

In Figure 2.1 below is displayed the organizational structure of the US Cyber Command, its component organizations and their roles, and its chain of command.

Figure 2.3: United States Cyber Command Organizational Chart[13]

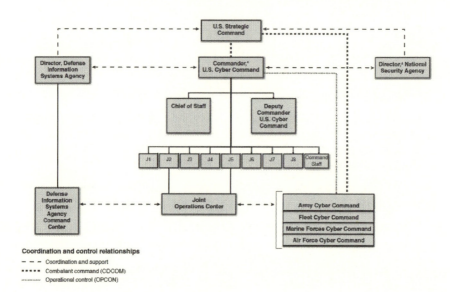

The establishment of Cyber Command reinforces the first pillar of the DoD strategy, to treat cyberspace as a military domain and touches on several of the drivers (introduced at the beginning of the chapter) including normalization and centralization. This should improve the training pipeline for cyber professions in the department. An authority now exists for articulating the job skills and experience requirements of professionals and over time this authority will impact a wide swath of human capital issues such as recruitment, training, career paths, promotions and leadership position selections.[44]

---

43   Noah Shachtman, "Dot-Mil Cyber Security Spending: Now Extra FUBAR," *Wired Magazine*, April 1, 2011, http://www.wired.com/dangerroom/tag/u-s-cyber-command/ (accessed August 29, 2011). Please note that it is labeled FOUO or "For Official Use Only." Normally this would not be publishable, but this chart has already been published by *Wired* magazine.

44   Gail Harris, "The Pentagon's New Cyber Command," *International Relations and Security Network (ISN)*, (20 December 2010).

Cyber Command has components in each of the Services. These currently include:

- United States Fleet Cyber Command (10th Fleet)[45]
- 24th Air Force (AFCYBER)[46]
- US Army Forces Cyber Command (ARFORCYBER)[47]
- US Marine Corps Cyberspace Command (MARFORCYBER)[48]

This means the Department of Defense cyber missions is more centralized than ever before. Yet according at least to the Government Accountability Office, there is still far to go:

> DoD's organization to address cyber security threats is decentralized and spread across various offices, commands, military services and military agencies. DOD cyber security roles and responsibilities are vast and include developing joint policy and guidance and

---

[45] United States House Armed Service Committee, *Statement of VADM Bernard McCullough before the House Armed Services Committee Subcommittee on Terrorism and Unconventional Threats and Capabilities* 111th Cong., 2nd sess., September 23, 2010, 1-10. http://democrats.armedservices.house.gov/index.cfm/files/serve?File_id=46 ab9cfd-c2a2-4529-a8bf-49413b1df8bf (accessed September 23, 2011)

[46] United States House Armed Services Committee, *Department of the Air Force Presentation to the House Armed Services Committee on Terrorism and Unconventional Threats*: *Statement by Major General Richard Webber,* 111th Cong., 2nd sess., September 23, 2010, 1-10. http://democrats.armedservices.house.gov/index.cfm/files/serve?File_id=8b 28f10f-e164-481f-93cc-0c0734195fb1 (accessed September 23, 2011)

[47] United States House Armed Services Committee, *"Statement of Major General Rhett Hernandez Before the House Armed Services Committee Subcommittee on Terrorism, Unconventional Threats and Capabilities,* 111th Cong., 2nd sess., September 23, 2010, 1-10. http://democrats.armedservices.house.gov/index.cfm/files/serve?File_id=06 7ffc96-e5c1-4cef-baa2-010d16e3be57 (accessed September 23, 2011)

[48] United States House Armed Services Committee, *"Statement of Lieutenant General George J. Flynn Before the Subcommittee on Terrorism, Unconventional Threats and Capabilities,* 111th Cong., 2nd sess., September 23, 2010, 1-10. http://democrats.armedservices.house.gov/ index.cfm/files/serve?File_id=d95a1fa0-48d3-4d57-93d3-ccaf4efbd848 (accessed September 23, 2011)

operational functions to protect and defend its computer networks.[49]

Figure 2.4 below, from the GAO, illustrates the important milestones of the last five years, with many new operational organizations, classes, and policies.

Figure 2.4 DoD Cyberspace Operations Timeline[50]

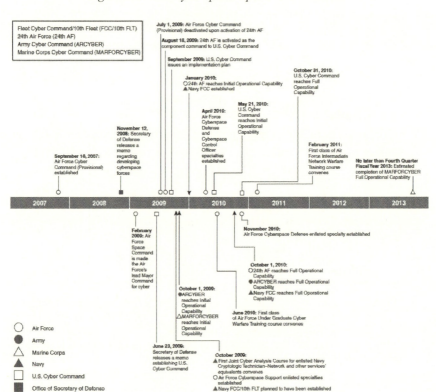

---

[49]   U.S. General Accounting Office. *Defense Department Cyber Efforts: DOD Faces Challenges In Its Cyber Activities*, GAO-11-75. Washington, DC: General Accounting Office, July 25, 2011.
      http://www.gao.gov/new.items/d1175.pdf (accessed September 9, 2011).

[50]   US Government Accountability Office, "Defense Department Cyber Efforts: More Detailed Guidance Needed to Ensure Military Services Develop Appropriate Cyberspace Capabilities," 8.

The Current DoD Cyber Strategy

In July 2011 the Department of Defense released an unclassified articulation of cyber strategy, the *Department of Defense Strategy for Operating in Cyberspace.*[51] This strategy was consistent with previous unclassified references, including testimony to Congress by CYBERCOM Commander General Alexander and an article in *Foreign Affairs* article by then Deputy Secretary of Defense, William Lynn. The five pillars of this strategy are:[52]

- Cyber must be recognized as a warfare domain, equal to land, sea, and air, requiring its own organization, equipment, and training;

- Defensive postures must employ new operating concepts, like active defense and advanced sensors, which go beyond "good hygiene" to include sophisticated and accurate operations;

- Cyber defenses must reach beyond .mil, partnering with other government agencies and private industry to enable a whole-of-government approach;

- Cyber defenses must be pursued with international allies to strengthen collective cyber security; and

- DoD must help leverage the cyber workforce and rapid innovation to maintain US technological superiority.[53]

Overall, the pillars acknowledge the limits of a nation's capability in the domain of cyberspace and seem accept the instability of the domain. While the first pillar addresses the domains uniqueness, subsequent pillars seem to show restraint in attempting to dominate the domain. Rather, they prioritize collaboration with state and non-state actors including the commercial sector, other government agencies, and international

---

[51] Department of Defense, "Department of Defense Strategy for Operating in Cyberspace" (July 2011).

[52] Lynn, "Defending a New Domain."

[53] US Department of Defense, *Department of Defense Strategy for Operating in Cyberspace*, July 2011. William Lynn, "Defending a New Domain," *Foreign Affairs* (September/October 2010): 97-108.

governments. While, "good hygiene" alone is seen as insufficient for adequate defense, it is paired with "response," which potentially leverages offensive capabilities to support deterrence and defense. Each of these pillars will now be examined in turn.

Cyber must be recognized as a warfare domain equal to land, sea, and air, requiring its own organization, equipment, and training.

Major US military organizational and conceptual approaches to combat are characterized by concepts of "domains" that traditionally included land and sea (or maritime), then later air and space. The DoD intends to treat cyberspace as a domain, signaling a serious change, marked first and foremost by the creation of Cyber Command.

While, the DoD recognizes that the domain of cyberspace is different due to its manmade nature, it has become just as critical to military operations as land, sea, air, or space. By considering cyber as a domain, it becomes easier to organize train and equip for operations. Furthermore, it helps DoD determine what organizations and structures are most adept at defending and operating in cyberspace – the drivers introduced earlier in this chapter. For example, Deputy Defense Secretary William Lynn cited the inherent uniqueness to the new domain as a reason that the loose confederations of cyber organizations in the Department were reorganized, and new command structures (Cyber Command) were established.[54] General Alexander added that cyberspace is a defensible domain and called for cyber conflict and cyberspace to be studied in the same way other domains have been studied "to understand how the principles of the military art apply there."[55]

One of the reasons cyberspace is recognized as a new domain is the military's requirements for command and control during ongoing operations, including operations in cyberspace. Current command structures are primarily geographical, with combatant commanders responsible for US military operations in geographic areas. But computer network operations can be regional and global at the same

---

[54]   Lynn, "Defending a New Domain."

[55]   United States Senate Armed Services Committee, *Advance Questions for Lieutenant General Keith Alexander, Nominee for Commander, United States Cyber Command: Hearing before US Senate Armed Service Committee,* 108th Cong., 2nd sess., October 15, 2004, 1-32.

time requiring a streamlined command process. As General Alexander articulated, "Because cyberspace is not generally bounded by geography, the Commander of US Cyber Command will have to coordinate with US agencies and Combatant Commanders that would be affected by actions taken in cyberspace."[56]

Future military operations in land, sea, air, or space will require close coordination with the cyber domain and vice versa. In fact, in the near future, if not already today, few military operations or objectives could be accomplished without cyber support due to the reliance of friendly and adversary forces on networked information systems for communication, intelligence, C3, and other vital functions. An even more recent DoD document, the 2012 Joint Operational Access Concept (or JOAC), recognizes that "cross domain synergy" is not only important but that,

> this integration will have to occur at lower echelons, generating the tempo that is often critical to exploiting fleeting local opportunities for disrupting the enemy system, and will require the full inclusion of space and cyberspace operations into the traditional air-land-sea battlespace.[57]

Another important aspect of treating cyber as a domain is that, "[a]s in any other domain, losses are inevitable, and joint forces projecting military force must be prepared to operate effectively despite such losses."[58] In testimony to Congress, General Alexander made a similar point that penetration of and damage to networks and infrastructure is inevitable and DoD must be able to "fight through."[59]

Defensive postures must employ new operating concepts, like active defense and advanced sensors, which go beyond "good hygiene" to include sophisticated and accurate operations.

The key strategy of *defense in depth,* a military strategy that delays the advance of an enemy rather than preventing it, is equally applicable to kinetic military operations as it is towards

---

[56] Ibid.

[57] Department of Defense, "Joint Operational Access Concept", p11.

[58] Ibid, p27.

[59] Alexander, "Advance Questions for Lieutenant General Keith Alexander, Nominee for Commander, United States Cyber Command."

operations in cyberspace. However, "active defense" has been a problematic term that the Department of Defense has long struggled to define.

According to Cyber Command, "active defense" includes the following elements:

- Build Defensible Systems
- Develop Culture and Practices
- Hunt Within Networks
- Mitigate Threats at the Boundaries
- Tip and Cue in Real Time
- Respond at Network Speed[60]

However, these six elements do not seem to include the offensive implications often associated with active defense. For example, then Deputy Secretary of Defense Lynn, wrote that, "Part sensor, part sentry, part sharpshooter, these active defense systems represent a fundamental shift in the US approach to cyber defense" and it is not apparent how sharpshooting matches to any of the six elements in Cyber Command's description.

DoD has long had limited defense operations that do seem to match the "sharpshooter" description which are known as "CND Response Actions" or CND RAs. Unfortunately, the military has said little about them. According to the National Research Council,

> CND RAs can only be used in response to intrusions that meet a certain threshold and are further limited in their scope, duration, and intended impact. Like all self-defense, CND RAs are tactical activities intended to address and mitigate a specific hostile action. ... Authority for CND RAs is described, constrained and granted through standing rules of engagement as established by the National Command Authority and

---

[60]   Undated Cyber Command briefing, http://www.afcea.org/ smallbusiness/files/CommitteeMeetings/PODCAST_Cyber_Command_Bri ef_February_2011/USCC%20Brief_unclass_AFCEA.pdf.

flowing through the secretary of defense, from the President's authority as Commander in Chief.[61]

However, other aspects of this pillar are more obvious. Computer "hygiene" is a form of proactive defense; by maintaining software patches and updating systems, the DoD seeks to make its network less penetrable. Sensors encompass intrusion detection devices and other related monitoring capabilities designed to detect and map intrusions and unauthorized activities when they occur.

Cyber defenses must reach beyond .mil, partnering with other government agencies and private industry to enable a whole-of-government approach.

With this statement, DoD articulates a clear requirement to help to improve the security of civilian infrastructure without which DoD missions could suffer dramatically. The DoD is responsible for protecting dot-mil only and has been energetic in trying to limit itself to that role and supporting the US Department of Homeland Security which has the lead in protecting the ".gov" and ".com" domains.

The DoD has publicly articulated that it will leverage its "ten years of concerted investment in cyberdefense to support broader efforts to protect critical infrastructure."[62] This strategy was further developed by the October 2010 Memo of Understanding between DHS and DoD, which aims to provide an enhanced ability to support cybersecurity missions for both parties.[63] Whether the DoD's assistance to Homeland Security in its efforts to secure the ".com" domain will optimally, or sufficiently, mitigate the risk imposed on critical infrastructure by cyber conflict remains unclear, but several programs are already underway including the DIB Cyber Pilot.[64]

---

[61]   William A. Owens, Kenneth W. Dam, and Herbert S. Lin, eds. *Technology, Policy, Law, and Ethics Regarding U.S. Acquisition and Use of Cyberattack Capabilities,* (Washington, DC: National Academies Press, 2009), p. 169.

[62]   Lynn, "Defending a New Domain."

[63]   "Memorandum of Agreement Between DHS and DoD Regarding Cybersecurity," (13 October 2010).

[64]   John D. Banusiewicz, "Lynn Outlines New Cyber Security Effort," *US Department of Defense,* June 16, 2011, http://www.defense.gov/news/newsarticle.aspx?id=64349 (accessed December 14, 2011).

Cyber defenses must be pursued with international allies to strengthen collective cyber security

Just as the DoD's systems are dependent on US civilian infrastructure, they are also dependent on global infrastructure. And, just as defensive constructs need to be collaborative with the private sector, within the US they are also linked to US allies. Many of these relationships in cybersecurity were developed through existing World War II era signals intelligence partnerships that have matured and advanced.

Given the global nature of the Internet, US allies play a critical role in international cyberdefense, such as allowing the DoD to gain more attack signatures, more sensors and forensic evidence, and like-minded colleagues to foster norms. Just as the United States' air and space defenses are linked with those of allies to provide warning of an attack from the sky, so too can the United States and its allies cooperatively monitor computer networks for intrusions. [65] Though intrusions could be attempted in a way or scale that makes international collaboration on monitoring less effective, shared warning and other collaborative efforts will greatly improve defense against many threat types.

DoD must help leverage the cyber workforce and rapid innovation to maintain US technological superiority.

The US government's utilization of new technologies has historically lagged behind that of private industry. This is principally caused by the federal acquisition process, which is widely viewed as cumbersome and too slow to support cyber forces and operations. This is why Secretary Lynn wrote that "[m]aking use of the private sector's innovative capacity will also require dramatic improvements in the government's procedures for acquiring information technology." Currently, systems are too frequently obsolete as soon as they are fielded. Consequently, the DoD is aiming to enhance IT acquisition through four key thrusts:

---

[65]   "Memorandum of Agreement Between DHS and DoD Regarding Cybersecurity," (13 October 2010).

1) Speed must be a critical priority. The Pentagon's acquisition process must match the technology development cycle. With information technology, this means cycles of 12 to 36 months, not seven or eight years.

2) The Pentagon must employ incremental development and testing rather than try to deploy large complex systems in one "big bang."

3) The US military must be willing to sacrifice or defer some customization in order to achieve speedy incremental improvements.

4) The Defense Department's information technology needs which range from modernizing nuclear command-and-control systems to updating word-processing software demand different levels of oversight. [66]

Moreover, the Department is looking to tap into the innovation of the private sector, with programs like Cyber Accelerator, DaVenCi, and DARPA's Cyber Fast Track. Through DARPA, is investing in fundamental research aimed at improving the government's ability to attribute attacks, blunt intrusions and enhance defense. [67] Recent DARPA projects have included the National Cyber Range, and DARPA has committed to increasing its funding of cyber research by 50% over the next 5 years.

DoD is also working with DHS to build a sensitive public-private partnership called the Enduring Security Framework. In this venue, the "chief executive officers and chief technology officers of major information technology and defense companies now meet regularly with top officers from the Department of Homeland Security, the Office of the Director of National Intelligence, and the Department of Defense."[68]

Steps are also being taken to improve DoD abilities by enhancing human capital. Workforce measures include increasing training and certification. And DoD is calling for more investment in high-speed sensors, advanced analytics, and

---

[66] Lynn, "Defending a New Domain."

[67] Ibid.

[68] "Memorandum of Agreement Between DHS and DoD Regarding Cybersecurity," (13 October 2010).

automated systems to back up trained cybersecurity professionals. [69] These steps will maintain superior human productivity, a factor that Secretary Lynn underscores alongside technology, stating "[t]he United States will lose its advantage in cyberspace if that advantage is predicated on simply amassing trained cyber security professionals. The US government must... confront the cyber defense challenge as it confronts other military challenges: with a focus not on numbers, but on superior technology and productivity."[70]

Other Operational Considerations

The centerpieces of DoD's cyber efforts are the DSOC and Cyber Command. However, there are still many other operational considerations. This chapter will now examine some of the most important, including the law, rules of engagement, intelligence gain/loss recommendations, and command and control.

Operational Implications of US and International Law

In its early, gestational period, CYBERCOM confronts difficult problems of bureaucratic authorities and legal guidelines, most of which are not new. US and international law restrict the range of actions available to the US intelligence community and military, and this is especially true for legal authorities that govern the conduct of cyber operations for military and intelligence purposes.

Implications of Domestic Law

US domestic law is currently ill-suited to the technological and policy demands of cyber operations, and creates false dichotomies between organizations that need to be integrated and coordinated. The most glaring of these problems can be found in the intersection of the various sections of the law governing military, intelligence, and criminal issues. Title 10 of the US Code provides the legal basis for the roles, missions and organizations of the Army, Navy, Marine Corps, Air Force,

---

[69]   Lynn, "Defending a New Domain."

[70]   Ibid.

Special Forces, Combatant Command, DoD Agencies and other military elements, while Title 50 of the United States Code focuses specifically on intelligence authorities.[71] Title 18 is also often used, as it covers cyber-related criminal actions, such as intruding into a computer and stealing personal data. To conduct their missions in cyberspace, the DoD has had to find a balance between these legal requirements. In the absence of legal remedy, the military has turned to doctrine, which is used by militaries to help codify the current best solution to problems,

Of these, Air Force doctrine has particularly good examples of how these domestic legal authorities affect cyber operations. For example, their doctrine explains how legal authority affects response to intrusions:

> Reaction to unwelcome activity can take several paths. At least three paths can be taken, which are not mutually exclusive. One path would be to prosecute perpetrators who commit acts that are illegal under the provisions of criminal law in USC Title 18. However, prosecution can be complicated by the need to gather forensic evidence and identify perpetrators, especially when cyberspace attacks cross national boundaries.
>
> If it appears that unwelcome activity has been instigated by foreign entities, US authorities may choose instead to engage in intelligence and counterintelligence monitoring under the authority of USC Title 50. Lastly, USC Title 10, which governs wartime actions, permits self-defense and even destructive kinetic responses depending on the severity of the original hostile behavior. A counterattack could include cyberspace, electronic, or physical action, or any combination of these.[72]

---

[71]   Title 10 also provides relevant language for the Intelligence Community, especially the portions of the intelligence community under DoD (which is the majority of the community).

[72]   Air Force, "Draft United States Cyber Operations - Never Published, AFDD 2-11" *Air Force*, 2008, http://www.au.af.mil/au/awc/cyberspace/documents/ AF%20Symposium%20AFDD%202-11.pdf (accessed 9 23, 2011).

Air Force doctrine also has an enlightening example of how the Service will organize itself based on the competing demands of the US legal code:

> Military forces under a combatant commander derive authority to conduct [network attack] from the laws contained in Title 10 of the US Code (U.S.C.). However, the skills and target knowledge for effective [network attack] are best developed and honed during peacetime intelligence … Intelligence forces in the national intelligence community derive authority to conduct network exploitation … from laws contained in U.S.C. Title 50.

> For this reason, "dual-purpose" military forces are funded and controlled by organizations that derive authority under laws contained in both Title 10 and Title 50. The greatest benefit of these "dual-purpose" forces is their authority to operate under laws contained in Title 50, and so produce actionable intelligence products, while exercising the skills needed for [network attack under Title 10]. "These forces are the preferred means by which the Air Force can organize, train, and equip mission-ready [network attack] forces.[73]

While designed to check the power of agencies to expand the scope of their mission, cross agency collaboration allows Cyber Command to utilized Title 10, Title 18, and Title 50 authorizing a wide flexibility of cyber actions. Yet, this flexibility is still limited by international law, which, at least in principal, should also limit the actions of enemy state-actors.

Implications of International Law

As discussed in the legal chapter, a critically important component of international law is the UN Charter. Article 51 of the UN Charter codifies the inherent right of self-defense by any nation against an armed attack, "Nothing in the present Charter shall impair the inherent right of individual or collective self-defense if an armed

---

[73]   United States Air Force, "Cyberspace Operations," Air Force Doctrine Document 3-12, (Washington DC, 15 July 2010).

attack occurs against a Member of the United Nations, until the Security Council has taken measures necessary to maintain international peace and security." Additionally, the UN Charter establishes that the Security Council can direct measures against any "threat to the peace," "breach of the peace," or "act of aggression."[74]

Article 2(4) of the UN Charter provides that states shall refrain from the threat or use of force against the territorial integrity or political independence of any state. States are prohibited from using "the threat or use of force against the territorial integrity or political independence of any state, or in any other manner inconsistent with the Purposes of the United Nations."[75]

Congressional testimony and a review of DoD policy have revealed that its operations, including those of the new Cyber Command, are conducted consistent with this and other international law principles. That is, well-established legal principles provide a framework from which we can deduce what is a threat or use of force in terms of hostile intent and hostile act, as reflected in DoD's Standing Rules of Engagement and Standing Rules for the Use of Force (SROE/SRUF). In response to questions asked of the first nominee to command the US Cyber Command regarding what constitutes use of force in cyberspace, DoD's view was articulated as:

> The President of the United States determines what is a threat or use of force/armed attack against the United States and authorizes DOD through [standing rules of engagement] to exercise our national right of self-defense recognized by the UN Charter. This determination involves an objective and subjective analysis that considers the facts surrounding a particular cyber attack, and is made within the bounds of US and international law. If the President determines a cyber event does meet the threshold of a use of force/armed attack, he may determine that the activity is of such scope, duration, or intensity that it warrants exercising our right to self-defense and/or the initiation of hostilities as an appropriate response.[76]

---

[74]   United Nations, "Charter of the United Nations," Art. 51, (24 October 1945).
[75]   United Nations, "Charter of the United Nations," art. 2, § 4, (24 October 1945).
[76]   Keith Alexander, "Advance Questions for Lieutenant General Keith Alexander," *US Senate*, (April 15, 2010).

Unfortunately, there is no international consensus on the meaning of the term "use of force," which renders legally ambiguous any particular response in kinetic as well as cyber conflict. [77] Consequently, the President, as advised by his National Security Council, must decide first whether any particular cyber attack amounts to a "use of force" or "armed attack" and second what is the appropriate kinetic or cyber response.

DoD has also cited the UN Charter's recognition of a state's inherent right to individual and collective self-defense to establish the legal justification for cyber actions. DoD has upheld the view that the United States has the right to evaluate its collective defense obligations when another state is threatened or subject to a use of force in the cyber domain. This normalizes cyber actions, as DoD would have the same response in other war-fighting domains. [78]

The Department's positions echo the views expressed in the deliberations of the National Research Council's study on *Technology, Policy, Law and Ethics Regarding US Acquisition and Use of Cyber Attack Capabilities*, which dove deep into the issues related to use of force in cyberspace. Particularly insightful was the NRC's observation that it is irrelevant whether an attack constitutes a "use of force." Rather, the effects of a given cyberattack should be "point of departure for an analysis of this question, rather than the specific mechanism used to achieve these effects." [79] The NRC's research articulated a caveat for economic-cyber warfare, stating that is entirely possible to imagine "cyberattack as a tool for pursuing goals related to economic competition and/or economic warfare." [80] The NRC acknowledges that although the laws of armed conflict and the UN Charter prohibit the use of force—cyber as well as kinetic force—in pursuit of purely economic or territorial gain, "the legitimacy of cyberattacks that do not constitute a use of force for economic gain is not entirely clear" [81]

---

[77]   bid.

[78]   Ibid.

[79]   William A. Owens, Kenneth W. Dam, and Herbert S. Lin, eds. *Technology, Policy, Law, and Ethics Regarding U.S. Acquisition and Use of Cyberattack Capabilities,* (Washington, DC: National Academies Press, 2009), 252.

[80]   Ibid., 259.

[81]   Ibid.

The NRC study also detailed the complexities of applying the laws of war to espionage activities. While espionage is illegal under domestic law, it is de facto legal under international law, for "No serious proposal has ever been made within the international community to prohibit intelligence collection as a violation of international law because of the tacit acknowledgement by nations that it is important to all, and practiced by each."[82] Since the collection of traditional intelligence collection may be perceived as a military threat, in cyberspace, it is difficult to distinguish between cyber attack and exploitation/espionage because both begin with exploiting vulnerability and gaining network access. Intent, therefore, is the key distinguishing factor.

Just as important as the declared US policy on "use of force" and "armed attack" are the complementary positions on the Law of Armed Conflict (LOAC), including proportionality, military necessity, perfidy, discrimination and distinction, and neutrality. According to General Alexander in Congressional testimony, the US has affirmed that the same LOAC principles that apply to kinetic warfare will also apply to actions in cyberspace.[83] This is an important statement, putting the United States on record that we will behave in a certain manner, according to US values and international commitments. Of course, how exactly these intricacies of LOAC will apply to cyber operations will depend on the nature of technology, future cyber conflicts, and the nature of cyber operations.

An example of how the military implements LOAC on a daily basis was released by the Air Force *Legal Reviews of Weapons And Cyber Capabilities.*[84] The document instructs the Air Force Judge Advocate General (JAG) to review weapons and cyber capability for their "legality under LOAC, domestic law, and international law" if they are not within a super-classified Special Action Program.[85] This demonstrates that, cyber capabilities have been normalized into this

---

[82]   Ibid., 260.

[83]   United States Senate Armed Services Committee, *Advance Questions for Lieutenant General Keith Alexander, Nominee for Commander, United States Cyber Command: Hearing before US Senate Armed Service Committee,* 108th Cong., 2nd sess., October 15, 2004, 1-32.

[84]   Secretary of the Air Force. (July 27, 2011). Air Force Instructions 51-402: Legal Reviews of Weapons and Cyber Capabilities. Air Force e-Publishing.

[85]   Ibid.

legal framework alongside traditional weapons, reflecting one of the implicit decisions made in cyber operations.

While the activity is largely normalized, the decision to not classify cyber capabilities as a subset of weapons is informative in and of itself. This distinction allows for important differences in operational procedure. For example, while the Air Force JAG can delegate the legal review for both weapons and cyber capabilities to a subordinate legal official in the Pentagon, these approvals can also be delegated to lawyers at subordinate AF Major Commands, closer to the acquisition programs or operational commanders.[86]

The long-term utility of LOAC will depend on whether other cyber conflict actors also adhere to its tenets. China and Russia, for example, have been unwilling to declare in cyber dialogues with US participants that that LOAC applies to cyber conflict. One could therefore imagine a future conflict in which the US adhered to LOAC while China did not, possibly with disastrous consequences for the former.

Rules of Engagement

In military operations, Rules of Engagement (ROE) guide the behavior of combatants, binding together strategy and operations with legal limitations. By establishing a set of standard practices, the US, NATO and many other militaries use ROE to provide guidance on when, where and how force shall be used. These rules can vary somewhat from operation to operation, but they are always founded in law and policy. They may be made public, but for the most part they are typically only fully known to the force that is using them, to prevent the adversary from finding weaknesses in them.

ROE are designed to flow from the law, but are also designed to protect forces and to enable mission accomplishment. Excessively tight ROE can hinder missions and place one's own forces at risk. Weak or loose ROE can facilitate escalation of conflict and result in unnecessary use of force, which can run counter to military objectives and perhaps result in a violation of rules and law of armed conflict.

---

[86]   Ibid.

It is not the intention of this chapter to enumerate specific ROE under which US cyber forces should, and will, operate. Rather, this effort seeks merely to highlight the recent consensus on some of the thornier issues of offensive cyber capabilities. Publicly available testimony to Congress, unclassified doctrine, statements by allied leaders and the review of law and policy elsewhere in this Chapter and monograph have allowed enabled the broad outlining of the current ROE.

According to the findings of the National Research Council, "some of the issues relevant to formulating ROEs for cyberattack might include:

- When to execute a cyberattack—what are the circumstances under which a cyberattack might be authorized?

- Scope of a cyberattack—what are the entities that may be targeted?

- Duration of the cyberattack—how long should a cyberattack last?

- Notifications—who must be informed if a cyberattack is conducted?

- Authority for exceptions—what level of authority is needed to grant an exception for standing ROEs?"[87]

As militaries do not routinely publicize their ROEs (to ensure that adversaries cannot find the potential cries of uncertainty to exploit), this section of this chapter will examine what can be known about how the Department of Defense tackles these questions.

General Alexander, the Commander of US Cyber Command, has testified, "The President of the United States determines what is a threat or use of force/armed attack against the United States and authorizes DOD through the SROE [standing ROEs] to exercise our national right of self defense recognized by the UN Charter."[88] Here the driver is normalization, treating the use of force in cyberspace the same as in any other area.

---

[87]   Owens, Dam, and Lin, eds., *Cyberattack Capabilities,* 169.

[88]   United States Senate Armed Services Committee, *Advance Questions for Lieutenant General Keith Alexander, Nominee for Commander, United*

The July 2011 GAO Report on Cyber Operations identified problems with the existing cyber ROE. According to the GAO, the *National Military Strategy for Cyberspace Operations*, the 2008 Unified Command Plan, the DoD Directive O-8530.1, and the Standing Rules of Engagement are not consistent and sometimes provide conflicting guidance. For example, under normal rules of engagement, any military commanders have the right to self-defense. When under attack, commanders are typically authorized to attack back. But because of the ambiguity surrounding the word "attack" in cyberspace, there is confusion about when shooting back is an available tactic.[89]

In his *Foreign Affairs* article, Deputy Secretary of Defense William Lynn called for a firmer foundation for rules of engagement:

> [Rules of engagement], when possible, distinguish between the exploits of a mere hacker, criminal activity (such as fraud or theft), espionage, or more serious attack, including attack against US infrastructure. Rules of engagement must help decision-makers determine what action is necessary, appropriate, proportional, and justified in each particular case based on the laws that govern action in times of war and peace.[90]

Since the publication of the *Foreign Affairs* article, the White House has issued this kind of specific guidance that, according to the Associated Press, "detail when the military must seek presidential approval for a specific cyber assault on an enemy and weave cyber capabilities into US war fighting strategy."[91] Some defenses are so limited that their use is pre-approved, but other, more offensive operations have been tightly controlled, as they are for other uses of

---

States Cyber Command: Hearing before US Senate Armed Service Committee, 108th Cong., 2nd sess., October 15, 2004, 1-32.

[89]   GAO, "Defense Department Cyber Efforts: DoD Faces Challenges in its Cyber Activities," (July 2011), 5, http://www.gao.gov/new.items/d1175.pdf.

[90]   Lynn, "Defending a New Domain."

[91]   Associated Press, "Obama hands military new cyber war guidelines" June 22, 2011, from http://www.cbsnews.com/stories/2011/06/22/scitech/main20073212.shtml.

military force. This guidance should accommodate much of the criticism from the GAO.

This description of limited authority to a subset of counteroffensive actions, such as the CND response actions described earlier in this chapter, seems in line with the new White House guidance. However, the new guidance goes further, clarifying the difference between offense and defense and what kinds of operations require the President's personal authority. Though the document remains classified, the media has reported important basic points, including that,

> As an example, the new White House guidelines would allow the military to transmit computer code to another country's network to test the route and make sure connections work — much like using satellites to take pictures of a location to scout out missile sites or other military capabilities.

> The digital code would be passive and could not include a virus or worm that could be triggered to do harm at a later date. But if the US ever got involved in a conflict with that country, the code would have mapped out a path for any offensive cyberattack to take, if approved by the president.[92]

These rules of engagement create a spectrum of available capabilities and predictable behavior that define what actions are permissible. The degree to which rules of engagement are publicly shared also determines the degree of confidence rival state actors will have in projecting likely US actions. If other nations know that the US military is actively searching for vulnerabilities, but not exploiting them, US military actions will be more predictable.

Intelligence Gain/Loss Recommendations

The dynamic between intelligence collection and intelligence use can be extremely difficult to balance. In the intelligence world, a source could provide valuable daily information, but if that

---

[92]   "Obama hands military new cyber war guidelines," *Associated Press*.

information is acted upon, the source's future capability could be lost. This is particularly sensitive in signals intelligence where intelligence gain/loss recommendations are routine occurrences. For example, during wartime should the US military leave an adversary's command and control node functioning, because of the intelligence it is producing, or destroy that node to deny it to the adversary and possibly forcing them to use a communication path we cannot monitor. In the cyber world, the same principles apply. If the military – or indeed any defender – acts on what they know, the adversary might change their methods to something undetectable.

The Commander of Cyber Command articulated the existing processes for intelligence gain/loss decisions, which are documented in a Tri-lateral Memorandum of Agreement among DoD, Department of Justice, and the intelligence community, and described in the classified National Security Planning Directive 38 (NDPD-38).[93] General Alexander also provided insight into the way this process normally works. In most cases, the supported combatant commander makes the gain/loss recommendation after the risk of loss is well articulated by the intelligence community. If there is disagreement, Cyber Command will be the focal point for highlighting it and making recommendations up the chain of command to the Secretary of Defense pursuant to the deconfliction process.[94]

The tension between intelligence gathering and military action is not limited to internal tension between the branches of the military. The distinction between military cyber action and intelligence gathering, disruption and exploitation, may necessitate different levels and degree of oversight from Congress.[95] Our international allies may also be affected due to

---

[93]   United States Senate Armed Services Committee, *Advance Questions for Lieutenant General Keith Alexander, Nominee for Commander, United States Cyber Command: Hearing before US Senate Armed Service Committee,* 108th Cong., 2nd sess., October 15, 2004, 1-32.

[94]   United States Senate Armed Services Committee, *Advance Questions for Lieutenant General Keith Alexander, Nominee for Commander, United States Cyber Command: Hearing before US Senate Armed Service Committee,* 108th Cong., 2nd sess., October 15, 2004, 1-32.

[95]   Owens, Dam, and Lin, eds., *Cyberattack Capabilities,* 132.

the technical architecture of the internet or their own ongoing operations.

The best publicly known example of this process is from a Washington Post article which discussed the takedown of a Saudi-based terrorist website.[96] The online discussion forum had been set up as an intelligence collection front by the Central Intelligence Agency and their Saudi Arabian counterparts to collect information from Islamic extremists who used it to exchange messages. Unfortunately, over time the site became somewhat too successful, with so much information being exchanged the military felt that the lives of American soldiers would be put at risk, and they recommended a cyber operation to take it down.

Both the CIA and the Saudi government were irate over the possible loss of what they felt was a valuable intelligence source. According to the article,

> "The CIA didn't endorse the idea of crippling Web sites," said a US counterterrorism official. The agency "understood that intelligence would be lost, and it was; that relationships with cooperating intelligence services would be damaged, and they were; and that the terrorists would migrate to other sites, and they did." [...]

> But the concerns of US Central Command and other defense officials prevailed. "Once DoD went to the extent of saying, 'Soldiers are dying,' because that's ultimately what the command in Iraq, what Centcom did, it's hard for anyone to push back," one former official said.

Unfortunately, the attack by the JFCC-NW offensive arm of Strategic Command apparently cascaded unexpectedly, "inadvertently disrupted more than 300 servers in Saudi Arabia, Germany and Texas."

---

[96]   Ellen Nakashima, "Dismantling of Saudi-CIA Web site illustrates need for clearer cyberwar policies," *The Washington Post*, 19 March 2010, http://www.washingtonpost.com/wp-dyn/content/article/2010/03/18/AR2010031805464.html (accessed September 5, 2011).

Command and Control of Cyber Operations

Cyberspace touches everywhere there is a microprocessor, affecting many of the US military's notions about commands having specific geographic responsibility. In 1998, the JTF-CND was given authority for "strategic" incidents which were widespread or critical, or affected more than one military service or command.[97] Yet tension remains. If a cyber attack is affecting a local command's networks, should not that local commander be in charge? Or should the command reside with a single cyber commander, since the attack may be part of a larger whole – and demands specialized capabilities not normally elsewhere?

Cyber Command has acknowledged that many cyber operations will originate at levels that put them within the authority of geographic and theater combat commanders. In such instances, it would play a supporting role.[98] Yet the very nature of operations in cyberspace defy geographic boundaries, and actions taken at specific targets could have unintended consequences with a global reach. In such a case, Cyber Command would assume primary command and control with geographical commanders lending support. However the mechanisms by which this command relationship would be implemented have not been established and the DoD is experimenting with several models to obtain the desired dynamic of command and control.[99]

This confusion became plan when, in 2008, the DoD suffered a major intrusion, nicknamed Operation BUCKSHOT YANKEE. According to a recent GAO report, afterwards

> US Strategic Command identified confusion regarding command and control authorities and chains of command because the exploited network fell under the purview of both

---

[97] JTF-CND Concept of Operations, 1998 and experience of author who was on the working group to create the JTF.

[98] US Government Accountability Office, "Defense Department Cyber Efforts: More Detailed Guidance Needed to Ensure Military Services Develop Appropirate Cyberspace Capabilities," 15.

[99] Ibid. 15-17

US Strategic Command, military services, and a geographic combatant command. This led to uncoordinated, conflicting, and unsynchronized guidance in response to the incident being issued in several forms via multiple channels from both US Strategic Command and Joint Task Force–Global Network Operations.[100]

The military has also struggled to find the best mechanisms to control day-to-day defensive operations. Examples of two different kinds of solutions come from the Air Force and the US Pacific Command.

The 24th Air Force is responsible for cyber operations and has established the 624 Operations Center to be the hub for command and control of defensive operations. The 624th appears to operate entirely similar to any other Air Force command and control organization, with Cyber Coordination Cell, Combat Strategy, Combat Plans and Combat Operations divisions – in parallel with the groups found in an Air Operations Center.[101] In addition, the 624 OC issues commands in ways familiar to airmen with a Cyber Tasking Order (to match an AOC's Air Tasking Order), Special Instructions (SPINS, just as from an AOC) and other, similar types.

Because it has both a regional role as well as a need to protect its own cyberspace, US Pacific Command has needed a different set of organizations, including a pilot for a Theater C4 Control Center which was later implemented as a Theater NetOps Control Center. This merged with another local center, run by the Defense Information Systems Agency to create the Theater NetOps Center – Pacific. Later, this was joined by the Cyber Fusion Center synchronize offense and defense organizations and provide decision support.[102]

---

[100]   U.S. General Accounting Office. *Defense Department Cyber Efforts: DOD Faces Challenges In Its Cyber Activities*, GAO-11-75. Washington, DC: General Accounting Office, 2011. http://www.gao.gov/new.items/d1175.pdf (accessed September 22, 2011).

[101]   "254th Combat Communications Group on Cutting Edge in Cyberspace", http://www.254ccg.ang.af.mil/news/story.asp?id=123177358.

[102]   Michael Collat, "Cyberspace Operations and the Need for an Operational Construct that Enables the Joint Force Commander," IANewsletter, vol 14, no 2, Spring 2011.

Summary and Conclusions

The organization and strategic changes the military has made in cyber were driven largely by necessity. The trends in military doctrine, policy, and operations were a series of decisions that were sometimes actively but mostly implicitly made in order to create an effective cyber defense and operational capability. While still evolving, the creation of Cyber Command allows researchers to ask what implicit decisions were responsible for its creation and if the right decisions were made.

Viewed through the lens of two decades, the creation of Cyber Command and the new DSOC mark a sharp transition. Key elements of this transition are summarized in the table below.

Table 2.2: Comparison of Military Cyber Operations During the 1990s and Today

Comparison of Military Cyber Operations		
Drivers	**1990s**	**2011**
Centralization or Decentralization	Completely decentralized with little oversight or coordination	Centralized
Normalization or Differentiation	Differentiated but part of larger doctrine of information warfare or information operations	Operationally normalized and treated like any other military capability, but differentiated organizationally with separate command
Military Goal	Military strategic superiority in cyberspace	Freedom of action in cyberspace and deny the enemy the same
Operational Coordination	The "Great Getalong" of informal coordination. Little ability to quickly assess right choices for intelligence gain-loss.	Four-star general with full command authority. Better ability to make intelligence gain-loss decisions.
Legal Questions	Unclear international laws Confusing domestic Title 10, 18 and 50 relationships	Laws of Armed Conflict Apply Confusing domestic Title 10, 18 and 50 relationships

Comparison of Military Cyber Operations		
Drivers	**1990s**	**2011**
Relationship of Military to Private Sector	Very separate, other than dependence	Pushing of "active defenses" starting with Defense Industrial Base and network providers

Conclusions

This chapter began by tracing the historical origins of the US military's cyber structure to its current state. The domain of cyberspace is unique, and while its history lies in early military communications and intelligence, responsibility for cyber operations were massively decentralized across Services, the Intelligence Community and DISA. The creation of the JTF-CND in the late 1990s was an attempt to address this failed model of total decentralization. This centralization has continued with the creation of Cyber Command and the DSOC.

What is unclear is if many of these decisions will continue along the current trajectory or not. While the close collaboration of intelligence and military operations with General Alexander dual-hatted as head of the NSA and Cyber Command, this could change. Former NSA and CIA director General Hayden has hypothesized that,

> Keith Alexander is the last intelligence officer to be the director of the National Security Agency. They will fill the position based upon the combatant command needs of the four-star CYBERCOM commander.[103]

If General Hayden is right, that could dramatically affect the trajectory of US cyber operations. Hayden thinks that the continual focus on offensive cyber operations will necessitate an agency culture that prioritizes cyber warfare. If that becomes the core focus of Cyber Command at the expense of intelligence or cyber defense, those

---

[103] Hayden, G. M. (2011, 9 7). Lunch: Evolving Threats to the Homeland And the Role of Intelligence. *The Evolving Terrorist Threat and the Importance of Intelligence to Protect the Homeland.* (D. J. Hamre, Interviewer).

services might be better served by a separate agency. However, this would also split agency resources, capabilities, and could diminish the ability to effectively collaborate. Additionally, the NSA has unique technical expertise at an institutional level, without with Cyber Command would lose some of its capabilities.

Many forces shaped current cyber doctrine, policy, and operations into their current form. Driving forces to normalize and centralize operations, coordinate across agencies, and develop a legal framework, help policy-makers, practitioners, and research communities develop a canon of knowledge. While firm answers cannot yet be provided, the research in this canon has captured a number of conclusions:

1. Cyber conflict did not evolve in a vacuum, but rather has its roots in the early evolution of electronic and information warfare.

2. The recognition of cyber as a domain was an important milestone for US cyber operations with far reaching and lasting effects.

3. The evolution of JTF into US Cyber Command and the 2011 release of DSOC highlight the need to balance unified command and a comprehensive, collaborative approach that reaches across service branches, domains, and the public/private divide for the cyber mission to be effective.

4. Operational and technical realities interact awkwardly with the current legal framework, highlighting the need for domestic reform and international consensus to provide clarity on the scope and definition of military actions in cyberspace.

5. Rather than focus on offensive operations or the pursuit of total defense, the US approach to cyber conflict is more nuanced, encompassing active cyber defense, technological superiority, and the pursuit of freedom of action to respond to threats and protect American interests in the cyber domain.

However, the list of questions only grows. How can cyber intelligence balance strategic goals against military necessity? Confronted with an increasingly complex organizational structure, how can cyber warriors and technicians respond to threats in real time with competing departments, legal authorities and strategic goals? New developments in cyber operations, although they have not resolved questions like these, have significantly advanced our understanding of them.

Chapter Three

Non-State Actors in Cyber Conflict

Introduction

Conflict in cyberspace engages a wider range of actors and activities than conflict in other environments or domains. Though consideration of cyber conflict at the political level has often focused solely on governmental actors,[1] this chapter argues that conflicts in cyberspace have been, and will likely continue to be, dominated by non-state activities. Most early attention in this area focused on the malicious intent and capability of individuals and small groups to cause disruption, particularly hackers or cyber-criminals, but largely ignored the potential for non-state attackers to achieve strategic effects. Particularly overlooked has been the fundamental role of non-state actors in cyber defense, given the essential role of the private sector across most of the globe in actually operating cyberspace. Thus, this chapter suggests ways to not just reduce maliciousness of non-state attackers but also improve the protective capability of non-state defenders.

As the United States considers its own strategy related to achieving national security objectives in the cyber domain, the fundamental role of non-state actors must remain at the forefront. Globally, we must consider the risks and opportunities related to involvement of non-state actors in cyber conflict. One

---

[1]   Such as Martin Libicki's *Cyberdeterrence and Cyberwar* (Santa Monica, CA: RAND, 2009) or Timothy Thomas' in-depth examinations of Chinese writing and operations, including *Dragon Bytes* (Ft. Leavenworth, KS: Foreign Military Studies Office, 2004) and *Cyber Silhouettes* (Ft. Leavenworth, KS: Foreign Military Studies Office, 2006).

aspect of this involvement is how these actors serve as both targets in and operators of cyberspace. In other conflict domains (sea, air, and outer space) the involvement of non-state actors in the conflict can, to a large extent, be avoided. The broad ocean, airspace and outer space are wide-open domains where conflict occurs with a high degree of freedom of action from involvement with non-military forces. While land combat often occurs in relatively open spaces, it increasingly involves situations where civilians are at risk, especially in urban environments. [2] In cyberspace, there is no analogous empty "space" and the activities of civil and military users are intertwined together. Moreover, the domain itself is composed of technologies, software, and hardware overwhelmingly created, owned and operated by non-state commercial actors with their own capital and for their own reasons.[3] Collaborative, multi-stakeholder, civilian institutions such as the Internet Engineering Task Force (IETF), World Wide Web Consortium (W3C) and Internet Corporation for Assigned Names and Numbers (ICANN) shape the protocols and coordinate the infrastructure that provide the capacity to transit the battlespace. The actions of the US, other governments, and all other actors in cyberspace largely depend on systems and networks engineered, owned, and operated by private sector actors.

To address the challenges and opportunities presented by the dominance of non-state activity in cyber conflict, it is essential to recognize and approach the cyber domain as an ecosystem of competing and collaborating actors. Each actor seeks a wide range of interdependent objectives within a global commons. In order to continue reaping the benefits of a vibrant, globally interconnected cyber ecosystem, the United States and

---

[2]   Insurgencies and other kinds of irregular warfare are obvious exceptions to non-state actors as non-combatants, and will be examined later in this work. We do recognize the increasing significance of armed groups and other non-state actors in 21st century conflicts.

[3]   Even in the areas of cyberspace dominated by states, such as military communication satellites, the underlying technology is still often civilian. Lockheed Martin, not the US military, produced the Defense Satellite Communications System with Boeing building the Wideband Global SATCOM system.

its partners need to improve its ability to control malicious non-state actors. This will require collaborating globally with the appropriate non-state actors to improve the health and resilience of this ecosystem.

The fundamental power of non-state actors is a key factor in the presence of cyber instability, as explained in Chapter One of this volume. The ability of small groups to gain significant disruptive capabilities, the presence of non-state actors in the battlespace, and the leading role of the private sector in creating the operating environment in cyberspace all create complicated risks for individual governments and their national security communities to effectively address with traditional approaches. The growth of a sophisticated Internet underground, which is capable of creating disruptive tools and providing the ability to organize malicious activity, very quickly allows a wide range of actors to rapidly emerge and wage cyber conflict using new approaches and the almost constant possibility of surprise and destabilization. These actors may begin attacking soft targets in a guerilla campaign outside the parameters envisaged by most state actors' emerging cyber doctrines and campaign strategies. The speed of cyber attack and the fear of surprise may cause overreaction and conflict escalation if actions conducted by relatively minor non-state actors are perceived as the initial phase of a more significant attack by state actors.

This chapter will discuss the involvement of non-state actors in cyber conflict. It examines the roles they have played in past conflicts, both on the offense and, less well recognized, on the defense. It is also important to set boundaries on scope. The chapter does not address general terrorist use of the Internet for purposes such as highlighting activities, recruiting, and fund-raising. It also does not directly address cyber crime, though it does discuss the significance of both organizations involved in cyber crime and how the financial resources generated by these activities are the primary engine by which the Internet underground develops disruptive tools and services, including botnets and sophisticated attack tools. These capabilities are then accessible to a wide range of actors involved in cyber conflict.

Non-State Actors And Conflict

Throughout history, non-state actors have both challenged and defended the status quo powers and influenced the power dynamics of the international system. Though non-state actors have been continuous participants in conflicts around the world from ancient to contemporary times, governments and militaries, especially those in the West, have often overlooked their role. Looking at their role as a disruptive political force, Schultz and Dew define non-state actors as

> [G]roups that challenge the authority of states, challenge the rule of law, use violence in unconventional, asymmetrical, and indiscriminate operations to achieve their aims, operate within and across state boundaries, use covert intelligence and counterintelligence capabilities, and have factional schisms that affect their ability to operate effectively.[4]

This definition usefully highlights both strengths and weaknesses of such groups as well as the unconventional and transnational nature of their operations. For our purpose, we must have a broader definition for non-state actors that include their role as targets and defenders in conflicts. For the purpose of this chapter, we will broaden the definition of non-state actors to *non-governmental actors who are participants in conflicts, including terrorists, protest groups, criminal organizations, corporations, multistakeholder organizations, ad-hoc collaborative groups, and individuals*.

Such non-state actors can be in conflict with state actors or working collaboratively with them or both. Across most of the globe throughout most of history, the existence of nomadic tribes made non-state actors a constant threat. The Mongols, Goths, Huns, and numerous others consistently encroached upon settled territories. The utilization of terrain, mobility, and specialized tactics to overcome more organized, but less mobile and versatile,

---

4   Richard H. Schultz and Andrea J. Dew, *Insurgents, Terrorists, and Militias*, (New York: Columbia University Press, 2006), 10.

state militaries is a recurring theme of guerrillas, raiders, insurgents, and other non-state actors. The Huns and Mongols enjoyed great success against both European and Asian empires by encircling their cavalry and avoid committing to a fight until their opponent had been worn down by maneuvering and arrow fire; this was in stark contrast to the ideas of formations, battle lines, and honorable combat that had dominated the militaries of the day.[5] Though such groups generally entered into conflict with little conventional military power, their predisposition to strike with novel, indirect, and asymmetric means had profound implications for the ability of states and empires ability to rule with stability. Cyberspace presents the same opportunities for smaller actors to have large-scale effects on states and the international system.

A striking example of such asymmetry is Proconsul Quintilius Varus's experience on the Roman empires German border in 9 CE.[6] Arminius, a former roman soldier, united several German tribes and led a guerilla war that eventually led to the defeat of Varus. The rebels were able to neutralize Roman military superiority by luring the Romans into marshes and forests where they fought on their own terms, rather then coming out onto the plain where the legion could employ the shock of power of its superior cavalry and lethal accuracy of its bowmen.[7] Historically, the use of local knowledge to pick the most difficult terrain has been used to advantage by rebels against traditional armies.[8] The analogous asymmetries will be important in cyberspace as well, particularly since the "terrain" of cyber space is owned and operated by non-state actors, as is demonstrated in the case studies below.[9]

---

[5]   John Keegan, *A History of Warfare*, (New York: Alfred A. Knopf, 1994), 161-162.

[6]   Gareth Wong, "Beyond the Velvet Curtain of Information: How the Future of Warfare will be Shaped," *Mindef Singapore*, April 24, 2010, http://www.mindef.gov.sg/content/imindef/publications/pointer/journals/20 07/v33n3/feature5.print.html?Status=1(accessed December 8, 2011).

[7]   Schultz and Dew, *Insurgents, Terrorists, and Militias*, 5.

[8]   Another excellent example of this is the Maccabee Revolt against the Seleucid Empire. See William T. Sorrells, "Insurgency in Ancient Times: The Jewish Revolts Against the Seleucid and Roman Empires 166 BC-73 AD" (Ft. Leavenworth, KS: US Army Command and General Staff College, 2005) http://www.dtic.mil/cgi-bin/GetTRDoc?AD=ADA436236 12, 15-21.

[9]   Schultz and Dew, *Insurgents, Terrorists, and Militias*, 5.

Non-state actors at sea have historically achieved strategic effect. The wide-open nature of the world's oceans makes it particularly difficult to track and control malicious activity caused by pirates. Pirate activity in the Aegean Sea was one of the principal factors that led ancient Crete to invest in the development of the world's first navy. [10] As piracy evolved, empires issued letters of marque, essentially waivers to commit piracy against foreign ships, to leverage pirates into privateers and utilize them to engage their enemies. The intended targets included hostile powers, economic rivals, and resented former colonies. [11] Using this veneer of legitimacy, privateers would activity destabilize trade, disrupt communications, terrorize travelers, and frequently required significant state resources to combat while the sponsoring empire maintained an element of deniability. [12] Privateers were non-state actors used as proxies in a specific environment. Characterizing their activities as offensive or defensive is often a matter of perspective but such action by proxies has often been significant in conflicts. Cyberspace now demonstrates the same use of non-state actors acting independently and as proxies for espionage and disruptive attacks; and states are considering the enlistment of private actors to empower their responses

Alternatively, non-state actors are often targets during conflict. People, tribes and ethnic groups as well as their belongings, homes and lands have frequently been the victims of the onslaughts of armies – from the Mongols' massacre of the inhabitants of Ryanzan, Russia or Joshua burning Ai in ancient Jordan to make it "forever a heap of ruins, as it is to this day." [13]

---

[10]   James A. Wombwell, "The Long War Against Piracy: Historical Trends" (Ft. Leavenworth KS: Combined Studies Institute Press, 2010), 1-2.

[11]   Schultz and Dew, *Insurgents, Terrorists, and Militias*, 5.

[12]   The practice of sanctioning state privateers was the norm for European powers until the Paris Declaration Respecting Maritime Law was passed in 1856, which abolished the use of the practice by its signatories. Though it did not sign the treaty, the US has abided by it since the Civil War. See "Declaration Respecting Maritime Law. Paris 16 April 1856," *ICRC*, 2000, http://www.icrc.org/ihl.nsf/WebART/105-10001?OpenDocument (accessed December 8, 2011).

[13]   Old Testament, Joshua, 8:28.

The principles of total war while first adopted in Europe have spread globally. Increasingly, conflicts have explicitly targeted all aspects of contending nations including the target population, its will, economic assets, and supporting infrastructures like transportation and energy that are essential for making military goods. This trend appeared to culminate with the advent of nuclear weapons. According to Thomas Schelling in the early 1960s:

> In the present era, noncombatants appear to be not only deliberate targets but primary targets ... at both ends of the scale of warfare; thermonuclear war threatened to be a contest in destruction and populations; and, at the other end of the scale, insurgency is almost entirely terroristic. We live in an era of dirty war.[14]

Cyberspace provides similar dynamics, blurring the distinction between state and non-state actors and civilian and government targets. It is difficult to distinguish targets on a network and thus far much of cyber conflict has focused on exploiting vulnerabilities of networks and systems owned by private actors. On the other hand, much of the malicious activity in cyberspace is conducted by a variety of non-state actors. There is no longer a clear line between state and citizen, either as a target or as a tool.

The (Brief) Decline of the Non-State Actor

Despite this long history of non-state-actor dominated activity, as both challengers and defenders of the political status quo, most Western military philosophy for the past four centuries assumes a basic state monopoly on the use of force. Karl von Clausewitz, a military theorist, locked this idea into military orthodoxy with his 1832 book *On War,* which put war squarely – and exclusively – in the domain of sovereign actions. As modern military historian John Keegan explains, "Clausewitz allowed the two institutions – state and regiment – that circumscribed his own perception of the world

---

[14] Thomas Schelling, *Arms and Influence*, (New Haven: Greenwood Press Reprint, 1966), 27.

to dominate his thinking so narrowly that he denied himself room to observe how different war might be in societies where both state and regiment were alien concepts."[15] Even within his own society, Clausewitz regarded irregular forces prevalent in Europe as either irreverent or uncivilized.

While Clausewitz discussed the purposes and nature of warfare, Grotius and others sought to impose limitations on the execution of warfare to prevent indiscriminate carnage. The concept known as "just war theory," in which wars are to be fought by states as a last resort when all other instruments of diplomacy failed, gained traction in the West. The role of non-state actors in such modern theories of just war is limited to that of the victim. That is, just war contends that non-state actors should generally neither be targeted nor enrolled in the attack.[16] The Law of Armed Conflict, which the US military must adhere to, is based around the principles of military necessity, distinction between combatants and non-combatants (including civilians, private property, and the wounded), and proportional response. As discussed in Chapter 4, many are now considering how these concepts apply to cyber conflict, including the significance of the Law of Armed Conflict and what boundaries might be applied to actions against cyber targets.

Throughout most of 20th Century, Clausewitz and Grotius still resonated with Western strategic thinkers. In the midst of the nuclear area, Thomas Schelling noted that military establishments' "favorite job is to deliver victory, to dispose of opposing military forces and to leave most of the civilian violence to politics and diplomacy."[17] However, as discussed in Chapter 1, Schelling also illuminated how military's forces, especially nuclear forces, could be used to threaten an adversary's people and infrastructures as a means of coercion and deterrence. The vulnerability of critical infrastructures to cyber attack has become a central concern for those tasked with the conduct and management of cyber conflict.

---

[15]   Keegan, *A History of Warfare*, 23.

[16]   These concepts in the Western world are rooted especially in the works of St Augustine (350-430) who argued that war can only be waged by properly instituted authorities. Read *The Just War* by Paul Ramsey for a fuller discussion.

[17]   Schelling, *Arms and Influence*, 13, 28.

The Return on Non-State Actors in Conflict

In the late 1980s and through the 1990s, the breakup of the Soviet Union, the disintegration of Yugoslavia, and the advent of failed states in places like Somalia and Rwanda have changed the focus of those concerned with conflict within the global political system. Conflicts were increasingly being fought for ethnic, racial and religious reasons, and that Western powers that entered into unconventional conflicts with traditional military forces were often ill equipped to achieve the outcomes they desired. As Schultz and Dew note, the principles that govern the form of warfare employed by the tribal warriors of Somalia were strikingly different from those that governed warfare in the West.[18] As the Western soldier confronted the tribal warrior, Western commanders quickly realized that these warriors had not heard of Clausewitz and Grotius. Rather, as Turney-High observed, they were fighting wars for socio-psychological purposes rather than political ones.[19]

For the tribal warriors in Africa, Central Asia, and the Middle East, war never had a Clausewitzean form: the norm for African clans and tribes was that states did not have a monopoly on the use of force. As Bozeman contends, "the pronounced revulsion against war that has pervaded many intellectual circles in the West" was not universally accepted across the globe. On the contrary: "the histories of Africa and Asia – all well documented now – are replete with references to culturally different theories and practices of warfare."[20] Ultimately, such cultures accept conflict and war as "normal incidents of life, legitimate tools … morally sanctioned courses of action."[21]

Western militaries are still trying to adjust their strategies, doctrine and tactics to reflect the indirect and asymmetric means

---

[18] Schultz and Dew, *Insurgents, Terrorists, and Militias*, 5. See also John Nagl, *Learning to Eat Soup with a Knife: Counterinsurgency Lessons from Malaya and Vietnam,* Chicago: University of Chicago Press, 2005. And, of course, Mao Zedong, *Selected Military Writings of Mao Zedong*, Beijing: Foreign Languages Press, 1968.

[19] Ibid.

[20] Adda Bozeman as cited in Schultz and Dew, *Insurgents, Terrorists, and Militias*, 27.

[21] Ibid.

contemporary adversaries employ in modern conflicts. Perhaps the most threatening aspect of this increasing prominence of the non-state actor is the potential for the formation of alliances with actors who wish to disrupt the status quo. Not required to operate within state or legal boundaries, non-state actors motivated often by financial gain and ideologies will seek to cooperate with other actors, so long as it is mutually beneficial. Political terrorism, while certainly cheaper than other forms of rebellion, requires funding for arms and logistics and resources for the militants. While terrorists can themselves engage in criminal activity, relying on robbery, extortion, kidnapping and drug trafficking to finance their activities, they can also partner with existing criminal enterprises. We increasingly see this kind of behavior in cyberspace, with hackers and other malicious non-state hackers partnering with the existing criminal underground to further their activities.

Joint action between terrorists and criminal enterprises potentially provides more opportunities for profit and political impact than either group enjoys when acting alone. [22] A contemporary example of this is the Revolutionary Armed Forces of Columbia (FARC) and the Colombian drug cartels. Formed in 1965, FARC sought to bring together communist militants and peasant self-defense groups – standing for the representation of the rural poor against Colombia's wealthy classes and in opposition to US influence in Colombia, the privatization of natural resources, the prominence of multinational organizations, and the rise of rightist violence. [23] Operating in roughly one-third of Colombia, FARC is comprised of nearly 8,000 guerillas and 110 operational units. According to the 2005 International Crisis Group Report, about 65 of the 110 operational units are involved in some aspect of the drug trade. Experts have estimated that FARC takes in between $500 million and $600 million annually from narcotics trafficking. While FARC has experienced setbacks at the hands of

---

[22]   Lyubov Mincheva and Ted Robert Gurr, "Unholy alliances? How Trans-state Terrorism and International Crime Make Common Cause," Annual Meeting of the International Studies Association, (March 24, 2006).

[23]   Stephanie, Hanson, "FARC, ELN: Colombia's Left Wing Guerillas," *Council on Foreign Relations*, August 19, 2009, http://www.cfr.org/colombia/farc-eln-colombias-left-wing-guerrillas/p9272.

the Colombian government in recent years and its members have decreased, its links to drug trafficking persist.[24] Simply disbanding such groups, however, is neither an effective nor adequate solution, others will simply take their place in the trade.[25] Even more alarming is the possibility of such groups acting as hired guns for foreign governments. In fact, FARC has been asked to serve as a shadow militia for Venezuela's intelligence apparatus, with the objective of assassinating political opponents of Venezuela's President.[26] As discussed further in this chapter, there are parallel dynamics in the criminal underground and its interactions with hacktivists, cyber militias, and other malicious actors, primarily the role of the Russian Business Network and the use of bots in Estonia to punish the country after the political decision to remove the Soviet-era statue.

The Role of Non-State Actors in Cyber Conflict

Just as the significance of non-state actors have often been overlooked in Western literature on warfare and conflict in the modern period, so too have governments and scholars alike underestimated the significance, often the primacy, of the non-state actors in cyber conflict.

Though in its nascent stages, the subject of non-state actors has yet to be fully addressed by thinkers describing the rise of the information age and cyber conflict. Those that have acknowledged the presence – and significance – of non-state actors can be said to fall into one of two schools of thought:

---

24 US National Counterterrorism Center, "Revolutionary Armed Forces of Colombia," http://www.nctc.gov/site/groups/farc.html.

25 In Colombia, thought the disbanding of the paramilitary United Self-Defence Forces of Colombia (AUC) between 2003 and 2006 was heralded a success, the region has now seen the emergence of similar, but smaller groups, such as the New Generation Organization (ONG). International Crisis Group, "Colombia's New Armed Groups," Latin America Report No. 20, May 10, 2007, http://www.crisisgroup.org/en/regions/latin-america-caribbean/andes/colombia/020_colombias_new_armed_groups.aspx.

26 Simon Romero, "Venezuela Asked Colombian Rebels to Kill Opposition, Analysis Shows," *New York Times*, May 10, 2011, http://www.nytimes.com/2011/05/10/world/americas/10venezuela.html?_r=1.

1.   Those who underestimate the ability of non-state actors to achieve significant strategic effects that result in serious threats to the stability of the political order, or

2.   Those who highlight the rise of non-state actors and their *potential* to pose significant threats.

Beginning in 1970s and into the 1990s, Alvin and Heidi Toffler unveiled a prescient vision for the emerging Information Age. In their series of books including *Future Shock* (1970), *The Third Wave* (1984), and *War and Anti-War* (1993), they contended that the Information Age, built on information and communication technologies, would overturn the status quo of nation-state power, "the deepest social upheaval and creative restructuring of all times."[27] New technologies proved to be double-edged swords. As they allowed for quicker and more expansive communication and collaboration between groups of people, they contributed to a shift in power from state to non-states. Just as the technologies allowed for remote access control of business operations, while not impeding the capability to compete with multinational competitors, it similarly enabled groups to infringe on the power of states. According to Joseph S. Nye, Jr., this diffusion of power away from governments is one of the great power shifts in this century.[28] Cyberspace is a perfect example of the broader trend. The largest powers are unlikely to be able to dominate this domain as much as they have others like sea, air or space."[29]

New technologies, the Internet in particular, have forced societies to develop strategies for understanding the full impact of, and coordinating, such revolutionary technology. In its early days, the Internet presented leaders not just with a new frontier that sought to redefine the relationship between citizen and state, but also with a domain potentially entirely independent of the state. A leading proponent of this point of view was John Perry Barlow, whose 1996 "Declaration of the Independence of Cyberspace" laid out the call for independence:

> You [governments] are not welcome among us. You have no sovereignty where we gather ... Where there are real

---

[27]   Alvin and Heidi Toffler, *The Third Wave*, (New York, NY: Bantam, 1984), 10.
[28]   Joseph Nye, *The Future of Power*, New York: PublicAffairs Press, 2011.
[29]   Joseph Nye Jr., "Cyberspace Wars", *New York Times*, February 27, 2011.

conflicts, where there are wrongs, we will identify them and address them by our means.[30]

The Tofflers foresaw the more violent implications of empowering non-state groups with new technology in their 1991 work *War and Anti-War in the 21st Century*, which hypothesized that "the Second Wave [Industrial Age] idea that national governments are the only ones that can wield military force is now obsolete."[31] Now armed with cyber weapons in a new domain for operations, individuals and groups could present military challenges to states and societies without needing to acquire portable biological labs, nuclear materials, or intelligence.

The key foundational works on significance of non-state actors in cyber conflict, however, remain those by Arquilla and Ronfeldt in the mid-to-late 1990s, such as "Cyberwar is Coming" and *In Athena's Camp*. While acknowledging that the cyber domain has the potential to enable all actors operating within it, Arquilla and Ronfeldt's analysis of non-state actors focused on offensive capabilities and actions.

> We offer a distinction between what we call 'netwar' — societal-level ideational conflicts waged in part through internetted modes of communication —and 'cyberwar' at the military level ... [Both] cyberwar and netwar may be uniquely suited to fighting non-state actors.[32]

In the pages of *In Athena's Camp*, they furthered the notion that "netwar" will be increasingly dominated by the actions of non-state actors:

> Many if not most netwar actors will be non-state and even stateless. Some may be agents of a state, but others may turn states into their agents. Odd hybrids and symbioses

---

[30] John Perry Barlow, "A Declaration of Independence of Cyberspace", February 8, 1996, https://projects.eff.org/~barlow/Declaration-Final.html (accessed December 8, 2011).

[31] Toffler, *War and Anti-War*, 270.

[32] Arquilla and Ronfeldt, "Cyberwar is coming!" *Comparative Strategy,* vol. 12, no. 2, (1993): 27.

are likely. Moreover, a netwar actor may be both subnational and transnational in scope.[33]

As a result of the increased statelessness, there will be a clear paradigm shift in the ways wars are fought: "Whereas cyberwar will usually see formal military forces pitted against each other, netwar is more likely to involve non-state, paramilitary, and other irregular forces."[34] As described in the case studies later in this chapter, this view has proved prescient.

While Arquilla and Ronfeldt may have seemingly overemphasized the speed with which such shifts in basic conflict dynamics could and would occur, other literature on the role of offensive non-state actors has inadequately addressed the significance and range of concerns, only tangentially discussing the role of non-state actors. For example, the National Research Council's most recent report, *Proceedings of a Workshop on Deterring Cyberattacks: Informing Strategies and Developing Options* (2010) and the Center for a New American Security's *America's Cyber Future: Security and Prosperity in the Information Age* (2011) acknowledge the dangers of offensive non-state actors, who remain, as of yet, undeterred. Though much of the technical literature does not focus on non-state actors, the Defense Science Board's 1996 report on "Information Warfare – Defense" and their 2000 report on "Defensive Information Operations," is noteworthy, claiming "offensive information warfare is attractive ... because it is cheap in relation to ... advanced military capabilities."[35]

However, the dynamics of cyber conflict are quickly changing. In the 1980s and 1990s, the malicious actors of greatest concern were individuals looking for an adventure, whereas cyber criminals in the past ten years have become much more professionalized – far better funded, with greater resources, more patient, and more organized. Despite the fact that most malicious activity in cyberspace, as of 2011, can be characterized as cyber crime rather than cyber conflict, the growing presence of an

---

[33]   Arquilla and Ronfeldt, *In Athena's camp: Preparing for Conflict in the Information Age,* (Santa Monica, CA: RAND, 1997), 278.

[34]   Ibid., 275.

[35]   Defense Science Board, "Information Warfare – Defense," (Washington DC, November 1996).

Internet underground that enables and feeds off this activity is of strategic concern. For instance, starting in the early 2000s many hackers started collecting credit card numbers, finding these could be easily sold in blocks to an emerging underground of websites specifically created to fence these spoils of hacking. As money flooded in, hacking became a serious business and gained the attention of organized crime. A number of in-depth studies now address cybercrime in a systematic way and provide insight related to the dynamics of the Internet Underground. [36] This rise of professional cyber criminals has been summarized this way:

> In the early years, cybercrime was clumsy, consisting mostly of extortion rackets that leveraged blunt computer network attacks against online casinos or pornography sites to extract funds from frustrated owners. Over time, it has become more sophisticated, more precise: like muggings morphing into rare art theft. [37]

The strategic significant of cyber crimes lies not in the types of attacks that these enterprises execute, but in their ability and potential to partner with political terrorists and states to inflict large-scale costs on, and damage to, their adversaries.

In writing on kinetic conflict, Richard Schultz and Itamara Lochard clearly identify the dangers of armed non-state groups and the implications for national security policy and military strategy. In their *Understanding Internal Wars and Conflicts*, Schultz and Lochard detail the tiered capabilities of various non-state groups and the potential they have to cause strategic effects. [38] Such a detailed analysis of non-state actors in cyber conflict, however, remains to be written. For cyber conflict to mature as a field of study, we require

---

[36]   Rick Howard, *Cyber Fraud: Tactics, Techniques and Procedures*, Verisign iDefense, (CRC Press: Boca Raton, FL, 2009); Aditya K Sood, Richard Enbody, Rohit Bansal, "Cybercrime : Dissecting the State of Underground Enterprise," *IEEE Internet Computing*, 03 May 2012. IEEE computer Society Digital Library; Symantec, *Symantec Report on the Underground Economy*, November 2008; McAfee, *A Good Decade for Cybercrime*, 2010.

[37]   Nart Villeneuve, *Koobface: Inside a Crimeware Network*, Information Warfare Monitor (2010).

[38]   Richard Schultz and Itamara Lochard, *Understanding Internal Wars and Conflicts*, London: Routledge Press, 2011.

equivalent analysis of non-state actors in cyber conflict. Specifically, it should combine a current assessment of skill sets with the conditions necessary for these actors to achieve strategic effects that would severely cripple a state adversary and/or result in a significant shift in power dynamics. The mere potential for strategic effect does not suffice; skills need to be evaluated within the context of the cyber environment. Our analysis later in the chapter endeavors to provide a start down this road.

Though other foundational works of research such as Dorothy Denning's *Information Warfare and Security* (1998), Gregory Rattray's *Strategic Warfare in Cyberspace* (2001), and the National Defense University's *Cyberpower and National Security* (2009) all discuss the roles of non-state actors as potentially disruptive actors, analyses of these actors' capabilities and roles as *defenders* of the status quo in cyber conflict remain largely unseen beyond the scope of partnering with government to protect critical infrastructure. As defenders, non-state actors have many other important roles to play. They run enterprise networks and are frequently involved in the detection and removal of malicious code from computer systems and networks. Non-state defenders are often comprised of either ad-hoc or sustained groups of individuals. While some of these may be non-governmental, volunteer organizations such as the Shadowserver Foundation or the Honeynet Project, others are incident response teams within companies sanctioned to conduct malware detection and removal, and alert those affected or involved. Non-profit organizations like Stop Badware seek to raise public awareness by providing publicly available information regarding websites which host malware as explained in more depth later in the chapter.

Additionally, because much of the cyber infrastructure is owned, controlled, and operated by the private sector, much of the governmental analysis on defending cyberspace is focused on critical infrastructure protection and public-private partnerships. This prominent theme of states consistently relying on, and partnering with, non-state actors in the private sector for cybersecurity, permeates through virtually all literature on critical infrastructure protection. While "partnership" appears to be the dominant term used to describe the needed relationship between governments and the companies that provide critical services, it all too often seems to suggest "control." Companies are increasingly expected to not only share information with the government, but also be willing and able to take necessary protective actions as specified by the government.[39]

Two key terms can be said to define this theme: dependence and partnership. In the early 1990s, Alvin and Heidi Toffler correctly noted that the gradual "civilianization" of war implies increasingly transferring "militarily relevant work" from "military-specific industries to civilian-oriented businesses.[40] Examples of such civilianization are evident when analyzing the rise of critical infrastructure companies, outsourced defense contracting, and the reliance of the Department of Defense on civilian IT and computer network defense.[41] As the private sector's monopoly over the creation and use of new technologies facilitated the rapid "civilianization" of war, the US government recognized the extent of the nation's reliance on critical infrastructure. By the mid-1990s critical infrastructure not only enabled the Internet and communications, but had become a key aspect of the electrical and financial industries.

Beginning with the Clinton administration, White House reports, policies and strategies all illuminate similar themes that identify the threat, vulnerabilities, our dependence on the network, and calls for cooperation between government and non-state actors. These began with the President's Commission on Critical Infrastructure Protection (1997) and Presidential Decision Directive 63 (1998) and continued through the Bush administration. In 2003, the first national cyber strategy, the *National Strategy to Secure Cyberspace* and Homeland Security Presidential Directive 7 were released. Since 2009, the Obama Administration has released the *60-Day Cyber Review*, *International Strategy for Cyberspace*, *Department of Defense Strategy for Operating in Cyberspace*, and the *Department of Homeland Blueprint for a Secure Cyber Future*.

In these documents, the White House and other executive departments acknowledge the need to partner with, without

---

[39]   Department of Homeland Security, *Blueprint for a Secure Cyber Future*, November 2011, 13.

[40]   Toffler, *War and Anti-War*, 226-227.

[41]   Such as the complete outsourcing of the Navy/Marine Corps Intranet – overseen by the Navy but run by HP.

controlling, the private sector to effective implement cyber security policies. The national policy recognizes that "the federal government could not—and, indeed, should not—secure the computer networks of privately owned banks, energy companies, transportation firms, and other parts of the private sector." [42] However, the influential report from the Commission on Cybersecurity for the 44th Presidency highlighted the apparent lack of an effective existing partnership between government and industry, noting that there is "almost universal recognition that the status quo is not meeting the need of either government or the private sector with respect to trust and operational collaboration."[43] Regarding such collaboration with non-state actors to defend critical infrastructure, the US government has specified that it is indeed the government, to be led by the Department of Homeland Security, which is at the center of such defense.[44] Still, it is the operational aspects of this intended collaboration that have remained undefined.

For instance, while the DHS interim National Cyber Incident Response Plan recognizes that NGOs "can provide assistance as needed and requested" to "help develop and implement sustainable strategies for effectively mitigating and addressing the consequences of a cyber incident," these NGOs are not featured in the rest of the response plan, which generally focuses on outlining mechanisms for coordination between government officials. [45] Though certainly headed in the right direction, this policy fails to fully consider how the private sector not just bears the brunt of cyber attacks but also is responsible for successful cessation of intrusions and defensive collaboration. Defensive non-state collaboration is best demonstrated in the case of the Conficker worm detailed in Chapter 5. [46] While key government players

---

[42]   US Executive Office of the President, *The National Strategy to Secure Cyberspace* (February 2003), 11.

[43]   CSIS Commission on Cybersecurity for the 44th Presidency, *Securing Cyberspace for the 44th Presidency,* Center for Strategic and International Studies (December 2008).

[44]   See Department of Homeland Security, *Blueprint for a Secure Cyber Future*, November 2011.

[45]   Ibid., 8.

[46]   For more detail, see Mark Bowden, *Worm: The First Digital World War*, New York, NY: Atlantic Monthly Press, 2011.

certainly contributed to the responsive measures taken, they were just one of many qualified players in the conflict. While essential, critical infrastructure protection efforts and existing public-private partnerships tend to focus on proactive remediation of potential vulnerabilities and furthering best practices rather than non-state actors roles in the actual conduct of cyber conflict.

Finally, we must acknowledge that the linkages between non-state and state actors are an important part of understanding the strategic significance and dynamics in cyber conflicts. As acknowledged by Graham et al in *Cyber Fraud: Tactics Techniques and Procedures,* the "most dangerous aspect of this organization, the Russian Business Network (RBN), was the connection between RBN's leadership and political power in local St. Petersburg's government and at the federal level," which provided the organization with protection from criminal prosecution.[47] Ultimately, this resulted in RBN ignoring numerous "takedown requests for fraudulent or malicious Web sites."[48] The RBN is also suspected of having played a central role in the politically motivated cyber attacks on Estonia in 2007, which will be described in more detail later in this Chapter.

To better understand the significance of the wide range of non-state actors and their role within the cyber conflict, it is necessary to understand the nature of the cyber environment and the ecosystem of actors within it. Actors in the cyber ecosystem play multiple roles, and thus the dynamics of interaction between them are in a constant state of flux and evolution. These roles are explored further in the following section of this chapter.

The Ecosystem of Actors in the Cyber Environment

The geographically malleable nature of the cyber environment and the inherently open architecture favor the offense. Actors – both

---

[47]   iDefense, "The Russian Business Network: Rise and Fall of a Criminal ISP," Updated March 3, 2008, Available at wired.com, http://www.wired.com/images_blogs/dangerroom/files/iDefense_RBNUpdated_20080303.doc.

[48]   Ibid.

state and non-state – can and do use the medium for competition, making it inherently dynamic and producing conditions of cyber instability. We must understand how these conditions are affected by the increasing number and range of actors that operate in and can disrupt the cyberspace ecosystem. This chapter uses as a concept the idea of the "environment" of the cyber domain and the "ecosystem" of actors within that domain. As Joseph Nye has observed, "The cyber universe is complex, beyond anyone's understanding and exhibits behavior that no one predicted and sometimes can't even be explained well."[49] This approach allows a deeper discussion of the complexities of actor interaction and conflict dynamics than traditional state focused analysis.

Like the other domains (air, space, land, maritime), cyber has its own characteristics and the equivalent of terrain. Understanding the forces that shape the environment and its geography are essential. Cyberspace is a man-made environment created by the connection of physical systems and networks managed by logical systems and rules established in software and communications protocols.[50] Both the laws of physics as well as the logic of computer code govern cyberspace. Cyberspace is unique in that hardware, software and logical protocols are man-made, allowing for control of the "geography of cyberspace." However, this malleability is limited by limits set by physical laws, logical proprieties of code, existing history, and the capabilities of people and organizations for change.

Key elements of the terrain are places where traffic in the domain flows through a limited number of devices including internet exchange points, submarine cables, cable landing stations, major data centers. Certain logical features such as the Domain Name System and the routing protocols can also enable large-scale, even system wide impacts on Internet traffic. Control over these "chokepoints" may prove essential in cyber conflict. Another

---

[49]   Joseph S. Nye, "Power and National Security in Cyberspace," in *America's Cyber Future: Security and Prosperity in the Information Age*, Vol. II, ed. Kristin M. Lord and Travis Sharp (Center for a New American Security: June, 2011), 5-24.

[50]   See William D. O'Neill, "Cyberspace and Infrastructure" in *Cyberpower and National Security*, eds. Franklin D. Kramer, Stuart H. Starr, and Larry Wentz, *Cyberpower and National Security,* (Washington, DC: Potomac Books, Inc., 2009), 113-146.

key feature of the environment is the speed at which electromagnetic waves move and bits travel in cyberspace. Global communications can happen almost instantaneously and vast amounts of data can rapidly transit great distances, often unimpeded by physical barriers and political boundaries.[51]

Cyber conflict can change and also be heavily influenced by cyber geography and its fast changing nature. Every time an attack occurs, it can remove devices from service that contain and route data, the attacks also remove pathways and create new chokepoints. Defensively, every time a patch is created and applied, the terrain changes as an operating system or application closes potential vulnerabilities. The emergence of new ISPs or protocols changes the environment to some degree. According to one characterization, "[m]ountains and oceans are hard to move, but portions of cyberspace can be turned on and off with the click of a switch"[52] The systems and infrastructures that make up cyberspace have varying degrees of interconnectivity. Individuals may use a small home network as an enclave not connected to larger cyberspace. Commercial enterprises may set up virtual networks that are intended to be logically segmented from interactions with the larger Internet. The Internet has become the prime example of a global network, wherever increasing numbers of devices and systems have significant interconnectivity moderated by software and protocol rules. In considering cyber conflict, understanding the nature and current state of the connectivity of systems and networks is essential in determining which actors can target key adversary centers of gravity. The chart below endeavors to provide a visual representation of the key features and complexity of the cyber environment.

Within this environment, actors in cyberspace interact as part of an ecosystem. An ecosystem more broadly can be understood as "the complex of a community of organisms and its

---

[51]   See Gregory J. Rattray, "An Environmental Approach to Understanding Cyberpower," in *Cyberpower and National Security*, ed. Franklin D. Kramer, Stuart H. Starr, Larry K. Wentz, (Washington, DC: Potomac Books, 2009), 255-274

[52]   Ibid., 256.

environment functioning as an ecological unit." [53] Their interconnections and interactions in pursuit of a wide range of collaborative and competitive objectives can be very usefully understood in a manner similar to other ecosystems. If we think of it in these terms, the "organisms" are the actors in cyberspace and the "non-living physical components" include the nodes of the global architecture described above. The range of significant actors in cyberspace include individuals, non-governmental organizations, individual hackers, hacker groups, hacktivists, universities, volunteer security groups, companies in the critical infrastructure sectors, security companies, other companies, terrorists, massed patriot hackers, organized crime, major Internet companies and carriers, transnational organizations, international organizations, and nation states. To effectively understand the interactions in the ecosystem and how they relate to conflict dynamics, we need to understand the nature and roles of non-state actors on the cyber ecosystem.[54]

This section does not strive to provide a comprehensive taxonomy of various actors in cyber conflicts across the globe. The charts provides a point of departure understanding the range of actors, their objectives and potential roles related to cyber conflict.

Table 3.1: Examples of Actors in Cyberspace Ecosystem	
Major Actors in the Cyberspace Ecosystem	**Examples**
Individual Hackers	Morris, Love Bug, Makaveli, Erik Bloodaxe, Analyzer, Iserdo
Small Hacker Groups	Masters of Deception, the 414s, Red Hacker Alliance
Organized Criminal Groups	Chinese Triad groups, Cosa Nostra, Russian mafia groups, Russian Business Network
Cyber Dissidents	SHAC, Anonymous, LulzSec

---

[53]   "Definition of Ecosystem," *Merriam-Webster*, http://www.merriam-webster.com/dictionary/ecosystem (accessed July 14, 2011).

[54]   For example, the Department of Homeland Security's white paper on the technical ecosystem, "Enabling Distributed Security in Cyberspace" (March 23, 2011).

Terrorists	Al Qaeda, Aum Shinrikyo
Massed Patriot Hackers	Chinese patriot hackers, Russian patriot hackers (conglomeration of individual hackers and hacker groups)
Individuals	You
Academe	University of Toronto, Georgetown University, National Defense University, Moscow State University, Stetson University
Commercial Enterprise Users	Hoover, Nestle, Huntingdon Life Sciences, Amazon, E-Bay, small businesses with web presence,
Security Companies	McAfee, Symantec, NeuralID, Delta Risk
Technology Producers	Microsoft, Google, Apple, Intel, Mozilla
Critical Infrastructure Operators	BP, Bank of New York, Constellation Power, NY Stock Exchange, Union Pacific
Network Operators	Google, Verizon, NTT Docomo, Global Crossing, PCCW (HK), AT&T
Cyber Security Collaboratives	ShadowServer Foundation, SANS Internet Storm Center, Forum of Incident Response Security Teams, Open Source Movement
Non-Governmental Organizations	Drewla, MSF, Falun Dafa
Nation States	United States, Russia, China, Brazil to include sub-actors in the departments, ministries, agencies, states, regions, counties, and localities
International Organizations	ICANN, IETF, ITU, NATO, ASEAN

As can be seen in the table below, non-state actors fill many roles across the spectrum of offensive and defensive activities in cyberspace, not just that of malicious attacker. We characterize a number of roles related to cyber conflict for this purpose that include:

- **User**: This actor uses cyberspace for legal or illegal purposes to gain information, communicate with others, or procure goods and services. Users may range from individuals, educational institutions, to large, global enterprise such as FedEx or Sony.

- **Attacker**: This actor intentionally initiates malicious activity against other actors in the ecosystem. "Attacks" may not always mean disruptive activities, but can also include subtler actions such as intruding into computers to steal data.

- **Target**: This actor is the object of intentional malicious activity by other actors in the cyber ecosystem.

- **Facilitator**: This actor has systems or plays a role in operating networks that have been compromised and used by attackers against targets. This includes situation where the facilitator is unwitting that their systems and/or networks are used for malicious purposes.

- **Provider**: This actor produces or provides information technology and/or services which are kept secure through periodic updates (such as Microsoft, Cisco, AT&T or Google).

- **Responder**: This actor helps to identify, understand, and/or respond to malicious activity against other actors (such as Computer Security and Incident Response Teams [CSIRTs][55] or McAfee).

- **Improver**: This actor helps to improve the overall health and resilience of the cyber ecosystem against malicious activity or other failures (such as helping to engineer a stronger Internet), or educates other actors on these issues.

A given actor may play many roles within the ecosystem. For example, Microsoft, Google or Nokia might play several roles at any one time, including user, target, source of the malicious activity, responder, or improver. Even an individual with a home computer may act as user, target and source of malicious activity. Government activities may also span all roles. In general, the more organized and well-funded an actor is, the more capable it will be on either offense or defense.

---

[55]   CSIRTs, also known as Computer Emergency Response Teams (CERTs), respond to computer and network failures, typically those by a malicious actor. They are typically part of a larger organization (such as the US-CERT that performs these functions for the US government).

Table 3.2 depicts the wide range of roles that individual actors can play in cyberspace (from individual citizens at top to national governments at the bottom). Protective roles are marked with an "O," while malicious roles are marked with an "X."[56]

Table 3.2: Major Actors and Their Roles in Cyberspace.

Major Actors	User	Attacker	Target	Facilitator	Provider	Responder	Improver
Individuals	O		X	X			
Individual Hackers	X	X					
Small Hacker Groups	X	X					
Organized Criminal Groups	X	X					
Cyber Dissidents	X	X					
Terrorists	X	X					
Massed Patriot Hackers	X	X					
Individuals	O		X	X			
Commercial Enterprise Users	O	X	X	X	O		
Security Companies	O	?	X	X	O	O	O
Technology Producers	O		X	X	O		O
Academe	O		X	X	O	O	O
Critical Infrastructure Operators	O	?	X	X		O	

---

[56] Some areas are marked with a question mark, as they represent industrial espionage or other schemes where one company may conduct malicious cyber activity against others. This activity may occur but is not a major focus of this analysis.

Major Actors	User	Attacker	Target	Facilitator	Provider	Responder	Improver
Network Operators	O	?	X			O	O
Collaborative Security Groups	O				O	O	O
Non-Governmental Organizations	O		X	X			
Nation States	O	X	X	X	O	O	O
International Organizations	O		X			O	O

Adding to the challenges identified in Chapter 2, which focuses on state-based military and intelligence concerns, we now must add the complexity stemming from the range of cyber conflicts that necessitate managing many actors with many roles. The malleability and constantly changing geography has profound implications for establishing and adapting effective strategy, operations, and tactics, and very likely may result in miscalculations related to perceptions of capabilities. An examination of the types of non-state actors in the cyber ecosystem, their evolution, potential strategic applications of their activities, and several case studies help illuminate their growing role in cyber conflict.

The Internet Underground

Much attention is given to the role and rising importance of the Internet underground in this Chapter. But who exactly is in this underground? The underground is populated by a diverse and generally distributed set of actors engaged in a variety of illegal activities with a wide range of motivations, including lone hackers out to prove their programming skills, forums and other community vehicles where hackers can share attack tools and techniques, dissident groups taking out sites to promote political goals, and criminal enterprises creating and renting out botnets or penetrating systems for financial gain.

Evolution of Cyber Conflict Involving Disruptive Non-State Actors

Many diverse non-state actors have conducted significant malicious activity in cyberspace for decades. Though their motivation, targets, capabilities and organizational structures have varied, the effects of their cyber operations have been highly destabilizing in terms of financial cost, disruption of service, lost or stolen data, and damaging confidence in both the network and affected institutions. Historical examples of individuals and small groups tend to be penetration activities motivated by financial gain or demonstrations of skill. However, we have recently seen the development of cause-based underground groups, an entry into the cyber domain by terrorist organizations, and alliances between states and these underground groups. These developments highlight the potential strategic significance of non-state actors in conducting disruptive cyber attacks and campaigns.

Categories of Actors

This section seeks to better offensive actors focusing on historically significant incidents, and the range of their capabilities, in particular on the intent and motivations behind various threatening non-state actors. Two particularly case studies are explored in depth: the use of patriot hackers and the Internet underground to attack Estonia in 2007 and the rise of Anonymous. Later the strategic implications of defensive non-state actors will be explored in further depth.

Individual Hackers

Attacks on e-commerce provide illustrations of individuals attacking for financial gain. In 1994, Russian hacker Vladimir Levin attempted to steal $10 million from Citibank.[57] By hacking the bank's cash management system, Levin attempted to impersonate account holders and transfer their funds to offshore accounts. He was successful in stealing over $400,000 before being arrested. In another Citibank attack in 2009, Russian criminals allegedly stole tend of millions of dollars. The criminals blocked access to Citibank's website by executing a Distributed Denial of Service (DDoS) attack and then gained access to the system for themselves. They used a tool called Black Energy, originally designed by a Russian hacker and easily available for sale and distribution on certain Russian language forums. Black Energy is now being sold as part of a $700 attacking kit called the YES Exploit System, which includes other crimeware that steals bank account credentials.[58] This bundling of successful attack software further lowers the barrier of entry to disruptive activity, facilitating less experienced hackers being able to participate in high level offensive actions.[59]

---

[57]   Federal Bureau of Investigation, Los Angeles Field Office Computer Crime Squad, Powerpoint presentation, 2001, http://media.ais.ucla.edu/BTseminars/ fbi_slides.pdf (accessed January 17, 2011).

[58]   Lance Whitney, "Report: FBI Investigating Citibank Cyberattack," CNET News, December 22, 2009, http://news.cnet.com/8301-1009_3-10420308-83.html.

[59]   For additional examples see the Morris Worm, *US v. Morris*, 928 F.2d 504 (2nd Cir. 1991), and Mafiaboy, Gary Genosoko, "FCJ-057 The Case of 'Mafiaboy' and the Rhetorical Limits of Hacktivism," *The Fibreculture Journal* 2006 http://nine.fibreculturejournal.org/fcj-057/ (accessed September 30, 2011), and the Love Bug, "The Love Bug: A Retrospective," *Rixstep,* http://rixstep.com/1/20040504,00.shtml.

Hacker and Criminal Groups

In the incident known as Solar Sunrise in 1998, Pentagon systems were attacked in what US Deputy Defense Secretary John Hamre insisted was "the most organized and systematic attack to date." The intrusions were suspected to come from Saddam Hussein's Iraq and came at a time of rising tensions in the region. However after an investigation by a joint task force, the incident was traced back to two California teenagers with an Israeli mentor, who was himself only 22 years old.[60] The teens were given probation while the Israeli, Ehuds Tenenbaum, was also given probation and a fine. This case illustrates the potential for misattribution wherein non-state actors conduct attacks that the targets believe came from another source, raising tensions between the target state and their believed assailants.[61]

Since the 1990s, the main thrust of small groups conducting cyber attacks has been criminal activity. As Misha Glenny argues, "No other sector of organized crime can match the growth rates of cyber crime...the profit levels are astronomical."[62] Though cyber crime does not rise to the level of cyber conflict, it is a particularly threatening trend because it often serves as an enabler to larger scale cyber operations that have the potential to cause significant strategic effects. Financial gains from cyber crime can and have been used to develop a major Internet underground of sophisticated technologists, such as the group formerly known as the Russian Business Network (RBN), who constantly seek to overcome any improvements in cyber defense.[63] Criminal technologists may also make available previously established and extremely large botnets

---

[60] Kevin Poulson, "Solar Sunrise hacker 'Analyzer' escapes jail," *The Register*, June 15, 2001, http://www.theregister.co.uk/2001/06/15/solar_sunrise_hacker_analyzer_es capes/ (accessed January 15, 2011).

[61] For additional examples see Cliff Stoll, *The Cuckoo's Egg*, (New York: Gallery Books, 2005) or the example of Dutch hackers accessing DoD systems, Jack L. Brock Jr., Testimony Before the Subcommittee on Government Information and Regulation, Committee on Governmental Affairs, United States Senate, November 20, 1991.

[62] Misha Glenny, *McMafia: Seriously Organized Crime*, (Vintage, 2009), 313.

[63] Rick Howard, *Cyber Fraud: Tactics, Techniques and Procedures*, Verisign iDefense, (CRC Press: Boca Raton, FL, 2009),171-207.

to third parties that can be used for spam, massive denial-of-service attacks, and similar criminal purposes with greater convenience and lower cost.[64] Recently, however, a new kind of hacker organization has emerged with distinctly different goals than financial gain, instead espousing a nationalist or idealistic cause as their organizing principle.[65]

Patriotic Hackers

As illustrated above, the earliest intrusions tended to be individuals working alone or small groups. Though some did have specific criminal or political roots, their actions were motivated more by teenage curiosity or financial gain than conflict or warfare. Since then, the universe of malicious actors has diversified, representing a shift in the ecosystem. Individuals in many countries have formed nationalistic groups to respond with malicious cyber activity to perceived slights. Some of these first "patriotic hackers" were Chinese hackers responding to the accidental bombing of their embassy in Belgrade in 1999 and a collision between Chinese and US military aircraft in 2001, which prompted competing attacks from the Chinese and US hacking communities.[66] The earliest patriotic hacker campaigns were tracked by Attrition.org, a website that archived defaced web pages from 1995 to 2001 and was used by both military and civilian cyber defenders to monitor malicious activity.[67] Patriotic hacking has since become a regular

---

[64]   Botnets are "networks of compromised computers used for nefarious means." See Jose Nazario, "Botnet Tracking: Tools, Techniques and Lessons Learned," 2007, http://www.blackhat.com/presentations/bh-dc-07/Nazario/Paper/bh-dc-07-Nazario-WP.pdf.

[65]   For additional examples see the 2007 attacks on Citibank: Misha Glenny, *McMafia: Seriously Organized Crime*, (Vintage, 2009), 313 and Lester Haines, "Brazil cuffs 85 in online bank hack dragnet," The Register, August 29, 2005, http://www.theregister.co.uk/2005/08/29/brazil_hack_arrests/, (accessed January 17, 2011).

[66]   Owen Fletcher, "Patriotic Chinese Hacking Group Reboots," *The Wall Street Journal,* October 5, 2011, http://blogs.wsj.com/chinarealtime/2011/10/05/patriotic-chinese-hacking-group-reboots/ (accessed December 8, 2011).

[67]   Robert Lemos, "Defaced-site archive retires", *CNET* News, May 21, 2001, http://news.cnet.com/2100-1001-258006.html (accessed January 15, 2011). The "because the volunteer staff can no longer keep up with the volume of

feature of both sides of the conflicts between Israel and the Palestinians, between India and Pakistan, and in Northeast Asia between Japan, South Korea, North Korea, and China.

Typical early patriotic hacking efforts were comprised of website defacement and some DDoS attacks, with important but not strategically relevant effects. The last ten years, however, have been driven by a "rise of the professional" – a drastic increase in the capability of non-state actors – as recent incidents have become increasingly organized and sophisticated. As discussed below, recent high profile patriotic hacking events have involved ties to national governments, both as allies and targets. It is quite conceivable we may also see patriotic hacking groups as targets, perhaps on different sides of an international dispute attacking one another to deny cyber advantage to the opposition.

Cyber Dissidents

The development of cause-based attacker groups also has another evolutionary branch, that of cyber dissidents. Like patriotic hackers, these dissidents are passionate individuals with varying degrees of expertise, but unlike the patriots they seek to promote a non-nationalist cause using cyber-attacks to proxy for or to augment political action and speech, usually targeted at their countries' institutions.

Cyber dissident groups are particularly problematic because they can increase in membership and momentum very quickly, especially if a particularly controversial target or goal is driving their activity. Law enforcement agencies have proven largely unable to keep pace with the growth of such groups. As new members are targeted, others appear. Hacking groups like Anonymous are decentralized by design, making it nearly impossible for arrests to decapitate the organization.[68] Unlike botnets, these groups generally use actual, distributed user effort to conduct their attacks, making proactive

---

defacements". This lack of staying power compared to government organizations is a common theme explored in further depth later in this analysis.

[68] Larry Dignan, "FBI's Anonymous challenge: Cast a wide net vs. distributed hacking group," *ZDNet,* July 19, 2011, http://www.zdnet.com/blog/btl/fbis-anonymous-challenge-cast-a-wide-net-vs-distributed-hacking-group/52665?tag=content;siu-container.

technical and forensic efforts to degrade their offensive capability extremely difficult. But as Michael Chertoff said, the biggest challenge is attribution: "In a decentralized group there are various flavors of bad guys. The FBI has to take out many bad actors—and associated servers—in hopes of getting a big score." Chertoff explains this predicament: "Do we respond if we don't know who had bad intent, but can locate the server that is a weapon against us? Do we take out the server in real life or cyberspace? There's not going to be a clear line and we may take that server out in physical and cyber domains." [69] With identities of members and leadership unclear, potentially very low barriers to entry for new members inspired by their cause, a distributed infrastructure and organizational model, and passion or outrage fueling their activities, dissident groups are extremely volatile actors with a growing disruptive capacity. Anonymous is studied in more detail in the case study below.

Terrorists and the Evolution of the Use of the Internet

With all of this malicious activity, one type of non-state actor has been noticeably absent up to this point: terrorist groups. [70] They do, as users, remain interested in developing cyber capabilities to fund their activities through crime, reach supporters, and disseminate their message. [71] One of the few examples of terrorists conducting attacks in the cyber domain is a case of malicious activity linked to Al Qaeda. Court records show that Mohamedou Ould Slahi told his interrogators at Guantanamo Bay, Cuba, that the group "used the Internet to launch relatively low-level computer attacks" and "also sabotaged other websites by launching denial-of-service attacks, such as one targeting the Israeli prime minister's computer

---

[69]   Larry Dignan, "Ex-DHS Chief Warns of Cyberwar with Hackers," *CBS News*, June 22, 2011,
http://www.cbsnews.com/stories/2011/06/22/scitech/main20073368.shtml
(accessed 12/31/2011).

[70]   Government of the United Kingdom, "Contest: The United Kingdom's Strategy for Countering Terrorism," (2011).

[71]   Hanna Rogan, "Al-Qaeda's Online Media Strategies," (Norwegian Defence Research Establishment, 2007)
http://www.opensourcesinfo.org/journal/2011/5/2/al-qaedas-online-media-strategies.html, 34.

server."[72] Such low-level, non-disruptive activity highlights that cyber terrorism to date, has been a much less significant concern than cyber crime or espionage.

However recent developments indicate that it may only be a few short years before terrorist groups are able to grow or purchase significant cyber capability. For example, the Lebanese-based extremist political-religious terrorist movement Hezbollah has been very active in cyberspace beyond using it for recruiting, propaganda, and an organizing tool. Significantly, Hezbollah has engaged in significant offensive cyber action against Israel and the United States, launching attacks during its conflict with Israel in 2006.[73] It is also evidenced by the high probability that Hezbollah hired a Russian botnet service to DDoS several key Israeli sites during the invasion. The attacks were mostly mitigated by Israeli defense efforts, but one key site that gave citizens on how to protect themselves from rocket attacks was down for several hours at a critical moment.[74] Interestingly, Israel had targeted Hezbollah for disruptive activity in an earlier, more widespread initiation of cyber conflict between Israel and its Arab neighbors in 2000, marking, perhaps, the first instance of a state mobilizing its cyber capabilities offensively against a non-state actor.[75]

With such a high level of digital engagement in fundraising and recruitment efforts, it is not unreasonable to expect terror groups may yet conduct significant disruptive activity in cyberspace rather than simply plan physical attacks there. Steven Chabinsky, the deputy assistant director of the FBI's Cyber Division, has testified to Congress that "Individuals with

---

[72] Alex Kingsbury, "Documents Reveal Al Qaeda Cyberattacks", *US News,* April 14, 2010, http://www.usnews.com/news/articles/2010/04/14/documents-reveal-al-qaeda-cyberattacks, (accessed January 17, 2011).

[73] Paula Newton, "Hezbollah and Cyber War," *CNN,* March 14, 2008, http://edition.cnn.com/WORLD/blogs/security.files/2008/03/hezbollah-and-cyber-war.html (accessed September 30, 2011).

[74] Anshel Pfeffer, "Israel suffered massive cyber attack during Gaza offensive," *Haaretz,* June 15, 2009, http://www.haaretz.com/news/israel-suffered-massive-cyber-attack-during-gaza-offensive-1.278094.

[75] Lee Hockstader, "Pings and E-Arrows Fly in Mideast Cyber-War," October 27, 2000, http://www.c4i.org/cyber-war.html (accessed September 30, 2011).

ties to al Qaeda are interested in attacking United States critical infrastructure systems."[76]

Alliances

A phenomenon of increasing frequency and concern is that of alliances between states and patriotic hackers in the underground. Such alliances need not be formal or bilateral, and may simply include a loose coalition of actors with shared interests. The United States and other governments may face real strategic threats when state adversaries cooperate with non-state actors to launch cyber guerrilla campaigns aimed at causing political and economic disruption against soft targets over months or even years. For example, a report from Israel that a DDoS attack from half-million infected computers "may have been carried out by a criminal organization from the former Soviet Union, and paid for by Hamas or Hezbollah," is an example of this new type of alliance.[77] Below are two tangible examples of these alliances achieving strategic significance. Estonia, while an important example of an alliance, is discussed later in this chapter as a full-length case study.

Estonia

In 2007, Estonia fell victim to one of the largest malicious cyber attacks against a state in history, arguably the first to achieve true strategic relevance. The attacks were less significant for their size, which were moderate for the time, but they nonetheless completely overwhelmed the country, particularly because Estonia was so dependent on e-services and e-governance.[78] Further, the Estonian

---

[76]   Angela Moscaritolo, "Critical condition: Utility Infrastructure," *SC Magazine,* February 1, 2010, http://www.scmagazineus.com/critical-condition-utility-infrastructure/article/161689/.

[77]   Anshel Pfeffer, "Israel suffered massive cyber attack during Gaza offensive", *Haaretz,* June 15, 2009, http://www.haaretz.com/news/israel-suffered-massive-cyber-attack-during-gaza-offensive-1.278094.

[78]   For more information about how Estonians and other responders view the attack five years later, see Atlantic Council, "Building a Secure Cyber Future: Attacks on Estonia, Five Years On," Transcript, May 23, 2012, http://www.acus.org/event/building-secure-cyber-future-attacks-estonia-five-years/transcript. Bill Woodcock of Packet Clearing House in particular

attacks are considered one of the first examples of cyber conflict that reached the nation-state level, as many of the attacks appeared to originate from Russia after political tensions between Estonian and Russia. The case study below addresses the events in Estonia, analyzing the nature of the disruptive operations and the actions of non-state defenders during the crisis.

Georgia

As in Estonia, the malicious activity in Georgia in 2008 was aimed at both state and non-state targets but this attack carried more overt fingerprints of Russian government involvement. As in the Estonian case, DDoS and misinformation defacement attacks were combined with a kinetic threat to achieve strategic level effect. In this case, the kinetic threat was a military invasion of Georgia by Russia. Russian organized crime was implicated as aiding the invasion with cyber operations. The attackers, according to one assessment, "were tipped off about the timing of the Russian military operations while these operations were being carried out" so that "any direct Russian military involvement was simply unnecessary."[79]

Researchers at Shadowserver reported that the Web site of the Georgian president had been rendered inoperable for 24 hours by multiple DDoS attacks several weeks prior to the physical invasion. According to Shadowserver the "command and control server that directed the attack was based in the United States had come online several weeks before it began the assault" and was likely a "dress rehearsal" for the attacks to come.[80]

Once the land invasion began, the Georgian President's website, media firms, communications and transportation companies were also attacked. The website of the Georgian National Bank fell victim to a propaganda-based defacement. Georgia's limited digital infrastructure was unprepared for the scale of the attack and was quickly

---

discusses why the attacks were not significant in terms of size, but had significant effects on Estonia.

[79]   US Cyber Consequences Unit, "Overview of the USCCU of the Cyber Campaign Against Georgia in August of 2008," (2009), 3.

[80]   John Markoff, "Before the Gunfire, Cyberattacks," *New York Times,* August 12, 2008, http://www.nytimes.com/2008/08/13/technology/13cyber.html.

overwhelmed. Georgia accused Russia of attacking its networks, but Russia denied all such claims. The cyber offensive impacted "the government's ability to spread its message online and to connect with sympathizers around the world during the fighting with Russia" in addition to internal disruptions.[81] While Israel initiated the first state on non-state and state-on-state cyber action during a physical war, and Estonia marked the first instance of an alliance forged between a state and dissident groups to take advantage of destabilizing physical disruptions in the target nation, the Georgia case marked the first known incident of a non-state cyber attack supporting an overt physical war between nation states.[82]

As for Russian involvement, there was evidence that Russian telecommunications firms hosted the servers running the control software for the involved botnets.[83] A Russian-language Web site, stopgeorgia.ru, also continued to operate and offer software for download used for distributed denial of service attacks to expand participation.[84] Other external software programs were traced to Turkey.[85] Botnet tracking revealed clear evidence of the involvement of the Russian Business Network's botnet infrastructure. "The attackers are using the same tools and the same attack commands that have been used by the RBN and in some cases the attacks are being launched from computers they are known to control," said Don Jackson, director of threat intelligence for SecureWorks.[86]

As the war began to wind to a close, so did the cyber attacks. Compared to the physical invasion and the cyber attacks in the Estonia case, the cyber offensive against Georgia had less effect because Georgia was simply not a very "wired" nation. However analysts examining the events asserted with "high confidence" that

---

[81]   Ibid.

[82]   Richard A. Clarke, *Cyber War*, Harper Collins, April 20, 2010, http://www.richardaclarke.net/cyber_war.php (accessed September 30, 2011) Chapter 1.

[83]   John Markoff, "Before the Gunfire, Cyberattacks," *New York Times,* August 12, 2008, http://www.nytimes.com/2008/08/13/technology/13cyber.html.

[84]   Ibid.

[85]   Dancho Danchev, "Coordinated Russia vs. Georgia cyber attack in progress," *ZDNet,* August 11, 2008, http://www.zdnet.com/blog/security/coordinated-russia-vs-georgia-cyber-attack-in-progress/1670.

[86]   Markoff, "Before the Gunfire, Cyberattacks."

"Russian government will likely continue its practice of distancing itself from the Russian nationalistic hacker community thus gaining deniability while passively supporting and enjoying the strategic benefits of their actions."[87]

Non-State Actors and Potential for Strategic Effect

The strategic potential of non-state actors is not limited to the types of examples above. It is both deeper and wider, with the possibility for strong disruption of states or critical infrastructure causing varied and diverse effects. This disruption may arise from collaboration and alliances between states and non-state actors, while other sources of strategically significant disruptive activity may arise from within the underground without any state direction or sponsorship.

Non-State Actors as Element of Advanced Persistent Threat

Non-state actors have played key elements in the recent rise of the Advanced Persistent Threat (APT). In such cases it can be very difficult to determine whether a particular action is conducted by the originating state, or by patriotic hackers or an organized criminal network. Much focus in APT analysis and policy discussion describes it as a means of conducting espionage or intellectual theft. However it is clear that many targets of APT efforts have little to offer by way of intelligence or economic advantage, such as water treatment facilities and electrical networks.[88]

These and other examples highlight a much more insidious and strategically significant application of APT network mapping of critical infrastructure and other potentially significant targets. Due to the persistent efforts and access when successful, APT can collect extensive information on network configurations and vulnerabilities. Conducting attacks against the same target or infrastructure sector conducted over the course of decades can also yield information about defensive efforts and patterns that can be

---

[87]   Project Grey Goose, "Russia/Georgia Cyber War – Findings and Analysis," October 17, 2008.

[88]   "Advanced Persistent Threats," *McAfee,* 2010 http://www.mcafee.com/us/resources/solution-briefs/sb-advanced-persistent-threats.pdf (accessed September 30, 2011) p. 2

exploited to reduce the effectiveness of a defensive response. Finally, if such penetrations by state affiliated or state sponsored non-state actors go undetected there is a possibility that attackers could leave malicious code dormant on critical machines. These factors prepare the battlefield for a significant cyber offensive as a component of a larger strategic conflict or as the basis for a long-term digital guerrilla campaign.

Advanced Capabilities for Sale

As mentioned above, many disruptive non-state actors draw on the support or direct involvement of skilled technologists to develop and manage advanced capabilities. Such technologists can be motivated by either belief in a cause or financial incentives. Once those advanced capabilities and supporting infrastructures are developed, we have observed a pattern of organizations repurposing or reselling their capability to third parties. For example, one of the most important pieces of malicious software for stealing credentials for online banking and other commerce is named Zeus, and can be bought for as little as $700 online.[89] Zeus provided criminal gains of $70 million to just one of the many groups using it.[90] According to the security company Symantec:

> Zeus provides a ready-to-deploy package for hackers to distribute their own botnet. The botnet is easily purchased and also freely traded online and continues to be updated to provide new features and functionality. The ease-of-use of Zeus means the Zeus bot is used widely and is highly prevalent, allowing the most novice hackers to easily steal online banking credentials and other online credentials for financial gain.[91]

Zeus highlights the concern around the rise of botnets-for-rent. A malicious individual or organization will develop a large

---

[89]   Nicolas Failliere and Eric Chien,"Zeus, King of Bots," *Symantec,* (2009), 1.

[90]   "More than 100 arrests, as FBI uncovers cyber crime ring," *BBC News,* October 2010, http://www.bbc.co.uk/news/world-us-canada-11457611, (accessed January 29, 2011).

[91]   Nicolas Failliere and Eric Chien,"Zeus, King of Bots," 13.

botnet through viral infection, but rather than jealously guard this capability for their own goals they will sell the computing power to one or more other groups. This allows other malicious actors to acquire large scale, unattributable disruptive capability very rapidly for relatively little cost. The Russian Business Network and groups like it have operated extremely successful business models on providing botnet-for-rent services. The demand, supply, and offensive capacity of for-sale attack tools and botnets will most likely increase in the future, demand which can be met because of the virus-like way these botnets propagate themselves through the network.[92]

Stuxnet

Attack tools are unlikely to remain limited to malicious code for accessing hosts, exfiltrating data, and conducting DDoS attacks. The possibility of highly advanced and potentially crippling malicious code being commercialized and widely available seems likely. Stuxnet, one of the most highly advanced cyber attack capabilities in history, could be a precursor to threats of the next decade. Stuxnet, according to recent reports was the result of a United States program, code-named Olympic Games, and was developed in conjunction with Israel to infect the nuclear facility software and hardware predominately used in Iran and delay the program for months to buy more time for diplomatic solutions.[93] Since its widespread discovery in 2010, there are already reports that the worm could be modified and redirected to other targets.[94] The "hacktivist" group Anonymous has posted a decompiled version of Stuxnet (having stolen it from the files of a security company) on the Internet, and at least one security researcher believes that the more dangerous binary version is "widely

[92]   Yurie Ito, "Managing Global Cyber Health and Security Through Risk Reduction," Unpublished Thesis, July 18, 2011, 11.

[93]   Jonathan Fildes, "Stuxnet Worm 'Targeted High Value Iranian Assets," *BBC,* September 23, 2010 http://www.bbc.co.uk/news/technology-11388018 (accessed September 30, 2011).

[94]   Mark Clayton, "Son of Stuxnet? Variants of the cyberweapon likely, senators told," *Christian Science Monitor,* http://www.csmonitor.com/USA/2010/1117/Son-of-Stuxnet-Variants-of-the-cyberweapon-likely-senators-told, (accessed February 11, 2011).

available." [95] Historically, military technologies rarely remain exclusively controlled by their inventors; the trend is toward proliferation. As advanced capabilities continue to be made available online, non-state actors will be able to acquire increasingly powerful capabilities to disrupt or destroy cyber systems and the actual physical infrastructure connected to them.

Anonymous and the Potential Rapid Emergence of Disruptive Force

Much attention has been paid above to the rise and achievements of Anonymous. With many members, no identifiable leaders, passionate causes, and a core of technologists able to mass-produce easy-to-use weaponized code, this attention is warranted. Efforts to disrupt the leadership and operations of such groups have resulted in arrests but have largely been ineffective, indicating in an organizational structure and growth able to outpace and survive law enforcement efforts.[96]

But it would be unwise to view Anonymous as a singular phenomenon. Anonymous serves as a model for a non-state actor as a potentially disruptive, rapidly emerging, and highly distributed organization. Much like a botnet-for-rent, a rapidly emerging group can quickly bring large-scale attack power to bear on a target with little warning. Unlike botnets and their controllers, however, these groups rely less on an emplaced command and control structure to attack, servers to confiscate, or an operator to arrest. With the notoriety of successful operations, the attacking power and depth of technological resources of a group may increase as more members join or sympathizers develop, a process made easier by the free distribution of simple attack tools to anyone willing to use them against the group's target. Furthermore,

---

[95] See David E. Sanger's reporting on this issue: David E. Sanger, "Obama Order Sped Up Wave of Cyberattacks Against Iran," *New York Times*, June 1, 2012, http://www.nytimes.com/2012/06/01/world/middleeast/obama-ordered-wave-of-cyberattacks-against-iran.html?pagewanted=all and David E. Sanger, *Confront and Conceal*, New York, NY: Crown, 2012, for more detailed information about Olympic Games and Stuxnet.

[96] Sam Biddle, "Anonymous Roars Back With 3GB Leak of Texas Police Chief Emails: "That stupid bitch got what she deserved" *Gizmodo*, September 1, 2011, http://gizmodo.com/5836741/anonymous-roars-back-with-3gb-leak-of-texas-police-chief-emails (accessed September 30, 2011).

the cause-based nature of such groups may attract sympathizers from the mainstream of even the state or institutions targeted, raising the possibilities of insiders sharing or leaking information and regular citizens supporting the activities of the group, both of which raise challenges to defense and response efforts. The disruptive ability, lack of vulnerable infrastructure for counter-attack, organizational resiliency, and operational flexibility of these groups combined with their ability to rapidly develop momentum and mobilize membership make them dangerous and strategically destabilizing, particularly as a guerrilla force.

Cause of Strategic Confusion and Inadvertent Conflict

Cyber conflict carried out through non-state actors can be directly disruptive, but it may also cause uncertainties about the origins of an attack, which can itself be strategically destabilizing. Mounting pressure to respond or assign blame for the disruptive cyber attacks will compete with the inherent difficulties of conclusively attributing the attacker. As in the Hezbollah example earlier, international collaboration between the Internet underground and alliances will further complicate the strategic picture. Additionally, it can be difficult to distinguish a rapid mobilization of attackers or botnets as a stand-alone event or the precursor to a larger cyber or kinetic military action.

If a dissident hacker group rents a botnet based across the globe without the knowledge of any government, let alone consent or direction, and conducts a strategically significant attack, should a military response be levied at the compromised computer or other targets in the host country? Should we wait for further investigation to find the identity of the group behind the attacks? There is no accepted standard of proof needed to determine which non-state actor or actors should be held responsible and if one or more states are also accountable. If non-state attackers plant misinformation regarding the origin of the disruptive cyber activity, it could further cloud a complicated strategic and diplomatic situation in the physical world.

These questions highlight some of the inherent challenges in developing a concrete response to cyber attacks in an increasingly murky cyber ecosystem. Assessment and retaliation will require nuanced approaches to maximize the effectiveness of any retaliatory action. Responding to an attack by retaliating against the wrong target would at best be a waste of strategic resources and at worst could weaken strategic alliances or start an unintended conflict or escalation.

A concrete example of the issues involved in this aspect of cyber conflict occurred in July 2009 when a botnet began a series of DDoS attacks on critical US and South Korean government sites, combined with a commercially available worm. The attacks came at a time of rising tensions with North Korea, following a test of a long distance missile just days earlier.[97] Little damage was done thanks to defensive efforts, but because of the timing and the targets, the North Korean government was the prime suspect, leading at least one prominent US lawmaker to call for retaliation before a more serious attack took place.[98] South Korean calls for response were not answered, because while the identity of the attackers remains unknown, many security analysts have questioned that North Korea was the responsible party.[99] Looking back, however, the sequence of events is troubling: the United States and South Korea quickly and definitively accused North Korea of the attacks, despite the fact that the responsible party was still in dispute, demonstrating clearly both the potential for the Korean peninsula to be a geo-political flashpoint and the instability of cyberspace.

Advantages and Disadvantages of Non-State Actors on the Offense

As described above, the disruptive capabilities of non-state actors are both diverse and significant. The types of actors are equally diverse, however they share some characteristic trade offs. These

---

[97]   Jose Nazario "Politically Motivated Denial of Service Attacks," *Arbor Networks,* http://www.ccdcoe.org/publications/virtualbattlefield/12_NAZARIO%20Politica lly%20Motivated%20DDoS.pdf.

[98]   Angela Moscaritolo "Cyber retaliation debate: Is North Korea guilty of DDoS?" *SC Magazine*, July 13, 2009, http://www.scmagazineus.com/cyber-retaliation-debate-is-north-korea-guilty-of-ddos/article/139968/.

[99]   "US Rules Out North Korea's Role in '09 Cyber Attacks," *The New New Internet,* http://www.thenewnewinternet.com/2010/07/06/us-rules-out-north-koreas-role-in-09-cyber-attacks/.

advantages and disadvantages, described below, illustrate the strengths and limitations typical of disruptive non-state actors.

Advantages

- **The barriers to entry are inexpensive and low:** Cyberspace offers unique advantages to non-state actors on the offense. Options and tools to achieve meaningful, successful attacks are relatively inexpensive and accessible.[100] Rentable botnets are on-demand armies, capable of massed attacks that can overwhelm many servers and target defenses for significant periods of time. In addition to network mapping and service disruption, attackers can also collect valuable information if their penetrations are successful. Even if not, there is perceived to be little risk in trying since it is difficult to authenticate user identities and many countries do not have strong legal norms against malicious cyber activity, making a law enforcement or military response more difficult than for physical crimes or attacks.[101] Finally, many attacks tools can be dual-use, achieving strategic ends as well as to raising money through extortion or selling stolen information, especially financial details and research.[102] This can allow non-state disruptive actors, especially the Internet underground, to fund themselves, resulting in the group sustainment and even the development of more dangerous capabilities.

- **Lean and agile organizational structure.** Non-state groups also tend to have flatter, more agile organization structures than their nation state counterparts. Non-state actors are less

---

[100] Symantec, "Attack Toolkits in 90 Seconds," *SymantecTV*, http://www.symantec.com/tv/news/details.jsp?vid=750972922001&om_ext_cid=biz_socmed_twitter_facebook_marketwire_linkedin_2011Jan_worldwide_attacktoolkits (accessed October 5, 2011)

[101] Wayne Arnold, "Philippines to Drop Charges on E-Mail Virus," *New York Times*, August 22, 2000, http://www.nytimes.com/2000/08/22/business/technology-philippines-to-drop-charges-on-e-mail-virus.html.

[102] Dan Goodin, "Sony Implicates Anonymous in PlayStation Network Hack," *The Register,* May 4, 2011 http://www.theregister.co.uk/2011/05/04/sony_implicates_anonymous/ (accessed October 5, 2011).

burdened by managerial oversight, constrained by regulations or ethics, nor beholden to a large and diverse constituency. They are able to pay talented staff, often with high salaries or a percentage of the illegal gains from their activities. If resources need to be reallocated, organizational processes changed, or priorities refocused, non-state actors would be able to do so with far more agility than a nation state. This also comes into play if parts of the group are killed or arrested; many such organizations are distributed and adaptable thus able to more easily recover from their own disruption. [103] In terms of organizational capacity, non-state actors have fewer constituent responsibilities and less resistance to change than the large-scale defensive apparatuses of states, though not without their own trade offs in terms of institutional support.[104]

- **Ability to achieve effects globally.** Cyberspace gives attackers a global reach. Since borders in cyberspace are largely porous, attackers can conduct their activities much faster and cheaper than using conventional operations. Collaboration between groups in different nations and locations, while not common, is rendered much simpler using digital communication and data sharing. This applies to the sharing and bundling of attack tools and techniques between groups. Attackers also avoid, or at least extremely mitigate, the risk of discovery and arrest before reaching their targets that is inherent with physical travel between nations.

- **Potential to leverage the Internet Underground to make alliances.** Non-state actors can mitigate some risks of discovery, tracking, and retaliation by collaborating with other members of the underground to gain new capabilities. As members of the underground community, non-state actors will enjoy advantages in deepening contacts with other actors in those circles. These relationships could be bilateral, such as cause-based groups identifying and renting botnet networks, or communal, exemplified by the exchange of malicious code and robust attack kits on hacker forums.[105]

---

[103]   Arquilla and Ronfeldt, *Networks and Netwars*, 72.

[104]   Gregory J. Rattray, *Strategic Warfare in Cyberspace* Cambridge, MA: The MIT Press, 2001), 164-167

[105]   Rick Howard, *Cyber Fraud: Tactics, Techniques and Procedures*, Verisign iDefense, (CRC Press: Boca Raton, FL, 2009).171-207.; Gunter Ollmann, "Want

Disadvantages

- **Human capital.** The primary challenge posed to the non-state actor attacking in cyberspace is one of human capital. States have the human capital to plan extensive and protracted operations in advance, knowing that they can draw on a large pool of people with a range of skillsets to accomplish tasks requiring varying degrees of specialization.[106] States can generally decide on an action, and then assemble the team needed to do it. In contrast, most non-state actors rely on existing membership to plan and execute operations. New members with particular skill sets can be recruited, but this is a lengthy and risky process. There are significant operational security concerns around expanding membership in a disruptive non-state organization due to law enforcement infiltration efforts.

- **Organizational stability.** Disruptive non-state actors face considerable pressures against their organizational longevity. For individuals and group members, particularly criminal and terrorist organizations, the risk of detection and arrest are ever-present. If leaders or a significant portion of the membership are neutralized it could drastically reduce an organization's operational capacity as in the case of the Russian Business Network.[107] Non-state actors such as patriot hackers and dissident groups, have a more informal, distributed membership, which is resistant to the loss of any one member but presents its own challenges. Lacking a hierarchy and almost entirely consisting of volunteers, the

---

to Rent and 80-120k DDoS Botnet?" *Damballa,* August 28, 2009, http://blog.damballa.com/?p=330 (accessed October 6, 2011); Omkar Sapre, "Cyber Underworld: How it Works," *The Times of India,* September 22, 2011, http://timesofindia.indiatimes.com/tech/enterprise-it/security/Cyber-underworld-How-it-works/articleshow/10075465.cms (accessed October 6, 2011).

[106] For more discussion of this, see Rattray, *Strategic Warfare in Cyberspace,* Chapter 3, "Establishing Organizational Technological Capacity for Strategic Information Warfare."

[107] Rick Howard, *Cyber Fraud: Tactics, Techniques and Procedures,* Verisign iDefense, (CRC Press: Boca Raton, FL, 2009),171-207.

operational capacity of such groups waxes and wanes depending on their members' motivation and cohesiveness.[108]

- **Management.** Non-state actors also suffer disadvantages in project management and large-scale technology systems integration. Non-state groups are often transient, only coming together for short periods of time, enough for a few protests or efforts to breach a target, and rarely do they have overhead resources such as project managers to keep multiple streams of activity synchronized and moving smoothly. Accordingly, it is difficult for them to pursue goals over months or years as states can. Moreover, the capability of a nation-state like the United States, with enormous resources, would be very likely to be able to recover relatively quickly after a disruptive action unless an adversary is able to sustain the damaging attacks over a long period in the face of determined cyber and physical counterattacks. The lessons of previous bouts of strategic warfare, such as aerial bombardment in World War II, have demonstrated the tremendous difficulty involved in sustaining such large-scale attack efforts even for industrialized nations giving maximum effort. Non-state actors, even using cyber attacks, would be under enormous pressure and few, if located, could sustain destabilizing attacks in the face of determined state-level resources involving economic, diplomatic, and political power as well as cyber and kinetic force.[109]

- **Long-Term Resources and Expertise.** While national treasuries and taxes can fund the execution of an attack planned by a state, generally a non-state actor must rely on funding from small groups and individuals or through criminal activity. Governments seldom fund non-state actors directly and explicitly, though as mentioned above such alliances are becoming more prevalent. While self-funding

---

[108]   Josh Halliday, "Operation Payback fails to take down Amazon in WikiLeaks revenge attack," *The Guardian,* December 9, 2010, http://www.guardian.co.uk/media/2010/dec/09/operation-payback-wikileaks-anonymous (accessed September 30, 2011).

[109]   Gregory J. Rattray, *Strategic Warfare in Cyberspace* Cambridge, MA: The MIT Press, 2001), p. 185, 206

through crime can be very fruitful and allow an organization to expand its offensive capacity, it can also be time consuming and risky. In the case of cause-based group, both criminal activity and state sponsorship may distract from their overall purpose or taint their "purity" in ways unpalatable to their members. Anonymous, for instance, would lose much of its support and ability to orchestrate disruptive attacks if it re-purposed an operation intending to expose wrong doing or embarrassing decisions on the part of a financial institution into acquiring and selling its customers' banking information. Non-state actors will generally be far more constrained in their trade-offs between the resources available to them and the targets want to pursue. Some degree of organizational complexity is typically needed to consistently pursue difficult complex objectives over time. While the least bureaucratic non-state groups may have greater agility than nations, this is often a direct trade off for staying power and capability over time.

To further illustrate the strengths and weaknesses of disruptive non-state actors, the case studies on Estonia and Anonymous provide more detailed background on those subjects and will apply that framework to each case.

Case Studies

Estonia Case Study

In 2007, relations between Russia and most of its former vassal states were marked by tension and conflict, but the cyber conflict involving Estonia was the first use of cyber conflict for regional coercion. The event that ultimately sparked Russia's digital onslaught was the removal of a 6-foot-tall bronze statue from downtown Tallinn by the Estonian government. The Soviets had originally built the monument in 1947 to commemorate their war dead after driving the Nazis out of the region at the end of World War II. To the Estonians, the statue was a symbol of the Soviet occupation while the ethnic Russians saw it as celebrating the victory of their native countrymen over fascism. In 2007, after 16 years of Estonian independence, the Estonians decided to ignore numerous previous Russian warnings that the removal of the statue would be disastrous, and uprooted the statue to a military cemetery on the outskirts of town. While the pro-Russian riots that had broken out on April 27th were tamed by the morning of the 28th, the cyber attacks against Estonian infrastructure were only beginning to gain momentum by April 28th.

Three Weeks of Attacks

The attacks on Estonia came in three phases and the primary targets included both state institutions and non-state organizations, such as major Internet Service Providers, e-banking services, and news organizations.[110] The first phase of attacks was characterized by simple DDOS attacks that required little technical expertise. Examples of such an attack were the attacks targeting Postimees, an Estonian newspaper. Automated programs began to "spew posts onto the commentary pages of the Postimees website, creating a

---

[110]   Eneken Tikk, Kadri Kaski and Liis Vihul, *International Cyber Incidents: Legal Considerations*, NATO Cooperative Cyber Defense Center of Excellence, (2009), 22.
Ian Traynor, "Russia accused of unleashing cyberware to disable Estonia," *The Guardian,* Wednesday 16, 2007,
http://www.guardian.co.uk/world/2007/may/17/topstories3.russia.

two-fold problem: The spam overloaded the server's processors and hogged bandwidth."[111] To mitigate this attack, the comments feature on the website was disabled. Though this saved bandwidth, those attacks that did get through ultimately crashed the systems. Attackers continued to alter their malicious server requests to evade the filters put into place.

The second phase of attacks lasted from April 30th to May 18th and was characterized by a more prominent use of botnets. On May 2nd, traffic on the Postimees website increased exponentially yet again, with the number one country accessing the website being Egypt, closely followed by Vietnam and Peru. Asking Elion, the newspaper's Internet Service Provider (ISP) to increase bandwidth proved to be a very short-term solution.[112] On May 4th, DDoS assaults continued against government websites, banks providing e-banking services, and domain names services, while showing remarkable intensification and precision in concentration, which indicated the use of botnets.[113] Attackers used a variety of means to cover their tracks, including using global botnets, routing their attacks through proxy servers in other countries (including those in NATO countries) as well as spoofing IP addresses. On May 9th, a national holiday in Russia commemorating their victory over Nazi Germany, up to 58 websites were shut down as a result of a surge of attacks – mostly on government institutions, including official communication channels of the government.[114]

These disruptions were followed by strong DDoS attacks, enabled by the use of an 85,000-computer-strong botnet against the

[111] Joshua Davis, "Hackers Take Down the Most Wired Country in Europe," *Wired,* August 21, 2001, http://www.wired.com/politics/security/magazine/15-09/ff_estonia?currentPage=all, (accessed August 23, 2011).

[112] Joshua Davis, "Hackers Take Down the Most Wired Country in Europe," *Wired.com,* August 21, 2007 http://www.wired.com/politics/security/magazine/15-09/ff_estonia?currentPage=all (accessed October 5, 2011)

[113] Tikk, Kaska and Vihul, *International Cyber Incidents: Legal Considerations.*

[114] BBC News, "Putin in Veiled Attack on Estonia," May 9, 2007, http://news.bbc.co.uk/2/hi/europe/6638029.stm (accessed October 5, 2011). Mikko Hypponen, "9th of May" *F-Secure.com,* May 9, 2007, http://www.f-secure.com/weblog/archives/00001188.html (accessed October 6, 2011).

websites of government institutions from noon until midnight on May 15th, as reported by the CERT-EE.[115] Since network capacities had already been increased in response to the earlier attacks, the heightened amount of traffic did not pose significant problems. The waves of attacks targeted a large number of websites, including government institutions and critical infrastructure, especially the banking and financial sector.

Government Institutions

During the three weeks of attacks, numerous government sites were disrupted. The offices of the Government, Prime Minister, President, Riigikogu (the Estonian Parliament), and the State Audit Office all experienced DDoS attacks. Almost all national ministries and some state-level services, including the policy, also experienced severe disruptions.[116] A website defacement was executed against the Reform Party, Estonia's leading coalition, on April 29th, replacing the main page with a fake letter from the Estonia prime minister begging for Russia's forgiveness and promising to return the memorial statue.[117]

Information Infrastructure

CERT-EE reported numerous instances in which both governmental and commercial Internet infrastructure providers were targeted. Among the most frequently targeted were the domain name servers provided by the Institute of Chemical Biology and Physics and EENet, which administers the core Internet servers for the Estonian governmental and educational institutions. At least three major Internet Service Providers – Elion Ettevõtted, Elisa Andmesideteenused, and Starman –, experienced DDoS attacks against their servers and had their routers overwhelmed by attacks against other targets.[118]

---

115   Tikk, Kaska and Vihul, *International Cyber Incidents: Legal Considerations.*
116   Ibid., 22.
117   Patrick Jackson, "The Cyber Raiders Hitting Estonia" *BBC News,* May 17, 2007, http://news.bbc.co.uk/2/hi/europe/6665195.stm (accessed October 6, 2011).
118   Tikk, Kaska and Vihul, *International Cyber Incidents: Legal Considerations.*

Commercial Services

The attacks affected two of the largest Estonian banks. When combined, these financial institutions controlled about 75-80 percent of the total Estonian banking market.[119] When considering that 95-97 percent of banking services are provided and executed online in Estonia, such interruptions significantly hindered transactions. Newspapers and other media outlets were also hit, hindering information flow about the attacks.

Origin of the Attacks

A significant amount of attack traffic was proven to have originated outside Estonia. According to information from Arbor Networks and the State Informatics Centre, the attacks were utilizing hijacked computers dispersed worldwide in over 178 countries. Initially, a substantial number of participating computers belonged to tech savvy political sympathizers, such as the Kremlin-tied youth group *Nashi*, which years later claimed credit for organizing the attacks.[120] But while the first phase of attacks may have been driven by popular nationalistic fervor among the ethnic Russian hacker community, log analyses has demonstrated that the attacks during the second phase had characteristics uncommon to that of an ordinary online citizen protest. Specifically, the later attacks displayed more sophisticated

---

[119] The e-banking services of Hanapank and SEB Eestl Uehlspank were attacked on numerous occasions between from May 9 to May 15. Both banks reported having to shut down e-banking services to Estonian, and eventually, to all customers accessing the website abroad, for periods of 1.5 to 2 hours during this time. Tikk, Kaska and Vihul, *International Cyber Incidents: Legal Considerations*, 22.

[120] Chloe Arnold, "Russian Group's Claims Reopen Debate on Estonian Cyber Attacks," *Radio Free Europe/Radio Liberty*, March 30, 2009, http://www.rferl.org/content/Russian_Groups_Claims_Reopen_Debate_On_Est onian_Cyberattacks_/1564694.html (accessed December 8 2011). Noah Shachtman, "Kremlin Kids: We Launched the Estonian Cyber War," *Wired.com*, March 11, 2009 http://www.wired.com/dangerroom/2009/03/pro-kremlin-gro/ (accessed December 8, 2011).

command and control, requiring significant financial backing and specialist-level intellectual resources.[121] While there were no direct links to the Russian government, malicious activity was linked to nationalist patriotic hacker groups "following instructions provided on Russian language Internet forums and websites," [122] and conducted by at least by one youth group linked to the Kremlin.[123] It became apparent, though not conclusively provable and naturally officially denied, that the patriotic hackers were receiving considerable encouragement and guidance from Russian government officials.[124]

Strategic Effects

The attacks on Estonia had both strategic and economic effects. The societal effect stemmed from a revolution in state-citizen interaction in Estonia. Because a majority of Estonia's public services had been offered online for a number of years preceding these attacks, their unavailability challenged the status quo by

---

[121]   Joshua Davis, "Hackers Take Down the Most Wired Country in Europe," *Wired.com,* August 21, 2007
http://www.wired.com/politics/security/magazine/15-09/ff_estonia?currentPage=all (accessed October 5, 2011).

[122]   Ibid., 33.

[123]   One person claiming to have organized the attack is a leader of the Kremlin-backed Nashi ("Ours") youth nationalism group and also an assistant of a member of the Duma (parliament). See the Charles Clover, "Kremlin-backed group behind Estonia cyber blitz," *Financial Times,* http://www.ft.com/cms/s/0/57536d5a-0ddc-11de-8ea3-0000779fd2ac.html#axzz1F0wNeeJX and "Behind The Estonia Cyberattacks," *Radio Free Europe,* http://www.rferl.org/content/Behind_The_Estonia_Cyberattacks/1505613.html. Nashi had attacked the Estonian ambassador to Moscow and barricaded the embassy over the same incident that led to the cyber attacks. See the reporting from the *Moscow Times* at http://www.themoscowtimes.com/news/article/protest-at-estonian-embassy-called-off/197288.html and the *Washington Post* at http://www.washingtonpost.com/wp-dyn/content/article/2007/05/02/AR2007050202547.html).

[124]   Ian Traynor, "Russia accused of unleashing cyber war to disable Estonia," *The Guardian,* May 16, 2007
http://www.guardian.co.uk/world/2007/may/17/topstories3.russia (accessed September 30, 2011)

impairing the ease and speed with which the citizen interacted with the state. Digital news, banking, and government services constituted a norm of Estonian life, and the unavailability of services and information combined with website defacements fed the national sense of alarm over the Tallinn riots. Defense minister Jaak Aaviksoo described the incident as being a successful attack "aimed at the credibility of the Estonian government."[125]

> Because Estonia is a NATO member, they could have potentially raised either the Article 4 defense consultations or Article 5 collective defense measures of the NATO Charter, but the legal uncertainties and lack of clear adversary with clear responsibility prevented Estonia from seriously considering or pursuing that course.[126] However, NATO and the European Union were informed of the cyber attacks, and NATO and the US CERT sent experts to observe and assist in the response.[127] In response to the Estonian attacks and the increased potential for cyber attacks against states, NATO has included cyber attacks as a significant threat to NATO member states and raised the potential use of Article 4 or Article 5 powers if a future incident required such a response.[128] Since the 2007 Estonian incident, NATO has continued to improve its mechanisms for decision making in cyber crises and continues to clarify members' obligations under the NATO charter

The overload of servers of a number of different sectors incurred significant economic costs not only on large corporations and the government, but also on small and medium enterprises throughout the country. Banks and other financial institutions were

[125]   Robert McMillan. "Estonia Readies for the Next Cyberattack," *CSO Online*. April 7, 2007,
http://www.csoonline.com/article/589867/Estonia_Readies_for_the_Next_Cyberattack (accessed April 13, 2010).
[126]   Häly Laamse, "Estonia: Cyber Window into the Future of NATO," *Joint Forces Quarterly*, Issue 63, 4th Quarter 2011, 58-63, 60.
[127]   Tikk, Kaska and Vihul, *International Cyber Incidents: Legal Considerations*, 24.
[128]   Laamse, "Estonia: Cyber Winder into the Future of NATO," 60.

specifically targeted for weeks, compromising the means for reliable commerce. [129] In addition to the specifically targeted institutions, the overwhelmed network infrastructure caused disruptions to users of the major national ISPs. The economic effects of such disturbances are difficult to quantify, but experts have stated that the daily loss was significant relative to the size of the Estonian economy. [130]

Advantages and Disadvantages of Non-State Actors Applied to the Estonian Case Study

Advantages

- **The barriers to entry are inexpensive and low:** During the first phase of attacks, the surge in sympathizers joining the hacking efforts indicates that those who had an impulse to participate after hearing of the event were able to do so without significant challenges. Russian ethnic hacker communities contributed by encouraging participation, offering precise attack instructions in underground forums and chat rooms. [131]

- **Lean and agile organizational structure:** The attackers organized themselves very rapidly and, at least initially, organically. When the time came to ramp up the attacks and transition from an outburst of activity to a sustained effort, this transition was smooth and swift.

- **Ability to achieve effects globally:** Almost all of the attackers and attacking computers were based outside of Estonia. The botnets were alleged to be controlled from within Russia but utilized bots from dozens of countries. The destabilizing effects of their activity and the necessary

---

[129]   Ibid, 22.

[130]   Ibid., 25.

[131]   Joshua Davis, "Hackers Take Down the Most Wired Country in Europe," *Wired.com,* August 21, 2007, http://www.wired.com/politics/security/magazine/15-09/ff_estonia?currentPage=all (accessed October 5, 2011).

defensive response effectively cut Estonia and its people from the global network for an extended period of time.

- **Potential to leverage the Internet Underground to make alliances:** Coordination between individual hackers, hacker communities, and botnet operators was largely successful. The sustained nature of the effort, the initial swell of patriot hackers supported by dedicated users committing botnet resources to continue escalating the attacks, was key to the effectiveness of the overall attack.

Disadvantages

- **Human capital:** The initial numbers of patriotic hackers had to invest significant resources in recruiting new participants to build momentum and critical mass for the first attacks. Propaganda and ready-to-use attacking tools with instructions on use all had to be created and provided to interested parties who had varying degrees of technical skill.

- **Organizational stability:** The initial wave of attacks was fueled by large groups of patriotic hackers inspired to collective action. This popular attack was effective but not sustainable at a disruptive scale. It ultimately gave way to a much smaller group of motivated botnet operators in subsequent waves.

- **Management:** The botnet attacks were devastating but encountered stiff resistance from Estonian responders that the attackers could not counter. Gradually, their impact lessened as defenders were able to adapt to the attacks, reconfiguring infrastructure, hardening servers, and redistributing state resources to key sites like government services, banks, and newspapers.

- **Resources:** Though the possibility exists that state sponsorship accounted for some funding, there was largely no financial incentive or backing for the attackers. This is one possible reason for the cessation of the botnet attacks in the face of increased resistance from Estonian defenders; it simply wasn't worth it.

Estonia: Lessons Learned

An analysis of the offensive tactics employed in the cyber attacks against Estonia highlights two key themes that are characteristic of numerous other contemporary cyber attacks: the continued prominence and growing importance of *patriotic hacking,* and the emergence of a *spectrum of cyber conflict.*

Patriotic hacking

Defined as the active participation of civilians in hacking a perceived adversary of the state for political reasons, Estonia was by no means the first victim of patriotic hacking. Unique to Estonia, however, were the scope and duration of the attacks. Russian sympathizers, who believed they were taking action "pro patria", initiated a protracted three-week-long campaign against commercial, individual, and government targets. Such hacking, however, is severely destabilizing for both the target and the origin jurisdiction. The target jurisdiction, Estonia, found itself under attack on multiple fronts, with inflamed political rhetoric emanating from the Kremlin, physical protests on the streets by ethnic Russians and other sympathizers, and cyber attacks from Russian patriots residing in Estonia and elsewhere. Patriotic hackers went beyond the acceptable level of "freedom of expression," as they proceeded to challenge Estonian sovereignty through a presumably state-sanctioned action. The potential prominence of patriotic hacking in future conflicts poses severe challenges to international stability and governance, particularly it is easily exploitable by other state and non-state actors. The effects of politically motivated hacking can be greatly augmented by a state reaching out to this underground to encourage and support their efforts and by the patriot hackers colluding with or simply hiring criminal botnets.

Spectrum of Cyber Conflict

Though some have deemed the attacks on Estonia to be the first instance of a cyber war, it seems that the Estonian case is lower on the spectrum of cyber conflict and does not reach any thresholds for "cyber war".[132] As cross-border cyber attacks become more frequent and sophisticated it is particularly important to distinguish between attacks that do and do not rise to the level of cyber conflict, and cyber war. As previously mentioned in the capstone, allegations of cross-border hacking, whether the cyber operation is classified as an attack or as espionage, have a profound effect on both official and unofficial channels of diplomacy and determinations of applying international law. It was this differentiation that precluded the Estonian government from invoking Article 5 of the NATO – namely, that an attack against one is an attack against all – and thus defined the Estonian defensive posture and incident response mechanisms. As defense minister Jaak Aaviksoo explained, "At present, NATO does not define cyber-attacks as a clear military action. This means that the provisions of Article V of the North Atlantic Treaty, or, in other words collective self-defence, will not automatically be extended to the attacked country."[133] However, the question still remains: "If the member state's communications center is attacked with a missile...you call it an act of war. So what do you do if the same installation is disabled with a cyber-attack?"[134]

Estonia: Conclusion

As disruptive as the cyber attacks on Estonia were, it was their political nature that made headlines for weeks. As Jose Nazario of Arbor Networks has noted, "it's the backdrop nature of the those

---

[132] See Atlantic Council, "Building a Secure Cyber Future: Attacks on Estonia, Five Years On" for a fuller discussion of the arguments about the scale and significance of the Estonian attacks and whether they should be considered "cyber war" or a lesser form of cyber conflict.

[133] Ian Traynor, "Russia Accused of Unleashing Cyber War to Disable Estonia," *The Guardian*, May 16, 2007, http://www.guardian.co.uk/world/2007/may/17/topstories3.russia (accessed October 6, 2011).

[134] Nate Anderson, "Massive DDoS Attacks Target Estonia; Russia Accused," *ArsTechnica*, 2007 http://arstechnica.com/security/news/2007/05/massive-ddos-attacks-target-estonia-russia-accused.ars, (accessed September 4, 2011).

attacks that's novel, in comparison to other denial of service attacks."[135] At 100 or 200 megabits per second, the size of the Estonian attacks was that of a "common-size attack."[136] What differentiated the Estonian attacks was the diversity of targets and the sustained, protracted, politically driven campaign executed by a network of non-state actors, with strong ties to Russia. Moreover, the incident in Estonia, from a technical, legal, and policy perspective, also offered insight into approaches that can be employed to activate collective defenses, which will be discussed in a separate case study later in this chapter.

Rather than detail a specific incident, the following case study examines Anonymous as a template for cause-based dissident groups and will apply the strengths and weaknesses framework in that capacity.

---

[135]   Robert Vamosi, "Newsmaker: Cyberattack in Estonia – What It Really Means," *CNET*, May 29, 2007, http://news.cnet.com/Cyberattack-in-Estonia-what-it-really-means/2008-7349_3-6186751.html#ixzz1Wzz7xoxN (accessed September 3, 2011).

[136]   Ibid.

Anonymous Case Study

Originating in 2003, Anonymous is a civil disobedience collective that seeks to represent the multitude of active online users writing as "anonymous" but thinking and acting as one. Since 2003 this civil disobedience collective has sought to define and express its existence and purpose through the use of aphorisms: "We are Anonymous. We are Legion. We do not forgive. We do not forget. Expect us."[137] Their principles are somewhat nebulous but generally revolve around supporting the goals of Internet freedom through anonymity and exposing perceived hypocrisy by or damaging secrets of religious, political, and financial institutions.[138] Though infamous for their numerous attacks against the banking sector, as well as local and foreign government entities that are perceived to act against free speech and freedom of information, the collective is most well known for its staunch defense of Wikileaks. While the attacks executed are rather simplistic – the majority are Denial of Service (DoS) attacks and website defacements – the group's political ideology and loosely networked organizational structure pose a long-term risk to the stability of online communities. Furthermore, such loosely tied organizations are particularly challenging adversaries for law enforcement to combat.[139]

The Evolution of Attacks

The group has been particularly active since 2006. Each year, Anonymous executes a number of cyber attacks against a wide variety of targets, and while the collective made its name by attacking the Church of Scientology and anti-piracy groups, its recent infamy stems largely from its staunch defense of Wikileaks. In 2008, the group's preferred online activities were the

---

[137] "We are Anonymous, We are Legion," *Yale Law and Technology*, Novermber 9, 2009, http://www.yalelawtech.org/anonymity-online-identity/we-are-anonymous-we-are-legion/, (accessed September 6, 2011).

[138] "Hats, Hacks, Cracks and other Shenanigans," *Osarena,* 2011, http://osarena.net/2011/07/hats-hacks-cracks-and-other-shenanigans.html.

[139] Nicole Kobie, "How Dangerous is Anonymous," *PC Pro,* February 22, 2011, http://www.pcpro.co.uk/news/security/365440/how-dangerous-is-anonymous, (accessed September 7, 2011).

organization of protests and website defacements. By 2011, though Anonymous had been making headlines worldwide by hacking (seemingly) anyone and everyone that opposed or denounced free speech, their attacks did not appear to mature. The group continued to capitalize on their ability to mobilize online sympathizers to execute coordinated DDoS attacks, following up with website defacement that made their message clear.

Anonymous operations have included supporting anti-regime forces in protests associated with the Arab Spring, the 2011 Wisconsin Protests, discrediting the Church of Scientology, and Operation Avenge Assange, which focused on supporting the activities of WikiLeaks while attacking those working against it. [140] They have also engaged in actions at the local level, targeting the public transit system of San Francisco after it powered down cell phone towers in its stations to prevent local protesters from coordinating and exposing the private communications of the Texas police force in retaliation for the arrest of an Anonymous member. [141]

Anonymous and the Middle East

In 2011, Anonymous became an active participant and enabler in the revolutions that seemed to define the Arab world. Anonymous began its Arab Spring participation with the taking down of the Tunisian Government's website, as a response to both their censorship of WikiLeaks and their crackdown on the protests that would soon sweep throughout the Middle East. Later, the group exposed the names and passwords of the email addresses of government officials

---

[140]   John Leyden, "Anonymous Attacks Paypal in 'Operation Avenge Assange,'" The Register, December 6, 2010, http://www.theregister.co.uk/2010/12/06/anonymous_launches_pro_wikileaks_campaign/.

[141]   "'Anonymous' Targets BART: Hacker Group Goes After San Francisco Transit System After Cell Phone Shutdown," *The Huffington Post,* August 14, 2011, http://www.huffingtonpost.com/2011/08/14/anonymous-bart-cell-phone-shutdown-protest_n_926574.html (accessed September 9, 2011). Sam Biddle, "Anonymous Roars Back With 3GB Leak of Texas Police Chief Emails: "That stupid bitch got what she deserved" *Gizmodo,* September 1, 2011 http://gizmodo.com/5836741/anonymous-roars-back-with-3gb-leak-of-texas-police-chief-emails (accessed September 30, 2011).

from Bahrain, Egypt, Jordan and Morocco, demonstrating their avid support of the Arab Spring.[142] Seeking retribution for the Syrian government's then forthcoming Internet blackout, Anonymous vowed to attack Syria as well, following through by hacking the Syrian Defense Ministry in August 2011. It replaced the Ministry's website with an image of the pre-Ba'athist flag, a symbol of the democratic movement, accompanied by a message supporting the forthcoming uprising and encouraging the Syrian armed forces to defect and protect the members of this movement.[143]

Diversity of Targets, but Unity in Motivation

As seen in the group's participation in the Arab Spring, Anonymous has targeted a significant number of foreign governments' websites.[144] Anonymous has been actively pursuing non-governmental targets as well, both in the US and abroad. In Germany, for instance, Anonymous hacked the website of the Society for Musical Performing and Mechanical Reproduction Rights (GEMA).[145] What sparked this attack was the refusal of YouTube to pay GEMA a rate of 12-euro cents per video, which would have made videos from major labels available on German

---

[142]   Nancy Messieh, "Anonymous Reveals Passwords For Hundreds of Middle East Government Email Accounts," *The Next Web,* June 5, 2011, http://thenextweb.com/me/2011/06/05/anonymous-reveals-passwords-for-hundreds-of-middle-east-government-email-accounts/?utm_source=feedburner&utm_medium=feed&utm_campaign=Feed%3A+TheNextWeb+%28The+Next+Web+All+Stories%29 (accessed September 8, 2011).

[143]   Bill Chappell, "Syria is hacked by Anonymous and Pressed by Gulf Allies," *NPR,* August 8, 2011, http://www.npr.org/blogs/thetwo-way/2011/08/08/139094501/syria-is-hacked-by-anonymous-and-pressed-by-gulf-allies (accessed September 8, 2011).

[144]   These include Zimbabwe, Spain, Iran, Bahrain, Egypt, Jordan, Morocco, Israel, Libya, Malaysia, Syria, as well as Austria, Turkey, among others.

[145]   GEMA is the only organization in Germany that collects royalties on behalf of over a million local and foreign singers, composers, authors and music publishers. Lucian Constantin, "Anonymous Supporters Hack German Music Royalty Collector's Website," *Softpedia,* August 24, 2011, http://news.softpedia.com/news/Anonymous-Supporters-Hack-German-Music-Rights-Collector-s-Website-218466.shtml.

You Tube – thus making the company a clear enemy of anti-copyright and freedom of information activists.[146] A number of Anonymous attacks have hacked other targets, including game systems, the banking sector, and the transportation sector. In December 2010, Anonymous voiced its support of WikiLeaks, and began to hack major corporations, such as Amazon, PayPal, MasterCard, Visa, and the Swiss Bank PostFinance, that had succumbed to international pressure and stopped taking donations for the group.[147] The 2011 Bank of America document release is an example of a cyber attack in response to perceived improper business conduct. A representative of Anonymous has said that the "documents relate to the issue of whether Bank of America has improperly foreclosed on homes."[148]

Limitations

Anonymous' unity of purpose is not always a constant, however. While most of their operations can be considered successful, limits to their capabilities have also been shown amidst their larger successes. Operation: Payback, intended to cripple Amazon, one of the world's largest online retailers and hosting companies, for their decision to stop hosting any sites offering WikiLeaks content, suffered from a breakdown in coordination. Shortly before the planned attack, there was a disagreement about the target, with factions preferring instead to go after PayPal, which had stopped processing payments to WikiLeaks. While the PayPal faction did succeed at disabling that site, and the larger operation supporting WikiLeaks was considered a success, the resulting discord prevented Anonymous from reaching the mass of network traffic

---

[146]   Ibid.

[147]   "FBI Cracks Down on 'Anonymous' Over PayPal Hacking, Arrests 14," *International Business Times*, July 20, 2011, http://www.ibtimes.com/articles/183495/20110720/federal-bureau-of-investigation-fbi-paypal-online-security-anonymous-hacking-cyber-attack-wikileaks.htm, (accessed September 8, 2011).

[148]   Joe Rauch and Mark Hosenball, "Hacker group plans BofA e-mail release Monday," *AP Reuters*, March 13, 2011, http://ca.reuters.com/article/technologyNews/idCATRE72C3QA20110314, (accessed September 8, 2011).

needed to bring down its much more ambitious primary target: Amazon.[149]

Anonymous: Advantages and Disadvantages

Advantages

A loose coalition of Internet users, Anonymous is bound together through various social networking sites and imageboards. Further, the collective has neither a leader, nor a controlling entity. Ultimately, anyone who agrees with the Anonymous agenda can join the collective, as all members act independently to achieve the collective's greater goals. However, the mere act of being identified and attributed online as a member of the group serves as grounds for removal. As a result of this organizational structure, or rather lack thereof, Anonymous enjoys a number of advantages over its state and state-sanctioned counterparts:

- **The barriers to entry are inexpensive and low.** In several operations, crowd-sourced DDoS tools were employed – thus, to participate in a given operation one need only to know of and download the appropriate tool. The social networking sites and image board, while often providing the attacks tools also enable planning and coordination of forthcoming attacks.

- **Lean and agile organizational structure.** The flexible membership requirement allow for an easily adaptable organization. Further, the lack of central, or even regional, leadership allows for continuity of operations after law enforcement crackdowns.

- **Ability to achieve effects globally.** Since 2003, Anonymous has become a global network, with members worldwide. While physical presence is not necessary for operations that have effects abroad, it ensures that cyber

---

[149] Josh Halliday, "Operation Payback fails to take down Amazon in WikiLeaks revenge attack," *The Guardian,* December 9, 2010, http://www.guardian.co.uk/media/2010/dec/09/operation-payback-wikileaks-anonymous.

operations follow, and can in a timely manner, respond to local and regional political tensions, as well as kinetic conflicts. Further, a global presence can ensure the simultaneous coordination of cyber and physical protests.

- **Potential to leverage the Internet Underground to make alliances.** For example, in 2011 Anonymous cooperated with LulzSec on Operation AntiSec, a series of hacking attacks whose priority is to steal and leak any "classified government information, including email spools and documentation."[150] Primary targets have included the Government of Brazil and the United Kingdom's Serious Organized Crime Organization (SOCA).

While the aforementioned characteristics facilitate the relative ease with which executed operations can succeed, certain disadvantages impact Anonymous as well.

Disadvantages

- **Human capital.** Organizations like Anonymous are limited by the expertise of their membership. For precise operations, especially involving significant intelligence gathering on targeted organizations, a group like Anonymous would have to handpick those members that are capable of participating. However, since membership is open to virtually anyone who is capable of remaining "anonymous," expertise is not a prerequisite. Thus, if Anonymous were to ever carry out larger-scale, more sophisticated, and sustained attacks, it would be necessary to partner with other hackers or hacker group. To an extent, this has already occurred with Operation AntiSec. However, the potential for alliances through the underground can result in significant risks if Anonymous paired with extremist hackers, or agreed to team with an organization "sponsored" to execute attacks on behalf of a US state adversary.

---

[150] "LulzSec Teams With Anonymous, in Operation AntiSec," *Slashdot*, June 20, 2011, http://news.slashdot.org/story/11/06/20/1357223/LulzSec-Teams-With-Anonymous-In-Operation-AntiSec, (accessed September 8, 2011).

- **Organizational stability.** Advanced and sustained cyber operations require not only a unity of effort, but also stability of leadership, organization, and mission. While state adversaries may almost take such requirements as a given, these are not necessarily present in loosely organized non-state actors. Though Anonymous may be hedging its bets against having key leadership compromised by not having one, the group is simultaneously limiting its potential to achieve strategic effects.

- **Management.** Large scale operations, which have a greater change of achieving strategic effect, require project management capability, which is inherently difficult to achieve in a collective whose communication and collaboration is dependent on social media, chat rooms, and image boards.

- **Resources.** Significant resources may be necessary to sustain a disruptive impact against many targets. To date, Anonymous has not achieved sustained impacts; rather, most of their attacks have been of limited duration and specific in scope to a particular "hacktivist" cause.

Anonymous: Conclusion

Ultimately, Anonymous has demonstrated itself to be a highly destabilizing but limited scope collective of civil disobedience. Because the group's cyber operations are internally perceived as morally motivated, the collective has not prioritized causing significant economic costs.[151] Certainly, Visa, PayPal, MasterCard, and others have incurred losses, but these, within the greater context of the national economy, cannot be considered economically crippling. Rather, by going after financial targets and executing short-lived, as opposed to sustained, attacks, Anonymous has succeeded in becoming an attention grabbing, destabilizing force. The confidence that impacts of attacks by this group could be mitigated is necessary if cyber stability and security are to ever be achieved.

---

[151] Adam Murphy, "Anonymous: the Hacker Group/Peaceful Revolution," March 14, 2011, http://evtron.com/Evtron-Alpha/?p=2840, (accessed September 7, 2011).

The above case studies demonstrate the capabilities and limitations of malicious actors and their potential for strategic effects. The Anonymous case study is less about the current strategic effects of such "operations," but exhibits the potential for groups like Wikileaks and Anonymous to have an out-sized effect on cyberspace, nation-states, and the economy. Still, as emphasized at the beginning of this chapter, the cyber ecosystem is not populated by disruptive actors alone. In fact, defensive non-state actors have an extremely wide and deep presence both maintaining and existing within the global network.

Evolution of Cyber Conflict Involving Defensive Actors

Non-state actors also play a strong but largely unsung role on the defensive side of cyber conflict. *A major finding of this study is that non-state actors play critical roles on defense; indeed their role is arguably even more important than the state.* These companies, associations, universities and collaborative efforts fulfill multiple roles and have different motivations to contribute to defense. These motivations range from simply conducting cyber security research to a desire to make a profit to volunteering their time and resources to uncovering the tactics and identities of adversaries or improving security tools.

An important aspect of the defensive side of cyber conflict is the collaboration of individuals, groups, academics, and companies coming together – especially to conduct ad hoc response or collaborate on specific projects. At many levels there exists activity that organizes against the efforts and innovations of disruptive non-state actors. While a full survey of this diverse set of actors is difficult, this typology of actors, motivations, and activity can illuminate the roles they play in the cyber ecosystem and demonstrate their capabilities for strategic impact.

Categories of Actors

The breadth of actors on the defensive side of cyber conflict is at least as diverse as malicious and disruptive actors. These defensive actors vary in size and engagement, but all play multiple roles in maintaining the health of the cyber ecosystem.

Individuals

Individual and corporate users represent a very diverse and diffuse category of actors. However their aggregate impact on defensive efforts cannot be understated. Without users enabling and continually upgrading anti-virus software, applying patches, reporting incidents of hacking, and practicing good digital hygiene the effectiveness of many higher-level efforts to combat malicious activity would be severely degraded. They are also frequently the targets of ground-level malicious activity, usually for the purposes of criminal activity, such as the stealing of identity of banking information, and the construction of botnets. Transitioning from a target to a facilitator, for instance a virus turning the user's computer into part of a botnet without their knowledge, is far from uncommon and represents the majority of botnet zombies.[152]

Commercial Enterprise Users

Like individuals, businesses are simultaneously users, targets, and sometimes facilitators. E-commerce has been a major driver of economic growth. Each year, more and more businesses are taking their goods and services online to save costs and reach more consumers. Financial data collected or held by these companies is of great value to attackers in the Internet underground looking to finance their operations. Spoofing or phishing to trick customers into giving their information to seemingly legitimate sites or downloading disguised malware has become common. The use of DDoS attacks as a cover for exploiting security vulnerability in a company's network has also been on the rise. If a site has been compromised without detection, customer data is at severe risk and company resources may be used in other attacks. Even if not, the loss of productivity, intellectual property, as well as costs of

---

[152] Brian Prince, "US Home to Most Botnet PCs," *eWeek.com,* October 14, 2010, http://www.eweek.com/c/a/Security/Microsoft-US-Home-to-Most-Botnet-PCs-216614/ (accessed 10/7/2011)

defense and securing data when combatting intrusive attackers or experiencing a DDoS can be staggering.

Technology Producers

Technology producers are also key to fundamental defense in the provider and improver roles. In the United States, private manufacturers and software companies have long been drivers in innovation, satisfying the ever-increasing consumer and governmental desire for computing power and applications. Attackers can, and frequently do, exploit vulnerabilities in hardware and software. Designing technology products with security in mind can preempt vulnerabilities and limit the severity of attempts to compromise the product.[153] Private companies are also a source of security training, with firms such as Microsoft offering education in securing its products as well as organizations such as SANS Institute or Black Hat providing professional development opportunities.[154]

Fortunately there exist several incentives for defensive activity at the user and producer level. The presence of malicious code on a computer frequently causes unwanted, even crippling behavior. Crashes, data corruption, and reduced performance can impact daily activity causing minor annoyance to the loss of unique data.[155] Additionally, as more and more consumer shopping is done online, the risk to financial information and other personal data is a powerful concern more prevalent in individuals' minds than ever before. Likewise, intellectual property is now widely seen as the key to competiveness in the information economy.[156] For technology

---

[153]   Google, "Security Overview," *The Chromium Projects,* http://www.chromium.org/chromium-os/chromiumos-design-docs/security-overview (accessed October 6, 2011).

[154]   "Training Courses," *SANS,* http://www.sans.org/security-training/courses.php (accessed October 7, 2011).

[155]   "Impact of Computer Virus," Virus Protection, 2006, http://www.adprevent.com/Free_anti_virus_protection_removal_software_download/Impact_of_Computer_Virus.html.

[156]   Robert J. Shapiro and Kevin A. Hassett, "The Economic Value of Intellectual Propery," *SONECON,* October, 2005, http://www.sonecon.com/docs/studies/IntellectualPropertyReport-October2005.pdf (accessed October 6, 2011), 3.

producers, the risks of loss of consumer confidence and competitive advantage, and subsequently a loss of business, are powerful motivators for technology producers to patch vulnerabilities and design from a security standpoint. The integrity of their own systems is also of critical importance, both to protect their intellectual property and avoid costly disruptions of productivity or service.[157]

Security Industry

One of the main reasons for the increased public awareness of the importance of personal computer security has been the rise of a professional security industry to fill the roles of responder, provider, and improver. After it became clear that the Internet had some severe security flaws in the design, and that it was only a matter of time before malicious attackers exploited those flaws to cause disruption and impact legitimate users. Security companies, like McAfee and Symantec, arose to provide consumer level anti-virus software to fill the now evident need for people and businesses to protect their computers from disruptive code and intrusions. These companies have since grown and now offer a wide range of services, including Secure Socket Layer (SSL) certification, database security, security management, risk assessment, research on emerging threats, and compliance assistance. Commercial anti-spam service providers and botnet hunters, such as Fire Eye and Damballa have also developed services to combat malware and viruses.[158]

Academia

Universities and academia were early adopters of the Internet and also took note of the rise of malicious activity since its creation. They have proven to be engaged actors in the cyber ecosystem, as both proactive improvers and, occasionally, targets for malicious

---

[157] "The Impact of Worms and Viruses," *Check Point,* http://www.checkpoint.com/securitycafe/readingroom/internal_security/imp act_of_worms_viruses.html.

[158] Christopher S. Stewart, "FireEye: Botnet Busters," *Business Week,* June 16, 2011, http://www.businessweek.com/magazine/content/11_26/b423407271 2001.htm.

activity. Universities have always been tied to the development of computing systems and the network as well as the technologies to protect them, improving the ecosystem. This connection now continues in two important ways.

The first is, as one might expect, by conducting research on emerging cyber issues, identifying trends, creating frameworks of understanding, and using analysis of available data to draw conclusions or recommendations. Universities with sustained programs in cyber security and cyber conflict can lead to institutional areas of focus that provide resources and a collaborative mindset to the larger security community. For example, the University of Toronto's Munk School of Global Affairs' participation in the Information Warfare Monitor helped uncover a number of large scale cyber-attacks in 2010.[159] This research activity also serves to develop the next generation of cyber professionals, a key function for developing and maintaining long-term national defensive capabilities.

Some of this research, and the individuals conducting it, will yield immediate results suitable for practical, commercial application. This frequently results in startup "spin off" companies offering new and innovative defensive technologies or approaches to the government or other non-state actors. An illustrative example of one such company is Damballa, a cyber security firm specializing in anti-botnet activity. Using technology the founders developed at Georgia Tech, Damballa takes a unique approach to neutralizing the threat of botnets.[160] Rather than focus on finding and removing the malware itself, their methods revolve around degrading the command and control channels botnet owners use to mobilize infected computers. Once detected and neutralized, they begin a forensic process to attempt to track the botnet operators.[161]

---

[159]   "Shadows in the Cloud: An investigation into cyber espionage 2.0," *Infowar Monitor,* April 5, 2010, http://www.infowar-monitor.net/2010/04/shadows-in-the-cloud-an-investigation-into-cyber-espionage-2-0/.

[160]   "Damballa," *Georgia Research Alliance,* 2011, http://www.gra.org/Commercialization/CommercializationDetail/tabid/621/xmid/1158/Default.aspx.

[161]   Damballa, "About Damballa," 2011, http://www.damballa.com/company/.

Critical Infrastructure

Protecting the power grid, financial sector, and other essential services has been identified as a high priority for national security efforts. The embrace of IT in these sectors, such as SmartGrid in the electric power industry, has allowed them to operate more efficiently and effectively, but also places them at increased risk of disruption from cyber attacks. In response to these challenges, the Department of Homeland Security has coordinated the formation of many public private partnerships to protect critical infrastructure since the 2003 Presidential Directive on Critical Infrastructure Identification, Prioritization, and Protection.[162] There has been much discussion of the value and role of these public/private partnerships, but they remain a point of controversy in the public debate, as evidenced by the clashes over various pieces of proposed cybersecurity legislation on Capitol Hill.

Network Operators

Due to their daily and necessary role of keeping the network functioning, essentially "providing cyberspace" in terms of user experience, network operators and hosting play a key defensive role as responders, providers, and improvers. This category of actors is particularly diverse given the varied entities that must work in concert to enable network functionality, but some illustrative examples follow below.

ISPs, such as Comcast and AT&T, routinely observe and manage traffic along their networks. In the event of a strategic level cyber attack, their cooperation will be crucial to detecting, identifying, and potentially isolating the sources of malicious traffic. For instance, if a botnet was being employed to facilitate an attack, ISPs would be able to identify users' computers infected and suspend their access to the Internet, disabling portions of the attacking force.[163]

---

[162]   Jody R. Westby, *International Guide to Cyber Security* (American Bar Association: Chicago IL, 2004), 21

[163]   "The Role of Internet Service Providers in Cyber Security," *Institute for Homeland Security Solutions*, June 2009, https://www.ihssnc.org/portals/0/PubDocuments/ISP-Provided_Security_Rowe.pdf.

The Domain Name System (DNS) is another crucial network management function. The DNS converts web addresses into their numerical equivalents and connects users to their destination. Maintaining the integrity of the DNS is essential to preserving public confidence of the reliability of the network.[164] Dominant application and search providers like Google can also substantially contribute to the security effort. They do this both by providing and securing their own services as well as improving the ecosystem by promoting awareness and adding their intellectual and financial resources to organizations dedicated to the security effort such as CERTs and the National Cyber Security Alliance.[165] Network providers can also act to foster security culture, partnering with security vendors and consumer groups to encourage, or in some cases enforce through penalties or the threat of disconnection, adoption of improved security measures and responsible activity in cyberspace.

CERT Community

Computer Emergency Response Teams (CERTs/CIRTs) have emerged in the responder role as valuable centers of daily coordination between targets of malicious attacks and security experts. At the national level, the CERT Coordinating Center, hosted by Carnegie Mellon, acts a "twenty-four-hour-a-day point of contact to respond to security emergencies on the Internet."[166] It's important to note that while hosted and operated privately, CERT-CC does receive funding from diverse sources (including government), emphasizing its cross cutting role,. Important activities include confidential vulnerability assessments, distinguishing between individual incidents and larger patterns of attack, coordination between victims of a larger attack, assisting law enforcement with tracking down attackers, and assisting technology producers with developing and deploying patches to address vulnerabilities.

---

[164]   D. Atkins and R. Austein, "Threat Analysis of the Domain Name System," *Internet Society,* August 2004, http://tools.ietf.org/html/rfc3833.

[165]   "Google Joins National Cyber Security Alliance (NCSA) Board of Directors," *PR Newswire*, August 12, 2009, http://staysafeonline.mediaroom.com/index.php?s=43&item=47.

[166]   Rattray, *Strategic Warfare in Cyberspace*, 381.

This CERT model has been replicated in several industries and organizations below the national level, including the manufacturing, academic, and banking industries.[167] CERTs have been created in many countries and companies around the world and both CERTs and some of their larger backers, such as Microsoft and Cisco, use CERT forums to improve international coordination with one another.[168] While CERTs do strive to conduct research on improving security generally and to promote security issues through education, they are fundamentally reactive organizations by nature.[169] They have been very successful in their roles as a central point of contact for emergencies as well as coordinating the response to specific incidents. However their lack of authority over other actors and limited personnel keep CERTs as valuable resources for mitigating damage during attack but have yet to step up as leaders in national level strategic response.[170]

Cyber Security Collaboratives

As security challenges have gotten more complex and organized, so too have non-state efforts to combat that activity. Collaborative groups drawing from all types of actors discussed above have been developed to better pool resources and coordinate response to malicious activity. These groups take on multiple roles, including responders and improvers, and can generally be divided into two types: sustained and ad-hoc.

Sustained collaborative groups are ongoing and fluid associations of actors that conduct regular activity on their organizing issue. Examples include the Honeynet Project, the Internet Storm Center, the Shadowserver Foundation, and Stop Badware. The Honeynet Project is an international organization founded in 1999 that focuses on researching defensive tools and gathering information on malicious actor motivations and tactics. They also promote awareness of cyber hygiene and available

---

[167] Jody R. Westby, *International guide to Cyber Security* (American Bar Association: Chicago IL, 2004), 141-143
[168] "Alphabetical List of FIRST Members," *FIRST: Improving Security Together*, 2011, http://first.org/members/teams/index.html.
[169] Ibid., 141.
[170] Rattray, *Strategic Warfare in Cyberspace*, 381.

defensive tools.[171] The Internet Storm Center is a program of the SANS Technology Institute that has been monitoring malicious incidents since before 2000. It is completely voluntary, and "succeeds through active participation of people who use firewalls and intrusion detection systems and who understand how sharing the data from those systems is a powerful way to help themselves and the entire Internet community." [172] The mission of the Shadowserver Foundation is to "understand and put an end to high stakes cyber crime" by gathering intelligence on "the darker side" of the Internet. The Foundation is comprised of volunteers, who gather, track and report on malware and botnet activity as well as on electronic fraud. [173] Stop Badware originated at Harvard University's Berkman Center for Internet and Society in 2006.[174] It is currently an independent non-profit organization that focuses on how to protect users from viruses, spyware and other malware.

Some groups, however, arise out of a specific short-term need that brings together various non-state actors to respond, such as the Conficker working group, Shadows in the Cloud, and Project Grey Goose. The first consists of an initiative comprised of corporations such as Microsoft, non-profits such as Shadowserver Foundation, international organizations like ICANN, universities, government organizations, and volunteers whose mission is minimize damage incurred by the spread of the Conficker Worm.[175] The Conficker case is examined in more depth in Chapter 5. Shadows in the Cloud was a comprehensive report issued by the Information Warfare Monitor and the Shadowserver Foundation which detailed a massive espionage effort originating from the People's Republic of China against individuals and organizations associated with the Dalai Lama. The investigation uncovered the source servers, analyzed the

---

[171] "About the Honeynet Project," *The Honeynet Project*,
       http://www.honeynet.org/about.
[172] http://isc.sans.edu/
[173] Shadowserver Foundation, "Mission," December 31, 2005,
       http://www.shadowserver.org/wiki/pmwiki.php/Shadowserver/Mission.
[174] http://stopbadware.org/
[175] See their webpage for more info
       (http://www.confickerworkinggroup.org/wiki/pmwiki.php/Main/HomePage)
       or the case study on Conficker later in this chapter.

attacking tools, and recovered copies of many of the stolen files. [176] The capability to form such short-term alliances to respond to a rapidly developing situation is a distinct advantage of non-state actors, however these efforts tend to be goal oriented do not last once the issue has been addressed.

Parallel to the development of collaborative groups has been the idea of crowdsourcing security. The theory behind this is that by making technology and computer code open to everyone, the scrutiny of individual users with diverse backgrounds will more rapidly expose vulnerabilities that can then be fixed. This philosophy can not only improve general purpose software and operating systems such as Linux and Apache, but there is a growing stable of security tools created by open source software developers like Nessus (vulnerability scanning) and Sn0rt (intrusion detection).[177] This means the Open-Source community are improvers of the ecosystem but can also act as providers of fixes for community developed software.

Non-State Actors and the Potential for Defensive Strategic Effect

Non-state actors have found many avenues to bring collaborative capability to defense and resilience of the cyber ecosystem. Their activity in defense of the network is multi-layered and widespread. Importantly, they have become trusted sources of security information, often able to disseminate information faster and more openly than governments raising awareness of the rising cyber threats to states and companies. For example, the Information Warfare Monitor has helped pioneer an "open source" or "crowd source" analysis of cyber intrusions, as discussed above. Similarly, journalists and companies have released previously unknown

---

[176] "Shadows in the Cloud: An investigation into cyber espionage 2.0," *Infowar Monitor*, April 5, 2010, http://www.infowar-monitor.net/2010/04/shadows-in-the-cloud-an-investigation-into-cyber-espionage-2-0/.

[177] Cynthia Harvey, "Ten Open Source Security Apps Worth Considering," *Datamation*, April 27, 2007, http://itmanagement.earthweb.com/secu/article.php/11076_3673721_1/Ten-Open-Source-Security-Apps-Worth-Considering.htm.

information on key security events that might have been expected to come from government. In February 2011 information was shared about intrusions into oil and gas companies, revealed by McAfee[178], and an intrusion into a NASDAQ network brought to light by the *Wall Street Journal*.[179] Symantec was one of the first to produce and release a comprehensive breakdown and assessment of the highly sophisticated Stuxnet virus.[180] There are also numerous informal collaboration mechanisms, including the North American Network Operators Group (NANOG) and Shadowserver, where network operators identify and analyze emerging threats, crack encrypted communication channels, provide information to affected parties and orchestrate collaborative responses.[181]

Protectors of the status quo can also realize strategic effects through botnet reduction. With many of the large-scale attacks in recent years, such as those experienced by Estonia as described in the preceding case study, enabled by the significant attacking power botnets have given non-state actors on offense, botnets have become cyber weapons of strategic significance. Defensive efforts to degrade or destroy these bot networks greatly reduce the strategic capability of a potential cyber attacker. Reducing botnets cleans up the cyber commons and helps narrow the space malicious actors can call a safe haven in addition to its tangible impact on reducing the effectiveness of malicious activity, including DDoS attacks. Presently, botnet reduction is largely a private-sector   initiative   with   occasional   government

---

[178]   McAfee, "Global Energy Attacks: Night Dragon," White Paper, February 10, 2011, http://161.69.13.40/us/resources/white-papers/wp-global-energy-cyberattacks-night-dragon.pdf (accessed December 9, 2011).

[179]   Devlin Barret, "Hackers Penetrate Nasdaq Computers," *Wall Street Journal*, February 5, 2011, http://online.wsj.com/article/SB10001424052748704709304576124502351634690.html, (accessed February 11, 2011).

[180]   Nicolas Falliere, Liam O. Murchu, and Eric Chien, "W32. Stuxnet Dossier," *Symantec Security Response*, February 2011, http://www.symantec.com/content/en/us/enterprise/media/security_response/whitepapers/w32_stuxnet_dossier.pdf.

[181]   See the websites for NANOG and Shadowserver Foundation at http://www.merit.edu/nanog/ and http://www.shadowserver.org/wiki/.

collaboration. [182] Besides US-based security companies and collaborative efforts, the activity against botnets is occurring worldwide, with a number of private initiatives and governmental actions. EU nations like Germany, Finland, and the Netherlands, as well as Australia, Japan, and APCERT all have active private sector initiatives and partnerships with law enforcement.[183]

If some nations engage with nationalistic, malicious non-state cyber actors to create alliances, the US and other like-minded governments must appropriately respond. In order to do so, the government must work closely with non-state actors to build counterbalancing alliances for defensive purposes, reduce the risks of cyber attacks, improve resiliency, and preserve free speech, privacy and commerce in cyberspace.

Advantages and Disadvantages of Non-State Actors on the Defense

Advantages

Defensive non-state actors benefit from a number of advantages in cyberspace. Most importantly, they are globally distributed and are in control of most technical operations in cyberspace.

- **Operational Control of the Network.** Non-state actors control most operations in cyberspace. If motivated and enabled, these actors can do much to stop attacks and identify source of malicious activity. Most targets during a cyber conflict are likely to be non-state assets. Not only is 85% to 90% of critical infrastructure owned and operated by the private sector, but make up the

---

[182]   Yurie Ito, "Managing Global Cyber Health and Security Through Risk Reduction," Unpublished Thesis, July 18, 2011, 21.

[183]   Giles Hogben, "Botnets: Measurement, Detection, Disinfection, and Defense," *The European Network and Information Security Agency (ENISA)*, 2011, http://www.enisa.europa.eu/act/res/botnets/botnets-measurement-detection-disinfection-and-defence/at_download/fullReport (accessed October 6, 2011).

preponderance of cyberspace users.[184] Moreover, non-state actors are responsible for finding significant numbers of vulnerabilities (researchers and companies) and producing patches for them (technology producers).

• **Flexible Organization and Governance.** Though they lack the resources of a national intelligence or law enforcement organizations, non-state actors also lack the legal and territorial restrictions those groups face. Law enforcement officers must follow strict procedures on gathering evidence and intelligence collectors have tight restrictions, such as not collecting on their own citizens. And neither can act where they lack clear authorization. Non-state actors typically lack many of these restrictions. Similarly, if a line of inquiry or experimentation is not fruitful they are under no obligation to continue spending resources on it. Many of their technocratic peers are happy to share information with non-state groups looking to stop malicious activity – even though they might balk at a similar request coming from a law enforcement organization that did not have a search warrant. As Yurie Ito highlights, "A key factor in establishing effective cyber health and security regime will be an ability to modify or stop using approaches that have become ineffective and look for more effective models and approaches."[185] This concept is explained in more depth in Chapter 5.

• **Access to Technology Resources.** Non-state actors have access to subject matter experts within their companies, universities, or even through leveraging social networks. This augments one of the most significant advantages for non-state actors: their agility. A bureaucracy responding to a fast-paced cyber incident is limited not only by its delegated authorities, but by agreements it has in place with other domestic and international organizations. However, non-state groups can work together far more

---

[184]   Eileen R. Larence. "Critical Infrastructure Protection: Progress Coordinating Government and Private Sector Efforts Varies by Sectors' Characteristics." *US Government Accountability Office.* October 2006, 1.

[185]   Ito, "Managing Global Cyber Health and Security Through Risk Reduction," 11.

easily, lacking legal constraints or concern over legal precedent. In addition, non-state actors can take advantage of innovative tactics and technologies made available by collaborative efforts that would be extremely difficult for risk-averse public ministries to take.

- **Rapid Global Collaboration.** Non-state actors can set up ad-hoc collaboration with fewer legal impediments than states. For example, when presented with evidence of a massive intrusion, possibly by a foreign state, the response of many governments is to hand it to counterintelligence specialists for a classified, prolonged investigation. When presented with the same challenge, the researchers of the Information Warfare Monitor went public, exposing and embarrassing the Chinese government.[186] Google went ever farther, going public with their investigation while it was still underway, encouraging and empowering other non-state actors to participate in the investigation and publish their findings.[187] This approach of outsourcing, open-sourcing and crowdsourcing attribution is one a government would have tremendous difficulties executing on its own.

Disadvantages

- **Authority and Legitimacy.** A fundamental disadvantage to non-state actors on the defense is a lack of authority or legitimacy to conduct certain active defensive operations. There are laws preventing certain activity from corporations and in still other areas serious questions about what is acceptable activity and autonomy for non-state actors in various roles during an

---

[186] "Shadows in the Cloud: An investigation into cyber espionage 2.0," *Infowar Monitor*, April 5, 2010, http://www.infowar-monitor.net/2010/04/shadows-in-the-cloud-an-investigation-into-cyber-espionage-2-0/.

[187] Kristin M. Lord and Travis Sharp. "America's Cyber Future: Security and Prosperity in the Information Age Vol. 2" *Center for New American Security*. June, 2011, http://www.cnas.org/files/documents/publications/CNAS_Cyber_Volume%20II.pdf (accessed October 11, 2011), 74, 117.

attack. In particular, US non-state actors are constrained by the strictures of the 1986 Computer Fraud and Abuse Act, which makes it a crime to "hack back" or gain unauthorized access to a computer, even if it is engaged in criminal or offensive activity. Finally, the private sector actors have no authority to command one another, making certain important processes such as standards-setting and information reporting difficult.

- **Collaboratives are Fragile.** Legitimate non-state actors, from individuals to collaborative groups, tend to lack the organizational staying power of nation states. While states may exist for hundreds of years, continually building and evolving institutions, it is not uncommon for companies to fold and collaborative groups to dissolve. This inherent instability provides for certain key pieces of information to "slip through the cracks" as well as impeding efforts to develop or preserve an organizational memory about how to deal with certain threats or examine emerging ones.

- **Human Capital.** Non-state actors will tend to have smaller levels of human resources with fewer guarantees of needed skill sets in the long term to conduct sophisticated cyber operations. This lack of depth may force collaboration as an operation necessity, an approach unsustainable for a distinct organization. Effectiveness of personnel and partnerships will vary between management styles and operating environments. Finally, challenges posed by generational change may force some actors to shut down as their founders and key personnel transition out of the workforce.

- **Resources.** Non-state actors must be able to keep themselves financially solvent, and defensive actors will likely not be able to pursue illegal or illegitimate means to do so. Furthermore, private companies will be under scrutiny from shareholders and owners to provide a profit, whereas nonprofit groups and associations will face considerable and fluctuating budget pressures. Without the stable revenue of a state tax base, non state actors will face considerable pressure to make profits, and thus need to justify diverting those profits to defensive security efforts, or to operate on a nonprofit's tight and uncertain business model. Non-state actors also typically lack access to classified material as well as the institutional resources to gather and analyze such information.

Case Study

The following case study highlight the potential impact of non-state actors in defensive efforts, and will apply the strengths and weaknesses framework described above.

Estonia

In previous sections of this chapter, we have examined the significance of the cyber attacks on Estonia in 2007. Experts have claimed such attacks were the first instances of a "cyberwar" because of the politicized nature of the conflict, the numerous players involved, and the near invocation of NATO Article 5. Numerous cyber experts, practitioners and policy makers alike, have analyzed the conflict in terms of the players involved, the targets exploited, and their short- and long-term effects on the Estonian economy, the legal frameworks surrounding cyber security, and the stability of the international political order. However, perhaps the most noteworthy aspect of this incident has remained largely unexplored: the defensive collaboration between numerous non-state actors that emerged in Estonia. It is the aim of this case study to demonstrate the nature and implications of such collaboration by the defensive players in this cyber conflict.

Collaborative Reponses

Given the political context in which the cyber attacks were executed, Estonian officials were not incorrect in suspecting that Russia, or Russian hackers were behind this sustained and targeted onslaught. However without cooperation between several sets of non-state actors, including network operators, CERTs, and security professionals, such suspicions would lack support. These actors worked together to pool technical resources and leverage their control over the network to identify the source of the attacks and use that information to inform the defensive response of state and non-state actors alike.

Attributing the Attacks

Estonian officials and security experts were able to quickly identify some of the attackers by their Internet address; while many of these addresses were Russian, some were determined to belong to Russian state institutions.[188] This Estonian cyber conflict offers particularly valuable insight into the problem of attribution. That is, while high confidence attribution of the technical source of the attacks may be difficult to achieve, political context and historic trends can suggest probable culprits and provide direction for determining response. For instance, Merit Kopli, the editor of Postimees, one of the newspapers whose website was compromise remarked, "The cyber-attacks are from Russia. There is no question. It's political." Russia's ambassador in Brussels retaliated, claiming, "If you are implying [the attacks] came from Russia or the Russian government, it's a serious allegation that has to be substantiated."[189] In practice, Mikko Hypponen of F-Secure, a Finnish security company also wasn't fully convinced the attacks were directly linked to the Russian government, noting, "There is just one IP address that leads to a government computer. It is of course possible that an attack was launched from there, too, but the person behind it could be anyone, from the son of some ministerial janitor upwards."[190] In actuality, full-scale attacks such as these can originate from a number of infected machines worldwide, all part of a botnet, making it nearly impossible to identity the command and control center. Still, according to CERT-EE, the attacks mainly, although not exclusively, originated from sources outside of Estonia, and information provided by Arbor Networks demonstrated that the attacks were sourced worldwide, coming from as many as 178 countries.[191]

Public-Private Collaboration

The response to the attacks was coordinated by CERT-EE, with

---

[188]   Ibid

[189]   Ibid.

[190]   Anderson, "Massive DDoS Attacks Target Estonia; Russia Accused."

[191]   Tikk, Kaska and Vihul, *International Cyber Incidents: Legal Considerations*, 23.

the help of system administrators from both within and without the country.[192] The CERT team organized an online chat room, where defenders from across the geographic region and from all relevant organizations could exchange information and provide the Estonian authorities with real-time intelligence on attack targets and types, as well as communicate simultaneously with foreign CERTs and the international Internet security operations community.[193] Cooperation between the public and the private sectors was epitomized in the core team of defenders, which consisted of Hillar Aarelaid, head of CERT-EE; Kurtis Lindqvist, the man in charge of running Stockholm-based Netnod, which directs global Internet traffic; Patrik Fältström, an advisor appointed to the Swedish government in 2003 who has worked with the Internet and the DNS since 1987; and Bill Woodcock of Packet Clearing House. Aarelaid and his team began to track the sources of the attacks almost immediately, eventually finding a botnet comprising of mostly hijacked computers in the US

> "As Aarelaid identified a specific address, Woodcock and Lindqvist sent rapid-fire emails to network operators throughout the world asking for the IP to be blocked at the source. Their goal was to block traffic before it could enter Estonia's major international connections. One by one, they picked off the bots, and by dawn they had deflected the attackers. Internet traffic into the country hovered just above normal."[194]

Among the first technical responses to the Denial of Service attacks was the gradual increase of bandwidth of state information servers in order to allow for greater data traffic handling capacity and the filtering out of the malicious traffic. Other technical security measures included the application of security patches, firewalling,

---

[192] Ibid., 24.

[193] Gadi Evron, "Battling Botnets and Online Mobs: Estonia's Defense Efforts During the Internet War," *Science and Technology,* Winter/Spring 2008, www.bligoo.com/media/users/1/50369/files/Ataque%20Estonia.pdf.

[194] Davis, "Hackers Take Down the Most Wired Country in Europe."

use of attack detection systems, using multiple servers and/or connections, and blocking access. [195] Much of the defensive collaboration was enabled by the ISPs, which helped to reduce the data transmission capacity of incoming international connections to Estonia. While this certainly blocked a number of incoming attacks, it also blocked "genuine traffic." [196] Temporarily shutting off Estonia's connection to the global Internet proved a vital, though costly, component to the defensive effort to combat the attacks.

Ultimately, what made the Estonian response to the attacks memorable, was that necessary channels of communications had been established prior to the attacks, the individuals who made up the command structure that emerged as the public and private sector worked together was young, connected, and not limited by the structures of government bureaucracies. [197]

International Cooperation: NATO

The Ministry of Defense (MoD) organized international support for Estonia, informing the European Union and NATO, of which Estonia is a member, about the ongoing cyber attacks. In response, several member states offered to limit the attacks passing through their cyber territories. Though the issue was considered, Estonia chose not to formally invoke NATO Article 5, which deems that an attacks against one member state is an attack against the Alliance. Estonia did decide to request assistance in the form of points of contacts from NATO member states. While the US governmental institutions assisted in locating and shutting down sources of attack, foreign partners like CERT Finland were instrumental in providing contacts and assistance in reaching service providers and computer incident response coordination entities of other countries. [198] Tikk, et al, note that as news of international assistance became publicized, the number of incoming attacks gradually diminished. [199]

---

[195] Tikk, Kaska and Vihul, *International Cyber Incidents: Legal Considerations*, 24.
[196] Ibid.
[197] Bill Woodcock, "Lessons Learned From the Russia-Estonian Cyber Conflict," *Packet Clearing House*, June, 2007, lacnic.net/documentos/ixp/woodcock-caso_estonia.pdf.
[198] Tikk, Kaska and Vihul, *International Cyber Incidents: Legal Considerations*, 24.
[199] Ibid.

Organizing for Collective Self-Defense: The Cyber Defense League and the NATO Cooperative Cyber Defense Centre of Excellence (NATO CCD COE)

The Russian-Estonian cyber conflict and the subsequent successful collaboration between the public and private sectors sparked the creation of the Estonian Cyber Defense League in 2011. The aim was to create a National Cyber Defense Unit, intended to operate as part of the Total Defense League, Estonia's all-volunteer paramilitary force that operates as part of Estonia's national defense infrastructure and financed, in part, by the Ministry of Defense.[200] Filling the roles of responder and improver, the Total Defense League was erected to bring together cyber defense experts from the private sector and various government agencies, with the goal of conducting regular exercises and, according to Defense Minister Jaak Aaviksoo, engaging in cyber contingency planning.[201] To ensure that the objectives and activities of the new organization are in line with Estonian priorities, as well as NATO objectives in this field, a special liaison group will correlate its intelligence with the CCDCOE, further discussed below. Aaviksoo has said the main risk in cyber battles is "not technological, but a matter of strategic management, it is a question of how well we are prepared to react to attacks and how well the subsequent decision making processes are set in motion."[202] For this reason, the Cyber Defense Unit is comprised of 100 people tasked with organizing training, seminars, and exercises for experts in the field of cyber defense, to enable the acquiring of and sharing of practical cyber defense skills.[203]

---

[200] Gerard O'Dwyer, "Estonian MoD Proposes Cyber Defense Unit," DefenseNews, January 27, 2011, http://www.defensenews.com/story.php?i=5556484.

[201] Ibid.

[202] "Aaviksoo: exchanging experience is the key in averting cyber attacks," Estonian Ministry of Defense, April 11, 2010, http://www.mod.ee/en/aaviksoo-exchanging-experience-is-the-key-in-averting-cyber-attacks.

[203] Government formed Cyber Defence Unit of the Defence League," Estonian Ministry of Defense, 20 January 2011, http://www.kmin.ee/en/government-formed-cyber-defence-unit-of-the-defence-league, (accessed September 2, 2011).

Advantages and Disadvantages

The Estonian response is now widely considered a success in mounting defensive cyber operations. Its strengths should be examined but it was not without its drawbacks which are also worthy of consideration.

Advantages

- **Operational Control of the Network:** International coordination was a key aspect of the response efforts, and some of the measures undertaken had international impact. In particular, Estonian ISPs closing off that country's international connectivity for a period of time prevented a large volume of incoming DDoS traffic from reaching their targets. But it also completely isolated Estonia, and any traffic that would be routed through it, from the global network.

- **Flexible Organization and Governance:** Non-state actors such as ISPs, CERTs, and media institutions were able to engage with the changing situation by reaching out to one another, exchanging information, and experimenting with defensive efforts. They were able to do so as quickly as the situation required, without long approval processes, political considerations, and entanglements common to national governments.

- **Access to Technology Resources:** Response coordination efforts were not simply between institutional actors or between CERTs and governments. Responders were able to directly access the expertise of a wide array of information security professionals without requiring a significant formal coordination or approval.

- **Rapid Global Collaboration:** Preexisting procedures and forums for cooperating against a cyber threat such as CERTs, network operators, and information clearing houses made response efforts considerably easier to for actors to participate in. These response efforts were international in nature as well as domestic.

Disadvantages

- **Authority and Legitimacy**: Even though private sector efforts to resist the attacks were numerous and in some cases successful, state help was required for certain courses of action. The involvement of the defense ministry, as well as the political pressure applied against Russia while gaining international support for Estonia, were not spearheaded by the private sector. NATO, an international organization of governments, was seen as a place for an offensive response to the attack to be given legitimacy and now provides legitimacy for institutions created to respond to future attacks in Estonia and elsewhere.

- **Collaboratives are Fragile:** Once the attacks subsided, the Estonian response was held up as a useful model to other nations. But it required state support, both Estonian and internationally, to ultimately institutionalize the level of cooperation desired in the future in the form of the Cyber Defense League.

- **Human capital:** While responders did the best they could, this was an unprecedented attack in its political intent and nature up to that point in time. The system administrators and CTOs of the targeted financial, news, and government systems did not necessarily possess the national security background to understand what was happening. It took time and coordination from a larger segment of professionals, including those inside the government, for non-state actors to identify an appropriate, effective response.

- **Resources:** Targets of the attacks quickly found themselves out of bandwidth and out of options to respond with. Attempts were made to strip sites to the bare minimum of content, containing no graphics or extraneous material, but were insufficient. Ultimately it took ISPs closing the chokepoint of the international connection to regain control of the situation.

Estonia: Conclusion

The cyber conflict between Russia and Estonia was particularly demonstrative of the potential of successful defensive collaboration by non-state actors. Though the Estonians' "main line of defense was to close down the sites under attack to foreign Internet addresses, in order to try to keep them accessible to domestic users," they required the cooperation of domestic and foreign ISPs, as well as government officials and freelancing security experts. With the help of officials from NATO member states, multinational organizations, and ISPs, the Estonian response team was able to track, trace, and identify the attackers.[204] Out of this ad-hoc collaboration on the defense emerged the world's first "cyber militia," the Estonian Cyber Defense Unit. To date, no "democratic country in the world has a comparable force" as soldiers are willing to "put themselves under a single paramilitary command to defend the country's cyber infrastructure."[205]

The Estonian case serves as an excellent example of non-state actors reacting and collaborating for defensive purposes during a conflict. This is a useful corrective to the standard, monomaniacal focus on the offensive threat from non-state actors, since defensive actors are also a valuable strategic asset that should be considered when developing policy.

Recommendations

Cyberspace has evolved as a largely open and permissive environment. Its technological foundations make it accessible to a wide range of actors to pursue their goals in a malicious manner

---

[204]   Traynor, "Russia accused of unleashing cyberwar to disable Estonia."

[205]   Jorge Benitez, "Estonia Develops Volunteer Cyber Defense Force and Considers Drafting Techies," Atlantic Council, January 13, 2011, http://www.acus.org/natosource/estonia-develops-volunteer-cyber-defense-force-and-considers-drafting-techies, (accessed September 4, 2011).

and cyber conflict and its management have begun to emerge as a major dimension of this environment that government and private sector leaders must address if we wish to continue to reap its benefits. Chapter One illuminated the fundamental challenge of cyber stability as one that must be addressed. The empowerment of non-state actors at this point in time adds to concerns over cyber instability and we must begin to address these problems. Key focus areas should include:

- Supporting growing efforts to establish a clean, safe and secure cyber ecosystem to improve strategic stability by making key attack capabilities such as botnets much less accessible and powerful, especially to disruptive non-state actors. At the strategic level, this effort must include establishment of global norms, discussed further in Chapter 5, for both governmental and private sector actors related to achieving a clean, safe, secure Internet. As described in this chapter, commercial and collaborative non-state actors that operate and provide cyber security services will play an essential role in these efforts.

- Governmental and private sector intelligence efforts should focus on understanding different types and tiers of capability necessary for a non-state actor to achieve strategic effects. Increased monitoring and analytic metrics to ascertain when a potentially disruptive actor is emerging as a strategic player would allow government and actors to start counter-campaigns early before offensive players acquire strategic scale and threatening capabilities.

- In a similar vein, intelligence and analytic efforts should track new forms of disruptive activity by traditional disruptive players, such as new alliances among members of the Internet underground. Understanding gleaned from such observations will inform both proactive efforts to break dangerous linkages and as well as improving the readiness and effectiveness of defensive efforts.

- Explore efforts to draw human capital away from the Internet underground, similar to efforts to co-opt scientists and others involved in WMD programs in the former Soviet Union.

- Establish focused efforts to undermine and eradicate the Internet underground with the dual benefit of improving strategic stability and more effectively addressing cyber crime, especially financial fraud. Efforts should include:

  o Targeting of key people by law enforcement and counterintelligence organizations

  o Combating the spread of state-level tools within the underground, including norms against the use of Stuxnet-like capabilities and collaborative efforts to rapidly share information about the emergence and spread of similarly destructive software

- Support efforts to get rid of overly permissive aspects of the ecosystem including:

  o Technical efforts to improve authentication and identity management

  o Norms that have governments more strongly limit the permissibility of disruptive attacks with consistent enforcement and stronger penalties

  o For net operators, including ISPs, DNS operators, web hosts, and e-mail providers, raise expectations regarding combating malicious activity, set measurable targets for reductions in the presence of such activities and consider government oversight and penalties if voluntary efforts and achievement of goals proves ineffective. First, however, governments must enable private sector network operators through encouraging the development of business models that focus on providing a clean and safe cyber environment and discuss how to reduce legal concerns of these organizations.

- Governments should seek to establish and improve active operational collaboration with the range of private sector cyber defenders to maximize the speed and effectiveness of defensive efforts to identify and mitigate emerging threats as well as part of national and global defensive organizations that can effectively reduce the strategic impact of cyber attacks. The Estonian Cyber Defense Unit provides an example of structure that should be supported.

- Improved government – private sector collaboration efforts such include sharing of information of adversary capabilities and tactics and joint defensive response tactics. These efforts would be greatly enabled by personnel sharing and sharing in the operation of network security centers and incident response teams.

- As discussed in more detail in Chapter 5, government and private sector actors should consider setting up cyber risk reduction centers at multiple levels local to global focused both on ecosystem health as well as facilitating crisis stability through communications during a crisis.

Conclusion

Approaching the cyber domain as an ecosystem of competing and collaborating actors, each of whom can take on a variety of different roles, can help policy-makers better understand the challenges and opportunities that are presented by the increasing role of non-state actors in cyber conflict. While researchers and the policy community have traditionally recognized the offensive role of non-state actors, their defensive role remains largely overlooked. Yet the voluntary collaboration by non-state actors on the defense, whether it be universities, research institutions, non-profits, or individuals, have greatly contributed to the defense of the nation and the mitigation of the cyber threat. As the Estonia case reveals, knowing how to leverage these sources of defensive capability has proven to be an important tool of cyber defense, and will be necessary to improve strategic cyber stability and the health and resilience of the cyber ecosystem.

Chapter Four

Legal Constructs and Cyber Conflict

Introduction

This chapter presents an overview of the domestic and international legal framework for the field of cyber conflict. Some people have advocated for new laws to address cyber conflict while others have argued that, for the most part, existing law is sufficient as long as it is supplemented with policy and organizational reform. In some ways, the relevance and utility of law to cyber conflict depend on the fundamental determination of whether cyber conflict is either a unique activity requiring a completely new legal structure, or whether it is part of a societal and technical evolution to which existing legal principles should be applied and amended only when necessary. This chapter proceeds on the latter foundation.

Technology always poses new challenges, but the purpose of law is not to regulate specific technologies *per se*. Legal systems, along with community norms and economic markets, are mechanisms for managing the behavior of people, organizations, and countries in relation to domestic and international society. The law of cyber conflict must be founded in the same principles and norms that govern non-cyber activities. While some of the tools and opportunities of cyber conflict are new and unique, this chapter posits that it is first important to understand the scope and efficiency of existing law applied to cyber conflict before designing new regimes. Such analysis may show that inefficiencies are operational or political in nature, rather than legal.

This task is complex and substantial; certainly a full explication of all law applicable to cyber conflict is beyond the scope of this chapter. The aims of this chapter are to portray the general landscape of existing domestic and international law, including the respective strengths and weaknesses, and to identify possible avenues for development of domestic and international legal frameworks relevant to cyber conflict. Another related goal here is to give an overview of existing law that may affect cyber conflict behavior, both offensive and defensive. The US section is roughly divided into categories of warfare, crime, emergency response, and preparedness. It also briefly touches upon other areas of domestic law relevant to intelligence and critical infrastructure protection that may span these categories. This section concludes with two key observations: the need for operational personnel and defenders of information infrastructure to understand legal implications (the restrictive *and* the enabling laws); and the need for policy makers to clarify the cyber conflict applicability of certain laws established before the digital era.

The second section discusses international law and cyber conflict. This analysis first reviews cyber activities that typically fall below the threshold of the laws of armed conflict, namely cyber crime and cyber espionage. The section then assesses the potential application of international humanitarian law, and gives a short overview of the applicability of existing treaties often mentioned in the cyber conflict context. This section concludes with a comment on legal, technical, and policy norms and the role of international law. This section also addresses the theme of cyber conflict as a new or continuous problem, influenced by an emerging legal consensus among primarily American scholars of international law. This consensus, however, is not necessarily carried through into the international academic community and is also arguably not reflected in current state practice.

US Law[1]

Some experts feel that existing US law provides sufficient legal authorities to support cyber operations. Instead of new legislation, these scholars think the US needs a clarification of roles and cooperative relationships, a more coherent cross-agency strategy and response plan, a unified lexicon, and stronger leadership.[2] The other chapters of this publication address strategy, leadership, and issues of critical infrastructure; therefore this chapter will attempt to restrict itself to purely legal matters. While operational or political changes may also be needed to address cyber conflict, this chapter does not address these matters. As explained in the introduction, this chapter assumes the perspective that cyber conflict does not require a completely new, unique legal framework, but rather that it is part of a societal and technical evolution to which existing legal principles should be applied and amended as necessary.

This section takes a positivistic approach – focusing on the law as it *is*, rather than focusing on the law as it *should be*. This is an important distinction approach because, before making recommendations regarding the law or how the law may affect organizational, military, or critical infrastructure issues relevant to cyber conflict, one must first understand the facts, contexts, and rationales of the existing law that may be applied. Normative legal

---

[1]   The U.S. Law section of this chapter was written with the benefit of two virtual working groups. With credit and thanks to the participants of the working groups. Group One: Aaron Burstein, Robert W. Clark, John Laprise, Sallie McDonald, R. James Orr III, and Panayotis A. Yannakogeorgos. Group Two: Mark Becker, Susan W. Brenner, Kevin G. Coleman, Lawrence Dietz, and Maeve Dion. The working group reports are available at http://ccsalegalone.wordpress.com. The views expressed in the reports are the personal opinions of the individual participants and do not represent the views of any U.S. government agency or department. Thanks also to the working groups' project assistant Tyler Johnson and student intern Aaron Alva. The working groups provided a platform for discussion of many of the issues in this chapter; however, opinions and errors in this chapter should be attributed solely to the authors and not the members of the working groups.

[2]   See, e.g., Maeve Dion, Rapporteur, "Working Group One Report, Study Two Legal Issues: U.S. Focus," *White paper, Cyber Conflict Studies Association*, http://ccsalegalone.wordpress.com, August 11, 2010, 2-3,.

changes are better analyzed in relation to their specific substantive goals, rather than standing alone in some legal theory silo.

The legal and academic community has expounded on a wealth of topics related to harmful cyber incidents, including national cyber security threats,[3] cyber crimes and torts,[4] law enforcement issues and forensics,[5] civil liberty protections and societal concerns,[6] telecommunications regulation and other business matters,[7] and cyber warfare.[8] For purposes of this section,

---

[3]   E.g., Stewart D. Personick and Cynthia A. Patterson, eds., *Critical Information Infrastructure Protection and the Law: An Overview of Key Issues* (Washington, DC: The National Academies Press, 2003); Lin V. Choi, ed., *Cybersecurity and Homeland Security* (New York: Nova Science Publishers, 2006); Susan W. Brenner, *Cyberthreats: The Emerging Fault Lines of the Nation State* (New York: Oxford University Press, 2009).

[4]   E.g., Seymour Goodman and Abraham D. Sofaer, eds., *The Transnational Dimension of Cyber Crime and Terrorism* (Stanford, CA: Hoover Institution Press, 2001); Susan W. Brenner, *Cybercrime: Criminal Threats from Cyberspace* (Santa Barbara: Praeger, 2010); Byron Acohido and Jon Swartz, *Zero Day Threat* (New York: Union Square Press, 2008); Clifford Stoll, *The Cuckoo's Egg: Tracking a Spy Through the Maze of Computer Espionage* (New York: Pocket Books, 1990); Jonathan D. Hart, *Internet Law: A Field Guide, 6th ed.* (Washington, DC: BNA Books, 2008); Michael L. Rustad, *Internet Law in a Nutshell* (St. Paul, MN: West, 2009).

[5]   E.g., Anthony Reyes, Richard Brittson, Kevin O'Shea, and James Steele, *Cyber Crime Investigations: Bridging the Gaps Between Security Professionals, Law Enforcement, and Prosecutors* (Rockland, MA: Syngress Publishing, 2007); Bill Nelson, Amelia Phillips, and Christopher Steuart, *Guide to Computer Forensics and Investigations, 4th ed.* (Boston: Thompson Course Technology, 2009).

[6]   E.g., Steven Hick, Edward F. Halpin, and Eric Hoskins, eds., *Human Rights and the Internet* (Basingstoke: Macmillan, 2000), electronic version via ebrary.com; Athina Karatzogianni, *The Politics of Cyberconflict* (New York: Routledge, 2006).

[7]   W. Russell Neuman, Lee W. McKnight, and Richard Jay Solomon, *The Gordian Knot: Political Gridlock on the Information Highway* (Cambridge, MA: MIT Press, 1997); Miriam Wugmeister and Christin Lyon, eds., *Global Employee Privacy & Data Security Law* (Washington, DC: BNA Books, 2009).

[8]   Richard W. Aldrich, "The International Implications of Information Warfare," *Airpower Journal* (Fall 1996): 99-110; David J. DiCenso, "IW Cyberlaw: The Legal Issues of Information Warfare," *Airpower Journal* (Summer 1999): 85-101; Edward F. Halpin, Philippa Trevorrow, David C. Webb, and Steve Wright, eds., *Cyberwar, Netwar and the Revolution in Military Affairs* (New York: Palgrave Macmillan, 2006); Pia Palojarvi, *A Battle in Bits and Bytes: Computer Network*

legal issues of cyber conflict may be viewed in the contexts of warfare, crime, emergency response, and preparedness.

This section attempts to give an overview of various legal issues in these areas. The main conclusions are that (1) these legal concerns must be clearly understood not only by the legislators and executive decision-makers, but also by the operational personnel and private defenders of the information infrastructure; and (2) some of the legal matters, which were established before the digital era, require clarification to better suit the cyber conflict context. These conclusions are carried over into the International Law section of this chapter, showing that the need for awareness and clarification is not merely a domestic law problem.

Overview of Relevant US Law

Before discussing the details of the highlighted legal authorities for warfare, crime, emergency response, and preparedness, it may be helpful to see the 'big picture' of the US laws and jurisdictions relevant to cyberspace. The following table establishes the broad domestic legal framework for cyber issues:

Attacks and the Law of Armed Conflict (Helsinki: Erik Castren Institute of International Law and Human Rights, 2009); Gregory J. Rattray, *Strategic Warfare in Cyberspace* (Cambridge, MA: MIT Press, 2001); Michael N. Schmitt, "Computer Network Attack and the Use of Force in International Law: Thoughts on a Normative Framework," *Columbia Journal of Transnational Law* 37 (1999): 885-937; Michael N. Schmitt, "Wired Warfare: Computer Network Attack and Jus in Bello," *International Review of the Red Cross*, Vol. 84, No. 846 (2002): 365-98; Walter G. Sharp, Sr., *CyberSpace and the Use of Force* (Falls Church, VA: Aegis Research Corporation, 1999); Department of Defense Office of General Counsel, "An Assessment of International Legal Issues in Information Operations" (1999), http://www.au.af.mil/au/awc/awcgate/dod-io-legal/dod-io-legal.pdf; Thomas C. Wingfield, *The Law of Information Conflict* (Falls Church, VA: Aegis Research Corporation, 2000).

Table 4.1: Relevant US Legal Authorities

US Code	Title	Focus	Principal Organization	Role in Cyberspace
Title 6	Domestic Security	Homeland Security	Department of Homeland Security	Security of US Cyberspace
Title 10	Armed Forces	National Defense	Department of Defense	Secure US Interests by Conducting Military Operations in Cyberspace
Title 18	Crimes and Criminal Procedure	Law Enforcement	Department of Justice	Crime Prevention, Apprehension, and Prosecution of Cyberspace Criminals
Title 32	National Guard	First Line of Defense of the US	Army National Guard, Air National Guard	Support Defense of US Interests in Cyberspace
Title 40	Public Buildings, Property, and Works	Chief Information Officer Roles and Responsibilities	All Federal Departments and Agencies	Establish and Enforce Standards for Acquisition and Security of Information Technologies
Title 50	War and National Defense	Foreign Intelligence and Counterintelligence Activities	Intelligence Community Aligned Under the Office of the Director of National Intelligence	Intelligence Gathering Through Cyberspace on Foreign Intentions, Operations, and Capabilities

Table Reproduced from Chairman of the Joint Chiefs of Staff, The National Military Strategy for Cyberspace Operations (December 2006).

The table illustrates the relevant legal authorities, as determined by the Joint Chiefs of Staff in the 2006 *National*

Military Strategy for Cyberspace (NMS-CO).[9] The majority of these titles are discussed below. Titles 18 and 32 are main components of the following analysis and Titles 10 and 50 are reviewed briefly, since they have already been discussed at length in Chapter 2 and have been extensively analyzed in other publications.[10] Title 6 provides the Department of Homeland Security its cyber security authorities, including the maintenance of the National Cybersecurity and Communications Integration Center (NCCIC), which is also discussed below.

In addition to the above table from the NMS-CO, the US Cyberspace Policy Review in 2009 traced the development of the regulatory and legal framework for communications technology, focusing mostly on Title 47, which regulates telegraphs, telephones, and radiotelegraphs.[11] The Cyberspace Policy Review also shows the development of technology against the development of legal and regulatory frameworks.[12] One notable trend is that from 1988 through 1995, there were no significant cyber-related laws or executive orders, which represents a gap from the Computer Security Act of 1987 until the Telecommunications Act of 1996. This gap in the regulatory and legal framework is interesting given that information technology was booming in terms of technological progress and accessibility during this time period. However the adage that 'law lags technology' is often cited, and this gap may be one representation.

---

[9]   Chairman of the Joint Chiefs of Staff, *The National Military Strategy for Cyberspace Operations* (December 2006), http://www.dod.gov/pubs /foi/ojcs/07-F-2105doc1.pdf (accessed 26 May 2011).

[10] See, e.g., Owens, Dam, and Lin, eds., *Cyberattack Capabilities*; Steven R. Chabinsky, "Cybersecurity Strategy: A Primer for Policy Makers and Those on the Front Line," *Journal of National Security Law & Policy* 4 (2010): 27-39; Sean Watts, "Combatant Status and Computer Network Attack," *Virginia Journal of International Law* 50:2 (2009): 391-447.

[11] U.S. Executive Office of the President, "Appendix C: Growth of Modern Communications Technology in the United States and Development of Supporting Legal and Regulatory Frameworks" in *Cyberspace Policy Review* (May 2009), http://www.whitehouse.gov/assets/documents/Cyberspace_Policy_Review_fina l.pdf (accessed 26 May 2011).

[12] Ibid., at C-13.

Because Title 10 and 50 are crucial for the Department of Defense and Intelligence Community—both significant actors for the US in cyber conflict matters—it is important to at least provide an overview of these titles and their applicability to cyber conflict. Though both Title 10 and Title 50 of the United States Code (U.S.C.) can be applied to cyber conflict, these sections typically fall outside of the bounds of the authorities discussed below.[13] Title 10 defines the organization, roles, and responsibilities of the US military, including some elements of the military intelligence components. Title 50, on the other hand, provides authorities and restrictions mostly to the civilian agencies of the intelligence community. While there may be some overlap regarding Title 10 and Title 50 authorities,[14] the titles seek to differentiate between the roles and responsibilities of the two separate communities with separate missions and restrictions.

Title 10 is the legal basis for the roles and organizations of the Army,[15] Navy,[16] Marine Corps,[17] Air Force,[18] Reserves,[19] Combatant Command,[20] Special Forces,[21] and Department of Defense.[22] Section 111 of Title 10 establishes the organization of the Department of Defense, followed later by Chapter 6, which addresses the Combatant Commands.[23] Section 161(a) authorizes the President, with the "advice and assistance of the Chairman of the Joint Chiefs of Staff" and through the Secretary of Defense to

---

13   "Warfare" of course falls within Title 10 authorities, but the particular provisions of Title 10 are not discussed in full detail in Section 2.2 of this chapter. Rather, Section 2.2 provides an overview of Title 10 authorities.

14   For discussion of ambiguous authorities for intelligence activities, namely counterintelligence, and the Department of Defense overlap, see Michael J. Woods and William King, "An Assessment of the Evolution and Oversight of Defense Counterintelligence Activities," *Journal of National Security Law & Policy* 3 (2009): 169-219.

15   10 U.S.C. §§ 3001-4842.

16   10 U.S.C. §§ 5001-7913.

17   Ibid.

18   10 U.S.C. §§ 8010-9842.

19   10 U.S.C. §§ 10001–18506.

20   10 U.S.C. §§ 161-168.

21   10 U.S.C. § 167.

22   10 U.S.C. §§ 111-119.

23   10 U.S.C. §§ 161-168.

"establish unified combatant commands and specified combatant commands to perform military missions." Section 164 establishes the powers and duties of commanders of combatant commands, including authority over subordinate commands.[24] This is relevant for US Cyber Command (CYBERCOM) because it is subordinate to US Strategic Command (STRATCOM). Accordingly, Title 10 authorities govern both commands. More detailed functions are established in Department of Defense Directive No. 5100.01, including the provisions to "organize, train, equip, and provide land, naval, air, space, and cyberspace forces."[25]

While there are different intelligence authorities for military intelligence, Title 50, Chapter 5 of the US Code sets forth the powers and duties of the civilian intelligence agencies.[26] Section 401a defines "intelligence" as "foreign intelligence and counterintelligence" and also defines the "intelligence community."[27] Sections 402 through 404o2 define the roles for the intelligence agencies, including the responsibilities and authorities for those organizations and their directors.[28] Accountability and reporting mechanisms for intelligence activities, including covert action, are defined in the subsequent subchapter. "Covert action" is

---

[24] 10 U.S.C. § 164(d).

[25] U.S. Department of Defense Directive No. 5100.01, "Function of the Department of Defense and Its Major Components" (21 December 2010).

[26] In addition to Title 50, Executive Order 12333 establishes a number of authorities and restrictions of the U.S. intelligence community as well as the roles and responsibilities for specific intelligence agencies. See Exec. Order 12333 (as amended), United States Intelligence Activities, 73 Fed. Reg. 45,325 (July 30, 2008). Much of 50 U.S.C. Chapter 15 is taken from the National Security Act of 1947, (Pub. L. No. 235, 80 Cong., 61 Stat. 496,) which has been amended subsequently. See also the Intelligence Reform and Terrorism Prevention Act of 2004 (Pub. L. 108-458, 118 Stat. 3638) which amended parts of Title 50 and other sections of the United States Code as well.

[27] Per 10 U.S.C. § 401a(2), "foreign intelligence" is "information relating to the capabilities, intentions, or activities of foreign governments or elements thereof, foreign organizations, or foreign persons, or international terrorist activities." "Counterintelligence" is defined in 10 U.S.C. § 401a(3) as "information gathered, and activities conducted, to protect against espionage, other intelligence activities, sabotage, or assassinations conducted by or on behalf of foreign governments or elements thereof, foreign organizations, foreign persons, or international terrorist activities."

[28] 50 U.S.C. §§ 402-402o2.

defined in 50 U.S.C. § 413b(e)[29] and § 413b requires presidential findings for covert action and congressional notification.[30]

As shown below, cyber conflict involves various agencies, whose jurisdictions and authorities may be affected contemporaneously or sequentially; therefore rather than detailing the legal issues pursuant to each entity or jurisdiction, this chapter assesses the variety of authorities within four topical areas of concern.

Warfare

There is much public interest in the question of what may be defined as an act of war in cyberspace, and in options for response. Warfare is primarily a legal construct of international law, and as such, discussions of these questions have been allocated to the International Law section of this chapter. Other chapters of this publication, specifically Chapter 2, address the cyber-related organization and efforts of the US defense community.

One specific authority in the US code, though, should be mentioned in relation to issues of cyber conflict. The Communications Act of 1934 included a section on Presidential war powers. Codified at 47 U.S.C. § 606, these powers include, *inter alia*, the authority to close "any facility or station for wire communication" or to have "any department of the Government" to take over "the use

---

[29]   Per §413b(e), "covert action" is defined as "an activity or activities of the United States Government to influence political, economic, or military conditions abroad, where it is intended that the role of the United States Government will not be apparent or acknowledged publicly." It does not include "intelligence, traditional counterintelligence activities;" "traditional diplomatic or military activities or routine support to such activities;" "traditional law enforcement activities…;" or "activities to provide routine support to the overt activities…of other United States Government agencies abroad." Ibid.

[30]   50 U.S.C. § 413b(a) establishes the procedure for presidential findings and 50 U.S.C. § 413b(b) requires that congressional intelligence committees are "fully and currently informed of all covert actions…including significant failures." The National Research Council considered the implications for covert action on cyber attack and cyber espionage. William A. Owens, Kenneth W. Dam, and Herbert S. Lin, eds. *Technology, Policy, Law, and Ethics Regarding U.S. Acquisition and Use of Cyberattack Capabilities,* (Washington, DC: National Academies Press, 2009), 195-199.

or control of any such facility or station" [§ 606(d)]. Section 606(d) requires that for such authority to be exercised by the President, "there exists a state or threat of war involving the United States." The table below details the authorities, contexts, and potential relevance of section 606 to cyber conflict:

Table 4.2: Potential Applicability of 47 U.S.C. § 606: Presidential War Powers authorized in the Communications Act of 1934, as amended

Section	Title	Authority	Trigger	Potential Cyber Conflict Applicability
606a	Priority Communications	The President may direct that essential national defense and security communications shall have "preference or priority with any carrier subject to this chapter"	"Continuance of a war in which the US is engaged"; "necessary for the national defense and security"	Application to the Government Emergency Telecommunications Service (GETS) and the Wireless Priority Service (WPS); Prioritization of critical information infrastructure networks during a continuing war
606b	Obstruction of Interstate or Foreign Communications	Unlawful for any person to "knowingly or willfully…obstruct or retard or aid in obstructing or retarding interstate or foreign communication by radio or wire"	"Any war in which the US is engaged"	Unlawful to divert traffic if communications are therefore slowed or obstructed; Unlawful to participate in cyber attacks that slow or obstruct communications[31]
606b	Obstruction of Interstate or Foreign Communications	"The President is authorized…to employ the armed forces to prevent any such obstruction or retardation of communication"	"Any war in which the US is engaged"; Presidential assessment that the public interest requires use of the armed forces	President may use armed forces to protect civilian communications infrastructure; Could mean using CYBERCOM/DoD to protect civilian information infrastructure networks
606c	Suspension or amendment of rules and regulations applicable to certain emission stations or devices	"The President … may suspend or amend, for such time as he may see fit, the rules and regulations applicable to any or all stations or devices capable of emitting electromagnetic radiations … and may cause the closing of any station for radio communication or any	Presidential proclamation of "war or threat of war or a state of public peril or disaster or other national emergency, or in order to preserve the neutrality of the United States"; necessary for national defense and	President may alter telecommunications regulations; President may close ISP or other telecommunications provider, or geolocation services, or may hand over use and control of services and/or equipment to a government entity

---

[31] Note that these activities may also be unlawful under other provisions of the U.S. code, and additionally may be tortious or a breach of service contract.

Section	Title	Authority	Trigger	Potential Cyber Conflict Applicability
		device … suitable for use as a navigational aid beyond five miles, and the removal [] of its apparatus and equipment … or he may authorize the use or control of any such station [by a government entity]"	security	
606d	Suspension or amendment of rules and regulations applicable to wire communications; closing of facilities; Government use of facilities	The President may "(1) suspend or amend the rules and regulations applicable to any or all facilities or stations for wire communication … (2) cause the closing of any facility or station for wire communication and the removal [] of its apparatus and equipment, or (3) authorize the use or control of any such facility or station…by any department of the Government…"	Presidential proclamation "that there exists a state or threat of war"; necessary for national defense and security; but for no longer than six months "after the termination of such state or threat of war and not later than such earlier date as the Congress by concurrent resolution may designate"	President may alter telecommunications regulations; President may close ISP or other telecommunications provider, or may hand over use and control to a government entity

Despite various discussions as to what the Section 606 provisions could mean for cyber conflict, this legislation has not been clarified by Congress as to its relevance to our current digital era and future contexts of cyber war. Thus there is no definitive interpretation that this law applies beyond the originally intended "wire communication" facilities or "device[s] capable of emitting electromagnetic radiations between 10 kilocycles and 100,000 megacycles."[32] Also, the United States has not declared any thresholds for determining a "threat of war" in a purely cyber context.[33]

Further, the context of the 1934 act (and predicate authorization of similar war powers) involved the use of the communications facilities or equipment by the government for purposes of communication, specifically in the assistance and facilitation of war communications. At least one commentator has questioned whether

---

[32]   47 U.S.C. § 606.

[33]   See part 3.0 International Law for a discussion of war and threats of war that include hybrid contexts (kinetic and cyber).

section 606(d) is applicable if the purpose of government takeover is to use the facilities as weapons of war. Further, this commentator notes that § 606 was enacted as part of the Congressionally-authorized 'war powers' of the President (requiring a Presidential proclamation of war or a threat of war),[34] even though section 606(c) discusses situations of "public peril or disaster or other national emergency" in the alternative to war. It is therefore a matter of interpretation whether this specific authority may be extended beyond these contexts (war and pure communications). This authority is one of several laws identified in this chapter that require open debate and clarification by Congress.

Crime

When addressing the topic of cyber security law, one of the first issues generally discussed is cyber crime. Of all the legal areas addressed in this chapter, crime has received more legislative attention and perhaps has less of a pressing need for clarification. In the cyber conflict context, although the focus is not on the myriad of cyber crimes, some treatment of cyber crime is necessary. For example, in the realm of cyber defense, concepts of active self-help or self-defense are often raised (e.g., "hack backs").[35] Here the concern is not so much on self-help and defense constituting protective, preparedness actions, but rather on

---

[34]   Susan W. Brenner and Leo L. Clarke, "Civilians in Cyberwarfare: Conscripts," *Vanderbilt Journal of Transnational Law* 43 (2010): 1011-1076, 1046-47. It should be noted that contrary to this discussion in Section 3.0 below, Brenner and Clarke concluded that the Laws of Armed Conflict and the UN Charter also likely do not apply to cyber warfare, due to their similar development in the purely kinetic context. Ibid., 1031.

[35]   See, e.g., expert discussions of "Property Rights on the Frontier: The Economics and Self-Help and Self-Defense in Cyberspace" (Symposium, *The Journal of Law, Economics, and Policy*, George Mason University School of Law, September 10, 2004); Orin S. Kerr, "Virtual Crime, Virtual Deterrence: A Skeptical View of Self-Help, Architecture, and Civil Liability," *Journal of Law, Economics, and Policy* 1:1 (2005): 197-214; Richard A. Epstein, "The Theory and Practice of Self-Help," *Journal of Law, Economics, and Policy* 1:1 (2005): 1-31; Bruce P. Smith, "Hacking, Poaching, and Counterattacking: Digital Counterstrikes and the Contours of Self-Help," *Journal of Law, Economics, and Policy* 1:1 (2005): 171-195.

active efforts that are more investigative or prosecutorial in nature or are fueled by retribution. If conducted outside of recognized structures and authorities for law enforcement and national defense, these activities may be characterized as vigilantism. Such vigilante efforts, whether in retribution or in anticipatory self-defense, may themselves violate computer crime laws.

Although this chapter focuses primarily on federal law, it should be noted that the first computer crime laws were enacted by several states in the 1970s.[36] The federal Computer Fraud and Abuse Act[37] (CFAA) is the primary law addressing improper computer access, and it has both criminal and civil components. The law initially was directed only to federal government computers and information, but subsequent amendments enlarged the scope of the statute to cover any computer "affecting interstate or foreign commerce or communication." With the growth of the Internet and the global information infrastructure, almost all computer use affects interstate or international communication or commerce.[38]

The CFAA prohibits unauthorized access to information, unauthorized access to computers for purposes of fraud, the transmission of computer threats for purposes of extortion, the trafficking of computer passwords, unauthorized access to computers that causes damage or loss, and unauthorized access to government computers that affects the government's use of the computers. Grouped in these categories, the specific statutory prohibitions include:

Wrongful Information Access, Retention, and Distribution

- Unauthorized access to certain financial information and federal governmental information, as well as unauthorized access to information from computers affecting interstate commerce or communication [§ 1030(a)(2)].

---

[36]   "Adequacy of Criminal Law and Procedure (Cyber): A 'Legal Foundations' Study, Report 7 of 12" (Report to the President's Commission on Critical Infrastructure Protection, 1997).

[37]   18 U.S.C. § 1030.

[38]   Deborah F. Buckman, Annotation, "Validity, Construction, and Application of Computer Fraud and Abuse Act," 174 A.L.R. Fed. 101 (2011).

- Unauthorized access, retention, and dissemination of protected information relevant to national security or foreign relations [§ 1030(a)(1)].

Fraud

- Knowing, unauthorized access (with intent to defraud) to computers affecting interstate commerce or communication, when such access furthers the fraud and obtains something of value (more than merely the use of the computer, where such use is valued at less than $5,000 in a 1-year period) [§ 1030(a)(4)].

Threats for Extortion

- Transmissions (with intent to extort) that (a) threaten to cause damage to computers affecting interstate commerce or communication, (b) threaten to obtain (without authorization) information from computers affecting interstate commerce or communication, (c) threaten the confidentiality of information obtained (without authorization) from computers affecting interstate commerce or communication, and (d) otherwise request compensation related to damage of computers affecting interstate commerce or communication, when such damage was part of the extortion plan [§ 1030(a)(7)].

Trafficking in Passwords or Similar Information

- Knowing trafficking (with intent to defraud) in passwords or "similar information" by which a computer may be accessed without authorization, if the trafficking affects interstate commerce or if the computer is used by the US government [§ 1030(a)(6)].

Causing Damage or Loss

- Knowing transmission of "a program, information, code, or command" that intentionally damages a computer affecting interstate commerce or communication [§ 1030(a)(5)(A)].
- Intentional, unauthorized access to a computer affecting interstate commerce or communication, when such access recklessly causes damage [§ 1030(a)(5)(B)].

- Intentional, unauthorized access to a computer affecting interstate commerce or communication, when such access causes damage and loss [§ 1030(a)(5)(C)].

Interfering with Government Use of Computers

- Intentional, unauthorized access to nonpublic US government computers when such access affects the governmental use of those computers [§ 1030(a)(3)].

Under CFAA definitions, 'damage' includes "any impairment to the integrity or availability of data, a program, a system, or information" [§ 1030(e)(8)]. The term 'loss' includes "any reasonable cost to any victim, including the cost of responding to an offense, conducting a damage assessment, and restoring the data, program, system, or information to its condition prior to the offense, and any revenue lost, cost incurred, or other consequential damages incurred because of interruption of service" [§ 1030(e)(11)].

The statute is applicable to both the commission of offenses as well as *attempts* to commit the proscribed actions. Criminal sanctions incorporate both fines and imprisonment. [§ 1030(c)]. In addition to criminal punishments, the CFAA provides for civil actions for compensation and injunctive relief. In delineating the limitations of these civil actions, Congress clarified that the CFAA does not support actions for "the negligent design or manufacture of computer hardware, computer software, or firmware" [§ 1030(g)].

In addition to the CFAA, other federal statutes relevant to cyber conflict and defense include the crimes of malicious mischief against communication lines, stations or systems; and malicious mischief that interferes with the operation of a satellite. Title 18, section 1362 criminalizes damage to "any radio, telegraph, telephone or cable, line, station, or system, or other means of communication, operated or controlled by the United States, or used or intended to be used for military or civil defense functions." It is also unlawful to willfully or maliciously (a) "interfere[] in any way with the working or use of any such line, or system," or (b) "obstruct[], hinder[], or delay[] the transmission of any communication over any such line, or system." In addition to actual actions, both attempts and conspiracies are also criminalized under this statute. Punishment may include a fine and up to 10 years imprisonment.[39] Title 18, section 1367 similarly criminalizes and punishes intentional, malicious interference with the operation of communications or weather satellites, including obstruction or delay of satellite transmissions.[40]

The Fourth Circuit US Court of Appeals has broadly interpreted the law regarding malicious mischief against communication systems. In *United States v. Turpin*, two men appealed their convictions under § 1362 by arguing that the statute was not applicable to their actions in cutting down and stealing copper communication wire that was part of the CSX railroad company's internal communication system.[41] The US military used the CSX railroad for transporting military materials. The *Turpin* court affirmed the convictions, holding that the statute should be interpreted broadly, similar to the Sabotage Act, and that the Congressional intent was not to restrict § 1362 to imminent war efforts. The court therefore found that § 1362 may apply to public, commercial, and private facilities used by military or civilian personnel in national defense and preparedness functions.[42]

Neither the CFAA crimes nor crimes of malicious mischief incorporate affirmative defenses. In other words, in a cyber incident, any private sector responders must obey these laws;[43] any hack-back or other intrusions that may violate these laws are not legally justified by affirmative defenses such as 'self defense.' Although commentators have hypothesized, for example, that some legal self-help provisions may apply in the cyber context,[44] no court or legislature has yet determined the viability of such provisions.

---

[39] 18 U.S.C. § 1362.

[40] In contrast to section 1362, there is no explicit inclusion of attempts or conspiracies in section 1367. Further, unlike section 1362, this statute specifically exempts "any lawfully authorized investigative, protective, or intelligence activity of a law enforcement agency or of an intelligence agency of the United States." 18 U.S.C. § 1367(b).

[41] *United States v. Turpin*, 65 F.3d 1207, 1209 (4th Cir. 1995).

[42] *United States v. Turpin*, 1211-12.

[43] Note that the CFAA "does not prohibit any lawfully authorized investigative, protective, or intelligence activity of a law enforcement agency of the United States, a State, or a political subdivision of a State, or of an intelligence agency of the United States." 18 U.S.C. § 1030(f).

[44] See, e.g., Robert Lemos, "Is vigilante hacking legal?", *CNET News*, February 27, 2003, http://news.cnet.com/2100-1002-990469.html (discussing a

Another relevant federal law that regulates cyber crime investigations is the Electronic Communications Privacy Act (ECPA), [45] which addresses privacy of electronic communications in transit as well as stored communications. Amended numerous times since being enacted in 1986, ECPA provisions are found in various sections of the US code. ECPA, *inter alia*, provides some of the rules under which the government may access electronic data from service providers (note that other laws, such as the Fourth Amendment of the US Constitution, and respective case law, are also important to such access, but these laws are not addressed here).

In the United States, therefore, it can be seen that traditional rules regarding warrants, subpoenas, and other requests for information have been somewhat adjusted in the digital age. Under the 'stored communications' provision of ECPA, for example, if communications have been stored for fewer than 180 days, then in order to access the contents, the government generally must follow the traditional rules of criminal procedure for obtaining a relevant warrant. However, if the data has been stored for longer than 180 days, then the government may request disclosure of the contents under a lesser procedural bar. [46]

ECPA also amended the federal Wiretap Act (regarding interception of the content of electronic communications) and implemented rules regarding the use of pen registers and trap and trace devices (related to real-time access to traffic information, or

---

conference presentation by attorney Curtis Karnow who suggested that self help provisions of state nuisance laws may permit cyber victims to lawfully interfere to stop harmful program emitting from computer systems that the victim would not otherwise have authority to access).

[45]   Electronic Communications Privacy Act of 1986, Pub. L. No. 99–508, 100 Stat. 1848 (1986), as amended.

[46]   18 U.S.C. § 2703. For a more nuanced discussion of the details, *see* U.S. Department of Justice, Computer Crime and Intellectual Property Section Criminal Division, *Searching and Seizing Computers and Obtaining Electronic Evidence in Criminal Investigations* (3d ed., 2009) (particularly Chapter 3: the Stored Communications Act); Orin S. Kerr, "Applying the 4th Amendment to the Internet: a General Approach," *Stanford Law Review* 62 (2010) 1005-1050, 1043-44. (arguing that the lesser procedural rules under 18 U.S.C. § 2703(b) are unconstitutional).

non-content information of electronic communications).[47] It should be noted that a pen/trap device may be installed without a court order in emergency situations, which include threats to national security or an ongoing attack to a protected computer (as defined in CFAA, discussed above).[48]

As relevant to this chapter, in addition to such procedural rules, ECPA also criminalized unlawful access to stored communications. This parallels the Wiretap Act's provisions that criminalize the wrongful interception of real-time communications (including electronic communications).[49] Using language similar to the 'without authorization' or 'exceeding authorization' text of CFAA, ECPA prohibits wrongful access or altering of stored communications, and it also criminalizes the wrongful prevention of authorized access to stored communications.[50] Service providers have an exemption from these prohibitions.[51]

Service providers are also excepted from other ECPA provisions under certain conditions. For example, service providers may divulge the contents of stored communications "as may be necessarily incident to the rendition of the service or to the protection of the rights or property of the provider of that service."[52] This exception also applies to intercepted communications.[53] These exceptions allow for access needed for general provision and maintenance of the service, and also for protection of the service from fraud and damage. However, courts have held that in taking such protective actions (that without this exception would otherwise violate ECPA), service providers must adhere to a standard of reasonableness that balances the need to protect the service with the privacy interests in the communications.[54]

---

[47]   U.S. Department of Justice, Computer Crime and Intellectual Property Section Criminal Division, 151-52.
[48]   18 U.S.C. § 3125.
[49]   See 18 U.S.C. § 2510 et seq.
[50]   18 U.S.C. § 2701.
[51]   18 U.S.C. § 2701(c).
[52]   18 U.S.C. § 2702(b)(5).
[53]   18 U.S.C. § 2702(b)(2) (referencing § 2511(2)(a)).
[54]   U.S. Department of Justice, Computer Crime and Intellectual Property Section Criminal Division, 172-73 (citations omitted).

It can therefore be seen that certain aspects of cyber crime are relevant to issues of cyber conflict. There are restrictions to the interception of communications, for example, and to the wrongful access to stored communications. However, service providers are permitted such interception and access in order to maintain and protect their networks. Another important provision may be the emergency pen/trap authority, which is applicable to ongoing computer attacks as well as imminent threats to national security.[55]

Furthermore, some types of 'active defense' or active investigations, such as "hack back," may violate federal law.[56] This stance is supported by the public policy rationale that law enforcement activities are not the purview of private citizens. As discussed below, only the recognized state and federal authorities are empowered to suppress activities falling within the rubric of insurrection and public disorder. Private individuals or organizations are not invested with such lawful powers.[57] Thus, only a "lawfully authorized investigative, protective, or intelligence activity of a law enforcement agency" may be permitted certain activities that may otherwise be seen as violative of US criminal law.[58] It is important that private defenders of the US information infrastructure have clear understanding of these matters. It is equally important that "investigative, protective, or intelligence" law enforcement personnel, who have the broader legal authority to respond, are trained, well-equipped, and have the human resources necessary to handle such cyber conflict concerns.[59]

Emergency Response

In the context of legal issues relevant to cyber conflict, it is also important to assess the applicability of laws related to emergency response. These laws may include the statutory

---

[55]   Ibid., 158-59.

[56]   And state laws, but that is beyond the scope of this section.

[57]   *People v. Chambers*, 72 P.2d 746, 755 (Cal. App. 1937).

[58]   See, e.g., 18 U.S.C. § 1030(f).

[59]   This chapter section deals purely with legal issues; for discussions of military and operational matters, see Chapter 2 of the present volume.

authorities for response and management (and relevant judicial interpretations), as well as laws and court decisions that place prohibitions or limitations on various responding entities. As discussed below, for purposes of this section, 'emergency response' is not limited to situations resulting from natural phenomena, but may also include man-made incidents caused by human error or acts of terrorism.[60]

State Authority

In the United States,[61] it is primarily the responsibility of states to maintain safety and public order.[62] As the Supreme Court stated, "the state has no more important interest than the maintenance of law and order."[63] In emergency situations that cause disorder, or threaten to cause disorder, governors may utilize both civil and military forces under their commands. In using the military, a governor's decisions, "made in good faith and in the honest belief" that such actions are needed, are granted broad discretion.[64] While a complete survey of state laws is beyond the scope of this section, it should be noted that some state laws permit the governor to use the National Guard only if the disaster has already occurred or if there is an imminent threat to life and human safety.[65]

In general, though, governors may call on the National Guard for support in protecting life and property.[66] To enhance their individual capabilities, states have entered into agreements for sharing their personnel and resources in times of emergency.[67]

---

[60] Note that lawful responses in circumstances related to war, armed attack, etc., are addressed in Part 3.0 International Law of this chapter.

[61] Outside of the context of invasion and warfare. See Part 3.0 International Law in this chapter.

[62] 32 C.F.R. § 215.4(a).

[63] *Sterling v. Constantin*, 287 U.S. 378, 399 (1932).

[64] Id., 399-400.

[65] Maj. Gen. Timothy J. Lowenberg, "The Role of the National Guard in National Defense and Homeland Security," (white paper, National Guard Association of the United States), 4, http://www.ngaus.org/NGAUS/files/ccLibraryFiles/Filename/00000000045 7/primer%20fin.pdf, accessed March 14, 2011

[66] Ibid., 2.

[67] See, e.g., the Emergency Management Assistance Compact. Joint Resolution Granting the consent of Congress to the Emergency

While governors may use the Guard in 'state active-duty' status, the National Guard may also be commanded by state governors under authority of Title 32 of the United States Code. Such 'Title 32 duty' status means that the governor is using the National Guard for shared state-federal purposes, or for primarily federal purposes, and the use is funded by the federal government. These situations may originate with a governor's request for federal funding, or they may originate with a federal government request that a governor deploy the National Guard for certain purposes. An example of the latter would be terrorist attacks of September 11, 2001, when the federal government asked the state governors to have the National Guard secure US airports.[68]

A governor may therefore command the National Guard to undertake homeland defense activities, including the protection of private critical infrastructures,[69] while the units are in 'state active-duty' or 'Title 32 duty' status. The National Guard includes units specialized in certain areas, such as weapons of mass destruction;[70] chemical, biological, radiological, nuclear, and high-yield explosives;[71] and offensive and defensive cyber operations.[72] While the National Guard has more commonly been used in responses to natural disasters, "Protecting the networks and computer systems that are vital to a state's commerce and public safety is likely to become as much a part of the Guard's job as is stacking sand bags to keep floods from factories, hospitals and neighborhoods."[73]

Depending on the state law, a governor may use the National Guard to protect not only people and state property, but also

---

Management Assistance Compact, H.R.J. Res. 193, 104th Cong. (1996), Pub. L. No. 104-321, 110 Stat. 3877.

[68]   Lowenberg, "Role of the National Guard," 2.

[69]   32 U.S.C. § 901 et seq.

[70]   "Weapons of Mass Destruction Civil Support Team" (fact sheet, National Guard, March 2011), http://www.ng.mil/media/factsheets/2011/CST%20Feb%2011.pdf.

[71]   "Chemical, Biological, Radiological, Nuclear and High-Yield Explosive Enhanced Response Force Package," (fact sheet, National Guard, March 2011), http://www.ng.mil/media/factsheets/2011/CERFP%20Fact%20Sheet%20-MAR%2011.pdf.

[72]   See William Matthews, "Cyber Sentinels," *National Guard*, September 2008, 37-40, http://www.ngaus.org/ngaus/files/ccLibraryFiles/Filename/000000004212/cyber0908.pdf.

[73]   Ibid., 40.

property and critical infrastructure owned by the private sector.[74] In such circumstances, the National Guard is acting as the state militia.[75] However as discussed below, with regard to federal troops (including the National Guard in 'Title 10 duty' status), US law places some restrictions on the domestic use of the military for law enforcement functions.

Federal Authority

In most cases public order and safety are generally managed at the state and local levels. However, under certain circumstances, the federal government may assume the responsibility to maintain safety and public order; in those cases some legal restrictions may apply to the domestic use of the federal military (including the National Guard in 'Title 10 duty' status). Before detailing such circumstances, this section first reviews the federal structure for emergency response.

The Department of Homeland Security (DHS) is the principal federal agency for domestic emergency incident management. DHS manages the federal response to terrorist attacks, major disasters, and other emergencies; and coordinates the federal response resources during incidents of national significance.[76] All Federal departments are directed to give DHS their full

---

[74]   Ibid. (referencing comments from Col. Tom Thomas, commander, Delaware Air National Guard's 166th Network Warfare Squadron).

[75]   Any limitations in the constitutions and statutes of the individual states is beyond the scope of this section.

[76]   See Homeland Security Act of 2002, Pub. L. No. 107-296, 116 Stat. 2135 (Title V "Emergency Preparedness and Response"); Homeland Security Presidential Directive 5: Management of Domestic Incidents (HSPD-5) ¶ 4 (February 28, 2003), in H. Comm. on Homeland Security, 110th Cong., "Compilation of Homeland Security Presidential Directives" 23-24 (Comm. Print 110-B, 2008) ("The Secretary shall coordinate the Federal Government's resources utilized in response to or recovery from terrorist attacks, major disasters, or other emergencies if and when any one of the following four conditions applies: (1) a Federal department or agency acting under its own authority has requested the assistance of the Secretary; (2) the resources of State and local authorities are overwhelmed and Federal assistance has been requested by the appropriate State and local authorities; (3) more than one Federal department or agency has become substantially involved in responding to the incident; or (4) the Secretary has been directed to assume responsibility for managing the domestic incident by the President.").

cooperation and offer their available resources.[77] DHS coordinates the National Cybersecurity and Communications Integration Center (NCCIC), a watch and warning center to address threats and incidents against critical information technology and infrastructure. NCCIC integrates a number of existing DHS organizations, including the US-CERT and the National Coordinating Center for Telecommunications, and all assist DHS's National Cyber Security Center in coordinating cyber security across the federal government.[78]

Under Homeland Security Presidential Directive 5, the DHS Secretary and Secretary of the Department of Defense (DOD) are specifically tasked with "establish[ing] appropriate relationships and mechanisms for cooperation and coordination between their two departments" (¶ 9).[79] This relationship was further enhanced with an October 2010 Memorandum of Agreement between the departments to better coordinate incident response and the protection of governmental and civilian networks from cyber threats.[80] Still, during domestic incidents, the DOD Secretary "shall retain command of military forces providing civil support."[81] In this role, the DOD prefers to operate under the traditional, three-tier approach: (1) DOD (as ordered by the President or DOD Secretary) provides support to local, state, and federal law enforcement; (2) the National Guard (as ordered by the state governor), performs homeland defense and homeland security activities; and (3) the

---

[77]   HSPD-5, Paragraph 5; Department of Homeland Security, "National Response Framework" (2008); Department of Homeland Security, "Cyber Annex to the National Response Plan" (2004). Note that the Cyber Annex remained in effect with the evolution of the National Response Framework. Federal Emergency Management Agency, NRF Resource Center: Incident Annexes, http://www.fema.gov/emergency/nrf/incidentannexes.htm (accessed March 14, 2011).

[78]   For more information about NCCIC and other cyber coordination through DHS, see Department of Homeland Defense, *National Cyber Incident Response Plan*, Interim Version (September 2010).

[79]   A similar tasking is ordered between the DHS Secretary and the Attorney General. HSPD-5, Paragraph 8.

[80]   "Memorandum of Agreement Between The Department of Homeland Security and the Department of Defense Regarding Cyber Security," 13 October 2010.

[81]   HSPD-5, Paragraph 9.

US military (as ordered by the President or DOD Secretary) intercepts threats.[82]

In its *Strategy for Homeland Defense and Civil Support*, the DOD commented that "[n]ewly expanded authorities under Title 32 of US Code—and the National Guard's on-going transformation—provide Governors and state authorities with the authority to use flexible, responsive National Guard units for a limited period to perform homeland defense activities, when approved by the Secretary of Defense. For example, National Guard forces may, when the Secretary of Defense determines that doing so is both necessary and appropriate, provide security for critical infrastructure and support civilian law enforcement agencies in responding to terrorist acts."[83] With its "Total Force" approach, the DOD recognized that one of the "most promising areas for employment of the National Guard and Reserve forces ... [is] Critical Infrastructure Protection, including ... utilization of Reserve component forces for quick reaction requirements, when sufficiently trained and resourced, and local security at key defense and non-defense critical infrastructure sites, when directed." [84] Additionally, the DOD can then call upon civilian expertise that may reside in National Guard and Reserve forces.

As stated in the DOD's *Strategy for Homeland Defense and Civil Support*, the military may be directed to protect non-military "assets of national significance that are so vital to the nation that their incapacitation could have a debilitating effect on the security of the United States."[85] This situation may be envisioned "where the nature of the threat exceeds the capabilities of an asset owner and civilian law enforcement is insufficient."[86]

---

[82] Department of Defense, "Strategy for Homeland Defense and Civil Support" (2005), at 26-27, 30. Note that this Strategy was written following the release of the interim National Infrastructure Protection Plan (NIPP), but that the NIPP appears not to explicitly inform this DoD Strategy.

[83] Department of Defense, "Strategy for Homeland Defense and Civil Support" (2005), at 27.

[84] Ibid. 35-36

[85] Ibid. 18

[86] Ibid. 29

Posse Comitatus Act

One traditional restriction to the use of federal troops domestically is the Posse Comitatus Act (PCA). It is very important for both civilian and military leaders to understand the PCA; as discussed below, misunderstandings of the PCA have resulted in incident responders believing that the PCA restricted them from using the military when, actually, such use was lawful and may have greatly aided the response effort.

The Posse Comitatus Act prohibits the use of the federal military "as a posse comitatus or otherwise to execute the laws,"[87] with exceptions for situations authorized by the US Constitution or Congress.[88] The prohibition originated in a fiscal year 1879 Army Appropriation Act, in response to local use of federal troops as police forces in elections in former Confederate states.[89] Congress intended the statute to prohibit civilian law enforcement officers from making direct, active use of federal military personnel to execute the law.[90]

The PCA is founded on a traditional public policy to limit domestic military operations during times of peace.[91] As one court explained,

> [c]ivilian rule is basic to our system of government. The use of military forces to seize civilians can expose civilian government to the threat of military rule and the suspension of constitutional liberties. On a lesser scale, military enforcement of the civil law leaves the protection of vital Fourth and Fifth Amendment rights in the hands of persons who are not trained to uphold these rights. It may also chill the exercise of fundamental rights, such as

---

[87]　Jennifer Elsea, "The Posse Comitatus Act and Related Matters: A Sketch," *Navy Department Library*, Congressional Research Service, June 6, 2005, http://www.history.navy.mil/library/online/posse%20comit.htm.

[88]　18 U.S.C. § 1385.

[89]　*Chandler v. U.S.*, 171 F.2d 921, 936 (1st Cir. 1948) (citing Lieber, "The Use of the Army in Aid of the Civil Power," (War Department Document No. 64, Office of the Judge-Advocate General, Government Printing Office, 1898)).

[90]　*United States v. Red Feather*, 392 F.Supp. 816, 920-24 (D. S.D. 1975) (citing 7 Cong. Rec. 3579-86, 3846-49).

[91]　*Laird v. Tatum*, 408 U.S. 1, 15 (1972).

the rights to speak freely and to vote, and create the atmosphere for fear and hostility which exists in territories occupied by enemy forces.[92]

Perhaps more succinctly, a member of Congress stated that "[s]oldiers do not need to be reading Miranda rights with automatic rifles in hand; that is not their purpose. That is not what they are trained for. That is not what they do."[93]

Although no one has been prosecuted for violation of the PCA, the statute has been analyzed in judicial contexts relating to jurisdiction, exclusion of evidence, and defenses against indictments.[94] Courts have interpreted the PCA to prohibit non-authorized "military involvement" in civilian law enforcement actions only if such involvement "actually regulates, forbids, or compels some conduct."[95] Another circuit's test includes whether the federal military use "pervaded the activities of the civilian officials."[96] In contrast, there seems to be no precedent for finding PCA violations in civilian law enforcement's failure to prevent military law enforcement actions on the military officer's initiative.[97]

By the early 1980s, several events related to the PCA caused Congress to clarify matters. These events show how the PCA may be considered and interpreted differently by lawmakers, courts, and incident responders in the field. First, the country was experiencing rising imports of illicit drugs, and lawmakers believed that federal military resources should be available to law enforcement anti-drug efforts. Also, different courts had handed down contradictory opinions on the PCA in various cases, and Congress wanted to resolve these differing interpretations. Further, experience had shown

---

[92] *Bissonette v. Haig*, 776 F.2d 1384, 1387 (8th Cir. 1985).

[93] 107 Congr. Rec. H5,701 (July 25, 2002) (statement of Rep. Sandlin).

[94] See H.R. Rep. No. 97-71 (II), 5-6 (1981) (summarizing various cases and testimony to Congress).

[95] *Bissonette v. Haig*, 1390 (addressing law enforcement use of military troops at Wounded Knee).

[96] *Riley v. Newton*, 94 F.3d 632, 636 (11th Cir. 1996) (citations omitted).

[97] *Riley*, 94 F.3d at 636-37 (granting the civilian officer qualified immunity because it was not obvious that he was violating federal law when his "military passenger, lawfully present on a joint drug patrol, attempt(ed) on his own initiative to make an arrest that (led) to the application of excessive force").

that misunderstandings of the PCA had "cause[d] some commanders to deny aid, even when such assistance would in fact be legally proper," and Congress wanted to clarify its intent regarding PCA to help minimize conditions when ambiguities would result in the improper denial or refusal to use federal military resources for law enforcement purposes.[98]

In the House Report (II) for the Department of Defense Authorization Act of 1982, Congress summarized that existing laws create permissions for use of federal troops

- to protect federal property and parks, as well as foreign officials;
- in investigations of certain crimes against the President or members of the Congress, Cabinet, or Supreme Court;
- to enforce laws of neutrality, and customs laws;
- in executing warrants regarding certain violations of civil rights law;
- related to the loan of services, equipment, personnel and facilities to law enforcement agencies;
- for the removal of unlawful enclosures on public lands;
- in disaster response; and
- in the suppression of civil disorder.[99]

However, some of these uses are not actual exceptions to PCA; for example, although federal troops may be used in disaster response, they may *not* be used to enforce law during disaster response unless the disaster has resulted in civil disorder.[100]

Trying to sort out the various allowed and prohibited uses, a DOD Directive determined that *unlawful* military actions in civilian law enforcement functions included: interdiction of a vehicle, vessel, aircraft, or other similar activity; a search or seizure; an arrest,

---

[98]   H.R. Rep. No. 97-71 (II), 3-7.

[99]   Id., 5 (citations omitted).

[100]   John A. McCarthy, Randall Jackson, Sr., and Maeve Dion, "*Posse Comitatus* and the Military's Role in Disaster Relief," in "Hurricane Katrina Task Force Subcommittee Report," 34 (ABA Standing Committee on Law and National Security, ABA Section of State & Local Government Law, ABA Section of Administrative Law and Regulatory Practice, February 2006).

apprehension, stop and frisk, or similar activity; and use of military personnel for surveillance or pursuit of individuals, or as undercover agents, informants, investigators, or interrogators.[101]

The PCA has continued to be emphasized as an important policy and statute. For example, in legislative activities resulting in the Homeland Security Act of 2002, Congress reiterated the importance of PCA. Representative Harold Rogers had introduced an amendment authorizing the establishment of a Joint Interagency Homeland Security Task Force comprised of military and civilian individuals. Some of the dissenting arguments raised the issue of the PCA, and a manager's amendment was drafted to reaffirm that the PCA was still important.[102] The Rogers Amendment was passed and became 6 U.S.C. § 465; the manager's amendment became 6 U.S.C. § 466, noting, *inter alia*, that nothing in the US code chapter on Homeland Security Organization should alter the applicability and importance of the PCA.

The PCA does not constrain the President's ability to use the military to enforce law during certain public emergencies. As discussed above and as restated in federal regulations, emergency authorities permit "prompt and vigorous Federal action, including the use of military forces, to prevent loss of life or wanton destruction of property and to restore governmental functioning and public order when sudden and unexpected civil disturbances, disasters, or calamities seriously endanger life and property and disrupt normal governmental functions to such an extent that duly constituted local authorities are unable to control the situations."[103]

For example, a President may make such use of the military under statutory authority of the Insurrection Act that permits the use of the military to suppress disorder when insurrections or domestic violence make it impossible for law enforcement authorities to execute the law.[104] As the Supreme Court stated, this

---

[101] Department of Defense Directive No. 5525.5, Enclosure 4, section E4.1.3 (January 15, 1986, as amended December 12, 1989).
[102] 107 Congr. Rec. H5,701-2.
[103] 32 C.F.R. § 215.4(b), (c)(1).
[104] 10 U.S.C. § 301 et seq. The language of the Insurrection Act states, *inter alia*, that the President may use the military to suppress an incident that "(1) so hinders the execution of the laws of that State, and of the United States within the State, that any part or class of its people is deprived of a right,

executive authority to call on the military (whether exercised by the President or by a governor under equivalent state emergency authority) "is to be exercised upon sudden emergencies, upon great occasions of state, and under circumstances which may be vital to the existence of the [state or Union]."[105]

The Insurrection Act is therefore an explicit exception to the PCA. However, this exception has not been well understood. For example, in 1992, the President, under the authority of the Insurrection Act, authorized the Secretary of Defense to send military troops to help restore order during the Los Angeles riots. The 3,500-member Joint Task Force (JTF) was mostly made up of Army soldiers and Marines (who underwent a day or so of "civil disturbance training" before deployment). The Los Angeles police chief wanted to use the military to partition the city, and the county sheriff wanted to allocate soldiers "to police units and follow their orders in a 'rent a soldier' fashion." However, the JTF leader "apparently believed that he and his troops were constrained by the Posse Comitatus Act, and therefore could not legally participate in law enforcement activities." The JTF leader was wrong, and this confusion "seriously degraded the effectiveness of military support of local law enforcement in Los Angeles."[106]

As discussed in the examples above, various PCA misunderstandings have impacted incident response in a traditional emergency context; during cyber conflict, those misunderstandings may be increased. In the context of cyber conflict, therefore, the PCA and its 'exceptions' are very important to understand – as much for their impacts on operational decision-making as for their policy importance. The PCA is based on a policy to limit domestic military operations during times of peace; there is an aversion to activities that may give the perception of 'martial law.' It could be argued that this

---

privilege, immunity, or protection named in the Constitution and secured by law, and the constituted authorities of that State are unable, fail, or refuse to protect that right, privilege, or immunity, or to give that protection; or (2) opposes or obstructs the execution of the laws of the United States or impedes the course of justice under those laws." § 333.

[105]   *Sterling v. Constantin*, 399.

[106]   Thomas R. Lujan, "Legal Aspects of Domestic Employment of the Army," *Parameters* (Autumn 1997): 82-97,
http://www.carlisle.army.mil/USAWC/Parameters/Articles/97autumn/lujan.htm.

perception is muted in the cyber context, where the virtual response would not necessarily include images of uniformed soldiers patrolling Main Street. However, it is not just the public perception of PCA that is important, it is also the military and law enforcement communities' perceptions. The operational understanding of what PCA prohibits, and more importantly what it does not prohibit, may affect decisions regarding the military role in cyber incident response. While no authorities have specifically interpreted the PCA in the context of cyber conflict and defense, it is reasonable to assume that just as in a physical context, federal troops may provide information, equipment, training and advice to civilian law enforcement authorities. What may be more difficult to interpret are the cyber equivalents of non-authorized use of the military in domestic, civilian operations.

Therefore, not only should the general understanding of PCA be clarified to help limit unnecessary operational restrictions, but the concept of PCA in the cyber context should be openly debated, refined, and agreed to by the legislators, law enforcement, and military communities at the federal and state levels. A good starting point may be the DOD directive summarizing unlawful military actions in civilian law enforcement functions. From this directive, the dialog should address the cyber equivalents of interdiction, search or seizure; arrest, apprehension, stop and frisk, or similar activity; surveillance or pursuit; and undercover agents or investigators.

Other Legal Issues

In addition to the legal authorities covered above in the categories of warfare, crime, and emergency response, other domestic laws relevant to cyber conflict include authorities for surveillance and critical infrastructure protection. While these issues are not exhaustively discussed in this section, it is important to highlight their importance in US policymaking regarding cyber security and cyber conflict.

Intelligence Surveillance Authorities

The enabling authorizations for the intelligence community were discussed earlier, and this section focuses particularly on surveillance authorities for intelligence efforts. US surveillance authorities are separated between domestic intelligence and foreign intelligence. The Federal Bureau of Investigation (FBI) is the lead domestic intelligence agency, in addition to its law enforcement functions. Because of that dual role, the FBI must balance between its intelligence and law enforcement functions, which has been problematic in the past. Through the 1960s, the FBI focused heavily on espionage and foreign subversion cases, resulting in cases of abuses of power and infringement on US citizens' civil liberties. These abuses were fully disclosed during the Church Committee investigation into the intelligence community, which also resulted in intelligence reform and updated authorities for electronic surveillance.[107]

Passed before the Church Committee, Title III of the Omnibus Crime Control and Safe Streets Act of 1968, is one of two primary laws for electronic surveillance, but it focuses on law enforcement investigations. Title III, or The Wiretap Act, establishes the regulations for court-authorized surveillance during the investigation of domestic crimes.[108] The earlier section on cyber crime discussed related CFAA and ECPA authorities.[109] Title III prohibits the interception and disclosure of wire, oral, or electronic communications,[110] unless such interception and disclosure follows the procedures for authorization by an investigative or law enforcement officer.[111] Title III may apply to cyber crime investigations, but has limited application to other areas of concern for the field of cyber conflict.

The second of the primary domestic legal frameworks for surveillance is the Foreign Intelligence Surveillance Act of 1978 (FISA), passed in the wake of the Church Committee investigation. In order to conduct domestic electronic surveillance of persons

---

[107]   Loch K. Johnson, "Congressional Supervision of America's Secret Agencies: The Experience and Legacy of the Church Committee," *Policy Administration Review* 64:1 (Jan. 2004): 3-14.

[108]   18 U.S.C. Chapter 19, specifically 18 U.S.C. § 2511.

[109]   Title III has been amended by ECPA, the Communications Assistance for Law Enforcement Act, the USA PATRIOT Act, and the FISA Amendments Act of 2008. See U.S. Department of Justice, Office of Justice Programs, "Federal Statutes" (2010), http://it.ojp.gov/default.aspx?area=privacy&page=1284 (accessed 20 May 2011).

[110]   18 U.S.C. § 2511.

[111]   18 U.S.C. § 2517.

who are agents of foreign powers, FISA permits court orders at the approval of the Foreign Intelligence Surveillance Court (FISC). In addition to the FISC, a three-member court of review – the Foreign Intelligence Surveillance Court of Review (FISCR) – hears appeals of denials of applications. Court orders for electronic surveillance are authorized if the government successfully shows probable cause that the "target of the surveillance is a foreign power or agent of a foreign power."[112] This is a different kind of threshold than would be required to receive a warrant for a criminal case.

In order to use FISA, a *significant purpose* of the electronic surveillance must be to obtain intelligence in the United States on foreign powers or those connected to terrorist groups. [113] The question as to the purpose of the FISA warrant demonstrates two procedural issues that can greatly affect the collection of intelligence. The first is that minimization still applies when collecting intelligence under FISA, but unlike law enforcement warrants, minimization occurs after the collection.[114] As defined by FISA, "minimization procedures" are those adopted by the Attorney General "to minimize the acquisition and retention, and prohibit the dissemination, of nonpublicly available information concerning unconsenting United States persons consistent with the need of the United States to obtain, produce, and disseminate foreign intelligence information."[115] Typically, minimization seeks the protection of civil liberties in criminal investigations, particularly in criminal investigations, and means the limitation of non-material information, for example, conversations with family members unrelated to the investigation at hand. Within a law enforcement investigation, minimization "occurs up front rather than during retention or dissemination in part because electronic

---

[112]   50 U.S.C. § 1804.

[113]   The previous standard was "primary purpose" under *United States v. Truong Dinh Hung*, 629 F.2d 908 (4th Cir. 1980); the current standard of "significant purpose" was changed via the USA PATRIOT Act and reaffirmed in *In Re Sealed Case No. 02-001*, 310 F.3d 717 (FISCR, 2002).

[114]   For more discussion see Eric Rosenbach and Aki J. Peritz, *Confrontation or Collaboration? Congress and the Intelligence Community*, The Intelligence and Policy Project (2009), http://belfercenter.ksg.harvard.edu/files/IC-book-finalasof12JUNE.pdf (accessed 20 May 2011).

[115]   50 U.S.C. § 1801(h).

surveillance during traditional law enforcement investigations is episodic and short term"[116] These kinds of investigations differ from FISA investigations, which are occur for a longer period of time and include more monitoring.[117] While FISA minimization procedures are classified, it appears that "the government conducts FISA minimization after processing (including transcription, translation, and analysis), and the retained foreign intelligence enters an indexed storage system for retrieval."[118] Some have argued that the 2007 amendments have damaged the original intent of minimization.[119] Whatever the minimization procedures may be, what is initially collected and how it is then categorized has a significant effect on what intelligence may be collected.

The second, and more significant procedural matter, is the role of information sharing between law enforcement and domestic intelligence. Because of the concern about using intelligence information improperly against US citizens (prior to the terror attacks of September 11, 2011), a Department of Justice policy created barriers, often referred to as "the wall," that prevented the sharing of intelligence information with law enforcement and vice versa. However, The USA PATRIOT Act, passed in the weeks following the 9/11 attacks, included provisions that encouraged intelligence and law enforcement to exchange relevant information.[120]

FISA has been significantly amended by the USA PATRIOT Act, the Protect America Act of 2007 (PAA), and the 2008 FISA Amendments. The 2007 and 2008 amendments were passed after public discussion of the Terrorist Surveillance Program, which bypassed the FISA process to obtain court orders. The PAA legislated that communications that begin or end in a foreign country may be wiretapped without a warrant and instituted procedures for the government to certify the legality of the

---

[116]   William C. Banks, "Programmatic Surveillance and FISA: Of Needles in Haystacks," *Texas Law Review* 88 (2010), 1633-1667, 1647.

[117]   Ibid.

[118]   Ibid., at 1648.

[119]   Ibid., at 1649.

[120]   Also see *In Re Sealed Case No. 02-001*, holding that FISA may be used to collect evidence for criminal prosecution. The opinion stated that as a legal matter, there was never a "wall" between intelligence and law enforcement sharing information and there is not one currently.

acquisitions.[121] The 2008 FISA Amendments added additional safeguards to national security surveillance conducted without a warrant, reaffirmed the PAA policy of permitting interception of foreign communications received domestically without a warrant, and provided immunity for telecommunications companies from lawsuits for "past or future cooperation" with governmental surveillance for intelligence purposes.[122]

Because both Title III and FISA relate to electronic intercepts, they are important for both law enforcement and intelligence intercepts in cyberspace. Additionally, some kinds of cyber exploitation may be considered surveillance, and if these activities are conducted domestically or targeting US persons, they may be subject to either Title III or FISA.[123] As noted by the National Research Council, application of FISA to cyber conflict is still unclear, but at least one case of a Title III warrant has authorized cyber exploitation.[124] Accordingly, these authorities may be used more frequently in the future for investigations and intelligence collection related to cyber conflict.

It is also important to emphasize that FISA and Title III apply to US persons, including American citizens and permanent residents in territory under US control. FISA and Title III do not apply to surveillance conducted outside of the United States. Foreigners abroad without a nexus to the United States do not have Constitutional protections.[125] This distinction in surveillance

---

[121]   The Protect America Act of 2007 (P.L. 110-55, 121 Stat. 552).

[122]   Foreign Intelligence Surveillance Act of 1978 Amendments Act of 2008 (P.L. 110-261. 122 Stat. 2436).

[123]   Owens, Dam, and Lin, eds. *Cyberattack Capabilities*, 287.

[124]   Ibid., (citing U.S. District Court Western District of Washington, Application and Affidavit for Search Warrant, June 12, 2007,: //politechbot.com/docs/fbi.cipav.sanders.affidavit.071607.pdf).

[125]   "Electronic surveillance" is defined under FISA to exclude surveillance activities that take place outside the United States, 50 U.S.C. § 1801(f): "The acquisition by an electronic, mechanical, or other surveillance device of the contents of any wire or radio communication sent by or intended to be received by a particular, known United States person who is in the United States, if the contents are acquired by intentionally targeting that United States person, under circumstances in which a person has a reasonable expectation of privacy and a warrant would be required for law enforcement purposes." See also, *United States v. Verdugo-Urquidez*, 494 U.S. 259 (1990) (the Fourth Amendment does

protections is complicated by the fact that technology has changed significantly in the decades since enactment of FISA; many of the world's communications are transmitted via fiber-optic cables, a large number of which pass through the United States. In some of the reform debates, it was argued therefore that FISA should be amended to allow for "foreign intelligence surveillance of non-US persons from within the country." [126] The Protect America Act of 2007 subsequently authorized warrantless surveillance of foreign-to-foreign communications passing through the United States, as well as "warrantless surveillance of US citizens communicating with people overseas, as long as the target was reasonably believed to be located outside of the United States." [127] The 2008 FISA Amendments authorized the same provisions. [128]

Thus the more "technology neutral" provisions of the 2008 FISA Amendments allow the Intelligence Community to adapt to the ever-evolving communications technologies and digital society. It should be noted that the 2008 FISA Amendments require reauthorization by the end of 2012, which may reopen debate on electronic surveillance and how technological developments affect surveillance authorities.

Defense Production Act

Another law that should be mentioned in the cyber conflict context is the Defense Production Act. Concerned about the lack of preparedness for supplying the defense community in the face of the Korean War, Congress passed the Defense Production Act of 1950 (DPA). [129] This law has many components, [130] among them the ability

---

not apply to the search and seizure by U.S. agents of property owned by a nonresident alien and located in a foreign country).

[126]   Rosenbach and Peritz, *Confrontation or Collaboration? Congress and the Intelligence Community*, 70.

[127]   Stephanie Cooper Blum, "What Really Is At Stake With the FISA Amendments Act of 2008 and Ideas for Future Surveillance Reform," *Boston University Public Interest Law Journal* 18 (2009): 269-314, 296.

[128]   Ibid., 299 (citing 50 U.S.C. § 1881a(b)(1)-(3) for a description of the communications requiring a FISA warrant under the FISA Amendments, which do not include foreign-to-foreign communications traveling over U.S. networks).

[129]   National Research Council, *Defense Manufacturing in 2010 and Beyond: Meeting the Changing Needs of National Defense* (National Academies Press, 1999): 91.

of the President to prioritize contracts and supplies "necessary or appropriate to promote the national defense."[131] Certain provisions of the DPA have been reauthorized and amended numerous times; currently the DPA defines 'national defense' as

> programs for military and energy production or construction, military or critical infrastructure assistance to any foreign nation, homeland security, stockpiling, space, and any directly related activity. Such term includes emergency preparedness activities conducted pursuant to title VI of The Robert T. Stafford Disaster Relief and Emergency Assistance Act [42 U.S.C. 5195 et seq.] and critical infrastructure protection and restoration.[132]

Under such a definition, the prioritization authority of the DPA for contracts and supplies is not meant for only wartime use, or even for use only in declared national disasters; it can be used to support homeland security activities such as the protection and restoration of critical infrastructure.

The incorporation of critical infrastructure into the definition of national defense, and thus the protection of critical infrastructure as a component of the DPA, dates from the 2003 reauthorization and amendments.[133] In the 2009 amendments, Congress stressed that the DPA is to be used for homeland security and critical infrastructure protection purposes in addition to more historical concepts of national defense.[134] Emphasizing the equally important roles of defense and homeland security, the President in 2010 announced that the newly-created Defense Production Act Committee (as established by the 2009 DPA reauthorization) would be chaired

---

[130] See 50 U.S.C. App. § 2061 et seq.
[131] 50 U.S.C. App. § 2071.
[132] 50 U.S.C. App. § 2152(14).
[133] Defense Production Act Reauthorization of 2003, Pub. L. No. 108-195, 117 Stat. 2892 (2003).
[134] See, e.g., Defense Production Act Reauthorization of 2009, Pub. L. No. 111-67, 123 Stat. 2006 (2009), at Sec. 2 Declaration of Policy, Sec. 8 Definitions (adding 'homeland security').

by the Secretaries of Defense and Homeland Security on an annually rotating basis.[135]

Although the DPA does not speak specifically to telecommunications or cyber conflict, these matters clearly fall into 'critical infrastructure protection' and 'homeland security.' And thus, while past commentators have been concerned that he DPA may not be properly interpreted to apply in the cyber conflict context,[136] the 2003 and 2009 amendments should combine to permit such interpretations. Questions and concerns may still remain regarding policy and operational matters (e.g., regarding the plans and policies for determining prioritization in a cyber crisis; and the need for a coherent, cross-agency understanding of potential cascading failures).[137] However, in this case, Congress has clarified that the Presidential prioritization authority of the DPA does apply to the protection and restoration of critical infrastructure and other homeland security activities beyond the historical definitions of national defense.

Protected Critical Infrastructure Information

Another relevant legal provision is the exception of certain critical infrastructure information from the federal freedom of information laws, an exception that may encourage information sharing in the cyber conflict context. The Homeland Security Act of 2002 included a section titled the "Critical Infrastructure Information Act of 2002."[138] The goal of this section was to protect critical infrastructure information that was voluntarily shared with the government.

Information could include vulnerability assessments, incident reports, continuity of operations plans, risk assessment or audits, etc.[139] When submitted to a federal entity, the information is exempted from disclosure under the federal Freedom of

---

[135]   The White House Office of the Press Secretary, Presidential Memorandum Designating the Chairperson of the Defense Production Act Committee (June 1, 2010).

[136]   See, e.g., Lee M. Zeichner, "Use of the Defense Production Act of 1950 for Critical Infrastructure Protection," in Joint Economic Committee of the United States Congress, Security in the Information Age: New Challenges, New Strategies (2002): 74-88.

[137]   Ibid. at 78, 80.

[138]   Pub. L. No. 107-296, 116 Stat. 2135, at Sec. 211 et seq.

[139]   Ibid. at Sec. 212.

Information Act; correspondingly, when submitted to a state entity, the information is exempted from state and local freedom of information laws. The information is also restricted from use in civil litigation and other purposes outside of the scope of critical infrastructure protection and security.[140]

DHS has established a Program Office to manage the Protected Critical Infrastructure Information (PCII) program. Program activities include the creation of policies for accreditation and oversight of participating government entities, as well as procedures for the submission, acceptance, and storage/safeguarding of information.[141]

The PCII program has primarily been used by state and local agencies in submitting information to the federal government.[142] So far there has been no test case in the courts to provide a more solid grounding on which the private sector may trust in the PCII protections. In 2009, though, one case did interpret part of the Critical Infrastructure Information Act provisions relating to PCII submitted by state governments to DHS. As a result of this case, in the jurisdiction of California, such information may *not* be protected from disclosure under the state freedom of information laws.

In that case, a group had filed a freedom of information request for information that the county of Santa Clara had properly submitted to DHS and for which the county had received validation under the PCII program.[143] The court found that the Critical Infrastructure Information Act was not an applicable bar to the petitioner's freedom of information request because the act only protected PCII provided *to* state and local governments, not PCII provided *by* state and local governments.[144]

---

[140]   Ibid., Sec. 214.

[141]   Department of Homeland Security, How Protected Critical Infrastructure Information (PCII) Is Protected,
http://www.dhs.gov/files/programs/gc_1193088517704.shtm (last reviewed/modified Oct. 22, 2009); see also Department of Homeland Security, Protected Critical Infrastructure Information Program Procedures Manual (April 2009),
http://www.dhs.gov/xlibrary/assets/pcii_program_procedures_manual.pdf.

[142]   Encouraged by the development of tools such as the Automated Critical Asset Management System (ACAMS) for example.

[143]   *County of Santa Clara v. Superior Court*, 170 Cal. App. 4th 1301 (6 Dist. 2009.), at 1312.

[144]   Ibid., 1316-19.

There appears to be not much public, readily-available data on the statistics of usage for the PCII program, or on the value of such program. In March 2011, the Federal Register ran a notice from DHS on its planned 'Protected Critical Infrastructure Information (PCII) Stakeholder Survey.' If the survey proceeds, it may provide fruit for further discussion; however, the survey appears to be focused on procedures and relationship-building, rather than legal matters, so it may not have too much relevance to these discussions.

Furthermore, the Critical Infrastructure Information Act is based on voluntary information sharing, with no obligation to share vulnerabilities or incident reports,[145] and so its effect on the cyber conflict and security contexts, particularly regarding private sector information, may be debatable. Regardless, the law may promote information sharing in the cyber conflict context,[146] even if certain interpretations, as in California (discussed above), may limit its utility.

Conclusion

This section has focused on four cyber conflict-relevant categories in the domestic legal framework—warfare, crime, emergency response, and preparedness—and also included several other titles of the US Code that may be applicable to cyber conflict. While presented as a positivist overview of the current legal framework, the above analysis has also demonstrated a trend of continued uncertainty regarding some aspects of US law in the context of cyber conflict. These legal concerns must be clearly understood not only by the legislators and executive decision-makers, but also by the operational personnel and private defenders of the information infrastructure.

---

[145]   The United States has not yet passed laws requiring such disclosure or reporting.

[146]   Another law that encourages information sharing is the authorization in the 2002 Homeland Security Act for the DHS Secretary to create an advisory council to the President on matters of critical infrastructure protection and to exempt this council from the Federal Advisory Committee Act. Consequently, the Critical Infrastructure Partnership Advisory Council was established in 2006. 71 Fed. Reg. 14,930 (Mar. 24, 2006).

For the most part, it seems that daily practitioners are in fact the most aware of the restrictions and boundaries of US law, but there must be an understanding between both sets of actors because they must work together to offer solutions to the problems of cyber conflict.

An additional recommendation based on the above analysis is that some of the legal matters, which were established before the digital era, require clarification to better suit the cyber conflict context. While some authorities still apply or have been updated, the pace of technology requires a reexamination of the legal framework. It is vital that policymakers and practitioners clearly define their goals and priorities for cyber conflict policy before turning to the legal process to shape future authorities. As the United States continues to update and amend existing statutes, as well as draft new authorities, [147] it is imperative that policymakers, lawmakers, and practitioners maintain the above recommendations as priorities. The importance of clarifying authorities for the cyber context, and of ensuring understanding of all relevant authorities, is also reflected in the international law section below.

International Law

While many scholars, including those discussed below, are actively discussing these issues, the decisions that will most quickly and definitively shape the international law of cyber conflict will likely not be *a priori* legal analyses but will be political decisions made in the context of responding to a significant cyber event.[148]

---

[147] See. e.g. Office of Management and Budget, "Complete Cybersecurity Proposal" (12 May 2011), http://www.whitehouse.gov/sites/default/files/omb/legislative/letters/Law-Enforcement-Provisions-Related-to-Computer-Security-Full-Bill.pdf (accessed 26 May 2011).

[148] This reality is not necessarily limited to cyber issues. For example, as analyzed in a later section, as of August 2001, there was much legal analysis, including international court decisions, on the subject of state responsibility for the actions of non-state actors. At that time, the analysis was primarily distilled into two rough standards for allocating responsibility based on the level of state control of the non-state actors. However, after the September 11, 2001 terrorist attacks on the United States, the invasion

Nevertheless, it is important to understand the nuances of international law and to develop frameworks for understanding the boundaries and ramifications of legal and political decisions in this context. While a full primer on international law is beyond the scope of this chapter, some fundamental aspects of international law must be presented as a basis for discussing legal issues of cyber conflict. The various interrelated sources of international law include:

(a) international conventions, whether general or particular, expressing rules expressly recognized ...

(b) international custom, as evidence of a general practice accepted as law;

(c) the general principles of law recognized by civilized nations

(d) ... judicial decisions and the teachings of the most highly qualified publicists of the various nations, as subsidiary means for the determination of law.[149]

International law is far from clear-cut and well-defined as regards to physical conflict; the cyber dimension adds more layers of complexity, both legal and technical. In fact, no aspects of these international law sources, from (a) through (d), have yet been delineated in the cyber context.[150]

Afghanistan was justified to the international community, even though the United States did not show that Afghanistan "controlled" the al Qaeda terrorists in line with previous legal definitions. Thus it can be said that here international law was perhaps shaped more by political decisions in response to a significant event than by prior legal analyses.

[149] Pia Palojarvi, *A Battle in Bits and Bytes: Computer Network Attacks and the Law of Armed Conflict* (Helsinki: Erik Castren Institute of International Law and Human Rights, 2009): 11 (quoting Article 38(1) of the Statute of the International Court of Justice, 1945).

[150] Ibid. See also, Michael N. Schmitt, "Cyber Operations in International Law: The Use of Force, Collective Security, Self-Defense, and Armed Conflicts" in National Research Council, ed., *Proceedings of a Workshop on Deterring Cyberattacks: Informing Strategies and Developing Options for U.S. Policy* (Washington, DC: National Academies Press: 2010), 151-178, 152, 157; General Keith Alexander, "Advance Questions for Lieutenant General Keith Alexander, USA Nominee for Commander, United States Cyber Command," April 15, 2010, http://armed-services.senate.gov/statemnt/2010/04%20April/Alexander%2004-15-10.pdf (accessed 22 May, 2011).

Under international humanitarian law, the law of armed conflict is applied to situations of armed conflict between states. [151] As discussed below, it is fairly widely accepted that international humanitarian law applies to an international armed conflict that incorporates cyber techniques, and could also apply to a purely cyber conflict. [152] The law of armed conflict does not generally apply to other situations, such as acts of terrorism or riots (which may be instead be addressed in specific treaties or in domestic law). [153] One important requirement is that the international armed conflict involves two or more states. The cyber actions must therefore be ascribable to states; as discussed below, this requirement also applies to notions of state responsibility. It is this particular aspect that may be the most contentious in analyses of cyber conflicts, particularly for cyber activities not concurrent with traditional armed conflicts. Additional discussions of the problems of attribution are found in Chapters 2 and 3 of this publication.

A second significant tenet in international humanitarian law is the elucidation of 'armed conflict,' the finding of which is prerequisite to certain internationally lawful actions. [154] Although international armed conflict is rather highly regulated, [155] there is no clear legal definition of the scope of activities that constitute an 'armed attack.' [156] The majority of scholars addressing this issue support the position that 'armed attack' should be defined based upon its consequences, and thus whether the attack is conducted via cyber or kinetic means may be irrelevant. [157]

It is important to remember that in the cyber conflict perspective, the consequence-based approach (or any alternative approaches discussed below) has not yet been incorporated into the codified international humanitarian law. Nor has it been interpreted in international courts. As discussed below, some countries have

---

[151]   Palojarvi, *A Battle in Bits and Bytes*, 60.
[152]   See Palojarvi at 13, 60-74 and Schmitt, "Cyber Operations in International Law: The Use of Force, Collective Security, Self-Defense, and Armed Conflicts," 154.
[153]   Ibid., 60, 66.
[154]   Ibid., 47-74.
[155]   Ibid., 62.
[156]   Ibid., 60-68.
[157]   These considerations are further discussed in part in Chapters 1 and 2 respectively.

made statements advocating that international law should be applied in cyberspace. However at this nascent stage of policy-making regarding international cyber conflict these statements may appear more to be aspirational goals, rather than statements representing an acknowledgement of binding expectations and obligations under law.

This distinction can be important, since international custom is one source of international law, and in fact has been recognized as the 'most fundamental' source of international law. All member states of the United Nations acknowledge international custom as a valid source of law. [158] Customary international law includes principles such as prohibitions on the use of force, respect of sovereignty, and the restraint on interference in the internal affairs of a state. [159] The concept of international custom is quite nuanced; this chapter will not delve into too much detail, but certain understandings are relevant to the discussion of international law of cyber conflict.

First, international custom means that the activity at issue is both a general practice and is accepted as legally binding. Most applications and interpretations of international custom deem that 'practice' may include an action, an absence of action, or a statement. [160] As to the prevalence of the activity at issue,

> practice can be of a general, particular, or local scope. In the case of a particular or local practice the uniformity has to be proved. In the case of practice of a general scope, however, a practice does not have to be uniform but the exact formula of how many states should adhere to a given practice ranges from half of the participants to virtual unanimity of participants. [161]

It should be noted that if a state openly asserts an early and consistent objection to a certain international custom, that states

---

[158] P.P. Polanski, Customary Law of the Internet: In the Search for a Supranational Cyberspace Law (The Hague, T.M.C. Asser Press: 2007): 144 (citing Article 38 of the Statute of the International Court of Justice).

[159] Ibid., 180.

[160] Ibid., 147-154.

[161] Ibid., 158.

may be recognized as a 'persistent objector' and may, in effect, 'opt out' of the binding nature of the custom.[162]

In addition to 'general practice,' the concept of international custom requires that the practice is followed because the states believe that the law so requires. In other words, the general practice must also be a legal duty. This is a subjective feeling of being bound, that there is some legally-supplied consequence or sanction for violation. [163] In this aspect, it is important to differentiate aspirational goals or mere statements of international policy from existing rules of international law. Therefore, some statements of international policy may be non-legal social norms, and not legal norms that may, with a finding of general practice, be found to comprise international custom.[164] As discussed further in subpart 3.3.2 below, many organizations and countries have propounded principles and norms regarding behavior in cyberspace, including roles and responsibilities of states. Most of these principles are statements of international policy, or opinions of what the international policy should be.

Arguably, regarding particular rules of cyber conflict, the international community has not yet established general principles of a lawfully binding nature. Further, while there may be more than 150 different customary norms recognized in international armed conflict,[165] the application of these norms to cyber conflict must be further discussed and elaborated. Determinations on how custom is created, and how it is evidenced, are also relevant to discussions of international law of cyber conflict, and should be included in such analyses. These debates and determinations complement the scholarly debates of defining 'armed attack' in the cyber conflict context. Some of these issues are discussed in more detail below.

New developments in technology and shifting threats to international security continually pose challenges to the international legal framework. This was true for armored vehicles, new weaponry, and the development of chemical weapons. Similarly, the emergence of cyber conflict and the potential of

---

[162] Ibid., 160-162.
[163] Ibid., 147-150, 164-165.
[164] Ibid., 169-171, 180.
[165] Ibid., 196.

"cyber war" have caused international legal scholars to debate the applicability of international law to these new threats. This decades-old debate has continued as international legal scholars seek to find consensus regarding the application of the laws of war to activities in cyberspace.[166] Currently there is an effort to create a *Manual on International Law Applicable to Cyber Warfare*, spearheaded by a NATO-accredited center of excellence,[167] which may coalesce consensus. Still, there are no public indications of consensus on the rules of cyber warfare or on the willingness of nations to bind themselves to such rules via a specific international legal instrument that explicates such rules.[168]

Although the apparent novelty of cyber conflict has started to wane, activities in cyberspace continue to present challenges to the maintenance and development of international law. Firstly, the scope of activities that are potentially harmful but that are below an "armed attack" threshold, or even a "use of force" threshold, remains legally ambiguous. Secondly, the relationship of non-state actors, state responsibility, and armed conflict, developed in other contexts, is contested in cyberspace. Additionally, the foundational concept of state sovereignty may be viewed as dynamic in the context of cyber conflict. Lastly, the importance of state practice and the ensuing contradictions therein demonstrate that a lack of political consensus may inhibit any growing legal consensus.

---

[166] It may be important to note that the commentators and legal scholars on the issue of cyber conflict have thus far been primarily American scholars. The majority of international legal analysis is published by American scholars and policymakers in U.S. law journals, which influences subsequent analysis in the United States and around the world. The trends in this field are changing as other international lawyers address this issue, but non-U.S. sources continue to be limited, respectively, when discussing cyber conflict and the laws of armed conflict.

[167] NATO Cooperative Cyber Defence Centre of Excellence, "MILCW – Manual on International Law Applicable to Cyber Warfare," 2011, http://www.ccdcoe.org/249.html (accessed May 12, 2011).

[168] The manual, though, is based on existing international humanitarian law (developed for the physical / kinetic context), and so the manual likely will interpret and extrapolate existing law rather than introduce many new international obligations. Comment from Maeve Dion (May 13, 2011), participant in the initial scoping meeting for the manual, held at the Cooperative Cyber Defence Centre of Excellence, Tallinn, Estonia, Sept. 12, 2009).

This chapter proceeds by first differentiating activities of cyber crime and espionage before progressing to an assessment of cyber conflict and the principles of International Humanitarian Law (IHL), also known as the Laws of Armed Conflict (LOAC), as they may apply to cyber conflict. The subsequent section discusses state responsibility and its application to non-state actors and transboundary harm. The last international law subcategory provides an overview of some treaties that have been discussed in the context of cyber conflict activities (relating to cyber crime, outer space, telecommunications), as well as the proliferation of policy norms, as opposed to legal norms, regarding international cyber security and the implications for international law.

Cyber Crime, Cyber Espionage, and International Law

As is discussed in earlier chapters and the opening capstone, cyber conflict encompasses many kinds of activities, from hacking to espionage to denial of service attacks, all done in the interests of a broader strategic purpose. Such activities include computer network defense (CND), computer network attack (CNA), and computer network exploitation (CNE).[169] Each of these activities has implications for international law and coordination regardless of the identity of the actor engaging in these activities. The full spectrum of cyber conflict, therefore, implicates a wide area of international law, from law enforcement agreements, existing communications treaties, and traditional notions of duty of care, to the established framework of the laws of armed conflict. One scholar notes that there are at least three overlapping fields of international law that apply to cyberspace: Internet governance, multilateral public policy, and international security. [170] Within that framework, law enforcement coordination, data privacy concerns, and human rights and civil liberties fall into the multilateral public policy

---

[169] For an overview of these terms and their technical attributes, please see the Capstone of this volume.

[170] Sean Kanuck, "Sovereign Discourse on Cyber Conflict Under International Law," *Texas Law Review* 88 (2010): 1571-1597.

category, encompassing a wide array of sometimes-contradictory interests and legal frameworks.[171]

Because it must incorporate a strategic purpose, cyber conflict, as defined in the capstone, does not include cyber crime when the primary focus is monetary gain – hacking into banks, poaching massive numbers of credit card accounts, or spear-phishing for financial information. For the most part, this kind of cyber crime is a concern for national law enforcement agencies in cooperation with foreign counterparts and organizations like the International Criminal Police Organization (INTERPOL) as needed. In the context of cyber crime, the presence of harmonized laws is crucial to the facilitation of extraditions and prosecution. Overall, however, this is an issue of national law and cooperation and is generally not one of strategic national security importance. Still, this chapter discusses the Council of Europe Convention on Cybercrime in a following section, as it is an important milestone in the creation of binding legal instruments that are applicable to activities in cyberspace and has political significance for many of the important actors leading the debate surrounding cyber conflict.

Cyber attack, or CNA, is the focus of the following section about LOAC, and CND also plays an important role in the laws of armed conflict. CNE, however, falls into an ambiguous middle ground. As explained by Schaap, espionage is "the act of obtaining, delivering, transmitting, communicating or receiving information about the national defense of a 'victim' state where the 'collecting' state possesses an intent to use the information to injure the victim state, or to give an advantage to any other state."[172] Traditional state-to-state espionage, for example the espionage activities conducted by the United States and the Soviet Union during the Cold War or any other contemporary traditional espionage, is permitted under international law. Espionage is not illegal *per se* under international law, although most countries include espionage as a criminal offense in their respective national

---

[171] Ibid.

[172] Major Arie J. Schaap, "Cyber Warfare Operations: Development and Use Under International Law," *Air Force Law Review* 64 (2009): 121-174.

legal systems. Despite the criminalization of espionage domestically, the vast majority of states consider espionage crucial to the maintenance of national security and defense.[173]

The rules of espionage during wartime are clearly defined, beginning with the Lieber Code of 1863, which defined a spy as "a person who secretly, in disguise or under false pretense, seeks information with the intention of communicating it to the enemy." [174] The 1907 Hague Conventions [175] and Additional Protocol I to the Geneva Conventions[176] further codify customs regarding espionage in a wartime environment. These rules permit "the employment of measures necessary for obtaining information about the enemy and the country."[177] Thus, the rules of conduct concerning espionage in wartime have been codified multiple times over the past century.[178]

In contrast, the laws governing peacetime espionage, while also permitted by international law, are less well established than those of wartime espionage. [179] There is some discussion that espionage is actually illegal under international law, [180] but the overall consensus is that peacetime espionage is one of many legitimate tools at a state's disposal.[181] Indeed, Wingfield cites the 1961 Vienna Convention on Diplomatic Relations as "[explicit recognition of] the well-established right of nations to engage in

---

[173] See Wingfield, *The Law of Information Conflict*, 350-358; Schaap, "Cyber Warfare Operations."

[174] Instructions for the Government of Armies of the United States in the Field (Lieber Code), 24 April 1863, http://www.icrc.org/ihl.nsf/FULL/110?OpenDocument (accessed May 7, 2011).

[175] Convention (IV) respecting the Laws and Customs of War on Land and its annex: Regulations concerning the Laws and Customs of War on Land. The Hague, 18 October 1907 (Hereafter Hague Convention IV)

[176] Protocol Additional to the Geneva Conventions of 12 August 1949, and relating to the protection of victims of international armed conflicts (Protocol I), Geneva, 6 August 1977 (accessed May 19, 2011).

[177] Hague Convention IV, Art. 24.

[178] The following section on *jus in bello* further discusses ruses of war in the context of perfidy.

[179] It is important to note, however, that most espionage attempts in the current cyber environment occur in peace time conditions

[180] A. John Radsan, "The Unresolved Equation of Espionage and International Law," *Michigan Journal of International Law* 28 (2007): 595-623.

[181] Wingfield, *The Law of Information Conflict*, 350.

espionage during peacetime." [182] Traditionally, espionage is considered an effective mechanism for reducing tensions and avoiding suspicion because it provides unfiltered information on adversaries' capabilities and intentions. Conducting espionage can also develop certain rules that may not rise to international law. For example, during the Cold War, "Moscow Rules" defined well-understood norms for espionage activities, up to and including the discovery of spies.[183] Peaceful resolution, in war and in peace, of espionage-related disputes were generally possible without a substantial increase in tensions.

The dynamics of cyber espionage, however, are strikingly different from traditional espionage activities. CNE is particularly problematic because of the low costs to those conducting espionage and the large amount of data that can be collected in a relatively small amount of time. The collection of files and information that would have required either years to collect or a forklift to take out of the building can be extracted in a fraction of the time through the Internet or other networked systems. Many of the same tools and techniques used to engage in CNE are the same sets that are also used for CNA. Further, because both sets of activities exploit the same vulnerabilities, the distinction between CNA and CNE can be difficult to discern.[184] Since the factual distinction is complicated, so too is the application of existing legal frameworks and subsequent response options for states. As summarized by Wingfield, "The technology of computers and the Internet allows a lawful act of espionage to morph into an unlawful use of force at the speed of light."[185] One proposed method of telling the difference is based on the collection platform used,[186] but the lines are still unclear even using that model. Due to the factors discussed above, this section addresses how international law traditionally considers espionage and how that may apply in the context of CNE.

---

[182]   Ibid.

[183]   For a list of example "Moscow Rules," see Lisa Burgess, "A Former Spy Teaches a Crash-Course in Espionage," *Stars and Stripes*, 30 December 2003, http://www.military.com/NewContent/0,13190,123003_spy,00.html (accessed May 7, 2011).

[184]   Owens, Dam, and Lin, eds., *Cyberattack Capabilities*, 261.

[185]   Wingfield, *The Law of Information Conflict*, 349.

[186]   Owens, Dam, and Lin, eds., *Cyberattack Capabilities*, 261.

According to some scholars and practitioners, CNE is permissible as a subcategory of espionage: "Nations should treat political and military espionage in cyberspace as they treat it in the physical world."[187] Still, the threat of all kinds of cyber espionage or exploitation is much more significant than previous tools and techniques utilized by intelligence agencies. Policymakers and national security leaders should address this problem from the perspective that cyber espionage is permitted, but that the borders between espionage and a use of force in cyberspace are blurred. This has led some practitioners and policymakers to propose the development of "Cyber Moscow Rules."[188] Alternatively, CNE may provide a prima facie indication of hostile intent, against which the use of force and self-defense is sometimes authorized.[189] However, determining what threshold would need to be met would be perilous.

Accordingly, the rules governing CNE are unlikely to change legally because it is not in states' interests to stop such a vital activity. Therefore, international law is likely to still permit espionage, and CNE as a subset of that. Still, certain policy norms and rules short of international law may curtail the current pervasiveness and intensity of CNE. While states are unlikely to sacrifice a vital tool of national power, they may be more likely to agree to common restrictions on activity.

---

[187] James A. Lewis, "The Cyber War Has Not Begun," Center for Strategic and International Studies Paper (March 2010), http://csis.org/files/publication/100311_TheCyberWarHasNotBegun.pdf (accessed 19 May 2011).

[188] Matthew Devost, "The 21st-Century Security Setting: Identifying the Demand," Panelist Speech at 39th IFPA-Fletcher Conference on National Security Strategy and Policy: The Marine Corps: America's Expeditionary Force in Readiness (April 14-15, 2011), http://www.ifpafletcherconference.com/2011/transcripts/DevostTalk.pdf (accessed 16 May 2011). In his speech, Devost cites Bob Gourley, an author of this monograph, as his source for his discussion about "Moscow Rules for Cyberspace."

[189] Joint Chiefs of Staff, "Enclosure A – Standing Rules of Engagement for US Forces," in *Standing Rules of Engagement for US Forces*, Chairman of the Joint Chiefs of Staff Instruction (CJCSI 3121.01A), January 15, 2000.

Jus ad Bellum and Jus in Bello

The modern conceptions of *jus ad bellum* and *jus in bello* were first fully developed after World War I in the League of Nations, and *jus ad bellum* and *jus in bello* are cornerstones of contemporary public international law and the global dynamics of the international system.[190] *Jus ad bellum*, generally codified in the United Nations Charter, limits the resort to war and has implications for both state and non-state activities in cyberspace. *Jus in bello* limits acceptable wartime conduct and similarly has effects in cyberspace. These two principal legal concepts will be discussed separately in this section.

Three analytical models generally pervade the discussion of cyber conflict and international law.[191] The first is instrument-based, which focuses on the means of an attack. The second model, an effects-based approach,[192] determines the legality of an action under *jus ad bellum* based on the consequences of an activity. The last model employs strict liability, which posits that "[c]yberattacks against [Critical National Infrastructure should be] automatically treated as armed attacks, due to the severe consequences that can result from disabling those systems."[193] While there are some notable disagreements,[194] the effects-based model is generally accepted when applying *jus ad bellum* principles.[195] Under all three of these methods, a cyber attack can potentially be considered an armed attack. This contrasts with other approaches that argue that only kinetic attacks could be considered armed attacks under the U.N. Charter.[196]

---

[190]   Robert Kolb, "Origin of the Twin Terms *Jus ad Bellum/Jus in Bello*," *International Review of the Red Cross* 320 (1997), http://www.icrc.org/eng/resources/documents/misc/57jnuu.htm (accessed 7 May 2011).

[191]   For a comparison of these theoretical models, see Matthew J. Sklerov, "Solving the Dilemma of State Responses to Cyberattacks: A Justification for the Use of Active Defenses Against States Who Neglect Their Duty to Prevent," *Military Law* Review 201 (Fall 2009): 1- 85.

[192]   Sometimes called "consequence-based." Ibid., 54.

[193]   Ibid., 55.

[194]   Brenner and Clarke, "Civilians in Cyberwarfare: Conscripts."

[195]   See Sklerov, "Solving the Dilemma of State Responses to Cyberattacks," for a fuller discussion of benefits of effects-based approach compared to other approaches.

[196]   Brenner and Clarke, "Civilians in Cyberwarfare: Conscripts," 22.

An effects-based viewpoint does not consider as the primary determination of legality the methods of the attack, but rather what the attack's consequences are. This determination must depend fully on the facts of a specific scenario. Therefore, it is difficult to state now what activities in cyberspace may be considered uses of force or armed attack because that determination would be based on specific circumstances and would in fact be a political decision. While this may be criticized as a subjective determination, this method of determining the legality of activities is not limited to the spectrum of cyber conflict. Rather, it fits in the broadly accepted context of an effects-based approach to international law and the laws of armed conflict.

The applicability of LOAC to cyber conflict, including *jus ad bellum* and *jus in bello* principles, is generally endorsed by many US lawyers, practitioners, and policymakers. As General Keith Alexander, Commander of US Cyber Command, stated to Congress, "The law of war principles of military necessity, proportionality, and distinction will apply when conducting cyber operations." [197] Therefore, LOAC defines US military operations in cyberspace, providing one example of state practice in this field.

This position, however, contrasts with the position of Russia and many of its Shanghai Cooperation Organization allies. [198] Russia has proposed an alternative framework for cyber conflict, but this proposal has been rebuffed by some Western states, including the United States and the United Kingdom. Furthermore, these two countries have until very recently opposed any attempts to create an international treaty (especially those attempts endorsed by Russia), emphasizing that the current

---

[197]   General Keith Alexander, "Advance Questions for Lieutenant General Keith Alexander." See also Department of Defense, *Department of Defense Strategy for Operating in Cyberspace* (July 2011).

[198]   For a discussion of the Russian position compared to the U.S. and Chinese positions, see Roland Heickerö, "Emerging Cyber Threats and Russian Views on Information Warfare and Information Operations," User Report, Swedish Defence Research Agency, March 2010, www2.foi.se/rapp/foir2970.pdf. Section 6.1 is especially relevant.

LOAC framework should be sufficient for states' activities in cyberspace. [199] As summarized by a 1999 US Department of Defense document from the Office of the General Counsel, "The LOAC is probably the single area of international law in which current legal obligations can be applied with the greatest confidence to information operations." [200] To some degree, this position may contrast with the positions of international lawyers in other countries, where there is disagreement centered on the proper application of international law to cyberspace. It is therefore crucial that US policymakers and leaders understand the current landscape of international law when considering activities in cyberspace, including the perception by others in the policy and legal communities.

Jus ad Bellum

Contemporary *jus ad bellum* is codified in the U.N. Charter, primarily in Articles 2(4), 39, and 51, and recognizes and restricts the rights of states to resort to force. Article 2(4) of the Charter forbids the "threat or use of force against the territorial integrity or political independence of any state," whereas Article 51 recognizes a state's inherent right to self-defense. Article 39 establishes the Security Council's obligation to "maintain or restore international peace and security." All of these articles are important to the legal issues discussed here, and their applicability to cyberspace and activities constituting cyber conflict: use or threat of force, armed attack, self-defense, anticipatory self-defense, and active defense.

Use of Force

Article 2(4) prohibits the threat or use of force by all U.N. member states; this prohibition is also a matter of customary international law, regulating the resort to force for all states. In its entirety, Article 2(4) states that "[a]ll Members shall refrain in their international relations from the threat or use of force against the territorial integrity or political independence of any state, or in any

---

[199]   Kanuck, "Sovereign Discourse on Cyber Conflict Under International Law," 1588.

[200]   Department of Defense Office of General Counsel, "An Assessment of International Legal Issues in Information Operations."

other manner inconsistent with the Purposes of the United Nations." [201] Article 2(4) is crucial to the maintenance of international peace and security because it outlaws wrongful acts of aggression and regulates legitimate uses of force. And, as will be discussed in the section about Article 51, a use of force can be below the threshold of an armed attack, meaning that a responsive action is more restricted for a use of force than in the case of an armed attack. Scholars generally agree that even though Article 2(4) references "territorial integrity or political independence," any use of force is prohibited unless allowed under existing *jus ad bellum* principles.[202]

The same logic and prohibition applies to the threat of use of force as well. Examples of threats of force may include "verbal threats, initial troop movements, initial movement of ballistic missiles, massing to troops on a border, use of fire control radars, and interference with early warning or command and control systems."[203] As applied to cyberspace, Schmitt posits that "threats of destructive cyber operations against another State's critical infrastructure unless that State cedes territory" would be prohibited under Article 2(4).[204] Alternatively, an example of a threat that would *not* breach Article 2(4) is "threatening destructive defensive cyber attacks against another State's military infrastructure if that State unlawfully mounts unlawful cross-border operations."[205]

As identified in the National Research Council's *Technology, Policy, Law and Ethics Regarding US Acquisition and Use of Cyberattack Capabilities*, a number of unfriendly actions, including trade decisions, boycotts, severance of diplomatic relations, espionage, economic sanctions, and economic and political coercion, do not amount to a use of force.[206] Force as defined under the U.N. Charter does not include all forms of pressure, nor does it include economic or political sanctions.[207]

---

[201] Article 2(4), United Nations, Charter of the United Nations, 24 October 1945, 1 U.N.T.S. XVI.

[202] Schmitt, "Cyber Operations in International Law," 153.

[203] Owens, Dam, and Lin, eds., *Cyberattack Capabilities*, 242.

[204] Schmitt, "Cyber Operations in International Law," 153.

[205] Ibid.

[206] Owens, Dam, and Lin, eds., *Cyberattack Capabilities*, 242.

[207] Schmitt, "Cyber Operations in International Law," 154-155.

The question then becomes: what constitutes a use of force relevant to cyber conflict? As answered by Schmitt, "cyber operations that directly result (or are likely to result) in physical harm to individual or tangible objects equate to armed force, and are therefore 'uses of force.'" [208] Otherwise, cyber activities, including espionage, do not reach this 'use of force' threshold. It is these kinds of activities below Article 2(4) that remain the most problematic in international law.

The key question, as articulated by the 2009 National Research Council (NRC) Report, is "whether a cyberattack *with a specified effect* constitutes a use of force," [209] demonstrating that the key question, for many US thinkers in this area, is not whether the laws governing uses of force apply, but rather *how* these laws apply and what factually might trigger a determination of a use of force. Michael N. Schmitt and Thomas Wingfield are well-respected international legal scholars and they have both contributed heavily to the development of thinking about cyber conflict in relation to the U.N. Charter and the laws of war. Both acknowledge that seeking to apply principles in the U.N. Charter to cyber attacks is something the drafters did not anticipate and is consequently a difficult undertaking. Most scholars who advocate for the application of *jus ad bellum* to cyber conflict caution that there is still much to be determined and much depends on the circumstances of a specific incident. Adding to the uncertainty, state practice and statements in the area of international law and cyber conflict are nascent and in some cases contradictory, further complicating the determination of what may factually be considered a use of force.

However, the existing *jus ad bellum* principles can provide a degree of guidance for key problems in cyber conflict. In 1999, Schmitt developed a list of factors to determine "whether particular cyber operations amounted to a use of force." [210] These factors have generally been accepted as useful criteria for determining a use of force in cyber conflict. Schmitt's analysis balances state interest in preserving cyber options with state interest in avoiding harmful

---

[208]   Ibid., 154. While many in the American legal community accept this, its actual application or legal application has not been explicitly confirmed by states.

[209]   Owens, Dam, and Lin, eds., *Cyberattack Capabilities*, 252.

[210]   Schmitt, "Cyber Operations in International Law," 155.

outcomes. It is also important to note that the following factors build upon the traditional criteria developed by Jean Pictet: scope, duration, and intensity.[211] The Schmitt factors are:

1. *Severity:* Consequences involving physical harm to individuals or property will alone amount to a use of force. Those generating only minor inconvenience or irritation will never do so. Between the extremes, the more consequences impinge on critical national interests, the more they will contribute to the depiction of a cyber operation as a use of force.

2. *Immediacy:* The sooner consequences manifest, the less opportunity States have to seek peaceful accommodation of a dispute or to otherwise forestall their harmful effects. Therefore, States harbor a greater concern about immediate consequences than those which are delayed or build slowly overtime.

3. *Directness:* The greater the attenuation between the initial act and the resulting consequences, the less likely States will be to deem the actor responsible for violating the prohibition on the use of force. Whereas the immediacy factor focused on the temporal aspect of the consequences in question, directness examines the chain of causation.

4. *Invasiveness:* The more secure a targeted system, the greater the concern as to its penetration. By way of illustration, economic coercion may involve no intrusion at all (trade with the target state is simply cut off), whereas in combat the forces of one State cross into another in violation of its sovereignty. The former is undeniably not a use of force, whereas the latter always qualifies as such (absent legal justification, such as evacuation of nationals abroad during times of unrest).

---

[211] See Sklerov, "Solving the Dilemma of State Responses to Cyberattacks." Jean Pictet, Vice President of the International Committee of the Red Cross, was an international humanitarian law expert, the main author of the commentary of the four Geneva Conventions of 1949, and collaborator the commentary for the Additional Protocols of 1977.

5.   *Measurability*: The more quantifiable and identifiable a set of consequences, the more a State's interest will be deemed to have been affected. On the one hand, international law does not view economic coercion as a use of force even though it may cause significant suffering. On the other, a military attack which causes only a limited degree of destruction clearly qualifies.

6.   *Presumptive Legitimacy*: At the risk of oversimplification, international law is generally prohibitory in nature. In other words, acts which are not forbidden are permitted; absent an express prohibition, an act is presumptively legitimate. For instance, it is well accepted that the international law governing the use of force does not prohibit propaganda, psychological warfare or espionage. To the extent such activities are conducted through cyber operations, they are presumptively legitimate.

7.   *Responsibility*: The law of State responsibility governs when a State will be responsible for cyber operations. But it must be understood that responsibility lies along a continuum from operations conducted by a State itself to those in which it is merely involved in some fashion. The closer the nexus between a State and the operations, the more likely other States will be to characterize them as uses of force, for the greater the risk posed to international stability.[212]

This analysis, furthered and improved by Schmitt over a decade, represents some of the best legal thinking on cyber conflict. It is by no means a perfect solution, but it provides a good framework for future analysis.[213]

---

[212]   Text excerpted from Schmitt, "Cyber Operations in International Law," 155-156. This article lists the seventh factor of "responsibility," although it was not in Schmitt's 1999 article. See Schmitt, "Computer Network Attack and the Use of Force in International Law: Thoughts on a Normative Framework," 914 for discussion of the six original factors only.

[213]   For application of these factors to a prominent cyber incident, see Thomas C. Wingfield, "International Law and Information Operations," in *Cyberpower and National Security*, eds. Franklin D. Kramer, Stuart H. Starr, Larry K. Wentz

There has been some resistance to Schmitt's seven factors and the application of existing *jus ad bellum* principles to cyber conflict. Other scholars have also called for the creation of proposals to develop a new legal framework rather than using traditional laws of conflict and other rules of war. Kanuck, for example, writing before Schmitt published his factors, offers an alternative framework, "urging a reformulation of the international legal system by filling a particular niche that addresses the legal concepts of territory, aggression, and intervention."[214] He argues that these tenets of international law require reformulation. A few years later, Barkham also directly critiques Schmitt's seven factors.[215] Barkham views "presumptive legitimacy" as an irrelevant factor because legitimacy is not a factor in determining whether something is actually a use of force.[216] Barkham also emphasizes that the Schmitt factors do not address cyber activities below the Article 2(4) and Article 51 thresholds. Finally, Barkham offers other potential legal regimes for cyber conflict: existing treaty regimes (primarily the International Telecommunications Union) and the potential for a new regime, although Barkham notes the difficulties of non-state actors, compliance, and enforcement in these alternatives. Hoisington is another recent US scholar who questions Schmitt's analysis, in essence building upon Barkham's arguments about the "presumptive legitimacy" factor and the *ex post* analysis needed under the Schmitt factors.[217]

(Washington, DC: National Defense University Press, 2009), 525-542, at 531-533. Using the seven Schmitt factors, Wingfield finds that there was a high level of immediacy; moderate levels of severity, directness, and invasiveness; and low levels of measurability, presumptive legitimacy, and responsibility in the Estonian case. "This suggests that the attacks were quantitatively damaging enough, or qualitatively 'military' enough, to be properly characterized under international law as uses of force." Ibid., 532.

[214] Sean P. Kanuck, "Information Warfare: New Challenges for Public International Law," *Harvard International Law Journal* 37 (1996): 272-292, 274.

[215] Jason Barkham, "Information Warfare and International Law on the Use of Force," *N.Y.U. International Law and Politics* 34 (2001): 57-113.

[216] Ibid., at 85.

[217] Matthew Hoisington, "Cyberwarfare and the Use of Force Giving Rise to the Right of Self-Defense," *Boston College International & Comparative Law Review* 32 (2009): 439-454, 452-453.

While beneficial and supported by many American international law scholars, Schmitt's approach still demonstrates two fundamental deficiencies in seeking to apply Article 2(4) to cyber attacks. Firstly, the prohibition on the threat or use of force applies to states. It does not apply to non-state actors, including terrorist groups, organized crime, or individuals, unless they have a connection to a state.[218] This then touches upon the role of state responsibility for non-state activity, a concept and obligation discussed in detail later in this chapter. Secondly, public acknowledgement of state practice is lacking in this field, making it difficult, nearly impossible, to actually enunciate an authoritative international law regarding 'cyber use of force.'

In summary, one side of the debate argues, "almost *all* state activities in cyberspace that intentionally cause almost *any* destructive effect within the sovereign territory of another state are probably unlawful uses of force." [219] However, the National Research Council argues that questions of scale, thresholds, and intent complicate the determination of a hostile cyber action.[220] A contrary legal position holds that

> [b]ecause the UN Charter was written long before the Internet existed, it was clearly not intended to encompass cyberattacks; and because it was written in the aftermath of two World Wars, it clearly was intended to encompass kinetic attacks....It is therefore reasonable to assume these are the only type of attacks the Charter encompasses.[221]

This position further argues that accordingly, *jus ad bellum* and *jus in bello* do not apply to cyber attacks.[222] Therefore, while many scholars and practitioners consider *jus ad bellum* to apply, others refute that position, demonstrating limited clarity and a continuing debate.

---

[218] Schmitt, "Cyber Operations in International Law," 157. The degree of connection is a different legal problem that is discussed in detail below.

[219] Wingfield, *The Law of Information Conflict*, 114.

[220] Owens, Dam, and Lin, eds., *Cyberattack Capabilities* 256.

[221] Brenner and Clarke, "Civilians in Cyberwarfare: Conscripts," 22.

[222] Ibid.

One fundamental missing piece in the application of Article 2(4) to a certain threshold of cyber activity is state practice; "[u]nfortunately, unequivocal State practice in characterizing particular cyber attacks as (or not as) uses of force is lacking."[223] This is in part because very few states have acknowledged participation in cyber operations that might amount to a use of force. A second concern for states and their reluctance on this issue is the potential of escalating or destabilizing state relations. As Schmitt concludes, "[t]herefore, one can only speculate as to future State practice regarding the characterization of cyber operations." While some scholars have mapped out the positions of a few key states' positions on a variety of cyber issues,[224] the current level of state practice, discussion, and statements makes it nearly impossible to move proposed legal methods and criteria into state practice.

While concluding this section it is also important to note that there are two general exceptions to the prohibition on the use of force. First, a state may justify a use of force in self-defense, as will be discussed in further detail below. The other exception is present in Articles 39 and 42 of the U.N. Charter, which authorizes the U.N. Security Council to determine if there is a threat to the peace and to authorize a use of force if necessary to "maintain or restore international peace and security." In the words of a 1999 US Department of Defense document, "[n]othing would prevent the Security Council from finding that a computer network attack was a 'threat to the peace' if it determined that the situation warranted such action."[225] Such exceptions to the prohibition on the use of force are important as they provide legitimate options for states to defend themselves against cyber attacks from both state and non-state actors.

Armed Attack and Self Defense under Article 51 of the UN Charter

Article 51 is a main exemption to the prohibition on the use of force in the UN Charter, maintaining the right to self-defense when under attack. The article reads in full:

---

[223] Schmitt, "Cyber Operations in International Law," 155.
[224] Kanuck, "Sovereign Discourse on Cyber Conflict Under International Law."
[225] Department of Defense Office of General Counsel, "An Assessment of International Legal Issues in Information Operations," 15.

"Nothing in the present Charter shall impair the inherent right of individual or collective self-defence if an armed attack occurs against a Member of the United Nations, until the Security Council has taken measures necessary to maintain inter- national peace and security. Measures taken by Members in the exercise of this right of self-defence shall be immediately reported to the Security Council and shall not in any way affect the authority and responsibility of the Security Council under the present Charter to take at any time such action as it deems necessary in order to maintain or restore international peace and security."[226]

Article 51, however, does not define what constitutes an armed attack or the degree to which states may respond to an attack. The former is dependent on the facts of the situation whereas the latter is governed by the rules of *jus in bello*. Article 51 is also important because it distinguishes illegitimate uses of force (as dictated in Article 2(4)) with legitimate uses of force as an inherent right of states to defend themselves.

Based on state practice and legal scholarship, the following is a list of traditional kinetic activities generally considered to fall within the category of an armed attack:

- Invasion, bombardment, cross-border shooting
- Blockade
- Attack on land, sea, or air forces or on the civilian marine and air fleets
- Breach of stationing agreements
- Placing territory at another state's disposal
- Participation in the use of force by militarily organized unofficial group[227]

The above examples of armed attacks may help elucidate, *a priori*, examples of possible cyber armed attacks. Some have argued that in order for a cyber attack to qualify as an armed attack

---

[226] Article 51, Charter of the United Nations.
[227] Wingfield, *The Law of Information Conflict*, 111.

under the U.N. Charter, it must have the same physical consequences as a classic, kinetic armed attack, including "causing a generator to overheat and catch fire or rendering a train or subway uncontrollable such that it crashed."[228] Schmitt's seven factors above are also helpful to determine whether a use of force rises to the level of an armed attack and what a potential appropriate response may be. Still, an armed attack must reach beyond an Article 2(4) threshold to another degree of severity.

As articulated by Wingfield, "since the text of Article 51 recognizes this right of self-defense at the time an armed attack occurs, the pivotal focus point of any self-defense analysis is on the meaning of an armed attack."[229] Further, any self-defense action taken after an armed attack must comport with the laws of war, specifically necessity and proportionality, and must not be punitive or retaliatory.[230] That is, self-defense must be appropriate to stopping ongoing armed attacks, rather than actions to after the

---

[228]   Schmitt, "Cyber Operations in International Law," 165. See also: David E. Graham, "Cyber Threats and the Law of War," *Journal of National Security Law & Policy* 4 (2010): 88-102: "A cyber attack conducted for the purpose of shutting down a power grid would be deemed an armed attack….A cyber manipulation of information across a state's backing and financial institutions significantly disrupting commerce within that state would be viewed as an armed attack," 91; Joshua E. Kastenberg, "Non-Intervention And Neutrality In Cyberspace: An Emerging Principle In The National Practice Of International Law," *Air Force Law Review* 64 (2009): 43-64: "A cyber attack that causes physical destruction could constitute an 'armed attack' under the UN Charter," 54; Scott J. Shackleford, "From Nuclear War to Net War: Analogizing Cyber Attacks in International Law," *Berkeley Journal of International Law* 27 (2009): 192-251: "It is possible for a cyber attack to rise to the level of an armed attack as traditionally recognized under IHL," at 230; Schaap, "Cyber Warfare Operations:" "If a cyber attack results in physical damage, it may constitute an armed attack," 147; Charles J. Dunlap, "Perspectives for Cyber Strategists on Law for Cyberwar," *Strategic Studies Quarterly* 5 (Spring 2011), 81-99; Stephen J. Lukasik, "A Framework for Thinking About Conflict and Cyber Deterrence with Possible Declaratory Policies for These Domains," in National Research Council, ed., *Proceedings of a Workshop on Deterring Cyberattacks: Informing Strategies and Developing Options for U.S. Policy* (Washington, DC: National Academies Press: 2010), 99-121.

[229]   Wingfield, *The Law of Information Conflict*, 41.

[230]   Ibid. It should also be noted that while retaliation is forbidden, action to discourage attacks in the future is allowed.

attacks or after an invading power has departed. Though the response must be proportional, it need not be limited to the weapons used by the aggressor.[231] A necessary use of force is defined as "that degree and kind of force, not otherwise prohibited by the law of armed conflict, required for the partial or complete submission of the enemy with a minimum expenditure of time, life, and physical resources."[232] While *jus in bello* principles apply to an armed conflict situation, they also control responses to armed attack, even if the response is not in the context of an armed conflict or ongoing war.

However, just because a state has a right to self-defense, an armed response may not always be appropriate in response to an armed attack. As the ICJ writes in the *Nicaragua* case, "a state never loses its right to use force in self-defense in response to a use of force within the meaning of 2(4), however the right of self-defense under customary international law may not always justify an armed response."[233] The same logic can be applied to more severe attacks as defined by Article 51 as well. For clarification, as defined by Wingfield, "a use of force that rises to a certain scope, duration, and intensity threshold constitutes an armed attack within the meaning of Article 51 of the Charter of the United Nations that invokes a state's inherent right of self-defense."[234] Wingfield, however, emphasizes that continuing state practice and the particulars of any cyber incident would be necessary to determine the applicability of this definition to an activity in cyberspace.[235]

There is some growing consensus, although not fully established, that a cyber attack equal to an armed attack under Article 51 must have the same significant physical consequences as a kinetic armed attack. Building upon that interpretation, some argue that a response in self-defense is that "a state could have a right to self-defense in response to a CNA only when that attack

---

[231]   Ibid., 42.
[232]   Ibid., 43 (citing US Department of Navy, NWP I-14M, *The Commander's Handbook on The Law of Naval Operations*, Section 5.2 (1995)).
[233]   Wingfield, *The Law of Information Conflict*, 51 (citing *dicta* in *Nicaragua* ICJ case, which is discussed in detail in Section 3.2 of this chapter).
[234]   Ibid.,123.
[235]   Ibid.

rose to the level of an armed attack."[236] Additionally, in order for self-defense to be valid, there must be a certain level of proof provided by the responding state.[237] A valid exercise of self-defense would require irrefutable proof of aggression to satisfy state responsibility and to justify any sort of retaliation. In responding to an armed attack, a state is not limited to a specific kind of weapon or attack, as long as the response is in line with the *jus in bello* principles of necessity and proportionality.[238]

For US decision makers, General Alexander's statements further support this principle.[239] Overall, the US military has been quite vocal in asserting that the laws of war apply to cyber operations, emphasizing that states have responsibility for military activities in cyberspace originating from their jurisdictions. However, this consensus is by no means universal among international lawyers, let alone nations. While the United States is only one country, its continued advocacy of LOAC applying to cyberspace and corresponding practice may lead the way for customary international law to develop regarding cyber conflict. This process, however, is still continuing. The cyber warfare manual, sponsored by the NATO-accredited center of excellence, may provide further support to the development of international law.

Anticipatory Self Defense

Opinions differ as to whether Article 51 incorporates the customary rule of anticipatory self-defense or precludes that right. Generally, anticipatory self-defense means that a state, faced with an immediate and overwhelming threat, may respond with force in self-defense before the aggressor or initiator is able to attack. The customary rule establishes that anticipatory self-defense may occur when "the necessity of that self-defense is instant, overwhelming, and leaving

---

[236] Shackleford, "From Nuclear War to Net War: Analogizing Cyber Attacks in International Law," 230.

[237] Ibid.

[238] Schaap, "Cyber Warfare Operations," 148.

[239] General Keith Alexander, "Advance Questions for Lieutenant General Keith Alexander": "Regardless whether we know who is responsible, international law requires that our armed attack in self defense be proportional and discriminate," 12, and, "Returning fire in cyberspace, as long as it complies with law of war principles…, would be lawful," 24.

no choice of means, and no moment for deliberation."[240] Attribution is a key problem for the potential relevance of anticipatory self-defense to cyber conflict. If a country is unable to determine the source and state-sponsorship of the cyber attack, anticipatory self-defense is difficult, if not impossible, for a state to legitimately use. Of course, this matter may be somewhat moot if there is not sufficient time to act in an anticipatory manner.

Anticipatory self-defense differs from most conceptions of "active defense," which are considered to be aggressive actions after an attack has been launched, further complicating the analysis. The legality of, for instance, disarming an opponent when a cyber attack appears imminent is different from employing active defense. The legal debate is currently much more focused on active defense and this section will follow suit.

Either anticipatory self-defense or active defense (i.e. "hacking back") could be considered a uses of force or armed attacks depending on the circumstances (especially if the initial cyber threat cannot be evidenced with proof enough to justify the countermeasures). The legality of active defense is in dispute both for the laws of war and criminal law. In a basic scenario, a state under cyber attack may believe that the only way to stop an on-going attack is to "hack back" and disable a command and control server responsible for the attack. However, under the Council of Europe Convention and the domestic laws of its signatories, active defense by private actors is considered a cyber crime; the Convention is mute on the issue of state actors engaging in active defense, leaving the laws of war as codified in the U.N. Charter as the prevailing legal framework to consider.

Sklerov agrees that active defenses would be permissible should a cyber attack amount to an "armed attack" as part of the recognized right to self-defense by states;[241] however, without being able to ascertain the identity or intent of an attacker, it is difficult to determine whether an incoming "attack" is in fact an "armed attack" rather than a criminal act. Thus, most cyber

---

[240]   Yale Law School Lillian Goldman Law Library "British-American Diplomacy: The Caroline Case," (2008) http://avalon.law.yale.edu/19th_century/br-1842d.asp (accessed May 7, 2011).

[241]   Sklerov, "Solving the Dilemma of State Responses to Cyberattacks."

attacks are currently treated as criminal matters, wherein active defense would be prohibited under domestic law. In the case of a truly devastating cyber attack, regardless of the identity of the attacker, the harm done would likely be considered the basis for determining whether the incident amounted to an act of war. Yet, making that determination while an attack is in progress so that active defenses can be utilized to mitigate the harm might be difficult.

Graham therefore argues that correctly utilizing anticipatory self-defense in the cyber context is difficult and near impossible. [242] The main problem for skeptics is the problem of attribution. [243] If engaging in active defense, states must also be able to determine that the threat they are facing is in fact CNA and does not constitute CNE. If the threat is espionage and not a cyber attack amounting to a use of force, the legality of using an active defense in an anticipatory self-defense context is questionable and such action may be unlawful under international law. It is still important to note that any possible use of active defense or anticipatory self-defense in cyberspace must still fall in line with *jus in bello* principles, which are discussed in detail below.

Many scholars, policy makers, and practitioners find the legal answers regarding active defense and anticipatory self-defense to be unsatisfactory. Hoisington argues that "[a]llowing a state to exercise active defense measures in response to an attack on critical national infrastructure, without incurring liability, represents a preferable governing principle to the treatment of cyberwarfare under the existing *jus ad bellum* paradigm."[244] Additionally, Sklerov argues strenuously that permitting states to use active defenses is one of the only ways to secure cyberspace.[245] However, the legality of active defenses and cyber attacks employed for anticipatory self-defense is still questionable and remains one of the most significant unanswered questions in international law.

---

[242] Graham, "Cyber Threats and the Law of War," 90.
[243] Ibid.
[244] Hoisington, "Cyberwarfare and the Use of Force Giving Rise to the Right of Self-Defense."
[245] Sklerov, "Solving the Dilemma of State Responses to Cyberattacks," 79-80.

Jus in Bello

The rules of *jus in bello*, codified in the 1949 Geneva Conventions and the 1977 Additional Protocols, are triggered in armed conflict and also apply when a state responds in self-defense to an armed attack. While much of LOAC has developed over time as customary international law, Additional Protocol I codifies many principles. The United States has stated that its military's cyber operations adhere to these principles, but other militaries may not view *jus in bello* principles as applicable in cyberspace. The United States is not a signatory to Additional Protocol I, yet the norms cited in this section are binding as customary international law and the United States recognizes them as such.[246]

As stated above, even if it were generally accepted that the LOAC applies in cyberspace, the details of *how* the LOAC should be applied are not explicit.[247] Rather, militaries that engage in cyber operations will need to balance the specifics of a situation in which a cyber operation is an option against the framework of principles listed below. While proportionality dictates whether a target is legitimate, states have an obligation to use means that lessen the amount of collateral damage.[248] "If an information operation is sufficiently destructive to be considered an armed attack, then the response must be guided" by the principles discussed below. The following subsections discuss necessity, proportionality, discrimination, distinction, chivalry and neutrality, which form the basis of the laws

---

[246] Other provisions in Additional Protocol I not recognized as customary law by the United States have not been discussed, including provisions limiting long-term environmental damage. See Schmitt, "Wired Warfare: Computer Network Attack and Jus in Bello" for further discussion of environmental protection in armed conflict.

[247] Air Force General Kevin P. Chilton: "The Law of Armed Conflict will apply to this domain," quoted in Jeff Schogol, "Official: Not options 'off the table for U.S. response to cyber attacks," *Stars and Stripes*, 8 May 2009. Additionally, the East West Institute is currently engaging in a project to better establish the application of the laws of armed conflict to cyberspace: East West Institute, *Working Towards Rules for Governing Cyber Conflict: Rendering the Geneva and Hague Conventions in Cyberspace* (January 2011).

[248] Protocol Additional to the Geneva Conventions of 12 August 1949, and relating to the Protection of Victims of International Armed Conflicts (Protocol I), (8 June 1977), Art. 57(2)(a). (Hereafter Additional Protocol I) Also, Schmitt, "Wired Warfare: Computer Network Attack and Jus in Bello," 393-394.

of war.[249] Their application to cyberspace, whether in the context of an armed conflict or not, are not universally accepted, but they form an important foundation for US cyber operations.

Military Necessity

Military necessity requires that "military objectives are limited to those objects which by their nature, location, purpose or use make an effective contribution to military action and whose total or partial destruction, capture or neutralization, in the circumstances ruling at the time, offers a definite military advantage." [250] Militaries must limit unnecessary suffering, which is based on two factors: quantitatively only the amount of necessary force must be used and qualitatively the means and methods of war that are by nature inhumane must be avoided.[251]

In an armed conflict, the principle of military necessity dictates that militaries refrain from targeting purely civilian infrastructure.[252] In a cyber conflict, militaries must also conduct the same targeting analysis as in a kinetic context and must limit unnecessary suffering. An example of this could include a prohibition against targeting the international financial system, or even the food storage and supply, as this has limited military advantage compared with its effects on the civilian population.[253] Applying necessity to cyberspace also means that any countermeasures must be necessary for self-defense and not taken as a reprisal or out of revenge—but can be taken to discourage future attacks.

Proportionality

Under proportionality, a military commander must balance potential collateral damage against the "concrete and direct"

---

[249] Wingfield, "International Law and Information Operations."

[250] Additional Protocol I, Art. 52.

[251] International Committee of the Red Cross, "Practice Relating to Rule 70. Weapons of a Nature to Cause Superfluous Injury to Unnecessary Suffering," www.icrc.org/customary-ihl/eng/docs/v2_rul_rule70 (accessed 6 June 2011).

[252] Wingfield, *The Law of Information Conflict*, 442.

[253] Clarke and Knake argue for a treaty to prohibit cyber attacks on banking and financial systems as a potential starting point. Richard A. Clarke and Robert K. Knake, *Cyber War* (New York: Ecco, 2010), 245-247.

military advantage that he or she can expect to be gained. Additionally, Protocol I identifies an unlawfully indiscriminate attack as "an attack which may be expected to cause incidental loss of civilian life, injury to civilians, damage to civilian objects, or a combination thereof, which would be excessive in relation to the concrete and direct military advantage anticipated." [254] Some collateral damage is allowed, but it cannot be foreseeably disproportionate to the expected military advantage.

If the assets are dual-use, the attacker must balance the higher likelihood of collateral damage with the military advantage. Wingfield, citing Schmitt, notes three ways in which proportionality is most often violated: a lack of full knowledge as to what is being hit; the inability to surgically craft the amount of force being applied to the target; and the inability to ensure the weapon strikes precisely the right point. [255] One common misunderstanding is the incorrect assumption that proportionality requires a parity of force in responding to an attack.[256]

As applied to cyber conflict, some scholars emphasize that understanding the actual outcome of a cyber activity requires a high degree of intelligence that requires a long time to obtain; "the open question is how commanders should account for uncertainties in outcome that are significantly greater than those usually associated with kinetic attacks in the sense that there may not be an analytic or experiential basis for estimating uncertainties at all."[257]

Unlike nuclear warfare, there is no *Effects of Nuclear Weapons* [258] physics chart for cyber conflict, because of the inherent ambiguities in the technologies. The effects and consequences of a cyber attack on an electrical grid, for example, might be difficult to anticipate, making the determination much more difficult for a military commander. Given the global,

---

[254]   Additional Protocol I., Art. 51(5)(b).

[255]   Wingfield, "International Law and Information Operations," 536 (citing Michael N. Schmitt, "Bellum Americanum: The U.S. View of Twenty-First Century War and Its Possible Implications for the Law of Armed Conflict," *Michigan Journal of International Law* 19 (1998): 1051).

[256]   Wingfield, *The Law of Information Conflict*, 14.

[257]   Owens, Dam, and Lin, eds., *Cyberattack Capabilities*, 262.

[258]   Samuel Glasstone and Philip J. Dolan, *The Effects of Nuclear Weapons* (Washington, DC: U.S. Government Printing, 1983).

interconnected and interdependent information infrastructures, accounting for uncertainties in the cyber context complicates the balancing test for proportionality.

Distinction

Under distinction, a lawful military operation must distinguish between combatants and non-combatants and between military objectives and civilian objects.[259] Included within the principle of distinction is the obligation to limit civilian collateral damage as much as possible, including removing the civilian population, separating military objectives from civilian areas and other precautions.[260] However, as elucidated by Wingfield, it may be permitted "to collaterally damage civilian objects located so close to lawful military objectives that no reasonable precautions could have prevented the damage."[261] Wingfield elaborates that the implications for discrimination or distinction in cyberspace "would require the collection and analysis of information to produce the intelligence required" to distinguish between civilian and military objectives.

Therefore, militaries, when engaging in information operations, must "consider foreseeable secondary effects in target selection and mission planning."[262] The uncertainties of cyber attack make distinction between civilian and non-civilian objects and individuals more difficult. The use of hacktivists or patriotic hackers further complicates the picture because they do not fall cleanly within the categories of combatants or non-combatants. Additionally, the use of the same critical infrastructures by both civilian and military organizations makes the distinction between civilian and military targets much more difficult to determine, to the point that one scholar notes it is "almost meaningless in the context of modern ICT networks."[263]

---

[259] Additional Protocol, Art. 58.
[260] Ibid., Art. 58 (a)-(b).
[261] Wingfield, *The Law of Information Conflict*, 13.
[262] Ibid.
[263] Kanuck, "Sovereign Discourse on Cyber Conflict Under International Law," 1595.

Discrimination

Under the principle of discrimination, Wingfield also states that "[w]eapons that cannot be used in such a way as to discriminate between lawful and unlawful targets are themselves unlawful under the doctrine of indiscriminate effect."[264] This clear rule, however, is complicated by the environment and structure of cyberspace.[265] This is similar to the dilemma in the distinction principle. Because critical infrastructure and particularly cyber infrastructure tend to be dual use, discriminating between civilian and military targets is difficult. The large amount of dual-use infrastructure raises a number of questions, including: Does compromising the computers of non-combatants violate prohibitions against attacking non-combatants? What responsibilities does a nation have to separate civilian and military computer systems and networks?[266] The debate on dual-use infrastructure and international humanitarian law is one that the East-West Institute has embraced, bringing together scholars from the United States and Russia to analyze the scope of the Geneva and Hague Conventions applicable to cyber conflict.[267] While scholars may agree to some extent that the general concepts of international humanitarian law do apply, the exact application in practice is even less clear.

Chivalry

Chivalry prohibits perfidy or treachery but allows "ruses of war," which are actions that may mislead an adversary to provide strategic advantage, but do not violate LOAC. Examples of "ruses of war" include the use of camouflage, decoys, mock operations, and misinformation.[268] Perfidy and treachery are interchangeable concepts in international law and are defined as "[a]cts inviting the confidence of an adversary to lead him to believe that he is entitled to, or is obliged to accord, protection under the rules of

---

[264] See Wingfield, "International Law and Information Operations," and Owens, Dam, and Lin, eds., *Cyberattack Capabilities*.

[265] See Chapter 3 of this monograph for a discussion of the cyber ecosystem.

[266] Questions taken from Owens, Dam, and Lin, eds., *Cyberattack Capabilities*, 265.

[267] East West Institute, *Working Towards Rules for Governing Cyber Conflict*.

[268] Additional Protocol I, Art. 37.

international law applicable in armed conflict, with intent to betray that confidence"[269] Examples of treachery include feigning various actions or roles, such as surrender, incapacitation, non-combatant status or protected status (i.e. prisoners of war, medical personnel, the wounded, and sick).[270]

The principle of chivalry means that countries may not invite the confidence of an adversary with false representations as to the relevant protections under international law. As applied to cyberspace and the spectrum of cyber conflict, militaries should not purposefully pretend to be non-combatant operators of civilian infrastructure. While ruses may be permissible, the lines between ruses and perfidy may be more difficult to discern within cyberspace (e.g., regarding 'camouflage'). Similar to the analyses of other principles, attribution in cyberspace may complicate the operation of chivalry, making it difficult to discern between lawful combatants or non-combatants.[271]

Neutrality

While neutrality has limited *jus ad bellum* application, it is an important principle of *jus in bello* as it defines the rights and duties of neutral states. As clarified by Oppenheim, neutrality "may be defined as the attitude of impartiality adopted by third States towards belligerents and recognized by belligerents, such attitude creating rights and duties between the impartial States and belligerents."[272] The neutral nation cannot assist any belligerent militarily and "must act to prevent its territory from being so used."[273] While some have questioned the continued applicability of the neutrality principle in a post-Charter environment, others have continued to argue for its relevance. As Walker stated, "The overwhelming weight of authority is that neutrality continues in

[269] Gary D. Solis, *The Law of Armed Conflict: International Humanitarian Law in War* (New York: Cambridge University Press, 2010); Additional Protocol I, Art. 37(1).
[270] Additional Protocol I, Art. 37.
[271] Kanuck, "Sovereign Discourse on Cyber Conflict Under International Law," 1594.
[272] Damrosch et al, *International Law Cases and Materials, 4th ed.* (New York: West Group, 2001), Chapter 12.
[273] Owens, Dam, and Lin, eds., *Cyberattack Capabilities*, 247-248.

the Charter era. If so, the concept applies in the [information warfare] context as well." [274] Additionally, a Department of Defense discussion of the application of LOAC to cyber conflict applies neutrality to cyberspace, arguing that if a neutral is allowing its information systems to be used by a military force of a belligerent, the other belligerent may request that the neutral cease such action. If the neutral continues to assist the belligerent, the opposing belligerent "may have a limited right of self defense to prevent such use by its enemy."[275]

As analyzed by the National Research Council, CNA, or even CNE, is "likely to involve message traffic that physically transits a number of different nations."[276] There is no established principle of neutrality as it applies to cyberspace and therefore legal scholars must draw on analogies from existing frameworks. Under telephone and telegraph rules, as in the 1907 Hague Convention, a neutral party has no obligation to stop transit of signals, and action against a neutral is therefore restricted.[277] Using a different analogy, the law of the sea and law of naval warfare, Walker suggests that a nation under cyberattack may take action if the neutral state is unwilling or unable to stop use of its territory for those attacks.[278]

One scholar offers a definition of cyber neutrality as "the right of any state to maintain relations with all parties in a cyber conflict and the right not to support or take sides with any cyber belligerent."[279] Similarly, if neutrality is relevant in cyberspace, and some doubt that,[280] belligerents would not be able to use "for

---

[274] George K. Walker, "Information Warfare and Neutrality," *Vanderbilt Journal of Transnational Law* 33 (2000): 1079-1200.

[275] Department of Defense Office of General Counsel, "An Assessment of International Legal Issues in Information Operations."

[276] Owens, Dam, and Lin, eds., *Cyberattack Capabilities*, 268.

[277] Ibid., citing Hague Convention (V) respecting the Rights and Duties of Neutral Powers and Persons in Case of War on Land, Article 8. The Hague, 18 October 1907.

[278] Ibid., 269 (citing Walker, "Information Warfare and Neutrality")

[279] Kastenberg, "Non-Intervention And Neutrality In Cyberspace," 56-57.

[280] Kanuck, "Sovereign Discourse on Cyber Conflict Under International Law," 1593. Kanuck reviews the ways in which traditional neutrality may not apply, because of an inability of some states to monitor or control data packets from their networks and because some parts of cyberspace are uncertain depending on the legal norm that one analogizes from.

military purposes domain names or computer systems associated with neutral nations, to launch cyberattacks from computer systems in neutral states, or to take control of neutral systems in order to conduct cyberattacks."[281] Because of the transnational nature of cyberspace, the practicality of applying neutrality may be much more limited than in kinetic contexts.

As shown in this discussion of the principles of necessity, proportionality, discrimination, distinction, chivalry and neutrality, which the practical details of LOAC application may be unclear for the cyber context, there is growing consensus that general principles of LOAC are applicable. The specifics of how the spectrum of cyber conflict activities interacts with LOAC thresholds are still uncertain, but this analysis can be conducted as cyber conflict unfolds. This parallels in many ways the methods for determining an armed attack under the U.N. Charter or the legality of activities under *jus in bello*. By emphasizing the general areas of consensus while also making sure to incorporate other views, perhaps the international legal framework will be able to further policymaking in the near term. Despite the concerns and complications discussed in this section, it may generally be agreed that in the realm of international law, the LOAC likely is still the one area "in which current legal obligations can be applied with the greatest confidence to information operations."[282]

Cyber Terrorism

As Dorothy Denning has explained, "cyber terrorism is the convergence of terrorism and cyberspace. It is generally understood to mean unlawful attacks and threats of attack against computers, networks, and the information stored therein, when done to intimidate or coerce a government or its people in furtherance of political or social objectives." [283]

---

[281] Owens, Dam, and Lin, eds., *Cyberattack Capabilities.*
[282] Department of Defense Office of General Counsel, "An Assessment of International Legal Issues in Information Operations."
[283] Dorothy E. Denning, "Cyberterrorism," Testimony before the Special Oversight Panel on Terrorism, Committee on Armed Services, U.S. House of Representatives, 23 May 2000. Full testimony available at

Cyber terrorism, by its very definition, is conducted by non-state actors, although nation states may sponsor the attacks or use non-state actors as proxies. An additional characteristic defined by Denning is that the effects of cyber terrorism should be violent enough to inflict fear on the population; Denning further clarifies, "attacks that lead to death or bodily injury, explosions, plane crashes, water contamination, or severe economic loss would be examples."[284]

It is also important to note that non-state actors, who may or may not be acting with tacit or explicit state direction or acknowledgement, often conduct terrorism. The role of non-state actors in "cyber terrorism" has not been as significant as we may have anticipated ten years ago, and there is a significant divide between views on whether the cyber terrorist threat is significant or not. The gap between the projected damage of a cyber terror attack and the demonstrated cyber capabilities of current terrorist organizations triggers most of the debates around cyber terrorism: some believe that a "cyber 9/11" is a realistic scenario while others doubt the seriousness of the threat.[285]

Unlike espionage, terrorism is widely addressed in international law, although there is no single treaty addressing terrorism, nor one definition. While there are treaties that address different aspects of terrorism,[286] there is no UN convention on

---

http://www.cs.georgetown.edu/~denning/infosec/cyberterror.html (accessed 22 July 2011).

[284] Ibid.

[285] See a discussion of a possible "Cyber 9/11" scenario in Gregory Rattray and Jason Healey, "Categorizing and Understanding Offensive Cyber Capabilities and Their Use," in *Technology, Policy, Law, and Ethics Regarding U.S. Acquisition and Use of Cyberattack Capabilities,* eds. William A. Owens, Kenneth W. Dam, and Herbert S. Lin (Washington, DC: National Academies Press, 2009).

[286] The UN has a series of conventions addressing crimes against internationally protected persons, taking of hostages terrorist bombings, financing of terrorism, acts of nuclear terrorism, terrorist acts committed on board aircraft, unlawful seizure of aircraft, unlawful acts against the safety of civil aviation, protection of nuclear material, acts of violence at airports, safety of maritime navigation, safety of fixed platforms located on the continental shelf and marking of plastic explosives for the purpose of detection. A full list of the conventions and their full text is available at United Nations Treaty Collection, "Text and Status of the United Nations

cyber terrorism.[287] A few instruments address the international concerns of cyber terrorism. The OSCE's Ministerial Council Decision No. 3/04 "Combating the Use of the Internet for Terrorist Purposes" (2004) encourages "States to exchange information on the use of the Internet for terrorist purposes and identify possible strategies to combat this threat."[288] A further decision builds upon the earlier Council Decision, calling for increased cooperation and consideration of "taking all appropriate measures to protect vital critical information infrastructures and networks against the threat of cyber attacks."[289] However, there is little in international law on cyber terrorism that distinguishes it from other forms of terrorism or cyber's potential to have the effects of an armed attack or use of force under existing international legal rules.

State Responsibility

As discussed above, a general treaty on state conduct and responsibilities in cyberspace does not exist, but there are a number of international law resources that may be helpful in determining the scope of state responsibility in cyber conflict. One key source of guidance are the "Articles on Responsibility of States for Internationally Wrongful Acts," adopted by the International Law Commission (ILC) in 2001. Under these ILC Articles, a state is responsible for its internationally wrongful acts.[290] Such acts are defined by international law and may not be

---

Conventions on Terrorism," 2011,
http://treaties.un.org/Pages/DB.aspx?path=DB/studies/page2_en.xml&menu=MTDSG (accessed September 22, 2011).

[287] In addition, COE has a convention on the prevention of terrorism that addresses the offences covered by the UN conventions. Council of Europe, "Council of Europe Convention on the Prevention of Terrorism," Warsaw, 16.V.2005.

[288] OSCE, No. 3/04 "Combating the Use of the Internet for Terrorist Purposes" (2004).

[289] OSCE, No. 7/06 "Countering the Use of the Internet for Terrorist Purposes" (2006), 2.

[290] Article 1, Draft Articles on Responsibility of States for International Wrongful Acts, with Commentaries (2008). Available at http://untreaty.un.org/ilc/texts/instruments/english/commentaries/9_6_2001.pdf (accessed 30 July 2011).

rendered lawful by any national legislation or determination.[291] In general, this international law principle covers wrongful acts that result in physical damage.[292]

The following sections illuminate concepts of state responsibility that may be of particular interest in the cyber conflict context: state responsibility for non-state actors, and state responsibility for transboundary harm. Under the ILC Articles, actions of individuals may be ascribed to a state if "the person or group of persons is in fact acting on the instructions of, or under the direction or control of, that State in carrying out the conduct."[293] In conjunction with the doctrine of state responsibility for non-state actors' cyber conflict activities, there needs to be some focused international attention to what may constitute a cyber "internationally wrongful act" for which a state may be held responsible.

State Responsibility for Non-State Actors

As discussed in the previous chapter, the role of non-state actors on both the offense and defense for cyber conflict has increased significantly as cyberspace has matured. This progression and continuing importance has implications for the applicability of international law to the spectrum of cyber conflict. The central issue that defines the notion of state responsibility for non-state actors is the degree of relationship between the state and the private actors such that the otherwise private conduct may be imputed to the state.

Two key standards for defining this relationship are the "effective control" standard set forth in the International Court of Justice *Nicaragua* case and the lower-threshold "overall control" standard in the International Criminal Tribunal for the former Yugoslavia *Tadic* case. However, following the US response to the terrorist attacks of September 11, 2001 and justifications for using force against the Taliban regime in Afghanistan, the standard for state responsibility may have shifted again, thereby loosening the

---

[291]   Article 3, Ibid.

[292]   Michel Montjoie, "The Concept of Liability in the Absence of an Internationally Wrongful Act," in *The Law of International Responsibility*, eds. James Crawford et al., (New York: Oxford University Press, 2010): 505.

[293]   Article 8, Draft Articles on Responsibility of States for International Wrongful Acts.

relationship a state must have to be responsible for non-state activity. This confusion between the three thresholds, according to Schmitt, is actually a natural process of international law.[294]

In 1986, the judgment of the International Court of Justice in *Military and Paramilitary Activities in and Against Nicaragua* found that state responsibility for human rights violations of non-state actors required that the state have "effective control" over the non-state actors.[295] In the court's words, the nation's "participation, even if preponderant or decisive, in the financing, organizing, training, supplying and equipping of the [non-state actors], the selection of ... targets, and the planning of the whole of its operation, is *still insufficient* in itself ... for the purpose of attributing to the [nation] the acts committed by the [non-state actors]."[296]

The Court decided that the United States bore some responsibility for training, arming, and financing the *contras* in Nicaragua because the United States had breached its international obligation not to intervene in other states.[297] However, the Court decided that the United States did not bear responsibility for the international humanitarian violations committed by the *contras*. To have impute responsibility for the *contras* actions, the court determined that the United States needed to have "effective control" of the *contras*, meaning that the United States must have "directed or enforced the [*contras'*] perpetration of the acts contrary to human rights and humanitarian law."[298] As such, this is the definition of the "effective control" standard, and in the *Nicaragua* case, the ICJ found that the United States had not exercised such control.

The decision in the *Nicaragua* case contrasts with *Tadic,* a 1999 decision made by the Appeals Chamber of the International

---

[294] Schmitt, "Cyber Operations in International Law," 164.

[295] See Mark Gibney, *International Human Rights Law: Returning to Universal Principles* (2008): 21-23.

[296] As quoted in Derek Jinks, "State Responsibility for the Acts of Private Armed Groups," *Chicago Journal of International Law*. 4 (Spring 2003): 83-95. Emphasis added.

[297] Antonio Cassese, "The *Nicaragua* and *Tadic* Tests Revisited in Light of the ICJ Judgment on Genocide in Bosnia," *European Journal of International Law*, Vol. 18, No. 4, 649-668 (2007).

[298] International Court of Justice, *Military and Paramilitary Activities in and against Nicaragua* (Nicaragua v. United States of America), Merits, Judgment, I.C.J. Reports 1986, 14.

Criminal Tribunal for the former Yugoslavia. The Appeals Chamber in *Tadic* applied an "overall control" test to the actions of non-state "organized and hierarchically structured groups," meaning military or paramilitary units.[299] Overall control did not require specific instructions for individual operations. Rather, overall control meant that a state coordinated or helped in the general planning of activities in addition to equipping, financing, and training non-state structured groups.[300] This threshold is significantly lower than the threshold furthered in the *Nicaragua* case.

The *Nicaragua* and *Tadic* cases, as well as the ILC Articles, highlight the requirement of imputing "to states only those unlawful acts committed on behalf of the state."[301] While citing different thresholds of control, these three sources require that private actions be attributable to a state; a state cannot be responsible based only on complicity. This threshold for imputing state responsibility, however, may have expanded after the terrorist attacks of September 11, 2001. The United States argued that the attacks were an "armed attack" under the U.N. Charter and that the international law permitted US military action against the Taliban in Afghanistan.[302] The US argument was that the terrorist attacks committed by al-Qaeda could be attributed to the Taliban because it refused to change its policies toward or oust al-Qaeda despite US demands to address the terrorist network operating out of Afghanistan before September 2001.[303]

The United States did not argue that the Taliban exerted "effective control" or "overall control" over al-Qaeda. Rather the US position articulated that the Taliban was complicit in the attacks. For the most part, the international community accepted this argument and at least tacitly consented to the US use of military force against the Taliban. This is a significant shift in international response; the United States had made similar arguments after the 1998 terrorist attacks against US embassies abroad and invoked Article 51, but the

---

[299] Paragraph 120 of *Tadic* decision, in Cassese, "The *Nicaragua* and *Tadic* Tests Revisited in Light of the ICJ Judgment on Genocide in Bosnia."
[300] Ibid., Paragraph 131 and 137.
[301] Jinks, "State Responsibility for the Acts of Private Armed Groups," 89.
[302] Ibid., 84.
[303] Kimberley N. Trapp, "Back to Basics: Necessity, Proportionality, and the Right of Self-Defence Against Non-State Terrorist Actors," *International and Comparative Law Quarterly* 56 (2007): 141-156, at 149.

U.N Security Council did not give authorization for the ensuing US missile strikes in Sudan and Afghanistan. [304] However, in the aftermath of September 11, 2001, the Security Council determined that the terror attacks were a threat to the peace and security, triggering Chapter VII powers, including self-defense after an armed attack under Article 51. [305] Regional organizations also supported US military action in self-defense: NATO explicitly invoked Article V's collective self-defense provision and the OAS recognized the US's inherent right to self-defense after the attacks. [306]

Rather than receiving international condemnation for imputing state responsibility based on complicity, as opposed to effective control or overall control, the United States was generally supported by the international community, which created a foundation for the potential opening of the scope of state responsibility to "harboring and supporting" non-state actors. [307] At the very least, state responsibility for the actions of terrorists, as based on state practice, has expanded. Whether or not this is a positive development for international law can be debated, [308] but this expansion may have significant implications for cyber conflict. As one scholar argues, "[since] cyber operations resemble terrorism in many regards, States may equally be willing to countenance attribution of a cyber armed attack to a State which willingly provides sanctuary to non-State actors conducting [armed attacks]"[309]

To summarize, based on *Nicaragua*, for a state to have responsibility for the non-state actors' activities, it must direct or enforce the unlawful activities. Under *Tadic*, states must assist in coordinating the general planning of structured non-state groups. These thresholds may have shifted, however, over the past ten years following US actions and international acceptance in invading

---

[304]   Jinks, "State Responsibility for the Acts of Private Armed Groups," 85.

[305]   Trapp, "Back to Basics: Necessity, Proportionality, and the Right of Self-Defence Against Non-State Terrorist Actors," 151 (citing UN Security Council Resolution 1368 (2001)).

[306]   Jinks, "State Responsibility for the Acts of Private Armed Groups," 85.

[307]   Ibid., at 89.

[308]   Ibid. Jinks argues expanding "state responsibility" is problematic, ineffective, and counterproductive and can result in both "overapplication" and "underapplication," which can endanger security interests.

[309]   Schmitt, "Cyber Operations in International Law," 171.

Afghanistan and ousting the Taliban. However, it is not clear which of these standards should apply to non-state actors' activities in cyberspace. [310] Indeed, guidance on which threshold applies to activities of hacktivists or patriotic hackers is likely to only be cemented based on state practice following a cyber incident conducted by non-state actors that crosses the Article 51 threshold.

This new post-September 11th threshold might have special bearing on the cyber conflict because of the potential use of patriot hackers or the utilization of CNE and CNA by rogue governmental elements. If a state knows of such activities, then it should not encourage or support such activities and has an obligation to prevent those activities. While on a different scale, it is analogous to how Afghanistan was held responsible for al Qaeda's terrorist attacks. As explained by Schmitt, "Any cyber operation rising to the level of an unlawful use of force will entail responsibility on the part of the State when launched by its agents, even when they are acting *ultra vires* ["beyond power"]." [311] However, much like the discussions of Articles 2(4) and 51, such a determination must be made on "a case-by-case basis looking to the extent and nature of involvement by the State with the group and in the particular operations."[312]

At least one scholar cautions against using the theory of imputed accountability within the cyber conflict context; because it is difficult if not impossible to deter or detect all "unwanted activity" on or from a state's networks, the current state of technology may inhibit the application of state responsibility, regardless of the standard used. [313] Even if technologically possible, it may be arguable that countries would be unwilling to accept imputed responsibility for the full variety of potentially internationally-

---

[310]   For demonstration of the post-September 11 norms and potential application to cyberspace, see Schmitt, "Cyber Operations in International Law." On the other hand, Tikk, Kaska, and Vihul claim that "(t)he current view for attribution still requires some form of overall control by the state over the private actor." Eneken Tikk, Kadri Kaski and Liis Vihul, *International Cyber Incidents: Legal Considerations*, NATO Cooperative Cyber Defense Center of Excellence, (2009): 82.

[311]   Schmitt, "Cyber Operations in International Law," 157.

[312]   Ibid., 158.

[313]   Kanuck, "Sovereign Discourse on Cyber Conflict Under International Law," 1591.

unlawful cyber activities in their respective jurisdictions, demonstrating both the practical and legal considerations in this area.[314] Finally, it must be restated that even if the concept of attributing non-state actors' conduct to a country were clearly defined in one standard, there still must be agreement upon the cyber conflict activity that may be deemed an internationally wrongful act. This issue also pervades the next section on transboundary harm.

State Responsibility for Transboundary Harm

Customary international law recognizes responsibilities of nations regarding transboundary harm, grounded in the notion that property should be used in a manner that does not harm its neighbors. [315] As with traditional negligence definitions, the transboundary harm rule takes into account the foreseeability and avoidability of the harm, the potential harmfulness of the activity under question, and the requirement for diligence in regulating or otherwise limiting the potentially harmful activity.[316]

The responsibility to prevent transboundary harm has been recognized in international law in various circumstances. For example, in the *Corfu Channel* case, Albania was held responsible for failing to take reasonable steps to prevent transboundary harm from mines which Albania knew had been laid (it was not necessary to prove that Albania itself laid the mines). The mines damaged British ships and Albania was deemed responsible for the damages.[317] Other examples of state responsibility for transboundary harm may be seen in environmental law, in both case law[318] and in treaties. Thus,

---

[314] Ibid.

[315] Alan Boyle, "Liability for Injurious Consequences of Acts Not Prohibited by International Law," in *The Law of International Responsibility*, eds. James Crawford et al., (New York: Oxford University Press, 2010): 95-104.

[316] Ibid. 98.

[317] Christian Dominice, "Attribution of Conduct to Multiple States and the Implication of a State in the Act of Another State," in *The Law of International Responsibility*, eds. James Crawford et al., (New York: Oxford University Press, 2010): 283-84 (discussing the case in the International Court of Justice).

[318] E.g., the *Trail Smelter* case. Celine Negre, "Responsibility and International Environmental Law," in *The Law of International Responsibility*, eds. James Crawford et al., 804.

pursuant to the Rio Declaration on Environment and Development, states have a "responsibility to ensure that activities within their jurisdiction or control do not cause damage to the environment of other States or of areas beyond the limits of national jurisdiction."[319]

Other treaties will be discussed below, but here it should be mentioned that this transboundary harm rule may be reflected in a variety of agreements and policies. Within the information infrastructure context, for example, if individual countries come to any special arrangements between themselves regarding international telecommunications, these countries "should avoid technical harm to the operation of the telecommunication facilities of third countries."[320]

In another example, international agreements on outer space include the recognition that member states shall be responsible for national activities in outer space, whether conducted by state or non-state actors. When launching objects into outer space, member countries are responsible for damage caused "by such object or its component parts on the Earth, in air space or in outer space, including the Moon and other celestial bodies."[321] If an object launched into

---

[319]   Quoted in Council of Europe Ad-hoc Advisory Group on Cross-border Internet (MC-S-CI), International and multi-stakeholder co-operation on cross-border Internet: Interim report of the Ad-hoc Advisory Group on Cross-border Internet to the Steering Committee on the Media and New Communication Services incorporating analysis of proposals for international and multi-stakeholder co-operation on cross-border Internet (2010), http://a.cwsm.coe.int/team21/conf_internet/themes/MC-S-CI-Interim-Report.pdf, at 16.

[320]   International Telecommunications Regulations, Geneva, 1989, at Article 9.1. It should be noted that Conference Opinion No. 1 Special Telecommunication Arrangements (appended to the International Telecommunications Regulations, page 98) speaks further to a state responsibility for minimizing harm to third countries from such special arrangements. However, various countries elected to disassociate themselves from this opinion. E.g., Final Protocol Statement No. 39, part III (United States of America); Final Protocol Statement No. 44 (United Kingdom).

[321]   United Nations Treaties and Principles on Outer Space: Text of treaties and principles governing the activities of States in the exploration and use of outer space, adopted by the United Nations General Assembly, ST/SPACE/11 (2002), 5 (citing provisions of the Treaty on Principles Governing the Activities of States in the Exploration and Use of Outer Space, including the Moon and Other Celestial Bodies).

spaces causes damage "on the surface of the Earth or to aircraft in flight," the launching state may be responsible for the damage. Here the 'launching state' may be defined as not only the country "which launches or procures the launching of a space object," but also the country "from whose territory or facility a space object is launched."[322]

The transboundary harm rule could have traction in the cyber conflict context. This has been recognized by a Council of Europe working group which, in its draft report, has found that international law supports the principle that "[s]tates should, in co-operation with each other and with all relevant stakeholders, take all reasonable measures to prevent, manage and respond to significant transboundary disruption of and interference with the stability, robustness, resilience and openness of the Internet, or at any event minimise the risk and consequences thereof."[323] As stated earlier, though, in the cyber context there is yet no international agreement on the types of cyber activity that may establish state responsibility for transboundary harm. Solution options may include evoking the effects-based analysis discussed in the above section on LOAC, or establishing explicit agreements on responsibility as seen in the environmental and space law arenas. Further, in the cyber conflict context, recognition must again be made of the complications of attribution.

Other International Law Issues: Treaties, Norms, and Principles

The following section analyses a number of important international legal issues that do not fall within the law of war or state responsibility frameworks discussed above, but which are often raised

---

[322] Id. at 13-15 (citing the Convention on International Liability for Damage Caused by Space Objects).

[323] Council of Europe Ad-hoc Advisory Group on Cross-border Internet (MC-S-CI), International and multi-stakeholder co-operation on cross-border Internet: Interim report of the Ad-hoc Advisory Group on Cross-border Internet to the Steering Committee on the Media and New Communication Services incorporating analysis of proposals for international and multi-stakeholder co-operation on cross-border Internet (2010), http://a.cwsm.coe.int/team21/conf_internet/themes/MC-S-CI-Interim-Report.pdf, 16.

in discussions of cyberspace law. The first section reviews existing treaties that may be pertinent to cyber conflict. That section is followed by an analysis of recent statements, by countries and international organizations, on the importance of developing "norms" within international cyber law. These norms may be legal (as discussed above regarding practice and custom in international law), or they may be social or policy norms lacking legal weight; this discrepancy is briefly addressed before the conclusion to this chapter.

Treaties and International Agreements

Most treaties and agreements that arguably may be relevant to the cyber conflict context were not created to address the particular concerns of cyber conflict or cyberspace in general. Not all treaties are covered here; a few examples are presented to exemplify the current situation. Some treaties are further discussed in earlier sections of this chapter. This section first looks at the Council of Europe Convention on Cybercrime, and then briefly reviews various international agreements on telecommunications and space.

Cyber Crime and the Council of Europe Convention

While ordinary cyber crime has not generally been included as a component of 'cyber conflict' analyses, any discussion of the current international legal system and cyberspace would be remiss without some treatment of the Council of Europe Convention on Cybercrime (COE Convention), the only binding international treaty specifically addressing cyber issues. The Committee of Ministers of the Council of Europe adopted the convention in November 2001, when it was also opened for signature, and it entered into force in July 2004. Thirty-one countries,[324] including the United States, have ratified the COE Convention.[325] While an "observer" at the convention's negotiations, the United States was

---

[324] In May 2011 the United Kingdom noted its "landmark achievement" in ratifying the convention. The Prime Minister's Office, "UK-US Co-operation on Cyberspace" May 25, 2011, http://www.number10.gov.uk/news/statements-and-articles/2011/05/uk-us-co-operation-on-cyberspace-64136. See also Council of Europe, "Convention on Cybercrime, CETS No.: 185, Status as of: 6/6/2011," http://conventions.coe.int/Treaty/Commun/ChercheSig.asp?NT=185&CL=ENG.

[325] Another 16 have signed but not ratified the COE Convention. Council of Europe, "Convention on Cybercrime, CETS No.: 185, Status as of: 6/6/2011."

important in the drafting of the COE Convention.[326] After ratifying the convention in 2007, the United States did not create any new implementing legislation, as it argued its laws already met the requirements listed in the COE Convention.

The main parts of the treaty identify obligations within the categories of substantive cybercrime offenses, investigative procedures, and international cooperation. [327] Listed criminal offenses include: illegal access, illegal interception, data interference, system interference, and misuse of devices;[328] as well as computer-related forgery and fraud and copyright infringement.[329] Interesting to note is that the only content-related crime listed is child pornography. [330] However, the Additional Protocol to the Convention on Cybercrime addresses the criminalization of racist and xenophobic content.[331] The United States is not a party to the Additional Protocol, as it conflicts with the First Amendment of the US Constitution. In terms of investigative procedures, the COE Convention establishes minimum standards for investigation and prosecution to harmonize law enforcement cooperation. This includes provisions for extradition and mutual assistance as appropriate.[332]

---

[326] Michael A. Vatis, "The Council of Europe Convention on Crime" in National Research Council, ed., *Proceedings of a Workshop on Deterring Cyberattacks: Informing Strategies and Developing Options for U.S. Policy* (Washington, DC: National Academies Press: 2010), 207-223.

[327] Ibid.

[328] Chapter II, Section 1, Title 1, Convention on Cyber Crime, Council of Europe, Budapest, 23 November 2001, ETS No. 185, http://conventions.coe.int/Treaty/EN/Treaties/html/185.htm.

[329] Chapter II, Section 1, Title 2, COE Convention on Cyber Crime.

[330] Chapter II, Section 1, Title 3 COE Convention on Cyber Crime. In this sense, the main body of the COE Convention does not address content issues that may be categorized by crime in a couple of countries but not necessarily in the larger international community (e.g., matters of social concern or public safety that may not rise to levels commonly recognized as crimes in the international community).

[331] Council of Europe, Additional Protocol to the Convention on Cybercrime, Concerning the Criminalization of Acts of a Racist or Xenophobic Nature Committed Through Computer Systems, 28 January 2003, ETS No. 189, http://conventions.coe.int/Treaty/EN/Treaties/html/189.htm.

[332] See Chapter III, Section 1, Title 2, COE Convention on Cyber Crime for extradition and Chapter III, Section 1, Title 3, COE Convention on Cyber Crime for mutual assistance.

Other COE countries and non-COE countries are being encouraged to accede to the COE Convention. For example, both the Organization of American States and the Asia-Pacific Economic Cooperation have encouraged their member countries to create domestic legislation that adheres to the COE Convention on Cyber Crime.[333] The United Nation's Office of Drugs and Crimes also encouraged the consideration of such a global convention against cybercrime. [334] However, others have cautioned that the COE Convention is not one-size-fits-all and that perhaps different regional organizations should develop their own agreements to counter cyber crime. [335] For example, the United Nation's International Telecommunication Union has questioned the global applicability of the COE Convention. [336] Russia also does not favor the COE Convention, despite Russia's COE membership.[337] Russia's continued opposition may in part be explained by the fact it has proposed a treaty to limit the use of certain cyber tools, and Russia continues to view that proposal as a goal for international cyber relations.[338]

In addition to the COE Convention, the European Union has also cooperated to combat cyber crime within the European region. As explained in a 2007 policy document, this aim can be divided into three main operational strands: improving and facilitating coordination and cooperation between cyber crime units, other relevant authorities and other experts in the European Union; developing, in coordination with Member States, relevant EU and international organizations and other stakeholders, a coherent EU Policy framework on the fight against cyber crime; and raising awareness of costs and dangers posed by cyber crime.[339] The

---

[333]   Shackleford, "From Nuclear War to Net War: Analogizing Cyber Attacks in International Law," 244.

[334]   Ibid.

[335]   Robert K. Knake, "Internet Governance in an Age of Cyber Insecurity," Council on Foreign Relations, Council Special Report No. 56, September 2010: 17.

[336]   Vatis, "The Council of Europe Convention on Crime," 218.

[337]   Owens, Dam, and Lin, eds., *Cyberattack Capabilities*.

[338]   See Heickerö, "Emerging Cyber Threats and Russian Views on Information Warfare and Information Operations" and UN General Assembly, *Developments in the Field of Information and Telecommunications in the Context of International Security*, A/RES/53/70, 4 December 1998.

[339]   Commission of the European Communities, "Communication from the Commission to the European Parliament, the Council and the Committee of

Communication bolsters the COE Convention and encourages EU Member States to ratify the COE Convention on Cybercrime.

Overall, while the COE Convention is generally seen as a positive development in combating global cyber crime, there are some caveats as to its potential effectiveness.[340] First, the convention is still limited in scope of membership; in the decade since adoption, only 31 countries have ratified the convention. Second, the convention provides no enforcement mechanisms for uncooperative states that may impede cross-border criminal investigations either purposely or by negligence or mistake. One commentator notes that some of the signatories "include some of the worst cyber-criminal havens in Eastern Europe."[341] A final note on effectiveness must recognize that despite any binding legal agreements, investigating cyber crime can take a significant amount of time, effort, and forensics tools and skills, so cooperation might be hampered by practical considerations.

It should also be noted that an international agreement lacking the active participation of Russia and China might limit the utility of common cyber security efforts against crime, attacks, and espionage. Still, the COE Convention is an example of state cooperation on one of the most pressing issues in cyberspace. In that sense, it may provide an example for future cooperation, although governing cyber attacks may be more contentious than cyber crime.

Telecommunications

International conventions on telecommunications date to 1865, with the signing of the first International Telegraph Convention, which addressed rules for standardization of equipment, common operating procedures, and rules for international tariffs and accounting. This convention also established the International Telegraph Union (ITU), [342] which facilitated subsequent amendments and international agreements. [343] International

---

the Regions - Towards a general policy on the fight against cyber crime," Communication 2007/267 Final, May 22, 2007.

[340] See Vatis, "The Council of Europe Convention on Crime" for full evaluation of COE Convention.

[341] Knake, "Internet Governance in an Age of Cyber Insecurity," 17.

[342] Now the 'International Telecommunication Union.'

[343] ITU's History, http://www.itu.int/en/history/overview/Pages/history.aspx, accessed May 13, 2011.

communications mandates, such as the current International Telecommunications Regulations ratified in 1988, continue to be focused on efficient management and availability of international communications.[344] For example, member countries commit to providing a minimum quality of service.[345]

One provision of the International Telecommunications Regulations may be relevant to cyber conflict or crisis situation. If for any reason a member country suspends international telecommunication services, that country must notify the ITU Secretary-General, who will disseminate the notification to other member countries.[346] Other than this provision, these regulations do not speak directly to the cyber conflict material at issue in this publication.

Various countries have, of course, entered into agreements with each other regarding telecommunications and related issues, but similar to the International Telecommunications Regulations, these agreements are generally focused on the efficient operation of international communications.[347] Like many international agreements, these likely have special provisions exempting the signatories from liability when otherwise violative actions were prompted by defense and national security or international security concerns.[348]

---

[344] Geneva, 1989 (ISBN 92-61-03921-9), at Preamble (Paragraph 1), Article 1.3. Regulations available at http://www.itu.int/dms_pub/itus/oth/02/01/S02010000214002PDFE.pdf (accessed May 13, 2011). The ITU also manages, *inter alia*, international radio-frequency spectrum and satellite orbits. ITU Radiocommunication Sector, "Welcome to ITU-R," http://www.itu.int/ITU-R/index.asp?category=information&rlink=iturwelcome&lang=en (accessed May 13, 2011).

[345] Article 4.3, International Telecommunications Regulations.

[346] Ibid. at Article 7.

[347] E.g., Agreement between the Government of Canada and the Government of the United Mexican States Concerning the Provision of Satellite Services (1999), http://www.ic.gc.ca/eic/site/smt-gst.nsf/vwapj/SAT-ENG.PDF/$FILE/SAT-ENG.PDF (accessed May 13, 2011).

[348] Id. at Article VII. Essential Security Exception. "This Agreement and its Protocols shall not preclude the application by either Party of actions that it considers necessary for the protection of its essential security interests or to the fulfilment (sic) of its obligations under the Charter of the United Nations with respect to the maintenance or restoration of international peace or security."

Outer Space

The law of outer space also includes various treaties and international agreements; while not obviously directly applicable to cyber conflict, the topic is briefly mentioned here due to academic and theoretical analogies between cyberspace and outer space law.[349] Dating from the 1963 U.N. General Assembly's Declaration of Legal Principles Governing the Activities of States in the Exploration and Use of Outer Space,[350] several multilateral agreements on outer space have addressed topics such as the exploration and use of outer space and celestial bodies,[351] the rescue of astronauts,[352] and the registration and reporting of objects launched into space.[353] Member countries have committed that celestial bodies should be used for peaceful purposes, agreeing, *inter alia*, to not place weapons of mass destruction in outer space, and to not use the celestial bodies for military bases or weapons testing.[354] Thus, similar to the telecommunications agreements, international law of outer space has not particularly spoken to cyber conflict matters. However, as discussed above, concepts of transboundary harm are included in the international law of outer space.

Thus it can be seen that these treaties on crime, telecommunications, and outer space are not particularly eloquent on matters of cyber conflict. The agreements presented here are examples of this situation. However, the lack of explicit agreements and treaties may belie the reality of the increasing international dialog on norms and principles for activity in cyberspace. This movement is briefly addressed below.

---

[349] See, e.g., Shackleford, "From Nuclear War to Net War: Analogizing Cyber Attacks in International Law."

[350] United Nations Treaties and Principles on Outer Space: Text of treaties and principles governing the activities of States in the exploration and use of outer space, adopted by the United Nations General Assembly, ST/SPACE/11 (2002), v.

[351] Ibid., 4 (Treaty on Principles Governing the Activities of States in the Exploration and Use of Outer Space, including the Moon and Other Celestial Bodies), 27-35 (Agreement Governing the Activities of States on the Moon and Other Celestial Bodies).

[352] Ibid., 9-12 (Agreement on the Rescue of Astronauts, the Return of Astronauts and the Return of Objects Launched into Outer Space).

[353] Ibid., 22-26 (Convention on Registration of Objects Launched into Outer Space).

[354] Ibid. at 4.

Norms & Principles

Over the past few years, many states, intergovernmental organizations, and think tanks have furthered proposals for new norms and principles to govern activity in cyberspace. The majority of these norms, however, address policy issues and not necessarily international law.[355] This section discusses a number of recent proposals.

The difference between principles, norms and rules is an important one from a legal perspective, and making this distinction also helps in understanding and categorizing current proposals and their interrelations. The COE, ITU, and the UK, among others, have proposed "principles" for Internet Governance, focusing on achieving and maintaining cyber security and peace, governing the use of cyberspace, and supporting cyberspace norms accord. Principles are fundamental tenets that represent bases for general conduct or management that can underlie norms and rules. Norms are models or standards voluntarily or involuntarily accepted by a group. They can be defined by technology, policy, culture and many other factors. A normative approach to cyber security can therefore mean establishing or ensuring the conformity to norms and standards that may, but do not have to, be based in law. Rules, in turn, mostly refer to established and authoritative standards and therefore are often used in the context of regulation. From analyzing the current wording of the proposals below, no specific emphasis has been put on a regulatory approach to cyber security. Accordingly, nations and groups should develop principles for behavior in cyberspace through a variety of different means, activities, and processes.

More states have released cyber security strategies since 2008 and most of those strategies have emphasized increased international cooperation in this area. For instance, the Australian Cyber Security Strategy states that "[e]ffective cyber security requires coordinated global action."[356] This statement is also echoed in the cyber security and national security strategies of the United Kingdom, Canada, Estonia, South Africa, South Korea, Germany, and the Netherlands.[357] However, only the Estonian strategy explicitly calls

---

[355]   For an overview of the difference between policy norms and legal custom, see section 3.0 above.

[356]   Government of Australia, Australian Cyber Security Strategy

[357]   See, e.g., U.S. National Security Council and Homeland Security Council, Cyberspace Policy Review (2009): 37,;U.K. Cabinet Office, The National Security Strategy (2010): 33; U.K. Cabinet Office, The Strategic Defence

for the development of legal norms and regulation, declaring that "[p]olitical attention is important in initiating efforts at drafting international norms and regulation is necessary to ensure cyber security and to facilitate co-operation between countries."[358]

Since the release of its cyber security strategy, the United Kingdom has called for the development of international norms and principles, offering its own set at the Munich Security Conference in February 2011. U.K Foreign Minister William Hague introduced seven principles for international use of cyberspace:

1. The need for governments to act proportionately in cyberspace and in accordance with national and international law.

2. The need for everyone to have the ability – in terms of skills, technology, confidence and opportunity – to access cyberspace.

3. The need for users of cyberspace to show tolerance and respect for diversity of language, culture and ideas.

4. Ensuring that cyberspace remains open to innovation and the free flow of ideas, information and expression.

5. The need to respect individual rights of privacy and to provide proper protection to intellectual property.

6. The need for us all to work collectively to tackle the threat from criminals acting online.

7. [T]he promotion of a competitive environment which ensures a fair return on investment in network, services and content.[359]

---

and Security Review (2010): 62; Australian Government, Cyber Security Strategy (2009): 22; Republic of South Africa, Draft Cybersecurity Policy of South Africa (2010); Republic of Korea, Global Korea: The National Security Strategy of the Republic of Korea (2009); Federal Republic of Germany, Cyber Security Strategy for Germany (2011); Kingdom of the Netherlands, The National Cyber Security Strategy (2011).

[358] Estonian Ministry of Defense, Cyber Security Strategy of Estonia (2008).

[359] William Hague, United Kingdom Foreign Secretary, Speech at the Munich Security Conference: Security and Freedom in the Cyber Age - Seeking the Rules of the Road (Feb. 11, 2011), http://www.fco.gov.uk/en/news/latest-news/?view=Speech&id=545383882.

While these norms uphold common values and emphasize security, the only norm that addresses international law is the first, and it does not discuss developing new international norms, but abiding by existing international law. However, as demonstrated in various sections above, there is no firm consensus among scholars as to the current application of international law to cyber conflict, let alone among states.

In May 2011, the United States released its International Strategy for Cyberspace.[360] The strategy speaks to enhancing existing norms and furthering new principles for responsible behavior for cyberspace. The overall US goal is the promotion of "an open, interoperable, secure, and reliable information and communications infrastructure."[361] In pursuing that goal, the United States endeavors to "build and sustain an environment in which norms of responsible behavior guide states' actions, sustain partnerships, and support the rule of law in cyberspace."[362] A significant portion of the strategy is devoted to norms, which are separated into existing and emerging concepts, as shown in the chart below.

Table 4.3: Principles and Norms in the International Strategy for Cyberspace

Existing Principles	Emerging Norms
• *Upholding Fundamental Freedoms*: States must respect fundamental freedoms of expression and association, online as well as off.	• *Global Interoperability*: States should act within their authorities to help ensure the end-to-end interoperability of an Internet accessible to all.
• *Respect for Property*: States should in their undertakings and through domestic laws respect intellectual property rights, including patents, trade secrets, trademarks, and copyrights.	• *Network Stability*: States should respect the free flow of information in national network configurations, ensuring they do not arbitrarily interfere with internationally interconnected infrastructure.
• *Valuing Privacy*: Individuals should be protected from arbitrary or unlawful state interference with	• *Reliable Access*: States should not arbitrarily deprive or disrupt

---

[360]   U.S. Executive Office of the President, *International Strategy for Cyberspace* (May 2011).
[361]   Ibid., 8.
[362]   Ibid.

their privacy when they use the Internet.	individuals' access to the Internet or other networked technologies.
• *Protection from Crime*: States must identify and prosecute cybercriminals, to ensure laws and practices deny criminals safe havens, and cooperate with international criminal investigations in a timely manner.	• *Multi-stakeholder Governance*: Internet governance efforts must not be limited to governments, but should include all appropriate stakeholders.
• *Right of Self-Defense*: Consistent with the United Nations Charter, states have an inherent right to self-defense that may be triggered by certain aggressive acts in cyberspace.	• *Cybersecurity Due Diligence*: States should recognize and act on their responsibility to protect information infrastructure and secure national systems from damage or misuse.

The strategy indicates US commitment to traditional policy norms and application of some international law, as well as its interest in the development of new policy norms. While based in some ways in international law and the rule of law, the above principles and norms represent a mix of aspirational policy statements with acknowledgements of the binding nature of some international law on cyber activities.

In addition to the rise in state involvement in international cyber policy, the role of international forums and intergovernmental organizations has grown as well. The current Internet governance coalition consists of a number of multi-stakeholder groups, incorporating companies, states, academia, researchers, and individuals. Examples of this multi-stakeholder process and model include the Internet Corporation for Assigning Names and Numbers (ICANN), the Internet Governance Forum (IGF), and the Internet Engineering Task Force (IETF), among many others. Recently, the ITU Secretary General has suggested "five principles for cyber peace":

1. Every government should commit itself to giving its people access to communications.

2. Every government will commit itself to protecting its people in cyberspace.

3. Every country will commit itself not to harbor terrorists/criminals in its own territories.

4.   Every country should commit itself not to be the first to launch a cyber- attack on other countries.

5.   Every country must commit itself to collaborate with each other within an international framework of co-operation to ensure that there is peace in cyberspace.[363]

Again, while some of these norms touch upon international law and the need to develop a stronger framework, they do not directly state international legal norms, nor do they advocate for the development of explicit international laws of cyberspace.

The three sets of norms from the United Kingdom, United States, and ITU have some overlap, but also emphasize different priorities, demonstrating the sometimes-incongruous development of international policy norms for cyber issues. The table below summarizes the similarities and differences between these policy norms:

Table 4.4: Comparison of Norm Promotion Among U.K., US and ITU Statements

PRINCIPLES	PERSPECTIVES		
	UK Foreign Minister	US International Strategy	ITU Secretary General
Proportionate Government Action in Accordance with National and International law	Mentioned	Related to Self-Defense Norm	Not Mentioned
Universal Access to Cyberspace	Mentioned	Mentioned	Mentioned
Tolerance and Respect for Diversity of Language, Culture, and Ideas	Mentioned	Related to Fundamental Freedoms Norm	Not Mentioned

---

[363]   Hamadoun I. Touré, "The International Response to Cyberwar, in International Telecommunication Union," in *The Quest for Cyber Peace*, International Telecommunications Union and Permanent Monitoring Panel on Information Security World Federation of Scientists (January 2011): 86-103, 103.

PRINCIPLES	PERSPECTIVES		
	UK Foreign Minister	US International Strategy	ITU Secretary General
Innovation and Free Flow of Ideas	Mentioned	Mentioned	Not Mentioned
Respect for Privacy	Mentioned	Mentioned	Not Mentioned
Protection for Intellectual Property	Mentioned	Mentioned	Not Mentioned
Combating Cyber Crime	Mentioned	Mentioned	Mentioned
Promotion of competitive environment for fair investment return	Mentioned	Related to Innovation and Free Flow of Ideas	Not Mentioned
Upholding Fundamental Freedoms	Not Mentioned	Mentioned	Not Mentioned
Right of Self-Defense	Not Mentioned	Mentioned	Not Mentioned
Multi-stakeholder Governance	Not Mentioned	Mentioned	Not Mentioned
Cybersecurity Due Diligence	Not Mentioned	Mentioned	Mentioned
Commitment to Not Launch Cyber Attacks First	Not Mentioned	Not Mentioned	Mentioned
Commitment to Collaborate with Other Countries	Implied	Implied	Mentioned

The above table demonstrates the different priorities of three important actors. Generally, the United Kingdom and the United States are focusing on the same issues. On the other hand, the ITU Secretary General's statement relates specifically to establishing "cyber peace and therefore the emphasis is on state action only and does not incorporate norms regarding privacy, freedoms, or a multi-stakeholder process. Additionally, comparing the statements' attention to state or non-state activities, the US and ITU strategies contrast with those of the United Kingdom. Foreign Minister

Hague's principles explicitly emphasize the role of the private sector and individuals, using language that demonstrates the pervasiveness of the problems. On the other hand, the majority of the US norms and all of the ITU norms discuss nation-state behavior and expectations, in part to cooperate with private actors, but also to retain certain rights and obligations in cyberspace.

Other international and regional organizations are increasingly active in matters of international cyber policy. The Council of Europe, building upon the success of Convention on Cyber Crime, created an Ad-Hoc Advisory Group on Cross-border Internet with the mission to, *inter alia,* "examine the shared or mutual responsibilities of states in ensuring that critical Internet resources are managed in the public interest and as a public asset ... [and to] explore the feasibility of drafting an instrument designed to preserve or reinforce the protection of cross-border flow of Internet traffic openness and neutrality."[364] This advisory group is currently developing a framework of principles for Internet governance and state responsibility, including a duty to protect human rights in cyberspace and a responsibility to prevent and minimize transboundary harm and interference to the free flow of the Internet across borders.[365] As discussed above, the COE advisory group rests part of its draft work on the transboundary harm rule of international law. The COE group, therefore, is one of the few international or regional organizations explicitly using established principles of international law as a key foundation of its work.

Other international organizations active in furthering international cooperation and the development of cyber principles include the Group of Eight (G8), the Organization for Economic Co-

---

[364] Terms of reference of the Ad hoc Advisory Group on Cross-border Internet (Sept. 28, 2010), http://www.coe.int/t/dghl/standardsetting/media/mc-s-ci/MC-S-CI_mandate_2011_en.pdf.

[365] Council of Europe Ad-hoc Advisory Group on Cross-border Internet (MC-S-CI), International and multi-stakeholder co-operation on cross-border Internet: Interim report of the Ad-hoc Advisory Group on Cross-border Internet to the Steering Committee on the Media and New Communication Services incorporating analysis of proposals for international and multi-stakeholder co-operation on cross-border Internet (2010), http://a.cwsm.coe.int/team21/conf_internet/themes/MC-S-CI-Interim-Report.pdf.

operation and Development (OECD), and the Organization for Security and Co-operation in Europe (OSCE). In addition to the development of a "24/7 Points of Contact for High-Tech Crime," the G8 also established the "G8 Principles for Protecting Critical Information Infrastructure" in 2003.[366] These principles include the creation of emergency warning networks, identifying interdependencies in infrastructures, maintaining crisis communication networks, and increasing training and exercises. The Principles also emphasize improving national legislation based on international agreements, citing the COE Convention. The Principles do not discuss the development of international law. As France has made Internet issues a priority for its 2011 Presidency of the G8, the organization may address international law as it continues to focus on the issue.[367]

Both the OECD and the OSCE have been active in encouraging continuing dialogue on international cooperation and cyber space. The OECD has issued guidelines ranging from online identity theft prevention to information security.[368] In addition to its guidelines, the OECD also has a number of working groups and committees focused on cyber security issues. The two most prominent groups are the Committee for Information, Computer and Communications Policy [369] and the Working Party on Information Security and Privacy.[370] The OECD has not adopted any OECD Acts (the legal instruments of the group) regarding international cyber security. Meanwhile, the OSCE has hosted conferences over the past year on addressing threats in cyberspace. The most recent of these conferences was held in May 2011. A

---

[366]   G8 Justice & Interior Ministers, *G8 Principles for Protecting Critical Information Infrastructures*, May 2003, http://www.justice.gov/criminal/cybercrime/g82004/G8_CIIP_Principles.pd f (accessed 23 May 2011).

[367]   G20-G8 France, "The Internet: New Challenges" 2011, http://www.g20-g8.com/g8-g20/g8/english/-fiches/the-internet-new-challenges.420.html (accessed 23 May 2011).

[368]   Ibid.

[369]   OECD, "Information and Communications Policy," http://www.oecd.org/department/0,3355, en_2649_34223_1_1_1_1_1,00.html (accessed 23 May 2011).

[370]   OECD, "Information Security and Privacy," http://www.oecd.org/department/0,3355, en_2649_34255_1_1_1_1_1,00.html (accessed 23 May 2011).

conference the year earlier emphasized a "comprehensive approach" and the 2011 conference built upon that momentum.[371] The 2011 conference focused on "[exchanging] views on the desirability of developing norms governing state behavior in cyberspace."[372]

Other regional organizations are continuing to propose norms and expectations for behavior in cyberspace. In December 2008, Kazakhstan, China, Kyrgyzstan, Russia, Tajikistan, and Uzbekistan, comprising the Shanghai Cooperation Organization, entered into an agreement on Cooperation in the Field of International Information Security.[373] Under Article 2 of this instrument these countries regard development and use of information weapons,[374] preparation and waging information war,[375] information terrorism,[376] information crime,[377] but as key threats in cyberspace. Additionally, it appears these countries are also concerned about the role of content in cyberspace.

For example, the same article lists "dissemination of information harmful to social, political and economic systems, as well as spiritual, moral and cultural spheres of other states and natural and man-made threats to safe and stable operation of global and national information infrastructures" as a significant threat in cyberspace. To respond to these threats, the governments of these six countries have agreed to cooperate in a wide variety of

---

[371] OSCE, "OSCE Explores Next Steps in Strengthening Comprehensive Cyber Security," May 2011, http://www1.osce.org/cio/77412 (accessed 23 May 2011).

[372] Ibid.

[373] Shanghai Cooperation Organization, "Agreement between the Governments of the Member States of Shanghai Cooperation Organization on Cooperation in the Field of International Information Security," 2 December 2008.

[374] Ibid. Defined as information technologies, ways and means of waging an information war. (Annex 1 to the Agreement).

[375] Ibid. Defined as confrontation between two or more states in the information space aimed at damaging information systems, processes and resources, critical and other structures, undermining political, economic and social systems, mass psychologic brainwashing to destabilize society and state, as well as to force the state to taking decisions in the interest of an opposing party. (Annex 1 to the Agreement).

[376] Ibid. Defined as use of and/or attack on information resources in the information space for terrorist purposes. (Annex 1 to the Agreement).

[377] Ibid. Defined as use of and/or attack on information resources in the information space for illegal purposes. (Annex 1 to the Agreement).

activities aimed at implementing security measures, monitoring, responding to threats, developing relevant norms of international law, coordinating policies, etc.[378]

In September 2011, the group responded to the White House strategy by releasing an "International Code of Conduct for Information Security" as a formal document to the 66th UN General Assembly.[379] According to the Code, its purpose is to identify states' rights and responsibilities in information space, promote their constructive and responsible behaviors, and enhance their cooperation in addressing the common threats and challenges in information space, so as to ensure the Information and Communication Technologies (ICTs) including networks to be solely used to the benefit of social and economic development and people's well-being, and consistent with the objective of maintaining international stability and security.

The Code requests states voluntarily subscribing to it to pledge not to use ICTs including networks to carry out hostile activities or acts of aggression and pose threats to international peace and security; not to proliferate information weapons and related technologies. It also calls on states to cooperate in combating criminal and terrorist activities which use ICTs, to fully respect the rights and freedom in information space and to promote the establishment of a multilateral, transparent and democratic international management of the Internet.

In addition to the SCO agreement, other regions have noted the importance of an integrated approach to combating cyber crime. The Asia-Pacific Economic Cooperation (APEC) encourages Member Economies to adopt comprehensive substantive, procedural, and mutual assistance laws and policies that take into account the COE Convention in its 2002 Cyber Strategy.[380] Similarly, ASEAN has been involved in this issue, issuing the Singapore Declaration in 2003 and encouraging the development of national CERTs.[381] The

---

[378]   Ibid. Article 3.

[379]   "China, Russia, Tajikistan, Uzbekistan Jointly Submit Int'l Code of Conduct for Information Security To UN," *Xinhua*, 13 September 2011.

[380]   Asia Pacific Economic Cooperation, APEC Cyber Security Strategy, 2002. http://unpan1.un.org/intradoc/groups/public/documents/apcity/unpan012298.pdf (accessed July 30, 2011).

[381]   Nicholas Thomas, "Cyber Security in East Asia: Governing Anarchy," *Asian Security*, 5:1 (2009): 3-23.

Organization of American States (OAS) has worked towards a comprehensive strategy for protecting information infrastructures and an integral, international, and multidisciplinary approach for threats in cyberspace.[382] Guidelines on harmonization of the legal frameworks concerning ICTs in West African States are aimed at defining major orientations of the West African information society and supplementing existing legislation in the field.[383]

These organizations, and many others, contribute to the on-going dialogue.[384] At the same time, while many governments are discussing "norms," they are mostly seeking to develop policy or technical norms rather than strategic and political expectations. Different states and organizations often emphasize different norms or priorities, demonstrating a potential difficulty in organizing international momentum in a focused area. Additionally, because of the nature of cyberspace, some actors emphasize the end-user or non-state components, while other emphasize the role of states. These viewpoints do not necessarily have to cause conflict, but they may in fact cause friction going forward. The implications of this for the development of international law will be discussed below.

Interplay of international law with norms & principles

While scholars of international law may provide guidance by parsing the existing international law or providing interpretations by analogy, international law has not yet been explicitly elucidated in agreements, nor directly applied to resolve differences in cyberspace. According to Admiral Mike McConnell (USN, ret.), a former director of the US National Security Agency and former Director of National

---

[382]   These developments derive from OAS General Assembly Resolution AG/RES. 1939 (XXXIII-O/03), "Development of an Inter-American Strategy to Combat Threats to Cybersecurity."

[383]   Abdoullah Cisse, "Harmonization of the legal frameworks concerning ICTs in West African States: Proposed guidelines," 2007, http://repository.uneca.org/bitstream/handle/123456789/5384/bib.%203719 6_I.pdf?sequence=1 (accessed July 30, 2011).

[384]   Other examples include Asia-Pacific Economic Cooperation (APEC), Organization of American States (OAS), Internet Governance Forum (IGF), North American Network Operators' Group (NANOG), Meridian, International Multilateral Partnership Against Cyber Threats (IMPACT), East West Institute (EWI), and Asia-Pacific Computer Emergency Response Team (APCERT).

Intelligence, the international community needs to establish "practical policies and international legal agreements to define norms and identify consequences for destructive behavior in cyberspace."[385] This lack of clarity can only attribute to the inherently unstable cyber environment; instead of providing a framework for state and non-state behavior, this lack of explicit international agreement may only further destabilize the environment. At the same time, such a framework and its ensuring stability will take time: custom is build off of behavior, statements, and a sense of legal obligation. Treaties are long and arduous to negotiate and may require amending, which is even more impractical given the dynamics of cyberspace.

Experts have noted that "the single greatest difficulty encountered thus far in the development of a legal response [to the national security cyber threat] lies in the transnational nature of cyberspace and the need to secure international agreement for broadly applicable laws controlling offenses in cyberspace."[386] In addressing this threat, many states, intergovernmental organizations, and non-governmental organizations have emphasized norm development for acceptable behavior in cyberspace.

These norms, however, are not necessarily statements that acknowledge a legal duty. Customary international law encompasses legal obligations of adherence by states, whereas a norm about international behavior may not be universally adhered to, nor is it necessarily legally binding. By developing policy norms and offering them as statements of foreign policy, however, states and organizations may begin a process that results in future evolution of such norms into customary international law. This will be a slow

---

[385] Mike McConnell, "Mike McConnell on how to win the cyber-war we're losing," *Washington Post*, February 28, 2010, http://www.washingtonpost.com/wp-dyn/content/article/2010/02/25/AR2010022502493.html (accessed 23 May 2011). McConnell also stated that "(t)he United States must also translate our intent into capabilities. We need to develop an early-warning system to monitor cyberspace, identify intrusions and locate the source of attacks with a trail of evidence that can support diplomatic, military and legal options -- and we must be able to do this in milliseconds." Ibid.

[386] Paul Rosenzweig, Workshop Rapporteur, "National Security Threats in Cyberspace: Post-Workshop Report" (American Bar Association Standing Committee on Law and National Security, and National Strategy Forum. Annapolis, Maryland. 4-5 June 2009).

process that will include setbacks and compromises, but to combat instability in cyberspace, states, international organizations, companies, and other non-state actors must start this conversation.

The prior section, though, typifies the wide range of topics that may be included in national or organizational statements of policy. Such variety may be helpful in the general approach to cyberspace, but for the purposes of cyber conflict, the statements and discussions should be more particular. Whether states pursue explicit legal agreements or non-binding policy norms related to cyber conflict, it is important to identify both the end goals and consequential effects (e.g., to human rights, privacy, etc.) when deliberating the role of international law in cyber conflict.

Conclusion

As demonstrated above, there is some applicability of existing US statutes and case law to cyber conflict issues. These legal concerns must be clearly understood by all relevant actors, from legislators and policy makers to practitioners both in the private and public sectors. Further, some US law requires clarification to better suit the cyber conflict context, in particular those laws that were developed before the creation of the Internet and development of the digital society.

Similarly, international policymakers should strive for clarity and common understanding of how existing international law applies to cyber conflict. In the interpretations or development of additional international law on cyber conflict, countries and organizations differ in preference for proceeding with non-binding policy guidance or establishing new legal instruments. For purposes of management of cyber conflict, it is important that policymakers clearly identify their goals and also align their national actions to these goals; even in the absence of explicit legal agreements, such processes could evolve and eventually evidence general practice accepted as law.

As this chapter demonstrates, there is still much left to resolve regarding legal matters of cyber conflict. By providing an overview of the existing challenges and scholarly debates, this chapter sought not only to portray some of these uncertainties, but also to demonstrate areas of growing agreement that may affect future applications of law. Such emerging consensus may be best seen in the laws of armed conflict, but much depends on future cases and continuing state practice.

Chapter Five

Understanding Approaches for Addressing Cyber Conflict

Introduction

Three traditional approaches have dominated the challenges posed by achieving cyber security and managing cyber conflict: the Technical Approach, Criminal Approach, and the Warfare Approach. This chapter opens with a brief overview of these, before introducing three newer approaches that can be used to think about contemporary cyber conflict. The emerging approaches – Environmental, Public Health, and Irregular Warfare – illustrate how the strategic, operational, and legal implications of cyber conflict can be leveraged to foster the development of a new security environment. Each of these approaches offers fresh insights that can be particularly helpful addressing the challenges stemming from cyber instability.[1]

The "original" approaches are well established by states as the typical or traditional ways to approach cyber problems: they line up well with existing government departments and ways of

---

[1] The research in this chapter related to alternative approaches to addressing cyber conflict supported by this study remains a work in progress for CCSA. Parts of this chapter were originally published Gregory Rattray and Jason Healey, "Non-State Actors and Cyber Conflict," in *America's Cyber Future: Security and Prosperity in the Information Age*, Vol. II, ed. Kristin M. Lord and Travis Sharp (Center for a New American Security: June 2011) and Gregory J. Rattray, Chris Evans, Jason Healey, "American Security in the Cyber Commons," in *Contested Commons: The Future of American Power in a Multipolar World*, ed. Abraham M. Denmark and Dr. James Mulvenon, (Center for a New American Security: Jan. 2010).

thinking. Each has its own mindset related to the roles of non-state actors and contain implied norms and applicable regimes – though some approaches have a stronger normative focus than others. However, none of these approaches has been able to sufficiently tackle the issue of non-state attackers, either singly or collectively. Following Table 2 on the next page, which summarizes the traditional approaches, the chapter opens with an overview of their respective advantages and disadvantages, including how each might help address strategic instability in cyberspace.

Table 5.1: *Understanding Differing Approaches to Engage Non-State Actors in Cyber Conflict*

| | Traditional Approaches | | War | Emerging Approaches | | |
	Technical	Crime	War	Public Health	Environmental	Irregular War
Viewpoint	Non-state actors should improve technology and response for the best defenses	States should improve defenses by using law enforcement to stop non-state criminals	States should improve defenses and defeating states and non-state actors	State and non-state actors improve defenses as if it were pandemic threat	State and non-state actors could improve defenses if cyberspace is seen as polluted domain	Militaries could improve defenses if seen *as if it were* an irregular war
Relationship to Non-States	Enable benevolent non-state defenders	Stop malicious non-state attackers	Stop malicious non-state attackers	Primarily enable non-state defenders but also to stop non-state attackers	Both enable non-state defenders and stop non-state attackers	Stop malicious non-state attackers
Primary Role Belongs to	Non-state actors who are extremely active in all aspects of this approach	Governments as law enforcers	Governments as warfighters	Governments as cyber public-health coordinators (cyber WHO or CDC)	Both government (as lawmaker and regulator) and non-state actors (as NGOs, individuals)	Governments as warfighters
Role of Non-State Actors	As researchers, coordinators, inventors	Criminals, victims, or witnesses	Attackers or non-combatants	Important supporting roles equivalent to care providers, drug companies, etc.	As individuals that decide not to pollute or are regulated or incentivized	Irregular adversaries to be defeated
Generally How?	Enables non-state actors on defense	States lock up non-state cyber criminals	Improving state defenses and offenses	Improving defenses in both states and non-states	Enrolling non-states and states to improve defenses	Improving state defenses against non-state offense
Specifically How?	Non-states lead in many kinds of cyber incident coordination; improved and secure technology, standards	States undertake forensics, improve laws; train cyber-smart police, prosecutors and judges	States treat warfare in cyberspace as analogous to warfare in other domains	International agreements to measure and share data, respond to incidents, enroll non-state actors	Creating norms of behavior and legal regimes based on "pollution" of cyberspace	Change of mindset based on tenets and tactics of irregular warfare

	Traditional Approaches			Emerging Approaches		
	Technical	Crime	War	Public Health	Environmental	Irregular War
Enables Int'l Norms?	Weakly	Strongly	Strongly	Strongly	Strongly	Weakly
Possible Norms	"New standards and technologies should be secure from the start"	"Don't be a victim; practice safe clicking"	"International humanitarian law applies to cyber attacks"	"Practice safe cyber hygiene"	"ISPs should not allow botnet-polluted traffic through their systems"	"We must patch our systems to fight on more favorable terrain"
Possible Responses to "Strategic Instability"	Technologies with more resilience and agility	Quicker incident response and more sharing with non-LE personnel	Risk reduction centers and "hotlines" between militaries	Mandatory reporting and measurement, faster response	May allow more non-state actions (like botnet takedowns) to clean environment	Agile operations and rapid sharing within "whole of government" approach
"Natural" Lead Agency in USG	Commerce	Justice	Defense	White House or Homeland Security	Homeland Security	Defense

The Original Approaches: Technical, Criminal, and Warfare

This section will look at the three traditional approaches, in the rough order they were developed: first technical, then criminal and lastly warfare.

The Technical Approach

This approach dates back to the original technical origins of the Internet in the 1960s and, of course, earlier communications and computing technologies. One of the primary challenges is that the architecture itself exacerbates insecurity, in part because the original creators did not consider how the design of the network would enable malicious activity. For this and other reasons, offense consistently outpaces defense and the lack of authentication and identity regimes makes attribution of attacks far too difficult. These problems are exacerbated by the breakneck rate of technological innovation, which is far outpacing security innovation. All of these factors are sources for the current strategic instability in cyber conflict.

The technical approach has two branches, the first of which argues that the technical community can either invent a new, more secure cyberspace[1] and that cyberspace would be more secure if users chose secure technologies and properly implement to the tools they already have.

This approach is championed by the open-source software movement, as well as the key standards and coordination bodies (such as the Internet Engineering Task Force and Internet Society). This branch can perhaps best be characterized by one of the true early Internet believers, John Perry Barlow of the Electronic Frontier Foundation:

---

[1] In the past, any number of technologies were often promised to make the Internet and computing safe from trusted computing, public key cryptography, firewalls, intrusion detection devices, intrusion prevention devices and more.

Governments of the Industrial World ... I ask you of the past to leave us alone. You are not welcome among us. You have no sovereignty where we gather. ... Where there are real conflicts, where there are wrongs, we will identify them and address them by our means.[2]

Such thinking has unleashed innovation but has not (yet) significantly advanced cyber security by, for example, making it easier to defend than to attack.[3]

The second branch of the technical approach involves responding to incidents after they occur. The technical community has a long and generally successful history of coordinating incident responses analyzing sources of attacks. However, these efforts are often not fully trusted by governments, poorly funded, and tend to be ad hoc, created for each new outbreak of malicious software. They do not effectively conduct sustained efforts, such as eradicating botnets, which are comprised of network of computers infected by malware that "allows an attacker to take control over an affected computer."[4] They also do not possess the legal authority to enforce recommendations or take action against attackers or share lessons learned about technical methods and processes for information sharing and collaboration.

This is the only traditional approach that is not inherently governmental and involves primarily non-state actors. The norms among advocates of this approach are fiercely meritocratic and usually libertarian. Anyone with technical prowess generally can participate. However, while technical solutions can serve as a foundation for other approaches it so far has not, and likely cannot, solve the challenges facing the health and resilience of the cyber ecosystem on its own.

---

[2]   John Perry Barlow, "A Declaration of the Independence of Cyberspace," *Electronic Frontier Foundation*, https://projects.eff.org/~barlow/Declaration-Final.html (1996).

[3]   For example, according to Arbor Networks, despite a massive 1000% increase in the size of the single largest distributed denial of service (DDoS) attacks over five years, only 53% of network operators tried to mitigate the effects of outbound DDoS attacks and 66% did not proactively block sites associated with botnet command and control, malware drop sites and phishing servers.

[4]   Norton, "Bots and Botnets – A Growing Threat," http://us.norton.com/theme.jsp?themeid=botnet (accessed September 22, 2011).

The Criminal Approach

By the 1980s, it was relatively common for states to use their traditional law enforcement powers to bring criminal or civil cases against non-state actors taking malicious actions in cyberspace.[5] This has generally been an effective approach, especially since nearly all malicious cyber activity is a crime. Although there may be disagreements about particular laws, sanctions, and prohibited actions, the Criminal Approach has strong and widely understood domestic and international norms and formal legal regimes. There are long-standing traditions by which states will cooperate to reduce crime and bring criminals to justice. However limitations have plagued effective international efforts to reduce cyber crime: it is often very difficult to solve cyber crimes due to cross-jurisdictional difficulties; there is a lack of trained police, prosecutors, and judges; and there are significant problems with digital forensics and evidence.

A key disadvantage of the Criminal Approach is that it is inherently governmental and slow. While some corporations assist in investigations and may alert the government when attacks occur, the formal investigation and possible prosecution of crimes are left to governments. Non-state actors can prevent crime by taking preventive actions (such as not clicking on attachments from unknown people) and they can report crimes and give evidence, but otherwise there is little role for non-state actors in a cyber crime approach. Moreover, as discussed in earlier chapters, legal gaps between jurisdictions, both domestic and international, are one of the important reasons for strategic instability in cyber conflict, particularly given the usually transnational nature of cyber activity.

The Warfare Approach

Even though this was the last to arrive of the traditional approaches, "cyber warfare" has been a regular topic of discussion for nearly two decades.[6] *Time* magazine featured a cover article with that now-

---

5   For example, the United States enacted both the Computer Fraud and Electronic Communications Privacy acts in 1986.
6   As discussed in more detail in Chapter 2.

common phrase as early as 1995, and Richard Clarke and Robert Knake's 2010 book *Cyber War* has galvanized debate in the field. A Warfare Approach does not depend on any specific definition of "cyber warfare" since it is characterized by a militarized outlook on cyber conflict. Supporters and critics alike point to the United States as the leading advocate of this view, highlighting the formation of a Cyber Command as the first formal "militarization" of cyberspace.[7]

One advantage of the Warfare Approach is that it enables militaries to recognize the threat of cyber attacks as an offensive threat – and a possible offensive opportunity. Another advantage is that it leverages existing norms and regimes. For example, even if adherents of the Technology or Criminal approaches won't understand it, other national militaries will have a good idea what is meant by the statement, "the US has affirmed that the international Law of Armed Conflict, which we apply to the prosecution of kinetic warfare, will also apply to actions in cyberspace as discussed in Chapter 4."[8] The Warfare Approach also brings access to well-developed thinking related to risk reduction, such as hotlines between militaries and establishment of risk-reduction conflict prevention centers.

One downside of the Warfare Approach is that the use of overly militaristic language frames this issue in competitive terms, which undermines efforts to build international cooperation on cyber security measures. Similarly, a Warfare mindset leads many observers into a mistaken view of many malicious actions as "cyber war" rather than what they usually are: crimes (or even petty nuisances) or espionage. A wide range of troubling activities, from patriot hacking[9] to WikiLeaks hacktivism[10] to Chinese

---

[7]   William Lynn, "Defending a New Domain," *Foreign Affairs*, vol. 89, no. 5 (September/October 2010).

[8]   Keith Alexander, "Statement of General Keith Alexander, Commander of US Cyber Command, before the House Armed Service Committee, September 23, 2010," *US Department of Defense*, http://www.defense.gov/home/features/2010/0410_cybersec/docs/USCC%20Command%20Posture%20Statement_HASC_22SEP10_FINAL%20_OMB%20Approved_.pdf (accessed September 22, 2011).

[9]   Cable News Network, "Kosovo cyberwar intensifies Chinese hackers targeting U.S. sites, government says," Cable News Network, http://articles.cnn.com/1999-05-12/tech/9905_12_cyberwar.idg_1_hackers-web-servers-web-sites?_s=PM:TECH (accessed September 22, 2011).

espionage [11] has mistakenly been called "war," even though warfare and espionage are distinct activities. Using the term "warfare" will always be inappropriate for non-state malicious activity that causes no casualties, no physical damage, and loss of information or services that can be set right in only a few days. [12]

Another disadvantage is that, like the Criminal Approach, there is only a very limited role for coopting non-state actors in strategic defensive efforts within the warfare construct. [13] In its traditional sense, war is an activity for militaries – non-state actors can assist, but these actors are generally considered victims or are mandated or expected to support their government. [14] The military conducts most of the action, while non-state actors are limited to supporting roles or helping on "the home front." Cyberspace has flipped this traditional arrangement around, with non-state actors conducting most of the protection, response and defense activities. Of course, non-state actors can take a more direct role as combatants in Irregular Warfare, which is considered below as a separate approach.

Some militaries actively seek to bridge the gaps between their uniformed forces and non-state actors. The United States only has limited programs so far, such as assigning some National Guard and Reserve units to cyber defense or offense missions, [15] and a new IT Exchange Program to exchange cyber personnel between

---

[10] Mark Townsend, Paul Harris, Alex Duval Smith, and Dan Sabbagh, "WikiLeaks backlash: The first global cyber war has begun, claim hackers," *The Guardian*, http://www.guardian.co.uk/media/2010/dec/11/wikileaks-backlash-cyber-war (accessed September 22, 2011).

[11] Michael Evans and Giles Whittell, "Cyberwar declared as China hunts for the West's intelligence secrets," The Times, http://technology.timesonline.co.uk/tol/news/tech_and_web/article7053254.ece (accessed April 7, 2011).

[12] As a giveaway that CNN did not consider their story on the Kosovo "cyberwar" as *real* war (see footnote above), the story was in the Technology section.

[13] Obvious exceptions are pirates and privateers, whose legitimacy with states has waxed and waned with circumstances.

[14] Greg Rattray, *Strategic Warfare in Cyberspace* (Cambridge, MA: MIT Press, 2001), 311-313.While a somewhat dated example, AT&T was placed under Federal government control during both World Wars.

[15] For example, the 262 Network Warfare Squadron in Seattle, Washington which pulls from the local high-tech companies (see http://www.homelandsecuritynewswire.com/dr20111219-national-guardsmen-the-new-front-line-in-cybersecurity).

the Department of Defense and the private sector.[16] Other nations have gone much further: as explained in Chapter 3, Estonia is creating a Cyber Defense League as part of its all-volunteer paramilitary force,[17] while one of Iran's responses to the Stuxnet worm has been to develop cyber units for their Basij paramilitary, subordinate to the Iranian Revolutionary Guard Corps. [18] By providing clear incentives rather than direct control, China has taken an approach of indirect guidance to its hacking community, cracking down hard against those who target Chinese companies but ignoring hacking efforts against foreign entities.[19]

These traditional approaches have been useful but are generally inadequate to effectively enroll non-state actors to give cyber defense the edge over offense. While states of course do have a role in cyber defense, it may be more limited than currently understood.

Accordingly, this chapter now describes **three emerging approaches** which may be able to further address issues of cyber security and manage cyber instability and conflict: approaches based on public health, environmentalism, and irregular warfare. These approaches could be used within governments, between governments, by governments to engage with non-state actors, or by used by non-state actors on their own.

Emerging Approaches: Public Health, Environmental, and Irregular Warfare

The following approaches are emerging to supplement those described in the previous section. This section attempts to assemble what has been written thus far as well as provide additional insight.

---

[16]   See the official DoD website for details: http://dodcio.defense.gov/sites/itep/.

[17]   Tom Gjelten, "Volunteer Cyber Army Emerges in Estonia," *National Public Radio*, January 4, 2011,
http://www.npr.org/2011/01/04/132634099/in-estonia-volunteer-cyber-army-defends-nation (accessed February 11, 2011).

[18]   Kevin Fogarty, "Iran responds to Stuxnet by expanding cyberwar militia",
IT World, January 12, 2011, http://www.itworld.com/security/133469/iran-responds-stuxnet-expanding-cyberwar-militia (accessed February 11, 2011).

[19]   Mara Hvistendahl, "China's Hacker Army," *Foreign Policy*, March 3, 2010,
http://www.foreignpolicy.com/articles/2010/03/03/china_s_hacker_army?page=0,2 (accessed December 22, 2011), 3.

Public Health Approach

The Public Health Approach[20] uses the controlling of the presence and spread of biological diseases as an analogy for malicious cyber activities and focuses on practical ways to stop them from spreading. The approach brings useful thinking regarding the utility of norms and regimes, both for non-state actors as well as governments, including personal hygiene, actions to limit the spread of disease, mandatory reporting of infectious diseases, and agreed-to scientific and medical principles and metrics. This approach also allows very active roles for non-state actors, such as doctors, researchers, hospitals, and pharmaceutical companies.

Though the idea of a cyber equivalent for the CDC dates back at least to a 1996 study by RAND,[21] the idea has recently been refreshed and championed by Microsoft. Senior Microsoft executive Craig Mundie in 2010 told the World Economic Forum that "we need a kind of World Health Organization for the Internet."[22] The idea was further defined in a follow-up concept paper, "Applying Public Health Models to the Internet," by Scott Charney, another senior company executive.[23] At first, Microsoft's strategy "would require computers to pass a malware check before being allowed to connect." Since that would have put an undue burden on Internet Service Providers, Microsoft is now looking at the equivalent of issued health certificates that certify your computer is clean.[24] In a similar vein, the Department of Homeland

---

20 See Rattray, Evans, and Healey, "American Security in the Cyber Commons" for a more detailed treatment of cyber implications of a public health model.

21 Robert Anderson and Anthony Hearn, "An Exploration of Cyberspace Security R&D Investment Strategies for DARPA: The Day After in Cyberspace II," *RAND*, http://www.rand.org/pubs/monograph_reports/2007/MR797.pdf (accessed September 22, 2011).

22 Agence France Press, "At Davos, ITU Chief Calls for Anti-Cyberwar Treaty," Planetrussell's Preposterous, http://planetrussell.posterous.com/un-chief-calls-for-treaty-to-prevent-cyber-wa-0 (accessed January 15, 2011).

23 Scott Charney, "Collective Defense: Applying Public Health Models To The Internet," Microsoft, http://www.microsoft.com/mscorp/twc/endtoendtrust/vision/internethealth.aspx (accessed September 22, 2011).

24 Warwick Ashford, "RSA 2011: Microsoft details refined 'public health' model for internet security", *Computer Weekly*, February 16, 2011,

Security released a parallel white paper in March 2011 on the cyber "ecosystem," which covers similar ground as the public health model, such as conceptualizing on cyber security based on the human immune system.[25]

The Public Health approach offers many useful features that can be applied to cybersecurity. **First**, public health authorities put significant emphasis on mandatory reporting and measurement to enable early warning, which is currently missing in a cybersecurity environment of voluntary reporting and concern about protection of shareholder value. **Second**, public health and epidemiology have a focus on practical intervention to stop diseases from spreading, which in the context of cybersecurity could help preclude an attractive but likely pointless debate about re-designing the entire architecture. **Third**, public health might be a useful analogy to organize the cooperative resources of state and non-state actors reacting to an outbreak of malicious software – similar to how public health authorities work with universities, researchers and pharmaceutical companies to deal with biological outbreaks. **Fourth**, the public health model may be a way to enroll ordinary Internet users to understand their responsibilities. During cold and flu season (and especially during a pandemic) people increasingly understand they should take basic hygiene actions for their own safety and others. "Cyber hygiene" may be another way to highlight similar actions for users of cyberspace. All of these advantages can help reduce the strategic instabilities present in cyberspace, and must be explored in more detail.

---

http://www.computerweekly.com/Articles/2011/02/16/245452/RSA-2011-Microsoft-details-refined-39public-health39-model-for-internet.htm, (accessed September 22, 2011).

[25]   Department of Homeland Security, "Enabling Distributed Security in Cyberspace:
Building a Healthy and Resilient Cyber Ecosystem with Automated Collective Action," March 23, 2011, http://www.dhs.gov/xlibrary/assets/nppd-cyber-ecosystem-white-paper-03-23-2011.pdf (accessed September 22, 2011). For an even more extensive analogy of the immune system, see Martin Libicki's "Postcards from the Immune System" in *Defending Cyberspace and Other Metaphors*, 1997.

Measurement and Early Warning

"The mandatory reporting of communicable diseases" is the "lynchpin for public health."[26] Regular reporting of a baseline is important, because it allows researchers understand the "normal" amount of good and ill health in any given population and therefore find anomalies more quickly. The strength of international disease reporting and cooperation compels even authoritarian nations to participate. After being roundly criticized, both domestically and internationally, for a slow and secretive response to SARS, the Chinese government was significantly more active in international efforts to fight avian and swine flu.[27]

Once collected, public health authorities use a variety of common, standard measurements such as the incidence and prevalence of various illnesses as well as the density with the population and rate of spread. With this combination of mandatory reporting and common, scientific metrics, the public health community is typically able to provide early warning of spreading diseases, allowing time to find interventions and make informed risk-based decisions.

Corporations and governments, however, do not share adverse cyberspace information eagerly, for a number of understandable reasons. Reporting adverse information may cause a corporation to lose shareholder confidence or market share value. The information may be classified, or a government may feel sharing information would undermine its sense of national sovereignty. There is, however, good information to be found in the work of volunteer groups (such as the Internet Storm Center or

---

[26] Dan Geer, "Measuring Security," Geer Risk Services, http://all.net/Metricon/measuringsecurity.tutorial.pdf (accessed September 22, 2011). See slide 153 in Geer's presentation.

[27] Ellen Bork, "China's SARS Problem, and Ours," *The Weekly Standard*, April 4, 2003, http://www.weeklystandard.com/Content/Public/Articles/000/000/002/504jl pnl.asp (accessed September 22, 2011); Xinhua, "China to help ASEAN countries in fighting bird flu," December 12, 2005, http://www.chinadaily.com.cn/english/doc/2005-12/12/content_502767.htm (accessed September 22, 2011). Ellen Bork offers a discussion of the Chinese response to SARS. Xinhua offers information about the Chinese response to avian and swine flu in its report.

the Shadow Server Foundation) and companies that collect information and share it with the community (such as the Verizon Data Breach Investigations Report or ESET's virus radar).[28]

Information on public health threats are combined to alert users about incidents of widespread concern. Even though nations may have their own system for internal use (such as, Singapore's "DORSCON" system) these use common criteria and national authorities all look to the World Health Organization to be the global coordinator.[29] In the cyber defense community, there are a multitude of alert systems, each run by a particular company or for a specific industry or government sector, all using varying criteria.[30] There is far more confusion than in the public health system, largely because each group is pushing a system for its particular needs, its customers, or its financial gain. A cyber warning similar to the WHO pandemic alert phases makes sense for malware that spreads like a biological virus but may not be appropriate for other kinds of cyber incidents, such as a massive surprise cyber onslaught by an adversary's military forces.

Practical Intervention to Stop Outbreaks

Inoculation can help prevent computers from becoming infected with a disease. In biological terms, immunity can be natural (the effect of previous exposure) or acquired (perhaps with a vaccination).[31] In

---

[28]   The Internet Storm Center, The SANS Institute, for more information, see http://isc.sans.org/ See The ShadowServer Foundation, for more information, see http://www.shadowserver.org/ and Wade H. Baker, David C. Hylender, Andrew J. Valentine, "2008 Data Breach Investigations Report", Verizon Business Risk Team *See also*, Virus Radar Online, ESET, LLC, for more information, see http://www.virusradar.com/

[29]   Raffles Medical Group, "What is DORSCON?," *Raffles Medical Group*, http://www.rafflesmedicalgroup.com/web/Contents/Contents.aspx?ContId= 1196 (accessed September 22, 2011).

[30]   Such as the Multi-State ISAC's "Cyber Alert Indicator", Symantec's "ThreatCon Level", and the SANS Internet Storm Center's "InfoCon". See the table on "Comparison of Alert 'Phase' Systems" in Rattray, Evans and Healey, "American Security in the Cyber Commons."

[31]   The National Institute of Allergy and Infectious Diseases, "Immunity: Natural and Acquired," April 18, 2011, http://www.niaid.nih.gov/topics/immuneSystem/pages/immunity.aspx (accessed September 22, 2011).

cyberspace, users typically acquire immunity by patching their systems with the most up-to-date anti-virus signatures, which provide a degree of detection and protection from known threats.[32]

This protects the individual from infection, but more important to the public health of cyberspace, though, is the dynamics of inoculation in the larger community, especially the goal in epidemiology of seeking herd immunity. This is an important threshold where, though some individuals remain susceptible to the disease (because they were not yet inoculated or the inoculation did not work) the majority of individuals have been inoculated and are safe.[54] Once there is herd immunity, even if a diseased member of the herd get infected the illness cannot spread enough to be an existential threat to the rest and the herd will survive. Herd immunity in cyberspace is analogous and can be achieved when enough systems are immunized through patches and other defenses. Although individuals may lose data, there would be no successful widespread botnet attacks or pandemic dissemination of malware throughout the herd, the other hosts connected throughout cyberspace.

Another important choice in public health is choosing a strategy for inoculation. Public health professionals have choices when seeking to immunize a population. They can vaccinate against impact or vaccinate against transmission. Vaccinating against impact is designed to minimize the harm. In this case, the most likely to die or those who are exposed and critical to stopping the infection – such as health care workers, children, pregnant women, and the elderly – get protected first.[33] In cyberspace, this might means prioritizing defenses for the most important machines first, such as those holding sensitive data.

The main other immunization strategy, vaccinating against transmission, is designed to improve herd immunity.[34] By giving priority of immunization individuals who are likely to encounter

---

[32]   For an extended analogy of the similarities between the human immune system and cyber defense, see Martin Libicki, "Postcards from the Immune System," in *Defending Cyberspace and Other Metaphors* (Washington DC: National Defense University Press, 1997).

[33]   Geer, "Measuring Security," Slides 157-159.

[34]   National Institute of Allergy and Infectious Diseases, "Community Immunity ('Herd Immunity')," October 21, 2010, http://www.niaid.nih.gov/topics/pages/communityimmunity.aspx.

a great number of people (such as transit workers), the spread of the disease can be greatly diminished. In cyberspace, this might mean immunizing devices and systems that have a high degree of interconnectedness, such as routers and servers at the core of the Internet or online-media companies instead of home computers.

Quarantine and isolation are measures used to minimize disease propagation, though "there is a long history of quarantine powers being reserved to the state."[35] This method is susceptible to the risk of failing to isolate every infected person because of lack of detection or long incubation periods. Fortunately, in the cyber world, isolating infected computers is straightforward, using routing tables or the Domain Name System. However, control methods do have downsides: Operations can be disrupted by isolation procedures, and universal precautions can be applied but are typically are not enforced. For example:

> When the (2004) Witty Worm was imminent, U Cal Berkeley and Lawrence Berkeley Labs [LBL] took different approaches. UCB warned systems administrators to administer a patch. LBL scanned their networks and only those who had taken the patch were allowed on the network. UCB had 800 infections. LBL had one. Quarantine works if there are diagnostic tests.[36]

At the level of cyberspace as a whole, quarantining implies the ability and will to isolate a particular network from the rest of the Internet. Conducting this kind of quarantine requires a control strategy and, more important, the ability to enforce it. Quarantining might mean closing off domains, servers, or even individual computers that are passing malicious traffic or are known enablers of cyber crime.

Another important parallel is hygiene, typically the first step in combating sickness or pandemic.[37] To decrease their

---

[35]   Geer, "Measuring Security," Slide 155.

[36]   Ibid.

[37]   For example, see World Health Organization, "WHO Guidelines on Hand Hygiene in Health Care," 2009,

chances of contracting the disease, public health authorities encourage the public take precautions ranging from simple hand washing to wearing protective clothing or use special handling instructions for contaminated objects. In the cyber realm, precautions include installing the latest patches, avoiding emails (especially with links or attachments) from unknown people, browsing only safe websites, and keeping security software up to date. Cyber hygiene is an increasingly popular concept, featuring prominently in the recent DoD Strategy for Operating in Cyberspace.[38]

Beyond hygiene, detection and diagnosis are needed so the right treatment regimen can developed and begun. Detection of biologic agents is conducted primarily by medical practitioners (through testing or analysis of symptoms), by the patient (through onset of symptoms), through public health surveillance data, or through the local media, followed by diagnosis[39] Within the computer world, public awareness of malware, its causes, symptoms, and effects is not nearly as comprehensive. People generally know when they are ill or are experiencing atypical symptoms, but most users are oblivious to the fact that their computer systems have been compromised.

Treatment follows diagnosis. Though treatment for biological illnesses is often a drawn out and painful affair, it can be much easier for cyber systems. Unlike infected humans, computers can simply be "wiped clean" and their operating systems reloaded so as to remove the infection, provided that the time is available to reload the system, suitable data backups exist, and the original vector is patched so the newly cleaned system cannot be re-infected. Even viruses attacking the system's BIOS, the fundamental code used in a computers start-up process, can be cured.

---

http://whqlibdoc.who.int/publications/2009/9789241597906_eng.pdf (accessed September 22, 2011).

[38] Defense Strategy for Operating in Cyberspace, 2011, http://www.defense.gov/news/d20110714cyber.pdf.

[39] World Health Organization, "Working for Health – An Introduction to the World Health Organization," 2007, http://www.who.int/about/brochure_en.pdf (accessed September 22, 2011).

Public Health Case Study: Battling the Swine Flu and the Conficker Worm

Comparing the Conficker worm outbreak on the Internet in late 2008 with the H1N1 swine flu pandemic of 2009 provides insight into how responses to future Conficker-like events could improve if they use the public health system as a model.

Discovery and Outbreak

In September 2008, a Chinese hacker introduced a proof-of-concept exploit that formed the nucleus of the Conficker worm, which installed itself and propagated to vulnerable computers, infecting a wide swath of the Internet user populace.[40] Defenses at the time, based on anti-virus signatures, were inadequate to stop Conficker as it became one of the largest botnets ever. By comparison, the first outbreak of H1N1 flu occurred in Mexico City and spread from person to person through direct or indirect methods.[41] Just like Conficker, existing defenses generally were not able to defend against it, as the swine flu was sufficiently different from the seasonal flu against which people had been vaccinated.

The original strains of the Conficker malware were detected by "honeypots," networks created for the purposes of capturing malware,[42] which showed a rapid spread of nearly half a million hosts in the span of 24 hours.[43] The H1N1 flu also spread quickly. Just in the United States, the "CDC estimated that between 14

---

[40]   Byron Acohido, "The Evolution of an extraordinary globe-spanning worm: Conficker Timeline," *The Last Watchdog on Internet Security*, http://lastwatchdog.com/evolution-conficker-globe-spanning-worm/ (accessed September 22, 2011).

[41]   Cable News Network, "WHO raises pandemic alert to second-highest level," April 29, 2009, http://articles.cnn.com/2009-04-29/health/swine.flu_1_swine-flu-first-case-pandemic?_s=PM:HEALTH (accessed September 22, 2011).

[42]   Phillip Porras, et al., "An Analysis of Conficker's Logic and Rendezvous Points," *SRI International*, March 19, 2009, http://mtc.sri.com/Conficker/ (accessed September 22, 2011).

[43]   Cooperation Association for Internet Data Analysis, "Conficker as seen from the UCSD Network Telescope," May 27, 2010, http://www.caida.org/research/security/ms08-067/conficker.xml (accessed September 22, 2011).

million and 34 million cases of 2009 H1N1 occurred between April and October 17, 2009."[44] The rate of new infections eventually slowed, but the global number of infected continued to rise inexorably through June 2009, when the WHO moved to the highest alert, level 6, signifying a global pandemic.[45]

Cycles of Response and Mutations

Conficker's authors released a new mutation every four to eight weeks, thwarting the security community's efforts to detect and contain the worm. As defenders reverse-engineered its binary files (equivalent to determining its digital DNA), the makers of Conficker responded with countermeasures like purposely hard-to-fathom code, anti-debugging features, and suicide routines, resulting in a more resilient strain.[46] The first variant of the Conficker worm, Conficker. A, spread by directly exploiting computers that were not patched to fix the Microsoft Windows vulnerability it used to propagate.[47] To receive instructions and updates, Conficker. A relied on the Domain Name System (DNS) to receive instructions and updates. The next mutation, Conficker. B, featured additional propagation methods and expanded use of the DNS to spread more quickly and defeat defenses that had been hastily erected to block it. Conficker. C further increased its use of the DNS, and added the ability to receive updates and instructions from other infected computer via a peer-to-peer network.[48]

As it developed, the H1N1 virus mutated to become more

---

[44]   Centers for Diseases Control and Prevention, "Updated CDC Estimates of 2009 H1N1 Influenza Cases, Hospitalizations and Deaths in the United States, April 2009 – April 10, 2010," May 14, 2010, http://www.cdc.gov/h1n1flu/estimates_2009_h1n1.htm (accessed September 22, 2011).

[45]   MSNBC, "Swine Flu Events Around The World," http://www.msnbc.msn.com/ id/30624302/ns/health-cold_and_flu (accessed September 22, 2011).

[46]   Conficker Working Group After Action Report, June 2010 (published January 2011) available at http://www.confickerworkinggroup.org/wiki/uploads/Conficker_Working_Group_Lessons_Learned_17_June_2010_final.pdf.

[47]   Ibid.

[48]   Phillip Porras et al., "Conficker C Analysis," *SRI International*, http://mtc.sri.com/Conficker/addendumC/ (accessed September 22, 2011).

deadly over time, with researchers believing the "strain has been circulating among pigs for many years prior to its transmission to humans ... [and] derived from several viruses circulating in swine."[49] Over time the current strain might mix with seasonal flu to become either more transmissible or more hazardous. The 1918 Spanish flu is a bleak reminder as started mildly before returning the following seasons to kill an estimated 20 million to 100 million people worldwide.[50]

The responses to both Conficker and H1N1 showed a tremendous amount of global coordination. The table below summarizes the similarities and differences in response methods.

Table 5.2: Similarities in Response for Conficker and H1N1

Means to Stop Spread	Conficker	H1N1
Sanitization	Don't open unknown attachments or click on unknown links	Basic hygiene like washing hands and covering mouths
Coordination	Ad hoc Conficker Working Group with Microsoft, ICANN, CERTS, researchers, universities	Established coordination between UN (WHO), CDC (US), and other nations, laboratories
Immunization	Microsoft released patch MS08-067 to fix original Windows vulnerability	WHO launching largest immunization since 1955
Diagnosis	Researchers reverse engineered malware and examine behavior	Researchers examine virus DNA and behavior
Treatment	Remove trapdoors and control software after	Reduce symptoms, also Relenza and Tamiflu

49　Smith GJ, Vijaykrishna D, Bahl J, Lycett SJ, Worobey M, Pybus OG, Ma SK, Cheung CL, Raghwani J, Bhatt S, Peiris JS, Guan Y, Rambaut A., "Origins and evolutionary genomics of the 2009 swine-origin H1N1 influenza A epidemic." *Nature* 459, no. 7250 (June 11, 2009): 1122–5. doi:10.1038/nature08182.

50　Taubenberger, Jeffrey K., and Morens, David M. "1918 Influenza: The Mother of all Pandemics," *Emerging Infectious Diseases* 12, no.1 (January, 2006), http:// www.cdc.gov/NCIDOD/EID/vol12no01/05-0979.htm (accessed September 22, 2011).

	infection such as with Windows Malicious Software Removal Tool	
Ingress Detection and Filtering	Signature updates were released for popular scanning tools like NMap and Nessus	Nations stopped inbound travelers from infected countries or who showed flu-like symptoms[51]
Egress Filtering and Quarantine	Many infected networks were taken offline, including in France[52] were the measure meant fighters bases could not access flight plans so their missions were scrubbed	Travelers dissuaded from going to infected countries[53]. Those infected were quarantined until it was clear they had no symptoms[54].

Initial responses to Conficker underestimated its potential. Microsoft released a patch for the infection vector via its "Automatic Updates" feature. In addition, the US-CERT released an advisory on the vulnerability; however, both it and the Microsoft patch proved to be ineffective in preventing the outbreak.[55] By late December 2008,

---

[51] Xinhua, "Thermal camera placed at Istanbul airport to prevent swine flu," *China View*, April 29, 2009, http://news.xinhuanet.com/english/2009-04/29/content_11280748.htm (accessed September 22, 2011).

[52] Kim Willsher, "French fighter planes grounded by computer worm," *The Daily Telegraph*, http://telegraph.co.uk/news/worldnews/europe/france/4547649/French-fighter-planes-grounded-by-computer-virus.html (accessed September 22, 2011).

[53] For example, the European Union recommended travelers to postpone trips to the U.S. and Mexico. See the following article: Daniel Nasaw, Chris McGreal, Jo Tuckman, and Rachel Williams, "Europeans urged to avoid Mexico and US as swine flu death toll exceeds 100," *The Guardian*, April 27, 2009, http://www.guardian.co.uk/world/2009/apr/27/swine-flu-mexico (accessed September 22, 2011).

[54] Hong Kong kept nearly 300 people for seven days in a Wanchai hotel, the Metropark, which gathered international reporters outside. Taxis would routinely avoid streets nearby to avoid the spot, which also had a role in the earlier SARS outbreak. See for example, Sophie Leung, "Hong Kong Lifts Swine Flu Quarantine on 351 People (Update2)," *Bloomberg*, May 8, 2009, http://www.bloomberg.com/apps/news?pid=20601087&sid=aO8D7j8 zVdWA (accessed September 22, 2011).

[55] United States Computer Emergency Readiness Team, "Technical Cyber Security Alert TA08-297A," http://www.us-cert.gov/cas/techalerts/ TA08-297A.html (accessed September 22, 2011).

security experts realized Conficker was using the DNS as a method of command and control and individuals attempted to preemptively register the domain names it was using to prevent Conficker from spreading.[56] In early February 2009, as Conficker spread around the world, Microsoft announced the formation of a Conficker Working Group (a.k.a., the Conficker Cabal).[57] The working group brought together Internet organizations, companies, service providers, security experts, and academia to set a course of action in response to the growing threat. The working group focused promoting awareness and developing detection and eradication tools.[58] In comparison to the public health system, these responses were entirely ad hoc.

For its part, the public health system had existing monitoring systems and formal international mechanisms to share information and actual viruses. The WHO, having been preparing for such an event for years, convened their Emergency Committee for the first time. This group reported changes in the progress of the H1N1 epidemic using a well-tested pandemic alert level system to which governments and companies executed trigger- based action plans.[59]

Conclusion

Public-private relationships to detect and stop malicious Internet

56   Jim Giles, "The inside story of the Conficker worm," *The New Scientist*, June 12, 2009, http://www.newscientist.com/article/mg20227121.500-the-inside- story-of-the-conficker-worm.html?full=true (accessed September 22, 2011).

57   Internet Corporation for Assigned Names and Numbers, "Microsoft Collaborates With Industry to Disrupt Conficker Worm," February 12, 2009, http://www.icann.org/en/announcements/announcement-2-12feb09-en.htm (accessed September 22, 2011).

58   Conficker Working Group, "FAQ – Announcement of Working Group," http://www.confickerworkinggroup.org/wiki/pmwiki.php/ANY/FAQ (accessed September 22, 2011). For more discussion of the development, successes, and challenges of the Conficker Working Group see Mark Bowden, *Worm: The First Digital World War*, New York, NY: Atlantic Monthly Press, 2011, and the *Conficker Working Group: Lessons Learned*, June 2010 (Published January 2011), http://www.confickerworkinggroup.org/wiki/uploads/Conficker_Working_Group_Lessons_Learned_17_June_2010_final.pdf.

59   World Health Organization, "Current WHO phase of pandemic alert," http://www.who.int/csr/disease/avian_influenza/phase/en/index.html (accessed September 22, 2011).

activities are not nearly as institutionalized nor do governments have sufficient authority to stop malicious Internet traffic.

The lessons from Conficker are that the ecosystem is unstable but at least partially defensible. Approaches limited to only one government, industry sector, or company to combat malicious activity are prone to failure in the face of a malware pandemic. Instead, cyberspace needs global collaborative and enabling approaches to clean the global cyber commons to constrain Conficker-like threats of the future.

Organizing Non-State Actors for Cyber Response

The public health model enlists and energizes state and non-state actors to identify and stop diseases. At the international level, the WHO prescribes International Health Regulations, promotes information sharing, tracks volunteer reporting of diseases and trends, and performs monitoring, alert and response operations.[60] At the national level, The US Centers for Disease Control and Prevention functions similarly to the WHO, providing centralized monitoring and guidelines for acute response, as well as supporting state and local programs through funding and assessment tools.[61] State and local governments have their own monitoring, reporting and response functions.

Non-state actors have important roles to play as well. Hospitals, clinics and doctor's offices provide treatments and report findings to authorities. Researchers – whether at universities or pharmaceutical companies – improve on the latest discoveries to better understand the idea, develop counteracting medications, or develop other practical interventions. Pharmaceutical companies commit their resources to participating in global conferences and projects to limit the disease, while non-pharmaceutical companies teach their workforce about hygiene and may even stockpile medicines for their use.[62]

---

[60]   Ibid.

[61]   Centers for Disease Control, "About CDC Mission & Vision", January 11, 2010, http://www.cdc.gov/about/organization/mission.htm (accessed September 22, 2011).

[62]   As happened during pandemic preparation over the last several years, where banks would purchase medicines, stockpile them at local clinics, determined

Organizing cyber response around a public health model might mean additional government funds going to non-state actors, for example Shadowserver, Google, or ad-hoc working groups, to improve the responsiveness of the system as a whole. If the majority of a nation's cyber infrastructure is in the private sector, then perhaps more government spending should go to non-state organizations that have been critical to stopping outbreaks and responding to incidents.

Public Outreach on "Cyber Hygiene"

Public health efforts also stress education and outreach. During the winter cold and flu season, people will frequently see messages on how to protect themselves and others. The current guidance from the CDC includes: [63]

- Get a flu shot.
- Cover your nose and mouth with a tissue when you cough or sneeze. Wash your hands often with soap and water.
- Avoid touching your eyes, nose and mouth. Germs spread this way.
- Try to avoid close contact with sick people.
- If you are sick with flu–like illness … stay home for at least 24 hours after your fever is gone except to get medical care or for other necessities.
- While sick, limit contact with others as much as possible to keep from infecting them.

During times of increased concern, such as during a pandemic illness, there might be other parts to this advice, including increased caution on public transportation or in crowds, wearing protective masks, and the like.

---

fair principles for determining who would receive them and practiced disseminating them before the outbreak occurred. Based on the experience of the author.

[63]   Centers for Disease Control and Prevention, "H1N1 Frequently Asked Questions," Citrus College, http://www.citruscollege.edu/notifications/Pages/H1N1FAQs.aspx#preventi on2 (accessed March 5, 2011).

Most of these items fit into the category of common sense, or advice we've heard many times, which is why it may be fruitful to borrow this language in campaigns for people to improve their "cyber hygiene" in similar manner. For example, here is one list by the President's Special Advisor for Homeland Security and Counterterrorism[64]:

- Keep your security software and operating system up-to-date.
- Protect your personal information online.
- Know who you are dealing with.
- Learn what to do if something goes wrong.

Unfortunately, such a list for "cyber hygiene" can sound trite or so common sense they don't fully engage people – just like many people don't pay scrupulous attention to hand washing and sanitization until the midst of an influenza outbreak.

The public health approach, then, offers significant advantages for the cyber community, including mandatory reporting and measurement, practical intervention, cooperation between nations and state and non-state actors during an outbreak, and possibly also to use "cyber hygiene" to enlist ordinary Internet users. This is not the only practical new approach, as the following section on the environmental approach will show.

Environmental Approach

Driven by the initiative of grassroots organizations, non-profits, think tanks, and motivated individuals, there is a new awareness of the health of the planet. This same type of concern can be directly applied to the "environment" of a polluted cyberspace, full of viruses, malware, spam and botnet attacks. In the cyber environment as much as in the "real" environment, the actions of one person, one organization, or one nation can have serious and unintended downstream consequences. And, many of those people,

---

[64] The White House Blog, "Cybersecurity Awareness Month Part III," *The White House*, October 19, 2009, http://www.whitehouse.gov/blog/Cybersecurity-Awareness-Month-Part-III (accessed September 22, 2011).

organizations and countries might be willing to make better choices if they were aware of the downstream damage, were incentivized (with carrots and sticks) to make changes, and had reasonable options to do so.

This call for individual and collective actions is one of the main strengths of this approach: instead of being inherently governmental (as with Criminal, Warfare, or Irregular Warfare) the environmental approach has active roles for both states and all kinds of non-state actors. Where the other approaches focus on scaring non-state actors ("Don't be a victim!") an environmental approach might better motivate people and organizations to become involved in ensuring a healthy, clean future for the Internet. Accordingly, an Environmental Approach may be more palatable to international state and non-state actors than an overt national security approach, even though it directly and intentionally enhances national security and reduces strategic instability. A second main strength is the depth of norms and regimes, including existing international jurisprudence but accepted social conduct for individuals, corporations, and governments.

This approach, then, can provide new solutions for instability in cyber conflict by (1) giving an applicable mindset – and legal regime – to deal with these problems; (2) providing a meaningful and familiar role for non-state actors, and (3) tying easily into the global development agenda.

Applicable Mindset and Legal Norms

If cyberspace is indeed a new domain, like air, land, maritime and space, then it seems easy to believe that it would also experience forms of "pollution." Accordingly, the simple translation of concern for pollution in the *physical* environment to the *cyber* environment may be relatively simple with the right messages to the correct communities. Individuals and corporations that think it is unjust to throw a can from a window of their car or fail to recycle their trash may be willing to take positive and even intrusive actions to ensure their own computers are not launching spam or participating in distributed denial of service attacks. Major telecommunication providers might be more willing (or under more pressure) not to pass polluted traffic downstream: according a survey by Arbor Networks, 27% of network operators do not attempt to detect outbound or crossbound attacks and, of those that do, nearly half take no actions to mitigate such attacks.[65]

Further, if insecure computers and distributed denial of service attacks can be usefully compared to polluting industries and cross-border emissions, then perhaps the legal regimes that developed for those problems will be useful for cyber pollution as well. The most meaningful legal norm is perhaps the principle that the "polluter pays". In the 1930's the United States complained to Canada about sulfur dioxide emissions from a smelter of zinc and lead in Trail, British Columbia that were poisoning crops across the border. The international tribunal judging this "Trail Smelter" case determined that Canada should pay a hefty penalty and the smelter should refrain from causing further damage and measure its impact on the local environment:[66].

> ... the Trail Smelter should refrain from causing any future damage to the State of Washington from its sulfur dioxide emissions. To ensure this, it mandated that the smelter maintain equipment to measure the wind velocity and direction, turbulence, atmospheric pressure, barometric pressure, and sulfur dioxide concentrations at Trail. Readings from these instruments were to be used by the smelter to keep its sulfur dioxide emissions at or below levels determined by the Tribunal.

This principle has been extended in more recent decades through the United States Superfund law[67] and might be applicable

---

[65] Arbor Networks, "Worldwide Infrastructure Security Report: 2010 Report," February 1, 2011, http://www.arbornetworks.com/report, (accessed September 2011) 15-16.

[66] Center of International Studies and Research, "1937 Trail Smelter Case (TRAIL)," University of Montreal www.cerium.ca/IMG/doc/7-Trail_Smelter_Case.1937.doc (accessed December 24, 2010).

[67] EPA, "The Comprehensive Environmental Response, Compensation, and Liability Act of 1980 (CERCLA)," http://www.epa.gov/lawsregs/laws/cercla.html (accessed September 22, 2011).

to help hold individuals or organizations that "pollute" cyberspace through acts of omission or commission.

As with a classic tragedy of the commons, there is a flawed policy that "favors pollution":[68] The owner of a factory on the bank of a stream--whose property extends to the middle of the stream, often has difficulty seeing why it is not his natural right to muddy the waters flowing past his door. The law, always behind the times, requires elaborate stitching and fitting to adapt it to this newly perceived aspect of the commons. To enable a botnet attacker, the people who have allowed their computers to become compromised, and the telecommunication providers that pass the attack all have some level of complicity in a way that seems comparable to a "tragedy of the commons." None have taken action to stop the attack because it is not their problem. If insecure computers and botnet attacks can be usefully compared to polluting industries and cross-border emissions, then perhaps the legal regimes that developed for those problems will be useful for cyber pollution as well. This principle has been extended in more recent decades through the United States Superfund law.[69] It could potentially be used to hold individuals or organizations accountable for activities that "pollute" cyberspace, whether by of omission or commission. This would cast a wide net to hold polluters liable. The Organization for Economic Cooperation and Development has defined a concept of "extended polluter responsibility" which pushes the notion of "polluter pays" even farther, to consider that "manufacturers and importers of products should bear a significant degree of responsibility for the environmental impacts of their products throughout the product life-cycle."[70]

Of course, a more complete legal analysis of how this notion would apply to cyber is out of the scope of this study. However, it

---

[68]   Garret Hardin, "The Tragedy of the Commons," *Science*, http://www.sciencemag.org/cgi/content/full/162/3859/1243 (accessed November 11, 2009)

[69]   See footnote 454. The Comprehensive Environmental Response, Compensation, and Liability Act of 1980 (CERCLA), section 107(a).

[70]   Organization for Economic Cooperation and Development, "Extended Producer Responsibility," http://www.oecd.org/document/53/0,3343, en_2649_34395_37284725_1_1_1_1,00.html (accessed March 5, 2011).

is clear that there are norms and existing law that could be built upon this foundation to hold the polluters of cyberspace responsible and even liable for their actions.

Meaningful and Familiar Roles and Norms for Non-State Actors

Three decades ago, throwing a soda can from a car window may have attracted little notice[71]. It was an accepted societal norm that litter was someone else's problem. Today, however, the same action would be more likely to be met with shock and scorn, especially by younger people because the norms have changed. Now the mantra is "Think globally, act locally," [72] believing everyone can play a role in cleaning up the environment, whether it is putting litter in its place, recycling, saving energy, controlling downstream waste, or building environmentally friendly buildings. Even better, these messages of responsibility are perceived as borderless, embraced in particular by youth (who have grown up as cyberspace "natives") and the cultural elite. Individuals and non-state actors typically just do not give that much attention to cyber security and cyber conflict; however the global environmental movement is something that people get involved with of their own accord. Where the other models focus on scaring non-state actors ("don't be a victim!") an environmental model for cyber security and conflict can excite people to want to become involved.

Tying to a Global Development Agenda and Sustainability

The Environmental Approach also allows productive ties to the development and sustainability communities. Slogans such as "clean food, clean water, clean Internet" or building a "sustainable" Internet are more likely than language from warfare or crime to be resonant with international elites at non-profits, the World Bank and donor nations. Similarly, the United States could change the global debate if it were to propose, using the language of the environmental movement, a pledge "to bring botnets down

---

[71] As noted by William Gravell in a CCSA-led workshop in support of this study, August 10, 2010.

[72] Although the exact origin of the quote in unknown, a few authors and activists are cited as having originated the concept, including Patrick Geddes, David Brower, and Rene Dubos.

to their 2005 levels by 2020." However, many governments and people of other nations are also not convinced the United States has moral legitimacy in cyber conflict. The US is seen as creating potential mixed messages by loudly discussing cyber warfare while decrying malicious activity;[73] hosting more botnets command and control servers than any other country (33% of the total in 2008);[74] and being rated by international IT executives as the country of "greatest concern" for cyber malicious activity.[75]

Another major challenge in this regard, would be the establishment of appropriate metrics and measurement systems that could be applied consistently and globally. Such an undertaking may take providing assistance to developing countries as well as the establishment of a trusted, technically focused organization that is perceived to be neutral in the gathering and dissemination of such information.

Environmental Case Study: Botnets and the Regime for Ozone-Depleting Substances

The following case study compares the promulgation of botnets and defensive response to the spread of ozone-depleting substances (ODS) in the 20th century and the international efforts to combat them. Comparing the two demonstrates the benefits and drawbacks to applying the environmental model to current cyber security vulnerabilities and threats. The comparison may seem odd: ODSs confer some societal benefits, and therefore are deliberately

---

[73]   For example, see Economic Times of India, "US 'CYBERCOM' may trigger a new arms race: Chinese analyst," June 3, 2010, http://economictimes.indiatimes.com/infotech/software/US-CYBERCOM-may-trigger-a-new-arms-race-Chinese-analysts/articleshow/6007158.cms (accessed January 15, 2011).

[74]   Symantec Corporation, "Symantec Global Internet Security Threat Report Trends for July–December 07," April, 2008, http://eval.symantec.com/mktginfo/enterprise/white_papers/b-whitepaper_exec_summary_internet_security_threat_report_xiii_04-2008.en-us.pdf (accessed September 22, 2011).

[75]   Stewart Baker, "In the Crossfire Critical Infrastructure in the Age of Cyber War," *McAfee*, http://resources.mcafee.com/content/NACIPReport (accessed September 22, 2011).

manufactured by legal means, while botnets confer no such benefits and are assembled by bad elements of society. Yet the negative effects of the substances are very similar can be viewed as similar. Therefore, the regime governing ozone-depleting substances can perhaps guide attempts to improve cyber defense and non-state defensive collaboration.

Promulgation of Botnets and Ozone Depleting Substances

As discussed earlier, botnets comprise a significant threat to the stability of cyberspace. They can include computers and machines from across the world and can consist of thousands or even hundreds of thousands of computers, sometimes called "zombies." Often users may not know their computers are infected, as bots search for vulnerable and unpatched machines across the Internet, even patching those computers after infecting them to secure control of the machine. Common uses of botnets include distributed denial of service attacks, spamming, sniffing traffic, keylogging, spreading new malware, installing add-ons, or conducting mass identity theft.[76]

Chlorofluorocarbons (CFCs) and other ODS, like botnets, are byproducts of development and technological development, but CFCs spread quite differently than botnets. Developed in the 1880s, CFCs were first used as refrigerants and propellants for chemical sprays. CFCs are inert, nonflammable, nontoxic, colorless, odorless, and fairly inexpensive to produce, making them a useful and preferred substance for a number of products. However, CFCs and other ODS[77] degrade in the stratosphere, making the ozone layer very thin in some places, primarily over the Antarctic.

While the benefits of CFCs were clear for decades, scientists began hypothesizing about their harmful consequences to the ozone layer in 1974.[78] Scientific consensus further solidified in

---

[76] Paul Bächer, Thorsten Holz, Markus Kötter, and Georg Wicherski, "Know Your Enemy: Tracking Botnets," *The Honeynet Project*, August 10, 2008, http://www.honeynet.org/papers/bots (accessed September 22, 2011).

[77] Other ODS include halons, carbon tetrachloride, methyl chloroform, and methyl bromide, among many other substances.

[78] Mario J. Molina & F.S. Rowland, "Stratospheric Sink for Chlorofluoromethanes: Chlorine Atom-Catalysed Destruction of Ozone," *Nature* 249, no. 5460 (June 28, 1974): 810-812.

1977, and the following year the US banned the use of CFCs in aerosol sprays.[79] Facing mounting, but uncertain evidence about the damage of CFCs to ozone, nations began negotiations in 1982. In 1985 scientific consensus further solidified following the publication of an article in *Nature* about damage to the Antarctic ozone layer.[80] Two years later, additional scientific research further established that CFCs were probably responsible for the size of the Antarctic ozone hole.[81] The CFC regime started slowly, in part due to scientific uncertainty, but developed over twenty years into a comprehensive regime, currently regulating nearly 100 chemicals. The last CFC production facilities were closed in India and China in 2008, and recent research reaffirms the catastrophic effects CFCs would have had if they were not regulated.[82]

While the process of promulgation is different for botnets and ODS, they are similar in their effects. Both are long-term, pervasive problems in which all users share a portion of the cause and effect. Individuals have responsibility for producing and using CFCs, and individuals also have responsibility for patching their systems, running anti-virus software, and engaging in safe use of cyberspace. ODS and botnets also originate from individual users or organizations and are transmitted into shared spaces, making the effects of both substances a transnational and international concern.

Secondly, the role of the private sector in combating botnets and CFCs is crucial. Often, non-state actors are the most important, proactive groups that combat botnets. For example, the working group that tracked and limited the spread of the Conficker botnet was made of industry experts and others from the private sector.[83]

---

[79]   Pamela S. Chasek, David L. Downie, and Janet Welsh Brown, *Global Environmental Politics*, 5th Ed. (Boulder, CO: Westview Press, 2009).

[80]   J.C. Farman, B.G. Gardiner, and J.D. Shanklin, "Large losses of total ozone in Antarctica reveal seasonal ClO_x/NO_x interaction," *Nature* vol. 315, no. 6016 (May 16, 1985): 207-210.

[81]   Chasek, Downie, and Brown, *Global Environmental Politics*, 167.

[82]   P.A. Newman *et al*, "What would have happened to the ozone layer if chlorofluorocarbons (CFCs) had not been regulated?," *Atmospheric Chemistry and Physics* 9 (March 23, 2009): 2113-2128.

[83]   A Conficker Working Group report summarizing the group's work strongly criticized the U.S. government's role: "The group as a whole saw little participation from the government. One person put it as 'zero involvement, zero activity, zero knowledge.'" Conficker Working Group, "Lessons Learned,"

Regulation of CFCs occurred before industry buy-in, but it was the development of CFC alternatives that made companies like Dupont support regulation of CFCs.[84] Private research and coordination accelerated the phase out of CFCs and were helpful in furthering the ODS regime. However, industry continued to lobby against future regulation of CFC alternatives and additional ODS not in the Montreal Protocol.[85]

The last two similarities between botnets and ODS include the questionable nature of states' obligations and the importance of measurement. Because non-state actors develop both ODS and botnets, some argue that the solution should be entirely based in the private sector or in a non-state actor community. However, the ODS regime demonstrates that while non-state actors are crucial, there is an important role for states in coordinating and legitimizing non-state actions. The last similarity is the importance of measurement and monitoring. The CFC regime implemented mandatory reporting, monitoring, and scientific assessment, tracking the development of CFCs and informing future attempts to eliminate them. Measuring and reporting on the spread of botnets would be crucial to the success of any potential botnet reduction regime.

Collaborative Responses

The majority of botnets that are taken down are mitigated through significant non-state actor response and coordination. Conficker is the most significant example of non-state defensive collaboration, as discussed in the public health case study above. Projects like the Honeynet Project, which informs researchers and studies botnets, also contribute to cyber defense. Therefore, it is primarily the coordination between companies, research organizations, and universities that forms the basis of cyber defense. For example, Microsoft and other partners dismantled the Waledac botnet in

---

Conficker Working Group,
http://www.confickerworkinggroup.org/wiki/uploads/Conficker_Working_Gro
up_Lessons_Learned_17_June_2010_final.pdf (accessed September 23, 2011).
[84] Chasek, Downie, Brown, *Global Environmental Politics*, 167.
[85] Ibid.

2010 through coordinated technical measures authorized by a US court.[86] Microsoft focused on this botnet because of its size; the Waledec botnet was estimated to have sent up to 1.5 billion spam messages per day at its peak.[87] In order to take down Waledec, state and federal government, law enforcement agencies, and domestic and international groups collaborated, showing the importance of collaboration across a range of sets of actors.

A more recent demonstration of non-state cyber defense is the takedown of the Rustock botnet, which was active from 2006 until March 2011, sending out about 25,000 spam messages per hour from individual "zombie" computers.[88] The Microsoft Digital Crimes Unit led the takedown in collaboration with other Microsoft groups, anti-malware company FireEye, the University of Washington, and Pfizer.[89] After the US District Court for the Western District of Washington issued an order authorizing the takedown, ISPs, the Netherlands government, Chinese CERT (CN-CERT), and other organizations worked with Microsoft to take down the command and control servers.[90] While also demonstrating non-state action, the Rustock botnet takedown also emphasizes that state involvement – in this case a court order – provides legitimacy for non-state defensive actions.

Similarly, the creation of the ODS regime and ensuing regulations succeeded because of the leading role of a number of states, intergovernmental organizations, and other non-state actors. Still, the importance of states as a foundation for progress in the

---

[86]   Jeff Williams, "Dismantling Waledac," *Microsoft Malware Protection Center – Threat Research and Response Blog*, February 25, 2010, http://blogs.technet.com/b/mmpc/archive/2010/02/25/dismantling-waledac.aspx (accessed September 23, 2011).

[87]   Lance Whitney, "With legal nod, Microsoft ambushes Waledac," *CNET News*, February 25, 2010, http://news.cnet.com/8301-1009_3-10459558-83.html (accessed September 23, 2011).

[88]   See footnote 476.

[89]   Larry Seltzer, "How Microsoft Took Down Rustock," *PC Magazine*, March 18, 2011, http://www.pcmag.com/article2/0,2817,2382203,00.asp (accessed September 23, 2011).

[90]   Jeff Williams, "Operation b107 – Rustock Botnet Takedown," *Microsoft Malware Protection Center – Threat Research and Response Blog*, March 17, 2011, http://blogs.technet.com/b/mmpc/archive/2011/03/18/operation-b107-rustock-botnet-takedown.aspx (accessed September 23, 2011).

ODS regime cannot be denied. In 1982 negotiations began about CFC elimination, despite the lack of scientific consensus and the role of the European Community as a veto coalition. The US proposed binding regulations, but the ensuing 1985 Vienna Convention had no binding obligations and encouraged additional monitoring, research, and data exchange. Due to increasing scientific evidence of damage to the ozone the countries again returned to the negotiating table. While the lead states wanted a strong commitment to reducing CFCs immediately, the Montreal Protocol in 1987 was a fifty-fifty compromise.[91] Among the most important measures, the Montreal Protocol created scientific and technological assessment panels, reporting requirements, and potential trade sanctions. The 1987 agreement also created procedures for reviewing the effectiveness of the regime and strengthening controls through amendments. Still, the Montreal Protocol only regulated the eight most widely produced CFCs and did not offer substantial financial or technical assistance for developing countries.[92]

The regime has continued to strengthen over time. In 1989, the Multilateral Fund for the Implementation of the Montreal Protocol was established, which is replenished every three years and funds ODS-eliminating projects in developing countries. The Implementation Committee was established in 1992 and investigates reported cases of noncompliance. Overall, the regime has continually strengthened in response to new scientific evidence and technological innovations, accompanied by constant monitoring and reporting. While the ozone hole is still a significant concern, it is expected that it will fully recover in 2045-2060.[93] In the mean time, the ODS regime has contributed significantly to the reduction of CFCs in the atmosphere from 1.1 million tons in 1986 to 35,000 tons in 2006.[94]

Applying Lessons of the ODS Regime to Cyber Defense

---

[91]   Chasek, Downie, Brown, *Global Environmental Politics*, 166.
[92]   Ibid., 166-167.
[93]   Richard Black, "Arctic ozone levels in never-before-seen plunge," *BBC News*, April 5, 2011, http://www.bbc.co.uk/news/science-environment-12969167 (accessed September 23, 2011).
[94]   Chasek, Downie, Brown, *Global Environmental Politics*, 178.

The elimination of CFCs and other ODS depended on international regulation, but it also depended on individuals stopping the use of CFCs and private industry creating CFC substitutes. At first, industry and private actors led a strong anti-regulation campaign before the introduction of concrete scientific evidence and before industry developed CFC alternatives, and industry continued to lobby against further regulation of CFC alternatives as the regime expanded. Over time CFC alternatives have been phased out, in part because even if alternatives deplete the ozone layer at lower levels than CFCs, they still qualify as ODS. The importance of individual action and responsibility for transnational "emissions" applies to both substances. Additionally, eliminating the substance had primary benefits, but also secondary benefits.

Eliminating botnets increases security, but botnet takedowns also contribute to a cleaner ecosystem and may also improve the overall speed of Internet traffic. The same is true for CFCs – the main benefit is the reparation of the ozone layer, but the regime has also contributed to CO_2 reduction efforts.[95] In the same way, industry and the private sector is important in reducing cyber vulnerabilities and threats. Furthermore, non-state actors have taken the lead in eliminating botnets and combating other malware. Coordination amongst the private sector and between industry and government in cyber would help push cyber security coordination toward a CFC model. Examples like the Rustock botnet takedown demonstrate the important role of the private sector and non-state actors with strong support and authorization by the state.

Another key lesson from the history of the ODS regime is the importance of bringing significant actors into negotiations early, even if it means limited agreements initially. In the CFC regime, there were early negotiations before there was a scientific consensus. Furthermore, the European Community and developing countries comprised a strong potential veto bloc. The lead states in the CFC negotiations, however, knew it was important to have the

---

[95]   John M. Broder, "A Novel Tactic in Climate Fight Gains Some Traction," *The New York Times*, November 8, 2010, http://www.nytimes.com/2010/11/09/science/earth/09montreal.html?_r=2& scp=12&sq=ozone&st=cse (accessed September 23, 2011).

most significant CFC producers in negotiations at the beginning, even if it meant less progress in the near-term. As applied to cyber conflict and international cyber issues, this means bringing the most important actors together, even if an agreement on botnet mitigation is unlikely at first. For an international cyber regime to have any influence or legitimacy, the US, China, and Russia will have to be present and willing to discuss possible regulations and goals for cleaning cyberspace.

At the same time, the CFC regime demonstrates the importance of different standards for developed, transitioning, and developing countries. The CFC regime instituted grace periods, different standards according to levels of development, and staggered phase-outs. The Multilateral Fund also provides financial and technical assistance for countries to meet the phase-out targets. The same could be done for botnet reduction and elimination. While the goal is to reduce, or even eliminate, botnets, a regime could stagger reduction targets depending on the level of development and Internet connectivity in individual countries. Additionally, the CFC regime is also one of the most successful at implementing provisions, enforcing compliance, and managing funding for CFC reduction efforts. These are all crucial elements of any successful international regime.

Lastly, changing perspectives in the European Community and increasing domestic and international pressure on this issue bolstered the CFC regime and contributed to the creation of comprehensive regulations on the emission of CFCs. Public demands for action increased with more scientific certainty and awareness about the consequences of depleted ozone, including increased ultraviolent rays and higher risks for skin cancer. While the consequences of botnets are not as severe as those of CFCs, increased awareness of the dangers of botnets would potentially increase individual responsibility and motivate states to be more proactive in combating them. Changing the dialogue about botnets could result in more international action to combat them, both by states, private actors, and multistakeholder organizations

Conclusion

The key similarity between botnets and CFCs is that both kinds of "emissions" originate from individual users or developers and have transnational and international effects. By cleaning botnets and utilizing environmentalism, those interested in seeing a cleaner cyberspace may make significant progress in eliminating botnets. Because of the technical differences between the two emissions, the most helpful analogies focus on creating effective international policy and bolstering public awareness, two crucial components of any successful international regime.

Additionally, the example of the ODS regime demonstrates the potential value that industry and the private sector may add, as well as the potential dampening effect that private actors may have if they are not regulated by governmental and international regulation. Still, the most important lesson to draw from the ODS regime is the commitment to involving all significant actors, despite the fact that including all of the important actors may hamper initial agreements. As the same time, the ODS regime demonstrates that a well-regulated, but flexible regime provides a beneficial framework for reducing pollution that affects all in the ecosystem. The same could also be true for botnets in the future, as long as states and non-state actors continue and increase defensive collaboration.

The Environmental Approach may be a success because it can give a new applicable mindset and legal regimes, provide a meaningful and familiar role for non-state actors, and ties into the global development agenda. Indeed, environmentalism's main strength is that many people, including youth, immediately grasp the importance and are willing to work across borders for solutions. While this can provide important solutions for cyber conflict, it is not the only way. The next approach focuses much more strongly on what governments and, in particular, militaries can do.

Irregular Warfare Approach

The Irregular Warfare Approach [96] offers many solutions for conflict between non-state actors, between states and non-states,

---

[96]   Irregular Warfare is comprised of a wide range of operations, from insurgency and counterinsurgency; to terrorism and counterterrorism and stability and reconstruction tasks. Key authors who have written on the role of non-state

and between states that are not willing to acknowledge their role publicly – all of which is happening now in cyberspace and could dominate future conflict. Irregular warfare is characterized by adversaries that purposefully seek to blur traditional distinctions such as combatant and non-combatant, which are the heart of the norms of warfare. By this definition, most of what happens in cyber conflict is not actual "irregular warfare" in even a loose way. The vast majority is criminal activity and best covered by that approach. However, governments may profitably borrow existing mindset and methods from irregular warfare.

Lessons from Irregular Warfare

The following table includes tactics for irregular warfare. The original purpose of including this table was to highlight those applicable to cyber conflict with non-state adversaries. However, it became immediately apparent that not only did they overlap with each other but nearly every single lesson had some relevant wisdom applicable to cyber conflict. Though it is clearly out of the scope of this study to discuss every relevant lesson, a few highlights follow.

Table 5.3: Conducting Successful Irregular Warfare

Counterinsurgency[97]	Stability and Recovery Operations[98]	Counterterrorism[99]
Win hearts and minds of the populace (Lose moral legitimacy, lose the war).	Continue to pursue a holistic understanding of the adversary as well as other parties with equity or influence in the conflict.	Address the underlying conditions that terrorists exploit

---

actors in irregular warfare include Mao Zedong's *On Guerilla Warfare,* to Schulz, Farah, and Lochard, *Armed Groups: A Tier One Security Priority*, David Kilcullen's *The Accidental Guerilla*, General Rupert Smith's *The Utility of Force* and John Nagl's *Learning to Eat Soup With a Knife*.

[97] "Counterinsurgency" generally serves as an umbrella term for all operations undertaken to defeat an insurgency. See Nagl, John A, David H Patreus, Sarah Sewall, and James F Amos, *The U.S. Army/Marine Corps Counterinsurgency Field Manual* (Chicago: University of Chicago Press, 2007).

[98] SSTRO seeks to establish a safe, secure, environment in a host nation during or after a conflict or insurgency. MCO JOC (2006).

[99] Bruce Hoffman, *Inside Terrorism* (New York: Columbia University Press, 1999): 169.

Counterinsurgency[97]	Stability and Recovery Operations[98]	Counterterrorism[99]
COIN requires Unity of Effort	Plan for shifts in missions, skills, priorities and relationships.	Counter extremist rhetoric and disinformation coming from hostile groups.
Increased short-term risk is an operational necessity.	Introduce general purpose and specialized military and non-military capabilities based on priorities set for SSTRO.	Deny terrorists safe havens (both active and passive sanctuaries)
The primacy of the political requires significant and ongoing civilian involvement at virtually every level of operations.	Achieve and maintain a unity of effort among military and non-military forces.	Understand the terrorist's mindset and their operational environment.
Success in COIN relies upon non-kinetic activities like providing electricity, jobs, and a functioning judicial system.	Formalize termination of major combat operations where permitted by nature of the adversary.	Force terrorists to pay more attention to their organizational and personal security than to planning and carrying out attacks.
Non-military capacity is the exit strategy.	Plan for protracted combat operations with enemy elements that employ irregular methods.	
COIN is an intelligence-driven endeavor.	Take actions to prevent reestablishment of enemy sanctuaries.	
Take away the ability of the non-state adversary to hide.	Interact with the local population to gain their trust and cooperation.	
Logistic activities are integral to COIN operations, but are different than those of conventional operations.	Diversity of Effort: support expansion in the role of interagency, multinational, international and contractor players.	
	Synchronize combat force redeployment.	

Amongst the important lessons here, several rise to the top:

Political legitimacy. Succeeding in an irregular war is, at root, a problem of "winning the hearts and minds of the people." Governments often have no more legitimacy than any other group with a loud voice – and of course the Internet comes fully equipped with a multitude of loud voices.

Political legitimacy can come in many forms, but especially comes from having each person be convinced, on his or her own terms, that the government's cause is the right one and they personally need to take steps to further the government's agenda.

None of the US government actions to date (from Cyber Security Awareness Month to speeches, bulletins and warnings) have won the hearts and minds of people, perhaps because of the perceived difficulty of securing home systems, mistrust of government intentions, or perceived threats to privacy and free speech. Some may agree to the goals of government cybersecurity efforts, but are unconvinced of the need to pay any of the costs, whether it their own time and money to patch their home systems or the possibility of surrendering some privacy. To counter denial of service attacks, norms could usefully characterize these activities as significant threatening activity to the global cyber commons. In doing so, governments will have to recognize limits to their own credibility and seek partnerships with others seen as more trusted by Internet users.

Address the underlying conditions the adversary exploits. In irregular warfare, the underlying conditions might include a corrupt government, poverty and malnutrition, or perceived slights or tit-for-tat violence from other groups. In cyber conflict, these may all spur a group to malicious activity but the most important "underlying condition" is that the cyber domain is vulnerable to such activity because of unpatched computers and insecure protocols. Governments seeking to reduce these underlying conditions of vulnerability may be able to more hold subordinate departments and employees to account with an argument based on irregular warfare than one of "cyber hygiene" or "reducing pollution".

Take away the ability to hide. In cyber conflict, adversaries are able to hide in many ways in the "difficult terrain" of cyberspace, whether at rest (in villages/in infected computers) or in motion (on the jungle trail/traversing networks). Among the ways to take away the cyber adversary's ability to hide could be to rapidly isolate or fix home computers and squeeze botnet denial of service attacks out of the main backbone networks, cleaning the environment and allowing network operators and defenders a clearer view of the more sophisticated malicious activity attempting to hide under that malicious traffic.

Martin Van Creveld has pointed out that "[t]o remain hidden, insurgents must disperse—the more of them there are at any one place, the more easily found they are. They must also avoid movement as much as possible.[100]" In the cyber domain, insurgents are not very dispersed, nor do they avoid movement. Indeed many nation states and Internet domains are very well known as having concentrations (see next paragraph) while "movement" through Tier 1 networks is a must for nearly any attack to succeed. Accordingly, it might in fact be easier to deal with cyber "insurgents" than the physical kind, which might significantly reduce strategic instability.

Reduce sanctuaries. Sanctuaries in irregular warfare can include locations in-country or in neighboring countries where the adversary is able to move, equip, and rest with impunity. In cyberspace, sanctuaries are where nations do not have the ability to stop all malicious activity from their national territory or are unwilling to do so. These sanctuaries, which greatly add to strategic instability, might be reduced using methods from irregular warfare, but the Environmental, Criminal, and Public Health Approaches also can help.

Irregular Warfare Case Study:
Combating Terrorism and Fighting Malware

This section will compare lessons learned from Operation Enduring Freedom Afghanistan (OEF-A) against those from tackling two key outbreaks of malicious software, ILOVEYOU and Zeus trojan.

The Adversaries

The struggle for Afghanistan was not simply a conflict between two states: it was a protracted struggle between US and coalition forces on the one hand, and a constantly shifting array of anti-Western forces on the other. Like an ungoverned Afghanistan, cyberspace presents a variety of actors, with a largely ungoverned space to contest. The increased participation of non-state actors in activities in cyberspace is evident when examining the propagation

---

[100]   Martin Van Creveld, "War in Complex Environments: The Technological Domain," *Prism* vol. 1, no 3 (June 2010), 125.

of the ILOVEYOU worm, created and released by a Philippine citizen without the backing of the state,[101] and the Zeus trojan, originally attributed to an Eastern European crime ring, leveraging the capabilities of international recruits.[102]

To their advantage and their detriment, each of the jihadist groups in OEF-A had different ideologies and their own political agendas. Still, they banded together in a marriage of convenience in an attempt to oust the West. The groups included Al-Qaeda[103] (goal: establishment of pan-Islamic Caliphate), the Taliban [104] (goal: "Islamic Revolution" in Afghanistan), and the Haqqani Network[105] (goal: prevent extension of the Karzai government's authority into border region).

---

[101]   Steve Ragan, "Love Bug 10 years later: I love you - now open this email," *The Tech Herald,* May 4, 2010
http://www.thetechherald.com/article.php/201018/5596/Love-Bug-10-years-later-I-love-you-now-open-this-email (accessed May 5, 2011).

[102]   Kim Zetter, "5 Key Players Nabbed in Ukraine in $70-Million Bank Fraud Ring," *Wired*, October 1, 2010, http://www.wired.com/threatlevel/2010/10/zeus-ukraine-arrests/ (accessed May 5, 2011).

[103]   Established around 1988 by Osama bin Laden, Al-Qaeda helped fund and train thousands of guerillas from a number of countries to be part of the Afghan resistance against the Soviet Union. With cells worldwide, Al-Qaeda seeks to establish a pan-Islamic Caliphate, and it is reinforced by ties to Sunni extremist networks. See Bruce Riedel, *The Search for Al Qaeda: Its Leadership, Ideology, and Future* (Washington, DC: Brookings Institution Press, 2010).

[104]   Formed in 1994 by graduates of Pakistani Islamic colleges, in the Afghan province of Kandahar, Taliban members are Pashtun and are led by Mohammed Omar. The Taliban advocates an "Islamic Revolution" in Afghanistan. In 1996, the Taliban ousted the Afghan government and imposed Sharia law. The Taliban were initially trained by a para-military force of the Interior Ministry of Pakistan. In October 2001, the Taliban was removed from power by Coalition forces. Global Security, "The Taliban," Global Security,
http://www.globalsecurity.org/military/world/para/taleban.htm (accessed September 23, 2011). For further reading, see Ahmed Rashid, *The Taliban: Militant Islam, Oil and Fundamentalism in Central Asia* (New Haven, CT: Yale University Press, 2010).

[105]   Comprised of followers of warlord Jalaluddin Haqqani, this group has deep-rooted ties to Pakistan's ISI. It is one of the strongest factions of the Taliban and has strong ties to al Qaeda by way of senior figures in Pakistan's tribal areas. Matt Duppe, "The Haqqani Network: Reign of Terror," *Long War Journal*, August 2, 2008,
http://www.longwarjournal.org/archives/2008/08/the_haqqani_network.php (accessed September 23, 2011).

Havens for groups specializing in the creation or use of malicious software include Russia and Eastern Europe, China, and Brazil. For example, in October 2010, the Federal Bureau of Investigation (FBI) announced that the Zeus attackers were in Eastern Europe. Those charged and arrested were hired as "money mules," recruited to facilitate planning for fraudsters based in Eastern Europe. The group behind Koobface operated out of St. Petersburg, Russia[106] while those behind ShadyRAT and similar operations appear to be from China.[107] Those behind Conficker are thought to be from the Ukraine.[108]

Adversary Goals and Strategies

The diverse insurgent groups in OEF-A did not have an overall strategy, but the following represent some of the more common elements.

Reclaim power and impose God's rule over the land.[109] The insurgent strategy to oust the Westerners is based partly on a

---

[106]   Nart Villeneuve, "Koobface: Inside a Crimeware Network," *Information Warfare Monitor*, November 12, 2010, http://www.infowar-monitor.net/reports/iwm-koobface.pdf (accessed September 23, 2011).

[107]   Dmitri Alperovitch, "Revealed: Operation Shady RAT," *McAfee*, http://www.mcafee.com/us/resources/white-papers/wp-operation-shady-rat.pdf (accessed September 23, 2011); Information Warfare Monitor and Shadowserver Foundation, "Ghost Net and Shadows in the Cloud," *Information Warfare Monitor*, April 6, 2010, http://www.scribd.com/doc/29435784/SHADOWS-IN-THE-CLOUD-Investigating-Cyber-Espionage-2-0 (accessed September 23, 2011).

[108]   See Tim Greene, "Conficker talk sanitized at Black Hat to protect investigation," *Network World*, July 31, 2009, http://www.networkworld.com/news/2009/073109-black-hat-conficker-talk.html (accessed September 22, 2011).

[109]   New York Times reporters found a document in an Afghan house that explains the goals of Jihad: Establishing the rule of God on earth; Attaining martyrdom in the cause of God; Purification of the ranks of Islam from the elements of depravity. See: Global Security, "Al-Qaida," July 31, 2009, http://www.globalsecurity.org/military/world/para/al-qaida.htm (accessed September 23, 2011). Similar sentiments can be found in Norman Cigar's translation of Al Muqrin's *A Practical Course for Guerilla War.* The mujahideen strive to establish a "pure Islamic systems free from defects and infidel elements." See: Norman Cigar, *Al Aqida's Doctrine for Insurgency:*

belief they simply need to outlast the Coalition force. As is typical during insurgencies, the insurgent acquires more strength as the conflict continues, whereas the counterinsurgent gradually weakens as a result of resource constraints and falling morale. For this reason, mountain forces like those in Afghanistan follow a method of operations that consists of "continuous movement, hitting the enemy, and then movement again."[110]

Win the support of the population. To delegitimize Coalition forces, a 2009 revised Taliban Code of Conduct urges the Mujahedeen to "behave well with general public and make efforts to bring their hearts closer to them" and win over the support of the Afghan people by "avoiding the killing of civilians and fewer suicide bombings."[111]

Hide under the cloak and manipulate the dagger. To remain hidden insurgents employ guerilla tactics, manipulating the terrain and geography to their advantage. In mountainous Afghanistan, caves provide good cover, as do corn fields.[112]

The first two of these are also typical counterinsurgency approaches and exemplify the enemy-based approach. Though this may demonstrate the role reversal between the insurgent and counterinsurgent in contemporary conflicts, [113] it may also demonstrate an evolution in Islamic insurgent theory. Such changes are reflected in Mullah Omar's revised Code of Conduct,

'Abd Al- 'Aziz Al Muqrin's A Practical Course for Guerilla War (Washington, DC: Potomac Books Inc., 2009).

[110] Norman Cigar, Al Aqida's Doctrine for Insurgency: 'Abd Al- 'Aziz Al Muqrin's A Practical Course for Guerilla War (Washington, DC: Potomac Books Inc., 2009).

[111] Mullah Omar advocates this in a Taliban Code of Conduct published by Taliban leadership in 2009. See Mullah Omar, "Taliban: A 'Book of Rules'," The NEFA Foundation, September 10, 2009, www.nefafoundation.org/miscellaneous/nefa_talibancodeconduct.pdf (accessed September 23, 2011).

[112] Towering maize plants that can grow as tall as 9 feet high have provided insurgents with cover while they place IEDs near Forward Operating Base Keenan. Jon Boon, "Why Corn, Not Opium, is Afghanistan's Deadliest Crop," The Guardian, April 13, 2010, http://www.guardian.co.uk/world/2010/apr/13/afghanistan-deadliest-crop-corn-not-opium (accessed April 11, 2011).

[113] David Kilkullen, "Counterinsurgency Redux," Small Wars Journal, smallwarsjournal.com/documents/kilcullen1.pdf (accessed September 23, 2011).

which urges all Mujahideen to avoid killing civilians and advocated fewer suicide bombings, in an effort to win over the support of the Afghan people.[114]

Like the jihadist groups, adversaries in cyberspace too have different motivations and goals. Attackers using malware attacks can be motivated by money, by personal foibles as a form of seeking revenge or to further a particular political, religious or personal cause.

Collaborative Responses

To achieve a number of military and civilian goals, US Central Command executed multiple "Lines of Operation," attacking simultaneously on several fronts.[115] Such planning reflected the need to employ different strategies to pursue a variety of goals. Similarly, actors in cyberspace pursue a variety of goals, ranging from criminal to political, and targeting a number of different sectors, thus necessitating a multi-pronged response.

The Coalition had the several goals, including these below:

Remove Taliban from power and destroy their military capabilities. This was the objective at the outset of the invasion in 2001. The Allies employed the "Direct attack of leadership of al Qaeda and Taliban" line of operation, which relied heavily on targeted strikes, human intelligence operations, and aerial surveillance. [116] As the first American forces to deploy to Afghanistan in September 2001, CIA operatives joined with various anti-Taliban forces to pave the way for Coalition airstrikes

---

[114] An ISAF spokesman disagrees: "This is either a smokescreen to repair the Taliban's well-earned reputation for brutality, or insurgent groups are simply ignoring their leader," and "if this is the case, then the Karzai government, which has been steadily expanding government services and individual rights, is gaining more credibility." See: Afghanistan International Security Assistance Force, "New Taliban Code of Conduct…Not Matching the Reality on the Ground," http://www.isaf.nato.int/article/isaf-releases/new-taliban-code-of-conduct-not-matching-reality-on-the-ground.html (accessed September 23, 2011).

[115] Global Security, "Operation Enduring Freedom – Afghanistan: Planning and Implementing," http://www.globalsecurity.org/military/ops/enduring-freedom-plan.htm (accessed September 23, 2011).

[116] Ibid.

and the deployment of follow-on traditional and Special Forces for conclusive military operations.

Secure Kabul. Securing Kabul meant Coalition forces could refocus efforts on securing the Taliban stronghold of Kandahar. By mid December 2001, this goal was achieved.

Deny the enemy safe harbor/place to hide. The Allies pursued a strategy that was three-fold: Raid existing hideout locations during Capture-Kill missions; alter Afghan terrain to be more transparent – i.e. limiting or substituting corn crops because they provide good tactical cover for the insurgent; and win over Pakistan by cooperating with government and law enforcement in counterterrorism operations.[117]

Win the hearts and minds of the population. At the outset, the Coalition relied heavily on psychological operations (PSYOPS) to further this goal. Leaflets explaining the Coalition's mission and the role of the individual Afghan citizen were administered, and were complemented by packages of humanitarian aid dropped from aircraft. In the longer term, the Coalition sought to address the underlying issues that may lead more people to sympathize with the insurgents.

To stop malicious software, civilian (and sometimes military) authorities have different tasks:

Stop the Outbreak, then Protect, Detect and Remove. The first task for defenders is to recognize malicious software in the wild, then stop its spread (see the Conficker case study above for more detail). If computers are cleaned while the malicious software is still spreading, they can simply just become re-infected. Accordingly, defenders must remove the underlying vulnerabilities in all of their systems, see which of their systems are infected, and remove the malware (or as often happens, delete all software and reload it all again from scratch).

Identify the adversary. To identify the adversary behind Zeus, domestic and international law enforcement sought to scope the crime ring by tracking financial transactions. The initial takedown of the crime ring was a result of a tip from a financial

---

[117] Pakistan now serves as a main route for NATO supplies going to Afghanistan and a key ally in the Global War on Terror.

services firm to the FBI office in Omaha, Nebraska. FBI began opening cases against schemes that used electronic payments processed through Automated Clearinghouse.[118] Thus they were able to identify the individuals who created the bank accounts, tracing money to the higher echelons of the crime ring abroad.

In the case of ILOVEYOU, the principle investigators tracking the adversary were a team of individual collaborators who worked with the FBI. The main break in the case came when the FBI noted that the ISP Access Net in Manila was infected and tracked the infection to a Manila apartment.[119] Another major breakthrough found a link between the Love Bug and previously released viruses, which pointed to the AMA Computer College in the Philippines.[120]

Prosecute the Adversary. This can be problematic: Guzman avoided charges for his ILOVEYOU worm because there was no law in the Philippines criminalizing the illegal use of passwords.[121] And though the FBI and its counterparts believed that by finding, charging and, arresting the members of the crime ring that unleashed Zeus, the botnet would be taken down. However, after over 100 members of the ring were arrested, Zeus remains a robust network.[122]

Key Parallels

International support is important. In Afghanistan, United Nations backing provided political legitimacy, and international support was crucial to planning and executing military operations.

---

[118]   Associated Press, "Money Mules: Cyberthieves Rely on Human Foot Soldiers," *Fox News*, November 22, 2010, http://www.foxnews.com/scitech/2010/11/22/cyberthieves-human-foot-soldiers-money-mules/ (accessed May 3, 2011).

[119]   Leander Kahney, "Who Do Cops Call? Virus-Busters," *Wired*, http://www.wired.com/science/discoveries/news/2000/05/36275 (accessed September 23, 2011).

[120]   Ibid.

[121]   Reuters, "Four Worm Suspects ID'ed," *Wired*, May 12, 2000, http://www.wired.com/science/discoveries/news/2000/05/36303 (accessed May 7, 2011).

[122]   Five key members of the ring's upper echelon were arrested in Ukraine, 20 were arrested in the UK and 39 arrested in the U.S.

In cyberspace, international support is just as crucial. With more states adopting the multi-stakeholder model as cyber attacks continually cross physical borders, international cooperation is essential. In fact, the identification and prosecution of the attackers behind the Zeus Trojan and the ILOVEYOU worm would not have been possible without coordinated domestic and international law enforcement efforts. Actors in cyberspace can learn from OEF-A exercises, as multinational cyber exercises can demonstrate how security professionals can coordinate each other's cyber capabilities to respond to common threats.

Geography is key. Using Afghanistan's geography to their advantage helped the Coalition achieve two key goals: secure Kabul and deny the insurgent physical safe havens. Geography is not irrelevant in cyberspace, as actors in cyberspace constantly adapt to a malleable terrain. Each time a system is patched, the local geography changes. Further, the Domain Name System (DNS) accounts for the existence of tiered geography – changes in DNS management can have profound implications for the geography of all of cyberspace

As is evident from ILOVEYOU, legal sanctuaries play an active role in cyber conflict. Thus, denying legal and technical safe havens in cyberspace is crucial to combating cyber conflicts. The denial of technical safe havens can be achieved using an enemy-based approach where the defense seeks to detect, disable and remove malware from the infected systems. Alternatively, the population-centric approach can be implemented to deny the adversary legal safe havens. While the denial of technical safe havens in cyberspace requires close cooperation between ISPs and tier-one networks, denial of legal safe havens requires the establishment of domestic and international laws that criminalize hacking.

Resolving conflicts requires addressing the underlying issues. As the Counterinsurgency Field Manual states, the exit strategy for counterinsurgencies is the establishment of non-military capacity in the host nation. [123] In Afghanistan this means building up local, regional, and national government, as well as starting counternarcotics initiatives. Resolution of the underlying issues in cyberspace means

---

[123] U.S. Army and Marine Corps, *Counterinsurgency Field Manual* (Chicago: University of Chicago, 2006).

cleaning cyberspace, improving user awareness, creating more secure products, and stigmatizing illegal hacking activities.

Political legitimacy helps further cultural change. In Afghanistan, winning the hearts and minds of the population was facilitated by a coalition of forces backed by the UN, but it is still a difficult task, especially in the face of corruption in the government of Afghanistan.[124] Countering and mitigating cyber conflicts will require not simply securing systems, but deterring hackers and teaching users to work more securely. In addition, governments need to increase the perception they are interested in cyber security not to more fully monitor their citizens' online behavior but to stop online crime and conflict. Regular testimonies to Congress and full "privacy impact assessments" are important steps.[125]

Conclusion

The key similarities between the dynamics of cyber conflict and those of contemporary irregular warfare operations are that the offensive players employ the similar tactics of manipulating geography to their advantage while applying indirect force. In Afghanistan, as in the majority of contemporary cyber conflicts, the offensive players are non-state actors that wage asymmetrical force against a state. Counterinsurgency efforts in Afghanistan provide a helpful framework from which to approach cyber conflict management and mitigation. In both, international support and political legitimacy is a *sine qua non*. Further, political legitimacy was instrumental in the ability of the Coalition to secure the local population. The same will be true of cyberspace – where political legitimacy will be a necessary precondition for the creation of a safer, smarter, "cyber culture." Counterinsurgency tactics that focus on isolating the insurgent from the population can be applied to cyberspace: cleaning the cyber commons will increase transparency of the environment in which the

---

[124]   For example, see Viola Gienger, "Gates Seeks Afghan Anti-Corruption Steps as Drawdown Begins," *Business Week*, June 4, 2011, http://www.businessweek.com/news/2011-06-04/gates-seeks-afghan-anti-corruption-steps-as-drawdown-begins.html (accessed September 23, 2011).

[125]   For example, see US Department of Homeland Security, "Privacy Impact Assessment for the DHS system Einstein,"May 19, 2008, http://www.dhs.gov/xlibrary/assets/privacy/privacy_pia_einstein2.pdf (accessed September 23, 2011).

attacker operates, and make it more difficult for the attacks to hijack unsecured systems to execute operations. Finally, the careful manipulation of conditions allows for the reduction of sanctuaries – physical, cyber, and legal.

The three approaches above illustrate some of the opportunities and limitations of alternative frameworks for the problem of cyber instability and cyber defense. The following section discusses the relative advantages and disadvantages for the three emerging approaches.

Which Approach is Most Helpful in Which Circumstances?

Like the shifting strategies in Afghanistan, the approaches that policymakers, practitioners and researchers use to think about cyber conflict will greatly affect how they diagnose problems and develop solutions. According to Bruce Schneier:

> If we frame this discussion as a war discussion, then what you do when there's a threat of war is you call in the military and you get military solutions. You get lockdown; you get an enemy that needs to be subdued. If you think about these threats in terms of crime, you get police solutions. And as we have this debate ... the way we frame it, the way we talk about it; the way the headlines read, determine what sort of solutions we want.[126]

Yet the issues posed by non-state actors in cyberspace are so complex and multidimensional that no single approach can ever be sufficient. Instead, an integrated strategy must incorporate insights from different approaches to address different aspects of the problem such as the 2003 National Strategy to Secure Cyberspace did when clearly differentiating between approaches by declaring, "When a nation, terrorist group, or other adversary attacks the

---

[126] Bruce Schneier, "Me on Cyberwar," Oct. 1, 2010, http://www.schneier.com/blog/archives/2010/10/me_on_cyberwar.html (accessed September 23, 2011).

United States through cyberspace, the US response need not be limited to criminal prosecution. The United States reserves the right to respond in an appropriate manner."[127]

When is each approach most helpful in addressing cyber conflict and cyber instability? The **traditional approaches** (crime, warfare, technical, counterintelligence, and counterterrorism) remain extremely useful within their own communities and for specific problems. However, singularly and collectively they will remain insufficient to deal with non-state threats. Even with better technology, more prosecutions, and more users deciding to "Stop, Think, Connect" (in the words of a current public cybersafety campaign[128]) there will almost certainly still be a host of non-state adversaries taking advantage of a massive global population of insecure machines for criminal and other purposes.

The newer approaches (environment, public health, and irregular warfare) tend to have common elements: create norms to get individuals to care, patch your systems, take away places for attackers to hide, throttle back on botnet activity, and cooperate widely for solutions. Where these approaches differ is the source of support for creating and enforcing these norms.

To start, the **Public Health Approach** emphasizes global cooperation especially between governments and non-governmental organizations, which can be approached on the existing epidemiological response approach. This approach can be especially effective at stopping, detecting, and responding to rapidly spreading malicious outbreaks as seen during Conficker but could also be helpful to mediate interactions between individual computers, such as Microsoft's idea to prove proper hygiene with computer "health certificates".

The **Environmental Approach** may be most helpful to enroll young people, corporations, foundations and think tanks to clean the cyber environment and stopping sources of pollution emissions that cause significant downstream effects (like botnets). These

---

[127]   The White House, "National Strategy to Secure Cyberspace, 2003," February, 2003, http://www.us-cert.gov/reading_room/cyberspace_strategy.pdf (accessed September 23, 2011). See page 50.

[128]   See www.staysafeonline.org.

communities are more likely to engage in an Environmental project than one built on a Criminal or Warfare Approach. A main strength here is that, along with Public Health, this approach embraces non-state actors as a critical part of the solution – not just part of the problem, as happens with the Criminal and Warfare Approaches.

The **Irregular Warfare Approach** is best for helping the Department of Defense understand how to address cyber conflict with non-state adversaries. For example, DoD personnel are much more likely to understand their role in cyber conflict if they are told to eliminate safe havens and reduce places where adversaries can hide than if they are told to "improve cyber hygiene." Winning the hearts and minds of the denizens of cyberspace will be just as important to military success as it is in the sands of Iraq or mountains of Afghanistan.

Further Research and Conclusion

Current efforts to address the most pressing cyber security challenges facing the United States and the international community are not focused on understanding the fundamental causes and dynamics of cyber conflict. Without a proper conception of the nature of the cyber environment, policy, operations, and strategies will continue to be inadequate to the challenge and fail to address the symptoms and possible consequences of cyber instability. Now is the time to develop a set of robust conceptual frameworks for managing cyber conflict and its risks. If such a framework is not developed soon, the interests of the US and its allies seeking greater international security and cooperation may be seriously threatened by cyberspace's strategic instability.

In order to properly conceive of the nature of cyberspace, it is important that decision makers and thought leaders have a firm grounding in the nature of the cyber environment, how this impacts the dynamics of cyber conflict, and the measures available to address the sources and management of these conflicts. Understanding of the causes and dynamics of cyber conflict is in its early stages and support for research efforts in this emerging field will continue to yield significant results.

Current efforts to manage cyber security are not sufficiently focused on addressing the foundational conditions that make cyber conflict risks difficult to manage. Additional research on cyber conflict and statecraft must prioritize risk reduction, including

- Exploring how best to remove long-term conditions that are increasing conflict pressures (such measures must include the role and feasibility of implementing confidence building measures and establishing risk reduction centers for cyberspace);

- Further developing new approaches, such as environmentalism, public health and irregular warfare;

- Determining appropriate norms, especially those that most aid in stabilizing cyberspace, such as reducing support for proxies and cleaning the Internet ecosystem;

- Continuing international engagement through a variety of means and forums, particularly those with significant opportunities for non-state actors to influence the discussion;

- Investigating how governments can further enroll non-state actors, such has how best to acknowledge and support their having a more central role in defense.

If not addressed in a more comprehensive manner with effective mitigation approaches, the instability of the cyber environment will continue to pose a threat to national and international security. We will continue to face an insecure, unstable environment with increased threats and attacks against private and public networks. By increasing resources and dialogue and promoting transparency in the global system, this proposal will address key policy deficiencies.

Solving the problems posed by cyberspace will not be solved by one country or a handful working in concert – there must be a global solution to instability in cyberspace. The United States has limited influence in how to mitigate the factors that cause an unstable cyber environment and it must consider difficult tradeoffs. Still, solving these fundamental issues is possible and the United States is poised to lead the world into a more secure, stable cyberspace, but it cannot do it alone. It must engage actors around the world to clean up the ecosystem, institute normative expectations of behavior of state and non-state actors, and keep core principles of freedom and innovation as the foundation of cyberspace while also maintaining and increasing its security.

Yet, the United States enters the second decade of this century still as the global leader in cyberspace. The basis of this leadership has been the incredible energy of its innovative companies, the technical acumen of its people and the ability of the government to enable this activity and seek a globally interconnected Internet as the basis of a new cyber domain. We must remain global leaders as the cyber environment becomes more challenging as a source of malicious activity and threats to US security. This leadership must be informed by a better understanding of the strategic instability of cyberspace. By doing so, the United States will serve both its economic well-being, its ability to promote democracy and freedom as well as its security and that of those across the globe.

Appendix

Critical Infrastructure Primer

The critical infrastructure of the United States is currently vulnerable to a range of crippling attacks, especially in the cyber arena. However, public awareness of these vulnerabilities and detailed understanding of the risks is insufficient to support large-scale policy initiatives. The deliverable of this study will be a primer on US critical infrastructure vulnerabilities, written in a form that is easily accessible to a wide range of audiences, including Congress, the policy community, government policymakers, and the general public.

Introduction

The purpose of this report is to provide a general understanding of an otherwise complex issue. Critical infrastructures have been repeatedly identified as a core component of US national and homeland security, yet despite billions of dollars invested in the examining and securing of these infrastructures, the topic remains inaccessible to a large number of concerned citizens and policymakers.

In our attempt to make this topic accessible to a majority of readers, we have taken some liberties in simplifying some otherwise complex topics. The intent is not to dismiss these complexities, but rather to enable a discussion of critical infrastructures and their associated vulnerabilities within a broader audience. While the vulnerability of these infrastructures might be highly technical, the dialogue associated with the risk and security of these infrastructures must include a broader audience in order to develop the requisite support to advance critical infrastructure cyber security initiatives.

Understanding Critical Infrastructure

The term critical infrastructure is self-defining though not always easily explained. Infrastructures are the underlying technological and physical components that enable societies to grow and prosper. The term critical infrastructure refers to those infrastructures that are most important to a society or upon which the society is most dependent. For an exhaustive examination of how the definition of critical infrastructure has changed over time, we recommend the Congressional Research Report entitled "Critical Infrastructure and Key Assets: Definition and Identification, October 1, 2004".[1]

There have been many independent commissions and studies addressing the issue of critical infrastructure protection. Most notable was the 1998 President's Commission on Critical Infrastructure Protection (PCCIP). There have also been varying definitions of what infrastructures are defined as critical. For the purposes of this report, we recommend the critical infrastructure list provided by the US Office of Homeland Security's *National Strategy for Homeland Security* published in July 2002.

In this report, critical infrastructures are defined as follows (in no particular order):[2]

- Agriculture
- Food
- Water
- Public Health
- Emergency Services
- Government
- Defense Industrial Base
- Information and Telecommunications
- Energy
- Transportation

---

[1]   Congressional Research Service, "Critical Infrastructure and Key Assets: Definition and Identification," RL32631, October 1, 2004.

[2]   U.S. Office of Homeland Security, *National Strategy for Homeland Security*, July 2002, 30.

- Banking and Finance
- Chemical Industry
- Postal and Shipping

While a critical infrastructure might contain multiple and complex subcomponents, there is usually a key function that is performed by the infrastructure at its core. That key function defines the infrastructure with the mission performed being prioritized over the enabling technology. For example, let's take a look at the water infrastructure.

When you turn on your faucet in your home, the expectation is that clean and safe water will be provided. Given that water is the essence of human survival and the fact that most urban areas are not geographically positioned to utilize natural sources of water, it is easy to understand why water is considered a critical infrastructure. However, it is what happens behind the scenes that give us a narrow glimpse of the ever-growing complexity of critical infrastructure operations.

Key notional components of the water infrastructure include the following:

Component	Description
Reservoir	Used to collect or store water
Water treatment plant	Used to process water to ensure it is safe for human consumption and condition it as desired
Water pumps	Used to distribute water within a water system (some systems might be gravity fed)
Water pipes	Simplified term to describe the complex piping infrastructure used to get water from point A to point B
Water management systems	Control systems used to distribute safe water within the piping infrastructure
Waste water system	Another complex infrastructure used to collect and clean excess and dirty water

As you can see, the simple act of obtaining safe water by turning on the tap is dependent on a series of systems and physical components (usually the result of years of planning and implementation) that conveniently provide safe drinking water.

The same dependence is true for most of the infrastructures discussed in this section or in general. When you place a phone call or check your bank account balance online, you are utilizing a dynamic and complex infrastructure to complete the call or provide you with the information you requested (your bank statement) quickly and conveniently. When you travel via rail, road, or air there are complex infrastructures that ensure that you are able to transport yourself or cargo between two points.

In addition to providing a critical civilian infrastructure, as we'll see in the next section, the electric power infrastructure, a sub-component of the energy infrastructure, is not just an infrastructure in terms of delivery of electricity, but also fulfills a critical dependency for most other infrastructures. One might refer to it as a Supercritical Infrastructure.

Critical Infrastructure Dependencies

As noted above critical infrastructures and their subcomponents (which are sometimes critical infrastructures in their own right) can be quite complex. That complexity becomes readily apparent in the discussion of critical infrastructure dependencies. This report focuses on two types of critical infrastructure dependency: 1) infrastructure dependence on computers and information technology, and 2) infrastructure dependence on other infrastructures (e.g., water infrastructure dependence on electric power infrastructure).

Information Technology Dependencies

"The world isn't run by weapons anymore, or energy, or money. It's run by little ones and zeroes, little bits of data. It's all just electrons."

– Cosmo in the 1992 movie *Sneakers*

Nearly twenty years after that quotation was heard in *Sneakers*, it couldn't more true. The provision, management, and operation of critical infrastructures are highly dependent on information connectivity. In some instances, the very substance of the infrastructure (for example, finance and banking) is entirely represented by digital information. To put this in context, let's look at a simple example.

Thirty years ago, if you wanted to change the channel on your television, you would have to get up from your comfortable seat and physically tune the television via a manual interface (a knob) on the television's control panel. The same was true for changing the volume. Today, you can use a tiny computer chip inside a small remote powered by batteries that will communicate wirelessly with your television and other entertainment components from across the room. This simple innovation was enabled by many technological inventions resulting from years of research and millions of dollars in investment. Having remote control technology makes it easier for consumers to access a diverse library of content in a convenient way. The manual process was modernized and became dependent on information technology. If the batteries die in your remote, you have to get up and adjust the channel manually. If you look at many modern TVs, you will see that while they still have manual buttons, those buttons are much less user-friendly and are often located out of sight behind a panel. The *expected* mechanism for interacting with the TV is now the remote. This same analogy applies to the operation and maintenance of critical infrastructures as well.

Critical control functions that used to require human intervention have been automated and are now controlled via computer interfaces. For example, in the water distribution infrastructure, water pressure and pipe flows used to be controlled by manual valves turned and adjusted using the raw strength of a human laborer. Those control valves are now mechanized and controlled via computer software. In some instances, the software is smart enough to engage in some "supervisory control" on its own, physically adjusting the valves based on pre-defined rules and processes. In other instances, a human engineer monitors and modifies the settings for the valve, making her the equivalent of the person pressing the button on the TV remote. In order to know how to adjust the valve without being there, the controlling entity (software or human) needs to "acquire" status data such as flow rates, pressures, or fluid levels, which are transmitted from sensors in specific locations. These control systems are often referred to within infrastructure protection environments as SCADA, which is an acronym for Supervisory Control and Data Acquisition systems. Where SCADA was a term discussed in relative obscurity a decade ago, you will now find it mentioned in nearly every report on infrastructure or information technology security, particularly after the discovery and analysis of Stuxnet and other SCADA-focused worms.

In order to facilitate remote control of infrastructures over long distances, these control systems are connected to communication networks, originally via phone lines and modems, and most recently, through wired and wireless Internet Protocol networks. As we will discuss in Section 4, this connectivity and dependence on computer and communications technology introduces not only convenience but also significant vulnerability.

Infrastructure Interdependence

Most critical infrastructures are not only dependent on computer and communications technology, but are also dependent on other critical infrastructures. In our water infrastructure example, let's look at what other infrastructure dependencies are present within just one of the infrastructure sub-components.

Reservoir Operations	
Mission Component	**Dependency**
Monitor and control water intake from the reservoir and dam hydraulics (via SCADA system)	• Information and Telecommunications Infrastructure • Energy (Electric Power) Infrastructure
Operate pumping infrastructure	• Energy (Electric Power) Infrastructure
Physically maintain all required equipment	• Transportation Infrastructure (to access the reservoir and transport personnel/parts)
Maintain water quality at prescribed standard	• Government Infrastructure (to set and enforce standards)

As demonstrated in this oversimplified example, not only is the infrastructure dependent on modern computer and communications technology, but also on telecommunications, energy, and other infrastructures. In fact, it is probably safe to assume that without electric power there is no water. Given that without electric power most other critical infrastructures are not able to viably operate (at least over the long term), electric power deserves its status as a "supercritical infrastructure".

In many instances, failure of one infrastructure can have cascading impacts on other infrastructures. Take for example, a few dependencies of the banking and finance infrastructure, which quickly start to resemble a house of cards.

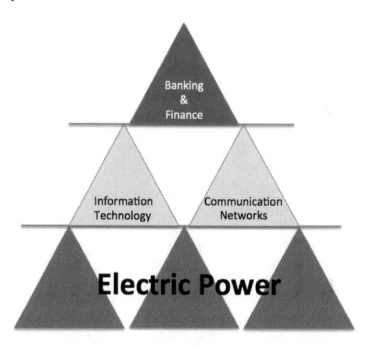

While banking and finance are critically dependent on information technology and communication networks, both IT and communications are dependent on electric power. As a result, banking and finance is also completely dependent on the energy infrastructure. In fact, given the dependence on information technology and communication networks within most critical infrastructures, *it is hard to identify a single infrastructure that is not directly or indirectly dependent on the energy infrastructure.*

In fact, government officials argue that the Internet is another Supercritical Infrastructure. One recent report explored the issue of critical infrastructure dependencies in much greater detail and proposes categories of critical infrastructure dependency. In a 2007 report on modeling interdependency in the critical infrastructure protection sector, the Idaho National Laboratory goes far beyond these relatively simple definitions.[3] Their report describes interdependence as the "interrelationship among infrastructures and its potential for cascading effects"[4] and categorizes interdependence in the following categories:[5]

- **Physical Interdependency**. A requirement, often engineering reliance between components. For example: a tree falls on a power line during a thunderstorm resulting in a loss of power to an office building and all the computers inside.

> "The Internet is fragile. Our economic and national security, privacy and civil liberties are fully dependent on the Internet....
>
> It is critical we improve our security posture. The threats are real. Malicious actors a continent away can exploit our networks. They're becoming better organized and sophisticated at exploiting weaknesses in our technologies."
>
> Keith Alexander - U.S. Cyber Command

- **Informational Interdependency**. An informational or control requirement between components. For example: a supervisory control and data acquisition (SCADA) system that monitors and controls elements on the electrical power grid. A loss of the SCADA system will not by itself shut down the grid, but the ability to remotely monitor and operate the breakers is lost. Likewise, this relationship may represent a piece of information or intelligence flowing from a node that supports a decision process elsewhere. An example is the dispatch of emergency services. While the responders may be fully capable of responding, an informational requirement exists as to answering where, what, and when to initiate response.

- **Geospatial Interdependency**. A relationship that exists entirely because of the proximity of components. For

---

[3]   P. Pederson, D. Dudenhoeffer, S. Hartley, and M. Permann, *Critical Infrastructure Interdependency Modeling: A Survey of U.S. and International Research*, Idaho National Laboratory, August 2006, 4-6.

[4]   Ibid., 4.

[5]   Ibid., 6. Internal citations omitted.

example: flooding or a fire may affect all the assets located in one building or area.

- **Policy/Procedural   Interdependency**.   An interdependency that exists due to policy or procedure that relates a state or event change in one infrastructure sector component to a subsequent effect on another component. Note that the impact of this event may still exist given the recovery of an asset. For example: after [the attacks of September 11, 2001] all US air transportation was halted for more than 24 hours, and commercial flights did not resume for three to four days.

- **Societal Interdependency**. The interdependencies or influences that an infrastructure component event may have on societal factors such as public opinion, public confidence, fear, and cultural issues. Even if no physical linkage or relationship exists, consequences from events in one infrastructure may impact other infrastructures. This influence may also be time sensitive and decay over time from the original event grows. For example: air traffic following the attacks of September 11, 2011 dropped significantly while the public evaluated the safety of travel. This resulted in layoffs within the airline industry and bankruptcy filings by some of the smaller airlines.

Supercritical Infrastructures and the Northeast Blackout

In explaining the concept of critical infrastructures in this document, we have also introduced the concept of Supercritical Infrastructures, with the electric power sub-component of the energy infrastructure serving as a perfect example. The importance of the electric power infrastructure is highlighted periodically with regional power failures, the most notable being the Great Northeastern Blackout of 2003.

The Great Northeastern Blackout of 2003 was a massive power outage that affected the Northeast and parts of the Midwest in the United States on August 14th. It was the second largest blackout in history, affecting 45 million people in the US and 10 million people in Ontario, Canada.

In February 2004, the US-Canada Power System Outage Task Force attributed the incident to FirstEnergy Corporation's failure to trim trees in part of its Ohio service area. However, there were also cyber causes that may have contributed to the blackout. A software bug known as a race condition existed in General Electric Energy's Unix-based energy management system, and at the time of failure the Blaster worm was spreading wildly, confusing and disrupting the response – and potentially even affecting the electrical system directly.

During the outage, cellular telephone and cable television coverage were disabled. Amtrak's Northeast Corridor railroad service was stopped north of Philadelphia, Pennsylvania, and all trains running in and out of New York City were shut down (note the cascade into the Transportation Infrastructure). Passenger screenings ceased, closing regional airports. In New York, flights were cancelled even after power had been restored to the airports because of difficulties accessing "electronic-ticket" information. Many oil refineries on the US East Coast shut down as a result of the blackout, and were slow to resume gasoline production. The American Stock Exchange relied on steam power to cool their trading floor and needed a backup steam generator to be able to open and close.[6]

In skyscrapers and other high-rise buildings, elevators stopped working along with building environmental and cooling systems. On the streets, vehicles were impeded by inoperable stoplights and excess pedestrian traffic. Fearing the worst, some citizens stocked up on food and water, resulting in near-term grocery shortages.

According to a study by the Anderson Economic Group, the impact on US workers, consumers, and taxpayers will total a loss of approximately $6.4 billion, due directly to the effects of the electric power blackout.[7] This blackout, while relatively short-term in a larger context, demonstrates how quickly the cascading impacts of a critical infrastructure failure can present themselves.

---

[6]   U.S. Financial and Banking Information Infrastructure Committee, *Impact of the Recent Power Blackout and Hurricane Isabel on the Financial Services Sector*, October 2003.

[7]   Patrick Anderson and Ilhan Geckil, "Northeast Blackout Likely to Reduce US Earnings by $6.4 Billion," Anderson Economic Group, August 19, 2003, http://www.andersoneconomicgroup.com/Portals/0/upload/Doc544.pdf.

Cascading failures extend beyond the electric power infrastructure as well. Take for example the 2002 strike that resulted in the shut down of the largest ports in California, including Long Beach. While the shutdown was the result of labor disputes, the cascading impacts affected manufacturing (plants unable to obtain parts) and food surety (grocery stores unable to receive expected food shipments. According to some experts, the costs per day of the shutdown exceeded $2 billion.[8] One could easily make the argument that transportation qualifies as a supercritical infrastructure as well.

Recognizing the criticality of these infrastructures and the critical interdependencies, we will now take a closer look at critical infrastructure vulnerabilities.

Critical Infrastructure Vulnerabilities

Critical infrastructure protection is a core component of our international security dialogue, not only because of our absolute dependence on these infrastructures in order to survive as a modern society, but also because these infrastructures are inherently vulnerable to disruption by a wide array of potential attackers.

For example, an attacker might target an infrastructure directly with a physical attack (e.g., a car bomb) or they might target computer and communications systems to disrupt the operation of the infrastructure. While one of these attack vectors is highly visible (a bomb explodes), the penetration of computer systems over global networks is not as observable, and an attacker's presence (or even the attack itself) might not be known or could be attributed to other causes such as a "software bug." The table below shows how infrastructures might be targeted:[9]

---

[8]   Chris Isidore, "Hope in West Coast port talks," *CNN Money*, October 3, 2002, http://money.cnn.com/2002/10/02/news/economy/ports/index.htm.

[9]   Adapted from Matthew Devost, Brian Houghton, and Neal Pollard, "Information Terrorism: Can You Trust Your Toaster?" The Terrorism Research Center, 1996.

Infrastructure Targeting Matrix		TARGET	
		Physical	Digital
Tool	Physical	Conventional bombing attack like Oklahoma City	Conventional bombing of a telecommunication switch
	Digital	Hack into or spoof Air Traffic Control to crash a plane	Hack into a bank to delete all financial records

This report will focus exclusively on the cyber vulnerabilities of critical infrastructure, providing further focus on what threat actors are likely to attack critical infrastructures.

Understanding Cyber Vulnerabilities in Critical Infrastructure

Let's say we just invented a new computer system that will help you navigate from your house to the nearest bus stop. In order to provide you with accurate directions, we'll ask you to carry a handheld computer. That computer system obtains your location through the global positioning system (GPS) and transmits the location to an even larger computer that contains a database of bus stop locations. It is programmed to receive your location, determine where the nearest bus stop is via its internal database, and then transmit directions back to you. It sounds like a simple process and programs are sold today that provide the same exact functionality. Let's look at the various ways a cyber attacker might attack our invention.

1. Target the GPS system so that our handheld computer cannot accurately determine where we are.

2. Target the bus stop database to introduce errors or deny access to information about nearby bus stops.

3. Target the communications between our handheld computer and the bus stop database. An attacker can flood the communications with more data that it can handle or "jam" our signal with noise.

4. Target the logic of our programming to exploit any potential weaknesses. For example, let's say our

software is designed to tell the user to move left or right and then a certain degree. The command "Turn right 90 degrees" would result in a right angle turn from 12:00 to 3:00 on a watch face. However, what if our system accepts a command called "Turn right 270 degrees"? We've now turned left!

5.   Target the power grid, which takes out the computer to which our handheld device was talking, and its database as well.

Our invention was not a complex infrastructure, yet with very little thought we were able to identify nearly a half-dozen potential attack vectors. Imagine targeting something as complex and interconnected as the energy infrastructure. The attack methods seem almost endless, which makes the challenge of securing the infrastructure that much more daunting. It also suggests that attackers have quite an advantage, as they only have to find one successful attack while critical infrastructure defenders must try to defend against every conceivable attack (or at least the most likely ones!).

Microsoft Windows 7 is said to contain 50 million lines of code. Imagine the possible attacks against software with that much complexity. Now layer that complexity on top of the complexity associated with the physical infrastructure components and infrastructure security becomes an enormous challenge. If we cannot secure our invention in the example above, how can critical infrastructure providers secure their infrastructures?

Within critical infrastructure an attacker would likely target the following types of systems:

Business Networks and Systems

Targeting the essential business operations network and workstations to disrupt the business management of a critical infrastructure. While this type of attack does not target the critical infrastructure components directly, it could impact infrastructure operations in the following ways:

- Reveal source code for customized infrastructure control systems

- Reveal sensitive information that allows the control network or systems to be compromised (e.g. details about the network or credential information)

- Provide a pathway to a control network through direct connectivity (e.g. hosts or networks segments connected to both control and business networks allowing an attacker to traverse between the two)

- Disrupt the business capability of the infrastructure operator by deleting critical employee or customer information

Control System Compromise

The direct compromise of control systems would allow an attacker to temporarily or permanently impact infrastructure operations. The same systems that are used to ensure safe and effective infrastructure operations can be targeted to disrupt the infrastructure system in a variety of ways, some of which might result in the shutdown or failure of the infrastructure.

For example, an attacker might increase the pressure in a water system causing physical failure of pipes, or might initiate an emergency shutdown sequence for an electric power grid or plant. There are a variety of ways in which control systems can be directly targeted to impact the infrastructure.

Control Network Compromise

Attacking the network that connects control systems together for critical monitoring and automated adjustment or allows a remote engineer to log into control systems. For example, an attacker to could flood the network with illegitimate traffic, which would disrupt legitimate communications on the network and impact the operation of critical control systems.

Potential Threats to Critical Infrastructure – Who and How

Given the interconnected nature of critical infrastructures and public and private networks, these infrastructures are subjected to the full spectrum of potential threats. We are just beginning to understand how to identify and classify the threats, and the appropriate defenses. Cyber conflict is a comparatively recent kind of warfare. If you wanted to study attack and defense strategy and tactics for conventional land warfare, there are literally thousands of years of material and "lessons learned" to review. However, the concept of computer network security as we know it today has been around less than fifty years, and the effectiveness of traditional institutions and concepts of national security (such as deterrence) has not even been fully determined.

Threat Actors

The first question in identifying potential threats is "Who might attack us?" The following is a set of categories identifying threat actors that might attack critical infrastructures.

- **Nation States**. Legitimate sovereign states with credible information warfare capability. Nation states might penetrate infrastructures to engage in clandestine collections (espionage), steal intellectual property, or engage in cyber conflict. Note that some of the potential impacts are indirect – individual Americans might not even know about a large-scale espionage attack against the Defense Industrial Base, but all Americans would be impacted by a reduction in our military preparedness or capability.

- **Funded Terrorists/Rogue Nations.** Sovereign states whose behavior does not conform with accepted international standards, or terrorist organizations such as al-Qaeda, whose level of funding and support gives them an increased capability level.

- **Unfunded Terrorists/Hacktivists**. Threat agents who have political or ideological goals, but generally lack the resources to mount significant coordinated attacks. The term "hacktivists" has been coined to describe activist groups who have turned to computer hacking as a means of promoting their agenda.

- **Organized Crime/Industrial Espionage**. Describes a set of well-funded threat agents who pursue an economic advantage or seek to amass power through criminal means. Given the substantial criminal economic opportunities presented, organized crime participation in cyber attacks is substantially increasing.

- **Insiders.** Can include critical infrastructure employees and contractors. This could be a typical disgruntled employee situation, but with much greater impact, particularly if a sabotaged system starts a cascading failure beyond what the employee originally intended.

- **Structured Criminal Hackers**. Individuals or small groups with significant expertise in attacking computer systems and networks. These individuals possess the capability to launch organized and persistent attacks that might not always be directly linked to economic gain.

- **Unstructured Hackers**. Generally unsophisticated individuals analogous to street thieves who prey upon unlocked cars. Often using open source tools, these threat agents can actually pose a disproportionate threat because of their relative lack of knowledge and the increasing power of the "point and click" tools available to them from open sources.

The great variety of threat actors poses a unique challenge to critical infrastructure operators. Even the less sophisticated threat actors pose a significant threat if they were to intentionally or unintentionally initiate a cascading failure within an infrastructure. If one subscribes to the theory that a million monkeys at a million keyboards eventually type the great works of Shakespeare, a million unstructured hackers at a million keyboards might eventually disrupt critical infrastructure operations. It is the cyber equivalent of the tree growing too close to the power line.

Attack Types

Threat agents are the "who" – attack types are the "how." The ways in which an attacker might target these systems is varied as well. For example, an attacker might target the cyber portion of critical infrastructures in the following ways:

- **Direct Compromise.** Where a device (normally a server, workstation, or networking device) is attacked via a known vulnerability using a procedure or publicly available tool.

- **Indirect Compromise.** Where an otherwise secure device is compromised by obtaining information such as a password from an already compromised device, or by exploiting a trusted relationship between the two devices. This mode of compromise is often referred to as the basis for the "domino effect," since one failure leads to another until an entire network has been compromised.

- **Compromise via Custom Attack Tool.** A direct compromise in which a special tool is designed and implemented for that specific purpose. This implies a high level of specialized knowledge and resources, so it is likely to come from only the largest and best-funded attackers. It also means that the existence of the tool is not likely to be public knowledge, thus allowing little or no opportunity to design a specific countermeasure to defend the infrastructure component.

- **Diversion Attack.** In which network traffic is misdirected, either for the disruption of operations, or to engage in criminal activity.

- **Insider Placement.** The deliberate positioning of human resources to gain access to a system or network for hostile purposes. This function can be accomplished not only by becoming employees of the target enterprise, but also working as contractors or consultants with comparable access, or even developers of software to be used on the target system.

- **Interception/Sniffing/Data Gathering.** Where various means are used to obtain critical data from or about the target network. While this attack often does not interfere with operations, it can be extremely damaging either through the release of proprietary information or by providing an attacker with critical information such as location of known vulnerabilities for later attack.

- **Malicious Code**. Where an attacker attempts to place unauthorized code into one or more hosts for purposes such as remote control or distributed denial of service (see next two bullets). This can be done either by building the code into an application, or by tricking a user into executing code (e.g., an email attachment), which is often called phishing or spear phishing.

- **Denial of Service Attack**. A single-source attempt to disable one or more hosts on a network by flooding the network with traffic or by disabling key network components.

- **Distributed Denial of Service Attack**. A more sophisticated and dangerous form of service denial, this attack involves the placement of remote agents on multiple (in some cases, thousands) of disparate hosts and then coordinating them in attacks on designated targets. The result is a far more intense version of the denial of service described in the previous bullet and is harder to defend against, because the sources of the attack are scattered across the network.

- **Directed Energy Weapons**. Typified by High Energy Radio Frequency (HERF) weapons. This class of attacks is included because one likely use of this type of weaponry is to disable electronics associated with an infrastructure. This type of weapon is a smaller version of the Electromagnetic Pulse (EMP) generated by a nuclear device.

- **Spoofing/Masquerading**. A more advanced form of the diversion attack, this attack inserts a hostile entity into the communications channel, either for purposes of intelligence gathering or for disruption of operation. It can be an extremely dangerous threat to integrity if information is modified and passed as authentic. Imagine the consequences if the SCADA systems discussed earlier suddenly began adjusting water valves or electrical feeds based on completely erroneous sensor information.

- **Legal Challenge**. Where an entity attempts to utilize the legal system to impede the operation of the target network. One example is the shutdown of the Department of Interior Internet connection in early 2002.[10]

- **Physical Threats to IT Resources**. Where an attacker utilizes calculated physical destruction of targeted information assets as part of a campaign to incapacitate the infrastructure. Sometimes the simple attack is the best choice. If critical control systems are identified as a legitimate target by an attacker (perhaps an international terrorist organization) and that attacker does not have the technical sophistication to attack it electronically, the attacker may target the control systems with a physical (e.g. bombing) attack. Some organizations have either no backup system at all, or a backup computer located in the same facility as the primary. In this case, one explosive device can take down a system for an extended period of time.

- **Supply Chain Compromise.** Attempted placement of malicious network devices into the enterprise environment either by compromising the manufacturing process, intercepting hardware between manufacturing and customer delivery (supply chain integrity), or tricking a company into installing hardware under false pretenses (free printer, etc.). In this case, the brand new computer (or printer, or network device) arrives already compromised and ready to harm the business or network.

As one can see, any a cyber risk management program for critical infrastructures must account for a large number of these attack types and a wide variety of potential attackers.

---

[10] Needs a cite or more context in the example. Not clear how that would work.

The Critical Infrastructure Protection Dilemma

It is not possible to guarantee perfect protection of any asset, let alone a complex infrastructure. Therefore, protecting critical infrastructure is about managing risk. Managing risk requires an understanding of vulnerabilities, threats, impact, and associated mitigation strategies. Unfortunately, with rare exceptions, critical infrastructure operators do not have enough information in any of these areas.

When looking at issues of risk management and critical infrastructure protection, the core objective is to find the appropriate balance with several central challenges:

Critical Infrastructure systems have been connected to open global communication networks.

The growth of the global Internet as a communications platform has enabled tremendous efficiency and societal gain. However, where critical infrastructure protection is concerned, it has also diminished some natural layers of protection. For example, if an adversary wanted to target critical infrastructure in the past, it required physical proximity to the target, which were controlled by multiple tiers of security including national borders and sometimes a physical security layer (fences, guards, etc.) around a particularly attractive infrastructure facility. It also required the means to negatively impact that infrastructure's operation, such as access to tools or explosives that could be used in the attack. Finally, attacks would be locally contained, as there were fewer interconnected infrastructures and fewer infrastructure interdependencies - so if you wanted to attack five electric power plants, you needed five teams (or the same team five times without getting caught) and five sets of tools and explosives. Now that these assets are connected, it's possible to attack all of them at once by using the connecting thread – the network.

To address this issue, infrastructure owners and operators will have to fundamentally address the notion of connectivity for the sake of convenience, as well as the desirability of connectivity through global communication networks. The core concept of interconnected networks will have to be examined in the context of critical infrastructure protection with clear pathways for reducing and mitigating the risks of placing critical systems on interconnected networks.

Cyber threats to Critical Infrastructure are difficult to identify and mitigate.

Our national security apparatus has typically been predicated on the use of "intelligence" generated by monitoring observable events and statistics. This intelligence helps to determine capability and analyze international relations and posturing in ways that can give us insight into intent.

In a cyberspace environment, determining intent and capability is a much more challenging proposition. At any given time, there are countless scans and attacks being conducted over the Internet. Many of these are actually automated attacks that are "crawling" across the network, attacking everything in sight without even having a particular target in mind. So critical infrastructures are targeted with rudimentary scans and attacks on a daily basis. Which of those represents a real threat, if any, and what sophisticated attacks are we missing in all this noise?

In order to adequately manage cyber risk to critical infrastructure, we must develop and maintain situational awareness of the threat and vulnerability environment. This will require new initiatives and approaches to the technical and human challenges associated with maintaining an accurate threat estimate. It is also critical to be able to attribute successful or attempted attacks – the concept of retaliation is meaningless unless the identity of the attacker is known.

Attacks against Critical Infrastructure are likely to have cascading impacts that cannot be accurately predicted.

Just as it is difficult to discern an adversary's capability and intent to launch a cyber attack against critical infrastructures, it is also difficult to model or determine what the impact of an attack or infrastructure failure would be.

Some of our best insights come from non-malicious or natural failures of critical infrastructures, such as the Northeast Blackout of 2003. The cascading infrastructure impacts from that blackout serve as a potential indicator of what a deliberate attack on a critical infrastructure might entail. For example, the failure of the electric power grid had cascading impacts in the following areas:

- Telecommunication systems
- Transportation systems
- Food surety (ability to safely supply food in urban environments)
- Water and wastewater systems

While a majority of the cascading impacts were mitigated through resiliency measures (e.g. backup generators), such measures are designed to sustain a dependent infrastructure for short periods of times and not against a sustained infrastructure failure.

In order to reasonably manage risk in critical infrastructures we must analyze and understand infrastructure interdependencies and the potential cascading impacts. This will require a cooperative effort amongst various infrastructure providers and between the public and private sectors.

While Critical Infrastructure Protection is a national security concern, the private sector owns and operates most of the infrastructures.

One consistent element of all the reports, commissions, and strategies written about critical infrastructure protection is the requirement for increased public/private sector cooperation. In general, the private sector is not anxious to be tasked or restricted by Government agencies. The private sector operates the critical infrastructure and engages in risk management based on best-available knowledge of potential threats and hypothesized impacts. When it comes to critical infrastructure, however, the private sector does not always have the threat intelligence necessary to properly manage risk. This is particularly true in the cyber threat arena.

The federal government needs to provide the private sector with reasonably robust intelligence on applicable cyber threats. It must facilitate cross-infrastructure analysis to determine not only the first-order, but also second and third-order impacts of cascading infrastructure failures. This knowledge, coupled with an understanding of the vulnerability environment, will allow for the reasonable management of risk. The private sector companies involved with critical infrastructure need to recognize that close cooperation is essential to protecting critical infrastructure and positioning itself to act in concert with government agencies for the common good.

Critical Infrastructure is inherently vulnerable to cyber attack

As discussed earlier, the critical infrastructure that enables a prosperous society, stable economy, and vital national defense is dependent on modern technology, including computer systems and networks. Those computer systems and network components were designed primarily to facilitate information processing, storage, and exchange. Security was not a major influence in their design. In most systems, security was simply not designed into the technology, resulting in the potential for numerous vulnerabilities. For example, a search of the National Vulnerability Database for the term "SCADA" reveals fifteen specific vulnerabilities, on top of the thousands of vulnerabilities that could impact the underlying operating system or application protocols.

The end result is that our infrastructures and their associated business networks exist in a state of vulnerability requiring constant vigilance and defensive action. New approaches and frameworks are needed to ensure uninterrupted operations and appropriately manage risk. Our approach cannot simply focus on mitigating the risk we currently have, but must strive to improve to overall security posture of the critical infrastructure to the point where it can resist the constantly increasing threats of the future.

Future Challenges – Future Opportunities

There is no question that numerous foreign and domestic entities have the capability to exploit critical infrastructure targets in the United States. Therefore, it is logical to ask why the critical infrastructure has not already been crippled or destroyed. The answer lies in a delicate balance of motivation and capability.

The United States occupies a unique and critical position in the world economy. It is also a major military and economic power. Accordingly, many potential attackers at the international level must think very carefully about issues such as fear of escalation, economic interdependence, and unpredictable cascading consequences. For example, a major attack on the Internet could bring it down not only in the US, but also all over the world. That would mean that the attacking country would also lose their Internet capability. Thus, even attackers have the capability, they currently lack the motivation to launch a major cyber attack against US infrastructure. On the other hand, there are groups who may want to attack despite the potential consequences, but do not necessarily have the capability to engage in sustained attacks (e.g., terrorist groups).

It would be a colossal mistake to assume that this delicate balance will continue indefinitely. The pendulum of intent and capability can swing in different directions rather quickly. Twenty years ago, the idea of hijacked airliners being used as weapons of mass destruction was simply not part of the American consciousness. With cyber attacks, we have the advantage of knowing about the danger in advance. We need to use this advantage by providing critical infrastructure operators with an opportunity to improve core critical infrastructure security before being subjected to an attempted large-scale attack.

Improving security will require new approaches, frameworks, and technologies that enable infrastructure operators to manage risk against a wide range of potential attackers and techniques.

It will also require that public policy makers and homeland security officials to act in close cooperation with the critical infrastructure providers to create a security-enabling environment for critical infrastructure operations. The challenges are formidable, but with sustained risk management initiatives, they are not insurmountable.

Conclusion

The day-to-day life of every American is supported by a complex set of interdependent infrastructures that we take for granted. Every time we flip a light switch, turn a water faucet, use a credit card or cross the street at the "walk" signal, we benefit from a vast set of interconnected systems. What most people fail to realize is how vulnerable all of this is to a computer-based attack, and that the more we "modernize" these systems, the more vulnerable they become. Tomorrow's smart, dedicated attackers can disrupt our entire way of life without leaving the comfort of their favorite chair.

There is much that can be done (and must be done) by both government and the private sector to reduce our collective vulnerability. Achieving a degree of security will require a national, long-term commitment of time and resources and unprecedented corporate cooperation. The effort to secure our critical infrastructure will be successful only if supported by all Americans, and the first step is helping everyone recognize the threat and the need for action. This paper is part of that first step.

Made in the USA
Middletown, DE
04 February 2021